Decay and Afterlife

Decay and Afterlife

Form, Time, and the Textuality
of Ruins, 1100 to 1900

ALEKSANDRA PRICA

The University of Chicago Press
Chicago and London

The University of Chicago Press, Chicago 60637
The University of Chicago Press, Ltd., London
© 2022 by The University of Chicago
All rights reserved. No part of this book may be used or reproduced in any manner whatsoever without written permission, except in the case of brief quotations in critical articles and reviews. For more information, contact the University of Chicago Press, 1427 East 60th Street, Chicago, IL 60637.
Published 2022
Printed in the United States of America

31 30 29 28 27 26 25 24 23 22   1 2 3 4 5

ISBN-13: 978-0-226-81131-4 (cloth)
ISBN-13: 978-0-226-81159-8 (paper)
ISBN-13: 978-0-226-81145-1 (e-book)
DOI: https://doi.org/10.7208/chicago/9780226811451.001.0001

The University of Chicago Press gratefully acknowledges the generous support of the Schwab Academic Excellence Award of the Institute for the Arts and Humanities at the University of North Carolina at Chapel Hill toward the publication of this book.

Library of Congress Cataloging-in-Publication Data

Names: Prica, Aleksandra, author.
Title: Decay and afterlife : form, time, and the textuality of ruins, 1100 to 1900 / Aleksandra Prica.
Description: Chicago : University of Chicago Press, 2022. | Includes bibliographical references and index.
Identifiers: LCCN 2021019307 | ISBN 9780226811314 (cloth) | ISBN 9780226811598 (paperback) | ISBN 9780226811451 (ebook)
Subjects: LCSH: Antiquities in literature. | Ruins in literature. | European literature—History and criticism.
Classification: LCC PN56.A67 P75 2022 | DDC 809/.93358—dc23
LC record available at https://lccn.loc.gov/2021019307

For my parents

A grey wall, a green ruin, rusty pike,
Make my soul pass the equinoctial line
Between the present and past worlds, and hover
Upon their airy confine, half-seas-over.
          LORD BYRON, *Don Juan*

Contents

List of Figures ix
List of Abbreviations xi

Introduction   1

I Foundations

1 Among Ruins: Martin Heidegger and Sigmund Freud   29
2 Afterlife: Hans Blumenberg and Walter Benjamin   48

II The Propitious Moment

3 Petrarch and the View of Rome   77
4 Poliphilo and the Dream of Ruins   112

III Living On

5 Ferdinand Gregorovius, Hildebert of Lavardin, and the Rupture of Continuity   133
6 Lucius Annaeus Seneca, Martin Opitz, and the Overcoming of Vanity   162

IV The Battleground of Time

7 Johann Jacob Breitinger, Andreas Gryphius, and the Reconsideration of Allegory   189
8 Thomas Burnet, Georg Wilhelm Friedrich Hegel, and the Realignment of Discourses   207

v Futures and Ruins

9 Johann Wolfgang von Goethe, Georg Simmel, and the
   Provisionality of Forms   233

   Epilogue   258

Acknowledgments 269
Bibliography 273
Index 293

Figures

1 Poliphilo among the ruins in *Hypnerotomachia Poliphili* (1499)   124
2 The pyramid in *Hypnerotomachia Poliphili* (1499)   125
3 Fragments in the ruined temple of deceased lovers seen by Poliphilo in *Hypnerotomachia Poliphili* (1499)   128
4 Ex bello pax detail, *pictura* (image), in Andrea Alciato, *Emblemata* (1621)   203
5 Ex bello pax detail, *subscriptio* (epigram), in Andrea Alciato, *Emblemata* (1621)   203
6 Ex bello pax, *pictura* and *subscriptio*, in Andrea Alciato, *Emblemata* (1531)   204
7 Johann Heinrich Wilhelm Tischbein, *Goethe in der römischen Campagna* (1787)   236
8 Michigan Central Station in Detroit (2015)   262

Abbreviations

AÜ	Walter Benjamin, "Die Aufgabe des Übersetzers" (1972)
BG	Walter Benjamin, "Über den Begriff der Geschichte" (1980)
BGS	Heinrich Düntzer, *Briefwechsel zwischen Goethe und Staatsrath Schultz* (1853)
BT	Martin Heidegger, *Being and Time* (2001)
CAG	Johann Jacob Breitinger, *Critische Abhandlung von der Natur, den Absichten und dem Gebrauche der Gleichnisse* (1967)
CD	Johann Jacob Breitinger, *Critische Dichtkunst* (1966)
CH	Walter Benjamin, "On the Concept of History" (2006)
CIN	Isaac Newton, *The Correspondence of Isaac Newton* (1960)
CM	Hildebertus, *Carmina minora* (2001)
FT	Johann Wolfgang von Goethe, *Fairy Tales, Short Stories, and Poems* (1998)
GA	Martin Heidegger, *Phänomenologische Interpretationen zu Aristoteles*, in *Gesamtausgabe* (1985)
GN	Johann Wolfgang von Goethe, "Novelle" (2007)
GS	Georg Simmel, *Georg Simmel, 1858–1918: A Collection of Essays* (1959)
GSRM	Ferdinand Gregorovius, *Geschichte der Stadt Rom im Mittelalter* (1988)
HCRM	Ferdinand Gregorovius, *History of the City of Rome in the Middle Ages* (1894–1902)
HG	Martin Heidegger, *Zu Hölderlin, Griechenlandreisen* (2000)
HP	Francesco Colonna, *Hypnerotomachia Poliphili* (1998)
IJ	Johann Wolfgang von Goethe, *Italian Journey* (2004)
IR	Johann Wolfgang von Goethe, *Italienische Reise* (1976)
LA	Martin Opitz, *Lateinische Werke* (2011)
LFM	Francesco Petrarca, *Letters on Familiar Matters* (2014)
LOA	Francesco Petrarca, *Letters of Old Age: Rerum senilium* (1992)
LW	Hans Blumenberg, *Lebenszeit und Weltzeit* (2001)
MA	Andreas Gryphius, *Majuma* (1991)

OGD	Walter Benjamin, *The Origin of German Tragic Drama* (1998)
OGW	Martin Opitz, *Gesammelte Werke* (1979)
PI	Martin Heidegger, *Phenomenological Interpretations of Aristotle* (2009)
RJ	Ferdinand Gregorovius, *The Roman Journals* (1907)
RT	Ferdinand Gregorovius, *Römische Tagebücher* (1991)
RVF	Francesco Petrarca, *The "Canzoniere," or "Rerum Vulgarium Fragmenta"* (1996)
SE	Sigmund Freud, "New Introductory Lectures on Psycho-Analysis and Other Works," in *Standard Edition of the Complete Psychological Works of Sigmund Freud* (1964)
SJ	Martin Heidegger, *Sojourns: The Journey to Greece* (2005)
SL	Francesco Colonna, *Hypnerotomachia Poliphili: The Strife of Love in a Dream* (1999)
ST	Thomas Burnet, *The Sacred Theory of the Earth* (1726)
TN	Don De Lillo, *The Names* (1989)
TT	Walter Benjamin, "The Task of the Translator" (2002)
TW	Seneca, *Trojan Women*, in *Tragedies* (2018)
WM	Hans Blumenberg, *Work on Myth* (1985)

Introduction

Tradition has it that when Scipio Africanus the Younger, commander of Rome's final campaign against Carthage in the Third Punic War (149–146 BC), looked upon the ruins of the city that had been razed on his order, he could not hold back his tears. Why Scipio cried—Was he overwhelmed by the delight of a glorious victory? Did he feel relief in light of his long-awaited success? Or were his tears an expression of empathy and remorse when he saw the disaster and the loss of the defeated?—is a question that has mystified generations of interpreters. It is imaginable that not even Scipio himself could have determined the reason with certainty. His first historiographers generously took the incident as a moment of prophetic insight and statesmanlike prudence. They conceded to the general that he had wept over the potential impending fate of his own country. Appian reports in his account of the events in the *Punic Wars*, that while contemplating ruined Carthage Scipio recited from Homer's *Iliad* Hector's verses on Troy's certain end: "A day will come when sacred Troy shall perish, / And Priam and his people shall be slain."[1] According to Scipio's teacher Polybios, his student worried that Hector's words were a prescient reference to Rome's fall, "which," he confessed, "he feared" when he thought about "all things human."[2]

In her essay "Imperial Ruin Gazers, or Why Did Scipio Weep?" (2010), Julia Hell detects in Scipio's tears for Carthage and Rome the manifestation of a discourse that tries to come to terms with the rise and fall of empires. According to Hell, this discourse is an element of all "imperial imaginaries"

---

1. Homer, *Iliad* 6.448–49.

2. Polybios, *Histories* (1995), 438–39. For full source citation of this and other works called out in text or notes, see the bibliography.

and the way they articulate space and time. At their core lie "scenarios" or "constellations" that organize power relations visually around ruins and their beholders and create a particular "mode of representation" that Hell calls "empiricist realism."[3] The term indicates that in the background of this form of representation one encounters a notion of the world that perceives it as "visible and understandable through observation."[4]

The focus on visuality and the gaze of the observer has informed much of Western scholarship on European ruins since the 1930s. In the time between Wilhelm Sebastian Heckscher's seminal dissertation on the aesthetic perception of Roman ruins from 1936 and Reinhard Zimmermann's comprehensive 1989 study about the form and significance of artificial ruins, the research landscape was clearly dominated by art history and the question how we *see* ruins in the literal sense.[5] A multitude of volumes emerged like, for example, Paul Zucker's *Fascination of Decay* (1968) that assembled art-historical materials on ruins or examined the history and reception of the ruin motif in prints and paintings.[6] In contrast to this surfeit, ruins have played a rather marginal role in literary research. Isolated analyses of Rome-reflections by individual poets and humanists, a study of the poetics of ruins in France, and discussions of ruins in the context of a theoretical and philosophical approach to fragments and totality are the rather small bounty yielded in the 1970s and 1980s.[7]

Against this backdrop, the cultural theoretician Hartmut Böhme stated in 1989 that future scholarship must address the lack of an aesthetic theory and the desideratum of a history of ruins as well as provide a sense of coherence for the many disciplines involved in ruin scholarship. In lieu of a proper introduction to the topic of the ruin, Böhme suggested that scholars read his

---

3. Hell, "Imperial Ruin Gazers" (2010), 170–71.

4. Hell, *Conquest of Ruins* (2019), 15. I will come back to this definition in the context of my reading of Freud in chapter 1. Catharine Edwards refers to the same scene but relates it to an expression of melancholy that is combined with Roman military power; see Edwards, "Imagining Ruins in Ancient Rome," 646.

5. Heckscher, *Die Romruinen*; R. Zimmermann, *Künstliche Ruinen*.

6. Zucker, *Fascination of Decay: Ruins; Relic–Symbol–Ornament*. Given the vast number of studies on ruins, the following surveil of scholarly works is necessarily selective and therefore limited: Vogel, *Die Ruine in der Darstellung der abendländischen Kunst*; Müller, "Die Ruine in der deutschen und niederländischen Malerei des 15. und 16. Jahrhunderts"; Simmen, *Ruinen-Faszination in der Graphik vom 16. Jahrhundert bis in die Gegenwart*; Du Pérac and Wittkower, *Disegni de le ruine di Roma e come anticamente erono*; Syndram, *Römische Skizzen: Zwischen Phantasie und Wirklichkeit*.

7. Deger, *Joachim Du Bellay*; Caprio, *Poesia e poetica delle rovine di Roma*; Mortier, *La poétique des ruines en France*; Dällenbach and Nibbrig, *Fragment und Totalität*.

rather subjective selection of art-historical, literary, and philosophical works, among them Heckscher's and Zimmermann's monographs and Zucker's illustrated volume, but also Georg Simmel's 1907 philosophical essay "Die Ruine" ("The Ruin"), Robert Ginsberg's article "Aesthetics of Ruins" (1970), and his own take on Tarkovsky's late films. These "fragments" were, in Böhme's view, a substitute that had to suffice until a work emerged that would finally prove suitable to comprehensively deal with the aesthetic and historical complexity of its subject matter. Given just how expansive Böhme's vision is, it is somewhat surprising that Rose Macaulay's *Pleasure of Ruins* (1953) is completely absent from his survey. It is possible that he dismissed its bold mélange of fiction and scholarly inquiry, in which the narrator's imagination repeatedly blends into her observations. However, it must have resonated with Böhme's objectives that Macaulay's book is also a tour de force through the history of Western civilizations, the dynamic of their rise and fall, and, above all, the aesthetics of their remains in images, texts, and architecture.[8]

Ever since Böhme's inventory of the state of ruin scholarship, the situation has changed dramatically, especially in terms of the volume and disciplinary range of research. In particular, there has been a considerable increase in ruin research in disciplines outside of art history. In literary studies, there is a focus on Romance and English literatures from the fourteenth to sixteenth centuries, with a preference for writers such as Petrarch (Francesco Petrarca), Joachim Du Bellay, and Edmund Spenser.[9] German studies have almost exclusively dealt with Romanticism's fascination with ruins and fragments.[10] Explorations of the baroque ruin were usually beholden to Walter Benjamin's *Ursprung des deutschen Trauerspiels* (*Origin of German Tragic Drama*; 1928) and consequently to a dialogue between literature, philosophy, and cultural theory.[11] From a combined philosophical and literary point of view, ruins have been studied as figures of thought with an intrinsic affinity to modernity. The 1996 volume *Ruinen des Denkens—Denken in Ruinen* (*Ruins of*

---

8. See Böhme, "Die Ästhetik der Ruinen" (1989); Simmel, "Die Ruine" (1996); Ginsberg, "Aesthetics of Ruins" (1970); Macaulay, *Pleasure of Ruins*.

9. Melehy, "Du Bellay's Time in Rome" (2001); Melehy, "Spenser and Du Bellay" (2003); Melehy, "Antiquities of Britain" (2005); Summit, "Topography as Historiography" (2000); Summit, "Monuments and Ruins" (2003); Vinken, *Du Bellay und Petrarca*; Hennigfeld, *Der ruinierte Körper*; Baker, "Ruin and Utopia."

10. Somewhat random examples are Bühlbäcker, *Konstruktive Zerstörungen*; Stadler, "Bedeutend in jedem Fall"; Grätz, "'Erhabne Trümmer'"; Schöning, "Zeit der Ruinen"; Baum, *Ruinenlandschaften*.

11. Van Reijen, *Allegorie und Melancholie*; Emden, "Walter Benjamins Ruinen der Geschichte." See also Benjamin, *Ursprung des deutschen Trauerspiels* (1991).

Thought—Thinking in Ruins) and Svetlana Boym's *The Future of Nostalgia* (2001), which associated the optic perception of ruins with the prospective longing for a potential future, set the tone for the discussions in subsequent years, in which the pairing of ruins and modernity became a constant that still persists and absorbs much of the scholarly attention.[12] One of the more recent publications on "modern ruins," to whose conceptual framework this book is deeply indebted, is Hell and Andreas Schönle's edited volume *Ruins of Modernity* (2010) that emphasizes the ruin's temporal complexity and its intricacies of meaning. In addition to the growing number of books and articles on ruins in literary studies and philosophy, there even exists the occasional sociological and historical analysis. Unsurprisingly, the engagement with ruins in art history and architecture endures to this day.[13]

Yet for all its advance, this progress that was supposed to surpass Böhme's provisional aesthetic theory and history of the ruin has proven to be a challenge. While many of the publications since 1990 are rooted within a particular field, they frequently emerged from scholarly backgrounds and research contexts whose ideologies were decidedly interdisciplinary and, in some cases, oriented toward cultural studies. Such research groups typically presented their findings in edited volumes that assembled miscellaneous contributions under the premise of the ruin's characteristic cross-disciplinarity. In that sense, Böhme's patchwork of aesthetic theory and history of the ruin was not only perpetuated but institutionalized. What is more, although the dominance of art history became less pronounced, the compromise between disciplinary and interdisciplinary research, which ultimately found its way into the majority of monographs as well, went hand in hand with a lasting emphasis on the visual and material aspects of ruins. They served as common denominators in a diverse situation and seemed best suited to uncover and explain the cultural and aesthetic qualities of ruined architecture, in whatever

---

12. See Bolz and Van Reijen, *Ruinen des Denkens—Denken in Ruinen*; Boym, *Future of Nostalgia*. Lacroix, *Ce que nous disent les ruines*, hypostatizes the Enlightenment as the era in which the perception of ruins changed radically and became part of modernity's criticism of classical metaphysics; Ginsberg's 2004 monograph *The Aesthetics of Ruins* (not to be confused with the 1970 essay of the same title) is a voluminous work on the perception of ruins, which—against a philosophical background and in systematizing, almost encyclopedic fashion—spreads out into a variety of cultural areas and humanistic fields, and can be regarded as philosophical and cultural-theoretical in character.

13. Turner, "Ruine und Fragment"; Sugrue, "City of Ruins" (2010); Fritzsche, *Stranded in the Present*; Cupperi, *Senso delle rovine e riuso dell'antico*; Zadek, "Der Palatin in den Publikationen Hieronymus Cocks"; Tschumi, *Architecture and Disjunction*; Siegmund, *Die romantische Ruine im Landschaftsgarten*; Vöckler, *Die Architektur der Abwesenheit*.

INTRODUCTION 5

medium it appeared.¹⁴ Conversely, studies on ruins in art and architecture that made extensive use of the written word, especially in its literary form, seldom seemed to favor literature for literature's sake but rather in order to embed and advance their art-historical argument further.¹⁵

This focus on the visual persists in contemporary works. In her recent book *The Conquest of Ruins* (2019), Hell investigates the political reception history of Rome's ruins by activating the hermeneutic tool of imperial imaginaries that structure her earlier Scipio essay. At their center, we once again encounter "ruin gazers," observers and imitators of Rome's grandeur as well as its decline. Visualization, albeit mainly through the medium of photography, is Françoise Meltzer's topic in *Dark Lens* (2019) that deals with the difficulty to represent disaster in view of the ruins of Nazi Germany. Susan Stewart's seminal *The Ruins Lesson: Meaning and Material in Western Culture* (2020) carries the reference to material culture in its subtitle and—for all the emphasis that poetic texts receive in this encompassing study of the cultural history of Western ruins—puts much of its weight on visual art.

In light of this scholarly landscape abundant with interest in the visuality and materiality of ruins, *Decay and Afterlife* seeks out a unique unoccupied place in an already exceptionally rich and voluminous corpus of thought by focusing on the textuality of ruins. In keeping with the Scipio example at the beginning of this introduction, this book distinguishes itself from much of ruin scholarship insofar as it argues that the general wept over a text. This means that throughout this study, my attention will not be directed at Scipio's gaze. Metaphorically speaking, I examine his memory of Hector's words in the *Iliad* instead, the thoughts it triggered, and the fact that Polybios and others incorporated the scene into their own writings about the commander. I seek to analyze the discourses that emerge when reflections on ruins travel through places, times, and, most important, texts. The guiding question is how we come to perceive ruins and their cultural significance if we move their discussion one step away from the immediate visual fascination and material urgency, and instead transfer it to a level of reflexivity that brings with it its own temporality, historicity, and intellectual dynamic.

14. Examples are Assmann, Gomille, and Rippl, *Ruinenbilder*; Hell and Schönle, *Ruins of Modernity*; Stoler, *Imperial Debris*; Kociszky, *Ruinen in der Moderne*; Bolz and Van Reijen, *Ruinen des Denkens*; Dillon, *Ruins: Documents of Contemporary Art*; even though published before 1989, Dällenbach and Nibbrig's *Fragment und Totalität* belongs in this group too. This is the case even for works that claimed to privilege texts; see, e.g., Forero-Mendoza, *Le temps des ruines*. Michel Makarius's 2004 volume *Ruins* includes paintings, drawings, architecture, photography, and literature of the past six hundred years.

15. Christopher Woodward's *In Ruins* (2001) is a case in point.

Apart from being a recurring characteristic of the discourses on ruins I discuss, reflexivity is also a feature of my methodology. *Decay and Afterlife* consists of dynamic readings that reflect on their own praxis through the medium of writing and strive to do justice to both the performativity *and* historicity of texts. The invocation of Reinhart Koselleck in a combined performative *and* historical focus on textual traits is no coincidence. The two features resonate with his understanding that the concept of human history and the very experience of reality rest just as firmly on the "autonomous power of words" that describe and communicate them as they depend on historical facts and deeds.[16] In this sense, the historical perspective on ruins is always mediated through the lens of literature in the widest sense, be it poetry, philosophy, or historiographical writings.

In what follows, I conceptualize the texts I analyze as *forms*. On the one hand, the term is intended to make a distinction apart from the forces of visuality and matter that have long dominated the discussion about ruins. By calling on philosophy's emphasis on the conceptual and abstract qualities of forms, I conceive of *form* as the eternal, atemporal, and intelligible aspect of objects that gives them shape, beauty, and identity.[17] On the other hand, forms as I understand them are more than just an antithesis to matter. The following chapters will show that textual forms build an interface where discourses, actual cultural phenomena, and practices meet, where the relationship between form and matter is less oppositional than a question of their reciprocal interpretation.[18] According to this line of argumentation, I focus on the temporality of forms; how they change, persist, and perish; how they are creatively renewed; and how they are set up against an impending threat of formlessness that discourses about ruins must always face. Most important, textual form is not perceived as antithetical to content but rather as a concept for which questions of composition, mediality, and materiality are just as important as the reference to semantics and semiotics.[19] In this sense, the scope of the term *form* as I use it here is broader than that of *discourse*. Forms may include discourses but reach beyond the mere discursive—that is reflective,

16. Koselleck, "Begriffsgeschichte and Social History" (1982), 409.

17. I am specifically referring to the Aristotelian and Platonic tradition. There has been a wealth of excellent research on form in recent years. The most important publications for this study are David Wellbery's "Romanticism and Modernity" (2010) and "Form und Idee" (2014). Also see Maskarinec, *Forces of Form in German Modernism*; Levine, *Forms*; Kornbluh, *Order of Forms*.

18. See Wellbery, "Romanticism and Modernity," 276.

19. To emphasize my understanding of form, I shall indicate in my readings those cases in which writers themselves draw on the distinction between form and content.

INTRODUCTION 7

methodical, or conceptual—traits of texts into the realm of techniques, rhetorical strategies, and design.

Against this background, my largely implicit dialogue with Koselleck should begin to come into view with greater clarity. Instead of following a conceptual history of the ruin and the terms that surround it, I track in my readings some of the many forms of histories that discourses about ruins have generated over time. My concern is with their parallels and resonances, their contrasts and tensions, their shared apprehensions and conflicting ideas. I examine their intellectual range and aesthetic principles and ultimately the ever-gripping question what keeps the ruins—symbolic and real—of a once grand past alive.

One of the leading premises of this book is that discourses about ruins are discontinuous. Ruins manifest a specific textuality that productively unsettles chronologies, histories, and meaning making as we have come to know them. Unearthing their intricacies means uncovering some of the temporal complexities in European cultures, languages, genres, and periods. This proposition is reflected in the structure of my study as well as in its broad historical scope. The individual chapters dialogically pair ruin-related texts and authors from the High Middle Ages to the turn of the twentieth century, traversing the lands of Europe where Latin, Italian, French, German, and English have been spoken. With each pairing, I address a specific problem of time—the propitious moment (part 2), the problem of living on (part 3), the battleground of time (part 4), and futures and ruins (part 5)—thereby connecting several temporal and textual layers. Scholarship has already paid close attention to some of the texts in my corpus, while others lie beyond the classical canon. In every case, the notion of ruins is manifest differently, yet each example brings to the foreground the ruins' inherently double-edged ability to both occasion and undo efforts to make sense of them.

The two concepts that bind my argument are *decay* and *afterlife*. As decay is to form, so is afterlife to time. Both establish a framework for analyzing how the threat of transience and formlessness, the turmoil of temporal discontinuity and the expectation of survival and endurance are intertwined in discourses about ruins. In light of their complexity and the considerable critical attention that both terms have received, their application for the purpose of this study requires further clarification.

For one, the function of *decay* is to subsume both forms and ruins under a common concept of processuality. The term emphasizes that neither forms nor ruins are static entities but subject to change—usually as a result of slow, fast, or even sudden disintegration. A glance at the etymology of the word *ruin* reveals that the aspect of transformation is inherent in its semantics but that this very indication of mutability was long cause for uneasiness. In classical Latin, the relatively rare occurrence of *ruina* refers to the process rather than the result of collapse.[20] The noun is almost entirely absent from medieval usage and—on those rare occasions when it is used—is limited to etymologically related adjectives and verbs.[21] Instead, it was much more common to linguistically treat ruins like intact edifices and speak of the temple, the thermae, or the theater that the ruins once used to be, thereby maintaining the illusion of integrity and immutability. By contrast, *decay* makes abundantly clear that ruins are elements in a course of events that alter them. The nature of this alteration is, however, not to render the object unrecognizable. Midas Dekkers observes in his praise of disintegration how decay is "the way of all flesh," a journey toward total collapse, on which we also come paradoxically into our own.[22] *Decay and Afterlife* traces this ambivalence between shifting shapes and evolving identities that Dekkers explores with respect to the human condition by focusing on the breakdown and renewal of forms that ruins represent and trigger and the relation of this process to the human perception of time.

My second eponymous concept, afterlife, serves to capture precisely this affiliation between time and transformation. The term *afterlife*—in German *Nachleben*—has often been cited as the summarizing punchline of Aby Warburg's work. As Georges Didi-Huberman points out, in Warburg's writings, "*Nachleben* refers to the survival (the continuity or afterlife and metamorphosis) of images and motifs—as opposed to their renascence after extinction or, conversely, their replacement by innovations"—the latter being a view famously adopted by Erwin Panofsky and Ernst Gombrich.[23] Against their advocacy for an understanding of art history as a sequence of periodizations and hierarchizations of stylistic features, Didi-Huberman introduces the idea of "impure time," a notion suitable for assessing the subliminal, anachronis-

20. For example, see *Oxford Latin Dictionary*, s.v. "ruina," 1666–67, and "ruo," 1669; Georges, *Ausführliches lateinisch-deutsches Handwörterbuch*, s.v. "ruina," 2422–23, and "ruo," 2428–29.

21. For instance, there is no entry for *ruina* in Du Cange, *Glossarium mediae et infimae Latinitatis*, or in Blaise, *Lexicon Latinitatis medii aevi*. Du Cange lists the noun *ruinatio*, translated as "destruction" from fifteenth-century sources (vol. 7, col. 235a). See also Zadek, "Der Palatin in den Publikationen Hieronymus Cocks, 82–86; Assmann, Gomille, and Rippl, *Ruinenbilder*, 7–14.

22. Dekkers, *The Way of all Flesh*.

23. Didi-Huberman, "Artistic Survival" (2003), 273. Didi-Huberman alleges that Gombrich's *Aby Warburg: An Intellectual Biography* was an attempt to make sure that the "hypothesis of survival not survive" (276) but that it was Panofsky's essay "Albrecht Dürer and Classical Antiquity" that "invalidated the concept of Nachleben for generations of art historians to come" (277).

tic dynamics of cultural forms and the manners in which they persist and change.[24]

Afterlife as a temporal hybrid that defies the self-evidence of advancing chronological time and the reflexes of periodization is at the heart of my own book, as well. However, Warburg's conception of the recurrence of visual tropes or pathos formulas (*Pathosformeln*) in Western culture does not serve as a main reference point. As detailed in chapter 2, my approach is based on Benjamin's discussion and simultaneous surpassing of the contemporary philosophy of life (*Lebensphilosophie*). In his 1921 essay "Die Aufgabe des Übersetzers" ("The Task of the Translator"), he understands afterlife as an "after-ripening" (*Nachreife*) of (literary) forms in various stages of metamorphosis beyond the original of a translation, for example.[25] This afterlife of the original in the form of its translation constitutes the work's fame and, according to Benjamin, its history. In this sense, form, fame, and history are deeply related in Benjamin's thinking, and history is what in his view requires reconsideration and rewriting. Yet there are elements in historical processes that persist. Benjamin expresses this concept by stating that succeeding forms help tease out and unfold the original's meaning. In adapting this position and combining it with my understanding of history as mediated through forms, I will—chiastically speaking—use the term *afterlife* when addressing both persistence in change and change in persistence.

There is a specific aspect of the Benjaminian understanding of afterlife that relates to Hans Blumenberg, Benjamin's dialogical partner in chapter 2. Afterlife and, with it, Benjamin's vision of history are subject to and depend on the liminal concept of death. Mortality is at the horizon of every transformation. For Blumenberg, the afterlife of forms is mainly a matter of cultural and, more specifically, aesthetic reception, yet its purpose is to console in the face of impending death and the challenges of a harsh reality. The fear of one's own transience is what Blumenberg captures by distinguishing "life-time" (*Lebenszeit*) and "world-time" (*Weltzeit*)—two concepts that will be of great importance for my readings—and by ascribing to humans an innate propensity to feel provoked by the imbalance between the shortness of the former and the long duration of the latter.[26] In the gap between the two temporalities—negotiating the conditions of (after)life beyond one's individual life-time, so to speak—forms take root.

---

24. Didi-Huberman, *Surviving Image* (2017).

25. See Benjamin, "Die Aufgabe des Übersetzers" (1972), 12. The English version translates *Nachreife* as "maturing process"; see "Task of the Translator" (2002), 256.

26. Blumenberg's framework is explained in Blumenberg, *Lebenszeit und Weltzeit* (2001).

A Brief History of the Discourses on Ruins and the Historical Scope of *Decay and Afterlife*

This introduction started by highlighting the orientation in *Decay and Afterlife* toward the textuality of ruins in a scholarly landscape that has long favored visuality. In this context, it should have already become apparent that the other main distinguishing feature of the present study is its historical scope. There are scholarly works that have a comparable longitudinal perspective—Susan Stewart's aforementioned *Ruins Lesson* being just one example—but they do not concentrate on texts with the same interest in discursivity. A textual focus often goes hand in glove with an emphasis on poetics and, as a rule, with a much more limited time frame that stays within designated periods. Andrew Hui's illuminating monograph *The Poetics of Ruins in Renaissance Literature* (2016), which inspired part 2 of this book, is a case in point.

Searching out the dynamics of collapse and survival in discourses about ruins that emerged not only over the course of eight hundred years of intellectual and literary history but that also thrived in diverse cultural regions of central Europe is an audacious and humbling endeavor. This is especially true if the guiding principle of investigation is less cultural historical than critical. It requires readings that combine the perspective of the *longue durée* with analytical depth and theoretical diligence, and it necessitates decisions that may not always seem obvious.[27] Like its subject matter, the achievements of such a project can therefore be fragmentary at best. Those modest conclusions that can be drawn, however, stem from the methodological presupposition that new outlooks on familiar issues are always the result of unfamiliar constellations. In what follows, I therefore elucidate my choice and combination of texts and authors by simultaneously locating them in two different paradigms. On the one hand, I place them within the history of discourses about ruins as it has been commonly told. This perspective is largely chronological and serves the purpose of providing the reader with a sense of development and continuity but also with an overview of some of the most important trajectories that reflections about ruins have taken since the Middle Ages. On the other, the pairings of works I propose in this book forcefully assert an anachronistic point of view. They suggest moments of kindred thinking that are related to specific temporal concepts and sometimes lie centuries apart. Positioning them in a traditional narrative reveals that these works are part of a historical context that has influenced and shaped them. At the same time, however, it evinces their potential for breaking new ground and exposing

---

27. *Longue durée* refers to my emphasis of a long-term historical scope.

their function in opening up for us new ways of *seeing* ruins—but now from the vantage point of the reader.

Following this introduction, part 1 ("Foundations") extrapolates the conceptual and theoretical foundations for this study by staging dialogues between Martin Heidegger and Sigmund Freud, on the one hand, and Blumenberg and Benjamin on the other. At the outset of the reader's journey through the ten chapters of this book, Heidegger and Freud express anxieties about an actual encounter with a ruinous past they know essentially from readings and hearsay but have never experienced (chapter 1, "Among Ruins"). Their physical approach to the ruins of Greece poses a challenge to their perception of reality and forces them to reflect on the epistemological premises and outcomes of the undertaking. I will show how both thinkers reconsider the discourses they have established and for which they are known. At the same time, they are prompted to ponder the status of the emerging textuality that ruins manifest in their travel reports. In other words, at stake are the relations between existing and new discourses, their defining features, and their mutability. Heidegger and Freud contemplate these aspects against the backdrop of a complex temporal setting that involves a tension between life-time and world-time.

Following this predominantly descriptive and narrative elaboration of my argument, the discussion in chapter 2 ("Afterlife") is decidedly theoretical. By connecting Blumenberg's terminological and conceptual decisions with the line Walter Benjamin draws between forms, historical processes, mortality, and his thoughts on the Thirty Years' War and the ruin in baroque German tragic drama, I show that for Benjamin history is based on forms in a shattered state. This discussion will lay the groundwork for a more detailed analysis of the war-related early modern discourses about ruins and also allow for a closer look at the dialectic between the concrete and metaphorical characteristics of ruins—or, using Benjamin's language, ruins and allegories.

Ideally, what readers should take away from part 1 of this book is how these four thinkers, when activated in unison, complement one another's thinking in spite of the very different, sometimes even countervailing, intellectual traditions to which they belong. They all strive to make sense of an overwhelming reality, the impositions and challenges of which come to the fore between the poles of decay and afterlife. They all in their own way activate *forms of coping*—that is, discourses that console, reassure, reevaluate, and renew the terms and categories of their intellectual approach to the world and simultaneously reshape the contexts from which the four thinkers argue.

Even a cursory glance at the history of discourses about ruins cannot overlook how ruins, when defined as fragments or remnants of architectonic buildings, characteristically appear as sites of colliding contradictions. These encounters—be they in the classical paintings of Hubert Robert, recent photo volumes on postindustrial ruins in Detroit, the symbols of vanity in the baroque, or Romanticism's nostalgic treatment of history—have in common that they are all conditioned by temporal factors. Ruins can be read as traces of former integrity, indicating a slow transition and the steady passing of time, or they can be seen as signs of radical ruptures and the suspension of historical and temporal experiences in traumatic events of sudden destruction. Susceptible to a wide range of meanings, ruins often rebuff rigid categories and instead stoke the imagination and aesthetic signification. It also makes them an ideal means for validating cultural shifts such as, for example, from the premodern to modernity.

In his 1936 dissertation on Roman ruins, Heckscher spoke of the romantic feeling for ruins (*Ruinenempfindsamkeit*) as a modern sentiment that displaced the sensation of horror that the ugliness of disintegration provoked in premodern beholders. According to his argument, the feeling emerged in the wake of a new approach to ancient ruins on Italian soil in sixteenth-century art, which followed a similar process in literature. As Heckscher puts it, these were the early stages when ruination started to acquire aesthetic and melancholic magic, developments that provided organic decomposition with metaphysical worth.[28] However, for this reevaluation and aesthetic realignment to occur, medieval notions of beauty and concepts of history had to be reassessed.

This medieval attitude toward ruins has been characterized by Peter Burke as one of indifference and lack of historical curiosity.[29] In aesthetic terms, the scarcity of premodern artistic depictions of dilapidated buildings was understood as the result of a specifically medieval—that is to say, Christian—concept of beauty that did not allow for ruins.[30] Thomas Aquinas's influential formal criteria that linked beauty to integrity, proportion, and clarity—in other words, to the original form that things had received from God[31]—needed to make room for the recognition and acceptance of the intrinsic

---

28. Heckscher, *Die Romruinen*, 1–3.
29. Burke, *Renaissance Sense of the Past*, 2.
30. For this assumption, see Heckscher, *Die Romruinen*, 2. Reinhard Zimmermann refers to Heckscher and explicitly mentions Thomas Aquinas as the main advocate for a Christian-influenced concept of the beautiful and its main property, which is integrity; see R. Zimmermann, *Künstliche Ruinen*, 137.
31. Eco, *Aesthetics of Thomas Aquinas*, 64–120; Heckscher, "Relics of Pagan Antiquity in Medieval Settings" (1938), 210–12.

value of ruins; namely, the aesthetic quality of their shattered materiality.³² There was also a practical side to the matter that had to be rethought: the custom of using Rome as a gigantic quarry and recycling rubble as building material—a custom that started in late antiquity and continued throughout the Middle Ages.³³ Panofsky argued that the reason for this "unsentimental" use of material from the past was the perception, prevalent in the Middle Ages, that a continuity existed between that epoch and antiquity, whose "corpse"—as he put it—was left "unburied," ready to be "galvanized and exorcised." The Renaissance, on the other hand, "stood weeping at its [antiquity's] grave and tried to resurrect its soul."³⁴

In the prevailing scholarly opinion, change became possible on the grounds of a shift in the core concepts of translation (*translatio*) and renewal (*renovatio*) in medieval historiography.³⁵ The idea of continuity with antiquity and especially with the Augustinian Empire that had triggered aspirations in later societies of revisiting and repeating its cultural and political success appeared to slowly yield to a sense of antiquity's irretrievable loss.³⁶ As a consequence, instead of repressing the factuality of decay that posed a threat to one's own existence while the belief in continuity prevailed, the past and its traces became objects of admiration and ennoblement—not despite but because of their imperfection.³⁷

One way to admit to the reality of loss was to dignify it with elegiac lament. Hildebert of Lavardin's Rome poems (which I will examine in chapter 5) are an early example of such sophisticated grief.³⁸ Yet it is Petrarch who ranks as the initiator of a clear shift in the perception of antique ruins. According to

---

32. It is important to once again mention that the term *aesthetic* as well as *aesthetics* in the Enlightenment and post-Enlightenment sense were unknown to the Middle Ages. The use of the terms in the present context refers to reflections on beauty as an objective quality of being. On this matter, see Eco, *Aesthetics of Thomas Aquinas*, 3. For the context of medieval German literature, see Braun, "Kristallworte, Würfelworte."

33. For the problem of preservation of ancient Rome and its impact on historical thinking, see the important study by Karmon, *Ruin of the Eternal City*. See also Böhme, "Die Ästhetik der Ruinen," 291; Zanker, "Die Ruine."

34. Panofsky, *Renaissance and Renascences in Western Art*, 113.

35. Heckscher, *Die Romruinen*, 33–37; Schramm, *Kaiser, Rom und Renovatio*; Heckscher, "Relics of Pagan Antiquity in Medieval Settings," 205. See also Kern and Ebenbauer, the introduction to *Lexikon der antiken Gestalten in den deutschen Texten des Mittelalters*.

36. In reference to the biblical book of Daniel, medieval interpretation considered the Augustinian Empire to be the last of four kingdoms, and the one that would see the arrival of the Antichrist. See Heckscher, "Relics of Pagan Antiquity," 205.

37. Heckscher, *Die Romruinen*, 15, 31–37.

38. Rehm, *Europäische Romdichtung*, 43–61; Heckscher, "Relics of Pagan Antiquity," 208.

Heckscher, the important innovation that can be associated with Petrarch is precisely his overcoming of a plaintive approach to ruins, even though his tone is still elegiac. Heckscher sees Petrarch's actual interest directed at the question of how ruins can be preserved *as ruins*. He makes a cautious claim about the poet's almost religious veneration of antique remnants, arguing that Petrarch's use of the noun *reliquiae* (relics) to denote dilapidated buildings serves as proof of this reverence.[39] When Petrarch first visited Rome in 1337, he indeed encountered a cultural situation in which there was a reluctance to acknowledge the existence of ruins at all and a language that lacked a general term to characterize them as independent objects of study and contemplation. The word *reliquiae* indicated a compromise, but one that added connotations to the idea and the phenomenon of decayed architecture that typically belonged to the realm of religious cult and devotion. Heckscher understands the way in which Petrarch employs the word as the quasi-secularized version of an effort to actualize the marvels and blessings of the past, while simultaneously acknowledging its historicity and its undeniable detachment from the contemporary world. On the perceived brink of a shift in worldview, Petrarch emerges with his choice of vocabulary as the forerunner and enabler of the new emotional value of *pietas* (piety) toward what is left of ancient times. He displays a hitherto unknown reverent respect for antique debris that would not acquire its own term until the fifteenth century: *ruina*.[40]

Petrarch's approach to ruins is only one instance that has been used, time and again, to define him as a watershed figure between the medieval and the modern. According to this line of argumentation, he is the first author whose texts marked the transition from a medieval focus on historical continuity to an acceptance of discontinuity and a permanent break with the past. His 1341 letter to his confessor Giovanni Colonna, in which Petrarch recapitulates their previous experience with the Roman ruinscape, has served as an almost iconic testimony to this claim. Concurrently, the poet was turned into a figure whose obsession with lost antiquity and ruined Rome was mirrored in the fragmentariness of his own self and of the work he produced. Both of these characteristics were considered to prove him to be a modern.[41]

Instead of rehearsing this argument once again and adding my voice to those who ascribe to Petrarch a foundational place in accounts of Western modernity, I ask in chapter 3 ("Petrarch and the View of Rome") what role

---

39. Heckscher, *Die Romruinen*, 26–27.

40. Heckscher, *Die Romruinen*, 28–29.

41. Heckscher and Böhme are only two out of a host of scholars who have perceived Petrarch as a figure on the threshold between periods. I will discuss this further in chapter 3.

INTRODUCTION   15

Petrarch's discourse about ruins plays in keeping the intellectual fragments of the past alive. The temporal concept around which my argument revolves is the propitious moment (as reflected in the title of part 2, "The Propitious Moment," which encompasses chapters 3 and 4). I focus on the textual dynamics of postponement, belatedness, the pressures of time, and the phantasm of the appropriate moment in time that inform much of Petrarch's historical and aesthetic self-positioning as well as his understanding of the political and historical events unfolding around him. My reading renders Petrarch a figure not of historical demarcation but rather of a flexible and fragile kairos. As I shall show, his texts circle around a constantly threatened and simultaneously perpetuated critical moment of reevaluation and renewal that arises from ruins and remains and guarantees their future significance.

The 1500s saw the consolidation of the relationship between decay and admiration that Heckscher had first identified in Petrarch's writings. Rome proved a powerful attraction for artists from north of the Alps whose work focused on the ruinscapes and helped promote the idea that ruins speak of the city's former greatness more eloquently than undamaged buildings ever could. This thought found its distinctive expression in the maxim *Roma quanta fuit ipsa ruina docet* (How great Rome was, its very ruins tell), which persistently reappeared as a popular motto in works of art and architecture.[42] At the turn of the sixteenth century, there was a sensitized awareness that the monuments and constructions of the past were worthy of memory and preservation, and the artistic and literary measures to oppose exploitation and neglect began to prevail against the still ongoing damage caused by the practice of ruin recycling. Greek and Roman antiquities became objects of archaeological interest and reconstruction efforts.

In this context, the ruin was featured as an independent object of printed graphics and text in the *Hypnerotomachia Poliphili* examined in chapter 4 ("Poliphilo and the Dream of Ruins"). My reading of the romance that was first printed in Venice in 1499 focuses on the narrative function of ruins and their role in establishing a propitious moment within the story that equips it with a time index. Illustrated with 172 woodcuts and written in a recondite combination of Latin and Italian, the plot tells of Poliphilo's dream in which

---

42. The motto famously appears as an inscription in Marten van Heemskerck's drawing of the *Septizonium* (1532–1536), or in the frontispiece of Serlio's *Terzo libro* (1540). See Curran, "Teaching and Thinking (About) the High Renaissance," 37; Torelli, "From Ruins to Reconstruction," 32; Guest Lapraik, *Understanding of Ornament in the Italian Renaissance*, 385. The thought was not foreign to Hildebert of Lavardin, who in his Rome poems points out the simultaneity of ruin and greatness. However, I will show that his focus is not greatness *because of* ruin but greatness *despite* ruin.

he follows his beloved Polia through landscapes replete with ruins of antiquity and marvelous works of architecture. The astonishing impact that the *Hypnerotomachia* and especially its illustrations had on Western European art, architecture, and the respective theories after the second half of the fifteenth century, is to a large extent due to its reception as a testament to an early Renaissance fascination with antiquity and evidence of a historical and antiquarian impulse. What has not been recognized clearly enough so far is that historicity is not a given in Poliphilo's dream, but that antiquity as well as Poliphilo's love story are initially depicted as timeless ideals. However, in the course of the story they are equipped with a historical and temporal index, manifest in the textuality of ruins or, more precisely, in the poetic description of ruined architecture. Ruin passages assume a prominent position in the narrative, breaking through a static lingering on the ideal by offering a reminder of its history, in one instance, and enabling the protagonist to read his own fate into the history of the world, in the other. This involves thoughts about death as the end of life-time and pondering on strategies to postpone it. In other words, the confrontation with ruins triggers a reframing of life-time and a reconsideration of world-time. With respect to both, the ruin is the space of reflection on the propitious moment, the one that links the past to the future, life to death, history to timelessness, and moves the narrative forward.

The seventeenth century was a time of deeply ambiguous experiences with ruins. On the one hand, Europeans struggled to come to terms with the catastrophe of the Thirty Years' War. On the other, in the second half of the century an emerging fashion of educational grand tours around Europe brought growing numbers of wealthy northern and western European youths and their entourage to the Eternal City, where the ruins—now displayed and canonized as must-visit sights—offered them the opportunity to explore Europe's cultural legacy.[43] The scientific, exploratory, archaeological, and conservatory enthusiasm that had been mounting since the late 1400s resulted in an abundance of artistic and literary output. At the same time and kindled by the long war, the idea of the ruin as a symbol of vanity, loss, and futility flourished. The early modern period had inherited the tradition from a Christian point of view that saw the ruin as a reminder of transience and a contrast to its own eternal order, but only now did it seem to have met its match in the historical reality of a universal disaster.[44]

---

43. Gampp, "Rom zwischen Tivoli und Washington," 225; Zanker, "Die Ruine"; Sweet, *Cities and the Grand Tour*, 99–163.

44. Related to the Christian understanding of ruins is the fact that since the late 1400s,

INTRODUCTION   17

Part 3, "Living On," explores the problem of the continuity of life-time and comprises chapters 5 and 6. The historiographer of medieval Rome and protagonist in chapter 5 ("Ferdinand Gregorovius, Hildebert of Lavardin, and the Rupture of Continuity"), Ferdinand Gregorovius, is a typical representative of the mid-nineteenth century as he seeks to combine late Romantic aesthetic techniques of self-fashioning in the light of decay with a universal historiography. In this chapter, Gregorovius enters into dialogue with the French theologian and bishop of Le Mans Hildebert of Lavardin (1055–1133), ruined Rome's most famous medieval mourner. Hildebert visited Rome at the beginning of the twelfth century and witnessed the devastation that Robert Guiscard's pillaging troops left behind in 1084. His poems *Roma* and *Item de Roma* process the experience with a look at ancient and Christian Rome, respectively. The poems are a benchmark in ruin discourse, and, as is the case with Petrarch's writings, they have been used to determine the bishop's historical position between humanist progressiveness and medieval conservatism. I shift the focus away from issues of epochal classification and instead examine how, on the one hand, the two poems address the experience of discontinuity as one of semiotic and semantic collapse. Continuity, on the other, becomes a matter of restoring semiotic orders and semantic points of reference by replacing the ruins with the cross, the remnants of ancient existence with the symbols of Christian life. How to live on and how to keep the fragments of a great but non-Christian past meaningful in a Christian context is the simultaneously universal and individual question that emerges from the textuality of ruins in Hildebert's case. It defines the aesthetics and specific historicity of his work and the significance of his position in the context of intellectual history. Roughly 750 years after Hildebert's Rome visit, Gregorovius includes the first poem in his *History of the City of Rome in the Middle Ages* and links the passage about historical discontinuity to an experience of ruin with regard to his own life-time. It is one of many examples where the historiographer, who was a witness to the political upheaval of the Italian Risorgimento, blends his biography with his opus magnum. Gregorovius's self-declared goal and

---

antique ruins started to appear increasingly often in paintings, frequently providing a frame or a backdrop of the main salvation historical scene. They bear witness to a conflicted Christian point of view, which, on the one hand, seemed to appreciate and even feed on the greatness of the past and, on the other, made a statement about the necessary and justified demise of what was perceived as the old, pagan world. See Makarius, *Ruins*, 22. Heckscher remarks that in medieval art the only way to visualize ruins was to show buildings in the very moment of collapse, see: Heckscher, "Relics of Pagan Antiquity," 211.

his most fateful task is to conquer the "universal being" (*Weltwesen*) Rome by means of thorough examination and aesthetic representation—in other words, by lending it semiotic and semantic substance. This, in turn, gives his life purpose. Here, as in the medieval example, the concept of historicity is based on textual and linguistic operations. Living on, however, takes on a secularized meaning in which the ruin of Rome is the yardstick by which Gregorovius measures the melancholy of his own existence and the political ambitions of the young Kingdom of Italy and world politics in general.

Chapters 6, 7, and 8 examine three works from the early to late 1700s paired together with texts from the early years of the Roman Empire and the eighteenth century. Chapter 6 ("Lucius Annaeus Seneca, Martin Opitz, and the Overcoming of Vanity"), the second of the two chapters in part 3, addresses the ruins of Troy and the devastation caused by the Thirty Years' War. I discuss how Seneca in his tragedy *Troades* (*The Trojan Women*) and Martin Opitz in his 1625 translation of the Stoic's work deal with a war-related semiotic breakdown and the question of how living on after and outside of meaningful sign relations is still possible. I posit that in Seneca's and Opitz's works we are faced with a borderline case of vanity, an experience of utter meaninglessness, brought about by the loss of a semiotically structured world, which in turn threatens the loss of life-time. However, in the early modern text the problem is aesthetically mediated. Instead of brooding over the pieces and fragments of an unredeemed world—a gesture that Benjamin ascribed to people of the baroque era—Opitz manipulates time and thereby reestablishes the early modern world as a network of signs in which life after the war is possible. What is more, Opitz's translation itself is a form of afterlife in the sense that Benjamin describes in "The Task of the Translator": With respect to the life of the original, the translation is as belated and deficient as it is indicative of a new beginning that emerges from the fragments, of which a translatable and translated work always consists.

Benjamin's celebrated claim in *The Origin of German Tragic Drama*—in the realm of thought, allegory is what ruins are in the world of things—underlies my analyses in part 4, "The Battleground of Time," which comprises chapters 7 and 8. These analyses focus on the dialectic between concrete and metaphorical characteristics of ruins and their respective temporal implications. I explore two seminal examples—the German poet Andreas Gryphius's allegorical play *Majuma* (1653) and the English theologian Thomas Burnet's treatise *The Sacred Theory of the Earth* (1684). Both authors struggle to establish a novel form of discourse capable of absorbing the knowledge of their time by merging the realm of thought with the world of things and by balancing the concreteness of ruins with allegorical abstraction.

INTRODUCTION 19

In chapter 7 ("Johann Jacob Breitinger, Andreas Gryphius, and the Reconsideration of Allegory"), I revisit with Gryphius's *Majuma* ruined Germany in the time shortly after the end of the Thirty Years' War by reading the play against the backdrop of Johann Jacob Breitinger's early Enlightenment criticism of German baroque allegory. In a situation between war and peace, Gryphius considers the nature of knowledge that emerges from the transition and contemplates its significance for the historical order of the postwar period. His work evinces, on the one hand, a very subtle reflection on allegory's ability to structure historical knowledge. On the other, *Majuma* is an example of an open aesthetic form that surpasses allegory's visual and verbal possibilities as well as what Benjamin described as "allegorical fragmentation," "arbitrariness," and brokenness.[45] The play experiments with ways to overcome ruination on both a highly abstract rhetorical and aesthetic plane and in the concrete postwar realm of a material world in shatters.

Chapter 8 ("Thomas Burnet, Georg Wilhelm Friedrich Hegel, and the Realignment of Discourses") takes readers on two trips to the Alps, the battleground of time for the English theologian Thomas Burnet and the German idealist philosopher G. F. W. Hegel. The aesthetic shock that Burnet experienced when he passed over the Alps on a grand tour to Italy in 1671 was the origin of his efforts to find a scientific explanation of why, in his mind, the earth was in a state of ruin. The understanding of ruin that Burnet presents to his audience using a genuinely literary discourse oscillates between abstraction and concretion. In the reception of his work, the tension galvanizes a realignment between theological and scientific discourses and the knowledge they contain about time and history. Hegel's encounter with the Alps in 1796 was unpleasant as well. Without mentioning the word *ruin*, he speaks of dead, formless masses, in which neither the eye nor the imagination can find a point of reference. And yet, I will suggest that Hegel's philosophical system emerges from a complex relation between abstraction and concretization at work in the Alpine decay and the spectacle of transformation that nature offers the viewer. It sets in motion the movement that will eventually result in the return of the spirit (*Geist*) to the ideal of cognition.

With the onset of the eighteenth century, Heckscher's historically deduced claim that a firm connection exists between ruins and a wistful, Romantic sense of beauty in the beholder seems to have finally achieved its proper realization. A passage from the 1763 work "Observations on Sculpture and Bouchardon" by the French poet Denis Diderot contains in a nutshell some

---

45. Benjamin, *Origin of German Tragic Drama*.

of the main aspects that account for the fascination with decay in European Romanticism and further enhances and redefines its aesthetic relevance:

> When any one has genius, it is there that he feels it; it is awakened in the midst of ruins. I believe that magnificent ruins strike much more forcibly than monuments which are entire and well preserved. Ruins are far away from towns; they menace, and the hand of time has sown among the moss, which covers them, a multitude of grand ideas and of sweet and melancholy sentiments. I admire the entire building; the ruin makes me shudder; my heart is moved, my imagination has more scope.[46]

The sequence gives ample evidence of Romanticism's specific focus: Emphasis is put on the self and its ruin-induced experience of overwhelming awe and melancholy. Individual creativity and the source of reflection and imagination are to be found in abandoned spaces, and the time-conditioned relationship between ruins and nature is foregrounded as the origin of grand ideas.

The eighteenth and nineteenth centuries mastered the art of staging, producing, intensifying, or mediating the intellectual and emotional attitudes enabled by ruins. One way to establish and control the experience was the erection of fake ruins in parks and gardens, a practice which was fashionable among the wealthy.[47] These so-called follies entertained an ambiguous relationship with time and space. On the one hand, follies gave familiar surroundings the prestige of a significant historical past—the precise nature of which depended on the choice of objects (towers, castles, houses, huts, etc.) and architectural styles (from antiquity, medieval period, etc.). On the other hand, their presence suggested the absence of history. Naturally anachronistic and misplaced, follies artificially perpetuated decay and provided the framework for personalized, historically nonspecific contemplation of the transience of all things worldly.[48]

Despite this possibility of the suspension of concrete historical time, however, the purpose of the folly is clearly to address the grave questions of existence. The melancholy romantic beholder typically ponders the fundamental

---

46. Diderot, "Observations sur la sculpture et sur Bouchardon (1763)" (1876), 43. For the English translation, see Von Grimm, *Historical and Literary Memoirs*, 381–82; translation modified.

47. The fashion of fake ruins is older than the eighteenth century, however. For an extensive study on the historical and conceptual complexity and variety of artificial ruins and an attempt to classify them, see R. Zimmermann, *Künstliche Ruinen*. According to Zimmermann, the first-known artificial ruin was a derelict house built by Girolamo Genga for the Duke of Pesaro in the early sixteenth century (77).

48. For an account of the excesses of the fashion, see Macaulay, *Pleasure of Ruins*, 30–32.

subjection of all things, including every living being, to the passage of time. What is more, follies are embedded in a discursive frame that contextualizes them and ennobles (artificial) objects to kindle the viewer's lofty thoughts. This is the "grand gesture" that has accompanied representations and perceptions of ruins for centuries and reinforced a close and somewhat paradoxical affiliation between decay, aesthetic pleasure, and reflective discourse.[49] Karlheinz Stierle once labeled Petrarch's walk among the ruins of Rome and his retrospective account of the event as one of the poet's "grand gestures."[50] The scene and its discursive processing were codified as a sort of substitute for what had been lost in the reality of decline.[51] Stierle thereby addressed Petrarch's skills in building on the key feature of ruins—namely, their potential to point beyond themselves. Romanticism has explicitly linked this faculty to the question of time and grandness.[52] In his aforementioned 1763 remarks on Bouchardon, Diderot spoke of "grand ideas" caused by the interplay between ruins and the natural world. Four years later, he reiterated the thought in his critique of Hubert Robert's paintings of ruins. Focusing on temporal specificities, he described the sense of grandness as a form of insight into the old age of the world, the persistence of time, and the ephemerality of human existence.[53] The same faculty of ruins to transcend materiality and visibility was also highlighted by the English writer Thomas Whately in his *Observations on Modern Gardening*, first published in 1770. He stated that while real ruins "present facts to the memory," purposefully imperfect buildings "suggest . . . subjects to the imagination." Memory and imagination are carried "to something greater than is seen," and this greatness lies in the old structure and its purpose, of which real and fake ruins have to be reminiscent in order to unfold their effect.[54] One could conclude that greatness is once again a function of time insofar as it emerges by way of comparison between former integrity

49. Rose Macaulay speaks of the perversity of the aspect of pleasure: Macaulay, *Pleasure of Ruins*, xvii.
50. Stierle, *Francesco Petrarca: Ein Intellektueller*, 267.
51. For example, see Böhme, "Die Ästhetik der Ruinen," 287–304.
52. Without mentioning grandness, the Greek historian Thucydides (c. 460–400 BC) gave a remarkable account of the referentiality of ruins that can also be deceptive and obscure historical facts. See M. Dillon and Garland, *Ancient Greece*, 8: "If the Spartans' city were to become deserted, and only the temples and foundations of buildings were left, I think that the people of that time far in the future would find it difficult to believe that the Spartans' power had been as great as their fame implied . . . , whereas if the same thing were to happen to Athens, from its visible remains one would assume that the city had been twice as powerful as it actually is." Cf. Thuc. 1.10.2.
53. Diderot, *On Art II*, 198.
54. Whately, *Observations on Modern Gardening* (2016), 116–17.

and present fragmentation. Regardless of whether they are fake or real, ruins expose a semantic flexibility that informs the grandness of the insight into time and transience that ruins allow. They reveal a versatility of meaning that provides a source for the aesthetic pleasure ruins can spark. Diderot reprimanded Robert aesthetically when he stated that the painter knew nothing of such enjoyments because he did not understand what caused "ruinous magnificence."[55] In a more general sense, grandness ultimately appears as an element in the relationship between the concreteness of ruins and the realm of abstraction that lies beyond their object-being.

The role that grandness plays also shows that throughout their history, ruins were routinely expected to attest to meaning in one way or another. When they were placed outside the paradigm of signification, it was usually to make the case that cultural processes were subject to demise and semantic dissolution. Böhme has argued that the loss of "meaning" began in Romanticism with the detachment of ruins from their relationship with images and their inclusion in poetic concepts. According to this line of argumentation, Schlegel's theory of the fragment, for instance, no longer exclusively established discourses or grand gestures around ruins; instead, ruin and fragmentation were now the main characteristics of discourses. The discourses themselves were broken, a trait that Böhme considered to be a modern element of Romanticism. This assertion of cultural decline and the placement of fragmentation at culture's discursive center has gained widespread acceptance as a defining feature of modernity. It accompanied the claim that semiotic and semantic relations had altogether failed due to the irreversible breakdown of the individual's capacity and willingness to create, recognize, or use them, let alone deal with the confusing abundance of signs and the excess of meanings they designate. Modernity seemed to mark the final disappearance of the grand gesture and, with it, the ultimate collapse of cultural signification.[56]

Yet this interpretation raises red flags. Apart from affirming problematic epochal demarcation lines, it overlooks the fact that in situations seemingly evacuated of meaning, the hermeneutic perspective on ruins and ruin—the urge to render them significant—nonetheless persists. Even in contexts where ruins are intended to counteract phantasms of ideality, integrity, completion, and closure, the related discourses often remain within a paradigm of meaning making.

---

55. Diderot, *On Art II*, 198: "Monsieur Robert, you still don't understand why ruins give such pleasure, independently of the variety of accidents they manifest."

56. See Böhme, "Die Ästhetik der Ruinen," 279.

With this persistence of meaning in mind, I engage Johann Wolfgang von Goethe's and Georg Simmel's self-positioning with respect to literary history and the history of philosophy in part 5, "Futures and Ruins." Both authors attest to an opening of discourses qua ruins to their transformative potential and their interminability, but not to the end of meaning. Chapter 9 ("Johann Wolfgang von Goethe, Georg Simmel, and the Provisionality of Forms") casts a light on Goethe's "Novelle" as a long-term undertaking. More than thirty years passed between the initial idea and the publication of the piece in 1828, a time during which the author grappled with the right form for the story and reflected on the meaning of an aesthetic theory for his work. The final version of "Novelle" establishes the ruin as a model and a concept for the reflection on art and literature. The ruin takes the place of privileged Goethean paradigms of aesthetic consideration such as the tableau or architecture. With this major shift, Goethe thinks through the temporality and historicity of aesthetics in a new way. Toward the end of his life, he unexpectedly postponed the realization of an ideal work of art and instead made an argument for the fundamentally provisional character of all things aesthetic. Their permanent transformative faculty is considered not from the point of view of "the minted form that lives and living grows," but rather under the perspective of decay.[57] Almost one hundred years later, the avid Goethe reader Simmel set out to show that in the ruin a synthesis between the opposing, dialectical elements of "form" and "life" is possible. The antagonism between form and life is what he understands as the tragedy of culture (*Tragödie der Kultur*).[58] According to Simmel, the ruin captures the tragedy in an image and brings the relentless movement to a halt. However, a closer look suggests that the ruin, instead of representing the unity of form and life, is a symptom or even a by-product of the impossibility of joining opposites. In fact, it is a liminal figure between form and life that keeps philosophical thinking in motion.

Meaning indeed seems to thrive in the most unexpected places. Hell has shown that the German historian Oswald Spengler's notorious intervention against late nineteenth- and early twentieth-century faith in progress, which he so verbosely sets forth in his 1918 volume *The Decline of the West*, ultimately led to the counterreaction of Nazi theorists and artists who opposed the claim of an imminent decline of Western civilization with the idea of an impending resurrection of the Roman Empire through Germanic supremacy.[59] The concept of ruin value mirrored this idea in the construction

---

57. For this oft-quoted phrase, see Goethe's poem "Urworte. Orphisch" (1980).
58. Simmel, "Der Begriff und die Tragödie der Kultur" (1996).
59. Hell, "Imperial Ruin Gazers," 171.

of buildings. Adolf Hitler's architect Albert Speer studied static and material conditions, capable of anticipating the future beauty of the ruined edifice—an eternal beauty, comparable to the Roman model.[60] War criminals of the twentieth century thus seem to have favored the idea of survival and sense making over the celebration of decadence. And the gaze of the "postmodern" subject—shaped and marked by a centuries-long tradition—continues to perceive ruins (and even mere rubble) as indicators of the richness of meaning, even when it is ambivalent or instable.[61] In 1984, the social theorist Niklas Luhmann claimed that "[a] muddle of objects is never meaningless. [A] pile of rubble . . . is immediately recognizable as such and one can immediately tell whether it is attributable to time, to an earthquake, or to enemy action."[62] Luhmann's example bespeaks an all-encompassing legitimacy of meaning, distinctive of experiential and analytical approaches to ruins and reiterated in grand gestures. The heap of debris, as understood by Luhmann, is a "confusion of signs" that presupposes semiotic and semantic orders.[63] In other words, meaninglessness is a phenomenon feasible only in the domain of meaning.[64] This dependence of meaninglessness on meaning suggests that, regardless of whether the breakdown of the hermeneutic paradigm is placed in Romanticism, the twentieth century, or the early twenty-first century, the interventions made by the advocates of a theory of decadence not only ignore the enduring importance of meaning making but also habitually neglect the fact that ruins *always* have been potential signifiers of *both* the abundance of meaning and its very lack.[65] Oscillating between object and process, concept and thing, nature and culture, survival and decay, and situated between the

---

60. Speer, *Erinnerungen*, 69.

61. Regarding the centuries-long tradition, see Hell and Schönle, introduction to *Ruins of Modernity*, 1.

62. Luhmann, *Social Systems*, 62.

63. Luhmann, *Social Systems*, 62.

64. Stäheli, "Hegemony of Meaning," 108. Systems theory's formal definition of *meaning* as the unity of the distinction between actuality and potentiality complicates things. Psychic and social systems seek to simplify their relations with a complex environment by choosing from a range of possible interactions, and this selection process uses and constitutes meaning. *Meaninglessness* can therefore be understood as the equivalent of unrealized possibilities of communication. In this sense of nonmeaning being a potentiality that has not (yet) been actualized, meaning incorporates even its own negation. Luhmann has been criticized for neglecting the role of subjects in the process of actualization.

65. For a perspective on the vicinity of ruins (especially of modernity) to the breakdown of meaning, see Hell and Schönle, introduction to *Ruins of Modernity*, 6. Not related to ruins but to the function of meaninglessness is Koschorke, "Nicht-Sinn."

dimensions of time, ruins are, after all, "uniquely ill-defined."[66] Yet they are simultaneously overwhelming in their countless semantic possibilities.[67] As Helmut Puff puts it, what a ruin is can be contained neither "spatially," nor "temporally," nor "structurally," since ruins have a "persistent ability to cross such divides."[68]

For the following study of ruins, one possible conclusion to be made from their elusive quality is to substitute the question about what ruins are with the question about the textuality they manifest and the discourses they excite. To this end, my work seeks out ways for capturing both the force of the propensity of ruins for meaning making and their alignment with senselessness. In a nutshell, this study's alternative approach to ruins involves replacing conclusive definitions with discursive spaces. In doing so, the dialogues constituting the story of *Decay and Afterlife* harness the tensions arising from ruins for their ability to disclose the dynamics of cultural events and processes. The book's epilogue offers not only a backward glance at discourses about ruins traversed over eight hundred years of European aesthetic and intellectual history of decay and afterlife but also an outlook onto ruins of the twenty-first century by reflecting on discourses that take up the coeval feeling of pending global disasters and place it into relation with both past history and concepts of possible futures that emerge in spite of the all-encompassing decay. Against the backdrop of tradition, the question that must be asked in closing is not whether and how utopia arises from debris. Instead, we must ask how we can address the provocation that yesterday's futures are today's ruined presents. As will be established over the course of these pages, the conclusion to be drawn must be that decay is and always has been a necessary condition of the transforming and transfiguring force of afterlife.

---

66. Hell and Schönle, introduction to *Ruins of Modernity*, 6.
67. Puff, *Miniature Monuments*, 27: ". . . ruins invoke traditions, visual codes and a wealth of significations."
68. Puff, *Miniature Monuments*, 24–25. More specifically, Puff refers to Heckscher's concept not of ruins but of "ruin thought," which he understands as receptiveness to "inspection through the ruin-gazer" and as an indicator for the intrinsic modernity of ruins.

I

Foundations

1

Among Ruins:
Martin Heidegger and Sigmund Freud

This chapter introduces some of the main conceptual and theoretical parameters of the book by staging a dialogue between the German philosopher Martin Heidegger and the Austrian neurophysiologist and founder of psychoanalysis Sigmund Freud. The prospect of an encounter with a ruinous past that they know essentially as mediated through art and literature causes both thinkers anxieties and reluctance to engage with an actual experience of decay. In taking a physical approach to the ruins of Greece, they find their perception of reality challenged and thus reconsider the established discourses for which they are known as they simultaneously ponder, through their travel reports, the status of the emerging textuality that ruins manifest. Heidegger and Freud contemplate the relations between existing and new discourses, their defining features and their mutability, against the backdrop of a complex temporal setting that involves a tension between life-time and world-time.

Heidegger on the Move

When Martin Heidegger embarked on his first journey to Greece in 1962, he finally redeemed a Christmas present his wife Elfride had given him no less than nine years earlier. The trip had been planned, repeatedly postponed, and eventually canceled, until—in the year of his seventy-third birthday—Heidegger determined that he was finally ready. Accompanied by Elfride, he left Germany on a spring day in April.[1]

---

1. C. Meid, *Griechenland-Imaginationen*, 376–77.

The long-lasting indecision that preceded Heidegger's adventure was a clear sign that the prospect of setting foot on the land that had occupied much of his thinking throughout his lifetime created no small anxiety for the reluctant traveler. In the travel journal *Aufenthalte* (*Sojourns*), a counterpresent for Elfride's seventieth birthday, he recorded his experience and reflected on the reasons for the delay: "The proposal and the gift of a journey to Greece . . . was followed . . . by a long hesitation due to the fear of disappointment" (*SJ*, 4; *HG*, 217).[2]

Lurking in the familiar unfamiliarity of Heidegger's destination were at least two potential disillusionments.[3] One was the likely incompatibility between present-day Greece and Heidegger's view of old Greece, whose significance as the birthplace and origin of premetaphysical thought he incessantly sought to recover. The other worry was that Heidegger's ideas about ancient Greece, cornerstones of his reflective efforts, would fail the test of reality and prove unfit to further sustain the unity of his philosophy. The physical encounter with Greece threatened to compromise the very core of his work.[4]

These concerns would linger with Heidegger once he boarded the ship in Venice and set out to visit the Peloponnese, the islands of Crete and Rhodes, and—on the way back to Venice—the island of Delos, the city of Athens, and Aegina and Delphi. While everyone else enjoyed the sights, Heidegger mulled over the purpose of the undertaking. It intensified his concerns that Friedrich Hölderlin, who was his literary source for all things Hellenic and subject of his utmost admiration, had never set foot in Greece (*SJ*, 1–2; *HG*, 215).

Heidegger starts his report with a quote from Hölderlin's 1801 poem "Brod und Wein" ("Bread and Wine").[5] The poet's virtual presence hovers over the

---

2. Heidegger, *Sojourns: The Journey to Greece* (hereafter cited as *SJ*). For the German text, see Heidegger, *Zu Hölderlin, Griechenlandreisen* (hereafter cited as *HG*). I will indicate the page numbers of the English translation followed by the page number of the edition of the German original after each quotation and at the end of a paragraph in instances where I summarize the content of Heidegger's account. The dedication of *Aufenthalte* in *Zu Hölderlin, Griechenlandreisen* reads, "Der Mutter zum siebzigsten Geburtstag. Ein Zeichen des Beschenkten" ("To the mother for her seventieth birthday. A token from the presentee"; translation mine).

3. In 1954 Heidegger had written to his friend Erhart Kästner that in his "thinking-romancing dialogues" he always lived in Greece ("Zwar lebe ich in den denkend-dichtenden Zwiesprachen immer dort"). Heidegger, "Brief an Erhart Kästner, 1.1.1954" (1986), 22.

4. In a similar argument, Peter Geimer claims that Heidegger's travels were characterized by the pressure to have an (appropriate) experience ("Erfahrungsdruck"). Geimer, "Frühjahr 1962," 51.

5. "Aber die Thronen, wo? die Tempel, und wo die Gefäße, / Wo mit Nektar gefüllt, Göttern zu Lust der Gesang? / Wo, wo leuchten sie denn, die fernhintreffenden Sprüche? / Delphi schlummert und wo tönet das große Geschick?" (But the thrones, where are they, the temples,

trip and implicitly permeates the philosopher's entire travel journal. With Hölderlin, Heidegger associated a far-reaching expectation that was also the reason for his eventual decision to visit Greece. The poet was at the center of the philosopher's critique of metaphysics and his attempt to renew—after the shift in his thinking known as the "turn" (*Kehre*)—"the question of the meaning of Being."[6] Heidegger's project of fundamental ontology and since the 1930s of the history of Being rests on the idea of two beginnings of philosophy. At the time of the first beginning before Plato and Aristotle, the meaning of Being was accessible. It has since been superseded by the preoccupation with beings. Yet the present moment is one of transition from the era of metaphysics to the other beginning (*der andere Anfang*), which, according to Heidegger, is not only a second beginning of philosophy but of history as well.[7] In this transition, Hölderlin's poetry plays a crucial role. It paves the way toward a better understanding of Being by using a language capable of addressing Being in its unfolding and therefore its historicity. It is a language that conveys—quite unlike philosophical concepts—what eludes definition.[8] In contrast to the inevitability of his own physical presence in Greece that Heidegger blames on a state of "poverty for poetic thoughts," he emphasizes in *Sojourns* Hölderlin's apparent superiority over any kind of actual experience (*SJ*, 2–4; *HG*, 215–16). He attributes this enviable privilege of not having to travel to the poet's ability to create, in his poetry, a historical experience of time (*SJ*, 1–2; *HG*, 215). In Heidegger's eyes, Hölderlin thereby proclaims the coming of a novel history and reveals glimpses of the mysterious nature of Being.[9]

Heidegger had laid out the meaning of the "other beginning" of philosophy and its relation with historical time decades before his trip to Greece in *Contributions to Philosophy*, first published 1936–1938. It is here that the idea of the first and second beginning of philosophy (and history) is combined

---

and where are the vessels, / Where the delight of gods, brimming with nectar, the song? / Where do the oracles gleam, striking far into the distance? / Delphi slumbers; where does the weighty destiny sound?). Hölderlin, *Sämtliche Gedichte und Hyperion*, 285–91; Ranson, "Brod und Wein; Bread and Wine." With a few exceptions, ß has been rendered ss throughout the entire book.

6. For Heidegger's critique of metaphysics, see Heidegger, *Being and Time* (2001). For the quotations, see Habermas, *Philosophical Discourse of Modernity* (1987), 137, 141. For the original German edition, see Habermas, *Der philosophische Diskurs der Moderne* (1985).

7. Andreas Grossmann points out that Heidegger's focus on Hölderlin that started in the 1930s was ultimately "a reflection on the essence of history and the problem of beginning." Grossmann, "Myth of Poetry," 30.

8. Grossmann, "Myth of Poetry," 31; Figal, *Martin Heidegger: Zur Einführung*, 136–39.

9. Müller-Funk, *Die Dichter der Philosophen*, 15.

with that of the "sojourn." In the introduction, Heidegger writes, "These 'contributions' question along a way which is first paved by the *transition* to the other beginning, the one Western thought is now entering. This way brings the transition into the open realm of history and founds the transition as a possibly very long sojourn."[10] The passage sets forth that *sojourn* is the interval between two efforts of coping with the problem of Being. Apparently, Heidegger still found himself in this transitional state when in 1962 he reflected on the term in his travel journal.

In the following pages I examine how Heidegger, in his endeavor to account for a second beginning of philosophy and a revival of the exploration of Being, reshapes his own philosophical discourse while lingering among the ruins of Greece. In the discontinuous temporal realm of his sojourns, Heidegger supplements, as I will show, the fragments of the past on the way to a new form of thinking that rests on the basis of old ideas. In this scenario, ruins are not just the setting in which the transformation of Heidegger's philosophy takes place. The changes emerge from their textuality, a discourse *about* ruins in the travel journal that Heidegger aligns with the discursive possibilities that Hölderlin's poetry offers. The resulting dynamic is one in which discourses sustain, include, and modify each other and guarantee one another's survival over time. Part of the complexity of Heidegger's thinking is that the resulting insights and evidence from a visit in the flesh to the ruins of antiquity are not, as one might expect, dependent on acts of seeing. In fact, the visual impressions Greek ruins make only count for Heidegger insofar as they can be directly absorbed into reflections and further deliberations. What ruins evince in a specific moment in time and what Heidegger hopes to detect among them is always already an element in a polyphony of discourses—those that precede and those that follow the immediate encounter with decay.

In Greece at last, Heidegger has seemingly surrendered to the travel imperative for the poetically ungifted. Yet each shore the ship approaches threatens a new mismatch with the beholder's expectations that have been shaped by his readings. "The first impression would not agree with the picture that the poet gives in book VI of the Odyssey," Heidegger states at the sight of Corfu (*SJ*, 7–8; *HG*, 218). The essence of Greece eludes the visitor who seeks to embed his experience in an already existing discursive framework. In Olympia, instead of overwhelming the beholder, the unfettered grandeur of the fallen column drums at the temple of Zeus and Hera disappoint Heidegger because

---

10. Heidegger, *Contributions to Philosophy (Of the Event)* (2012), 6 (emphasis in the original). For the German text, see Heidegger, *Beiträge zur Philosophie (Vom Ereignis)* (1989).

they fail to explain the former purpose of these consecrated buildings (*SJ*, 13–14; *HG*, 221–22). What he yearns to find, the proper character of Greece that could bring him closer to the essence of Being, lays buried underneath the debris, until in Delos a decisive moment transpires. Heidegger is on a hike through the island's ruinscape toward the peak of Mount Kynthos when the first indications of change make themselves felt. "In comparison with everything else we have seen up to now . . . the island looked on first sight deserted and abandoned, in such a way, though, that it couldn't have been the result of mere decline" (*SJ*, 30; *HG*, 231). There is, on this particular island, something hidden behind the immediate material decay that Heidegger intuits but that he cannot capture instantly. However, while guiding his readers up the mountain and through an elaborate reflexive process, Heidegger is on his way to identifying what he senses with the core of his philosophy. As he approaches the mountaintop, he gains ever more insight into the island's significance: "The island is called Δῆλος [*Dēlos*]: the manifest [*die Offenbare*], the visible [*die Scheinende*] . . . Δῆλος [is] the sacred island, the center of the Greek land . . . [It] reveals insofar as it conceals [*offenbart, indem sie verbirgt*]" (*SJ*, 30–31; *HG*, 231–32).[11] The conjunction of "the unconcealed (revealing) and the concealed (sheltering)"[12] is what Heidegger perceives as the truth, or "Ἀλήθεια" (*Alētheia*; *SJ*, 32; *HG*, 232) in Greek thought, which is the equivalent of an opening up of Being for human understanding.[13]

At the time of the first Greek trip, the concept of *Alētheia* had been on Heidegger's mind for almost four decades. The experience in Delos, although it was the first genuine encounter with Greece as an actual place, was therefore not a moment of surprising novelty. It much rather allowed for reflection and dwelling and eventually for the confirmation of *Alētheia* as the already established discursive center of Heidegger's thinking (*SJ*, 32–34; *HG*, 232–33). In Delos, the journey lost its air of restless compulsion. It merged into the state that Heidegger termed "sojourn" (*Aufenthalt*) and defined, in *Contributions to Philosophy*, as a transition en route to the rediscovery of Being.

---

11. According to Greek mythology, Delos is the birthplace of Apollo and Artemis.

12. Translation modified. What I translate with "unconcealed (revealing) and concealed (sheltering)" is the German "Unverborgenheit (Entbergen) und Verborgenheit (Bergen)." My translation replaces Manoussakis's variants inside the parentheses, "the unhidden" and "the hidden." *Entbergen* and *Bergen* are nominalized German verbs, and *Bergen* carries the meaning "sheltering," which the English *hidden* does not preserve. *Unverborgenheit, Entbergen, Verborgenheit*, and *Bergen* share the same etymological root.

13. For a discussion of Heidegger's ontological difference and the question of truth, see Van Reijen, "Heideggers ontologische Differenz" (2004), 525–30.

But the continuation of the journey reveals that the second beginning was not yet within reach. As the ship departed from Delos and set course for Mykonos, Heidegger contemplated whether, under the technological conditions of modern travel and the fast pace of modern times, the transitional temporal space of sojourns was or would inevitably become obsolete (*SJ*, 36; *HG*, 234). When Athens got within sight, the doubts had already turned into the pessimistic vision of the "growing desert of earth's inexorable destiny," the industrial age, "that denies sojourn" (*SJ*, 38; *HG*, 235, translation modified). In front of the belated traveler, the wasteland of modernity stretched as far as the eye could see. With the prospect of a smooth transition now uncertain, the recovery of Being was cast in doubt.

It would take another visit to the Greek ruins five years later to revive Heidegger's confidence in a second beginning of philosophy (*HG*, 249–73).[14] A weeklong cruise through the Aegean offered him the chance to revisit—with Hölderlin in mind and a collection of his poems in pocket—the old question about the future significance of the premetaphysical origins of Western history and thought. Walking around the Acropolis again, Heidegger muses that the sacredness of the place is still palpable even though the gods have abandoned it long ago. What is sacred, he states, appears insofar as it conceals itself (*erscheinend im Sichverbergen*; *HG*, 254). Clearly, Heidegger's wording suggests that on the Acropolis we are in the middle of another instance of *Alētheia* enabled by ruins. Yet this time around, the experience does not stop at the recollection of past philosophical achievements. The transgression of the boundaries of familiar ideas happens on the occasion of a visit to the well-preserved Temple of Hephaestus. Heidegger's impression in front of the nearly intact building is almost the reverse of the one he had five years earlier, when in Delos he recognized something more in the ruins than the material evidence of destruction. Paradoxically, integrity induces a sense of void. "Where did," he asks, "despite the unusually good condition of this temple-structure, its coldness, its murkiness, its emptiness come from?" (*HG*, 254).[15] It leads Heidegger to consider whether "we, the late-born [*wir Spätgeborenen*], need the fragment" (*HG*, 254). In contrast to the empty soundness of the temple's

---

14. Heidegger entitled this manuscript *Zu den Inseln der Ägäis* (*Toward the Islands of the Aegean*, usually translated as *On the Islands of the Aegean*). All translations are mine. I will indicate the page number of the German original either after my translation or at the end of a paragraph in cases where I summarize Heidegger's account.

15. In the original, "Woher kam jedoch, der ungewöhnlich guten Erhaltung zum Trotz, das Kalte, das Düstere, das Leere dieses Tempelwerks, was auch das ringsum Blühende nicht aufzuheitern vermochte?"

construction, he praises the ruins of the Acropolis that shine in the "light of supplementation [*im Lichte des Ergänzens*]" (*HG*, 255).

As indicated in the introduction to this book, the idea that true splendor can arise from incompleteness has haunted ruin discourses for a long time. Ruins scholar Wilhelm Sebastian Heckscher starts his 1936 reflections on Rome by quoting Stendhal's remark that the decaying Colosseum is more beautiful than the intact construction ever was.[16] The acknowledgment of beauty in decay was accompanied by an evolving recognition that the unique aesthetics of ruins was rooted in their former wholeness; in their broken state, they were an indication of future integrity. In other words, beauty essentially appeared to be based on a promise of totality, and supplementation was the means to bring that promise closer to its fulfillment.[17]

Heidegger's intuition that the fragment was a necessity for his generation seems to have sprung from a similar insight, except that he applied it to his own philosophical discourse. In the travel report, he states that the ideas that arose in Athens—the thoughts about the significance of the fragment—had an extrinsic, close to intrusive quality but that at the same time they blended in with familiar concepts. "They [i.e., the ideas] demanded entrance to my own thinking," he writes, and adds that his thinking had long known the necessity of supplementation (*HG*, 255). Not yet entirely part of his mind-set, the Athenian ideas seemed to be elements of an emergent kind of thinking that he could call complete and that he could embrace as his own.

The notion that Heidegger supplied his thinking with new ideas and, in the process, conquered unknown intellectual territory has been harshly contested—and with good reason. While it is blatantly obvious that at the time of the Greek journey Heidegger's reflections on Being were anything but a brand-new building brick in his intellectual edifice, it is perhaps more surprising that neither was the form in which he presented his search for what was properly Greek. His efforts in the travelogue to evoke a certain impression of eventfulness, singularity, and authenticity—for many critics a failed undertaking in itself—stand in odd contrast to previous, similarly structured discussions of the same topic.[18] This raises the question of what the real purpose of Heidegger's self-exposure to the risk of reality is. The peculiar iteration

---

16. Heckscher, *Die Romruinen*, 1.

17. Böhme, "Die Ästhetik der Ruinen" (1989), 287. See also Julia Hell's remarks on Freud in Hell, *Conquest of Ruins* (2019), 23. Hell does not address beauty but does pose the question why ruins speak to us. According to Hell, one of the reasons is that we "see what is missing" and know what would fill the void.

18. See Geimer, "Frühjahr 1962," 58–59. Geimer refers to the *Origin of the Work of Art* (1950) and an essay entitled *Aletheia (Heraklit, Fragment 16)* (1943).

on several levels seems to imply a certain immunity to change. One might even ask whether Heidegger—as Jürgen Habermas suggested with respect to his late work—was trying to shield his philosophy from "all empirical and normative questions that can be . . . handled in argumentative form," an attitude which, according to Habermas, fell in line with Heidegger's unapologetic commitment to National Socialism.[19] The use of Hölderlin to reaffirm the significance of the philosophy of Being has been perceived as mere exploitation of the poet.[20] From this point of view, Heidegger's assertion of the importance of supplementation, as well as the display of his anxiety about the uncertain outcome of his trip, come under suspicion of being calculated strategies instead of philosophical engagements with the unexpected and novel forms of thinking.[21] It seems that while on the surface Heidegger entrusted to Hölderlin the poetic retrieval of philosophy, his travel journals disguise a deeply rooted distrust in "that which is coming" and doubts that a new beginning of philosophy will ever materialize.[22]

As plausible as this assessment may be, the present analysis points in the opposite direction. It considers Heidegger's encounter with the remains of

---

19. Habermas, *Philosophical Discourse of Modernity*, 139.

20. There is a vast literature on the subject. See, e.g., Schmücker, "Monologisches Gespräch," 550–68; or Paul de Man's remark on the reasons for Heidegger's focus on Hölderlin in De Man, *Blindness and Insight*, 254: "It is the fact that Hölderlin says exactly the opposite of what Heidegger makes him say." See also Gosetti-Ferencei, *Heidegger, Hölderlin, and the Subject of Poetic Language*. Heidegger himself explicitly denied any aesthetic or literary-historical purpose of his Hölderlin-interpretation. See the preface to the fourth edition of volume 4 of the complete works: Heidegger, *Elucidations of Hölderlin's Poetry* (2000), 21: "The present Elucidations do not claim to be contributions to research in the history of literature or to aesthetics. They spring from a necessity of thought." For the German original, see Heidegger, *Erläuterungen zu Hölderlins Dichtung* (1981), 7.

21. I thank Lutz Koepnick for pointing out to me that it confirms Heidegger's tendency to shield his thinking from any kind of historical intervention that in his account of the 1967 trip to Greece he completely neglects to mention the coup d'état that had taken place less than a month before Heidegger set out on his second journey.

22. Julia Hell discusses Heidegger's perspective on novelty and how it relates to the past in the context of his understanding of the relationship between empires—particularly that of the Nazis—and historical time: "Heidegger . . . applied his early critique of historicism to the Nazis' appropriation of the past . . . For Heidegger, to think historically involved . . . a journey of discovery, searching for the otherness of the past. This originary otherness of the West could only be rediscovered in the encounter with ancient Greece in the *future*, through the work of remembrance reserved for philosophers and poets." Hell, *Conquest of Ruins*, 440. While I agree with Hell's assessment of Heidegger's critique of historicism's perception of the past as an imitable, re-presentable entity, I would add that for Heidegger only the poet's remembrance is a given. The philosopher's is jeopardized by a lack of confidence.

antiquity as a frame for the *reexamination* and *further development* of his key ideas in which Hölderlin assumes center stage. I will show that Heidegger opened his philosophy—the form of his thinking—to the influence of poetic discourse and transformation. Hölderlin's poetry is the supplement that actually alters Heidegger's philosophy and guarantees its afterlife beyond mere repetition.

Heidegger's dialogue with Hölderlin began in 1934-1935 with a lecture on Hölderlin's hymns "Germanien" and "Der Rhein," and it continued until the philosopher's death. This long-lasting engagement alone indicates the exceptional place that Hölderlin's work occupied in Heidegger's thinking. In *Contributions to Philosophy*, Hölderlin's poetry appears as the first manifestation of the transition from metaphysics to an understanding of Being in the second beginning of philosophy and a new beginning of history. But Heidegger's appreciation goes much further. In his view, the historical determination of philosophy depends on whether or not Hölderlin's poetic word can make itself heard. As I have indicated already, it is uniquely suited to express the significance of Being by revealing what is concealed. Heidegger insists that Hölderlin's poetry concerns us as (our) destiny (*Geschick*). The term is notoriously difficult to translate, and its meaning changes over the course of Heidegger's Hölderlin interpretations.[23] What can be clearly grasped, however, is the reference to the transformative ways in which Being gives itself to us through Hölderlin's poetic language if we are willing to listen.[24] In his 1946 lecture "Anaximander's Saying," Heidegger states that "a great deal depends on the manner, in which we ... open ourselves to the claim of destiny [*Geschick*]."[25]

Yet the confidence that Heidegger places in Hölderlin's poetry does not prevent him from simultaneously claiming that poetic change is based on philosophical conceptualization. With respect to our susceptibility to what is destined such that the second beginning can come into view, he rhetorically asks whether it can "ever happen without thinking."[26] Disclosing the meaning of Being thus appears to be the outcome of a cooperation between two discourses or the work of thought arranging and organizing the achievements of poetry.[27] At the same time, Heidegger did not take the convergence of his

23. For a discussion of the meaning of Geschick between destiny, ordering, history, sending, gift, appointing, furnishing and so on, see Guignon, "History of Being," 397-98.
24. I follow Iris Buchheim's article on Heidegger's Hölderlin reception: Buchheim, "Heidegger," 432-33.
25. Quotation from lecture as published in Heidegger, *Off the Beaten Track* (2002), 255.
26. Heidegger, *Off the Beaten Track*, 255.
27. Buchheim, "Heidegger," 433-34.

thinking with Hölderlin's poetry for granted. In his lecture "What Is Called Thinking?" from 1952 he writes, "It is still questionable with what right we, by way of an attempt to think, make mention of a poet, this poet in particular. And it is also still unclear upon what ground, and within what limits, our reference to the poetic must remain."[28] Heidegger circles around this thought, rephrases it several times, and tries to define the conditions under which it can be conceived: "On our way toward thinking, we hear a word of poesy. But the question to what end and with what right . . . our attempt to think allows itself to get involved in a dialogue with poesy . . . this question we can discuss only after we ourselves have taken the path of thinking." A few passages later, Heidegger seems to have approached an understanding of his own juxtaposition between the poetic and the philosophical:

> This much might be clear to us right now: we are not dragging Hölderlin's words into our lecture merely as a quotation from the realm of the poetic statement which will enliven and beautify the dry process of thinking. To do so would be to debase the poetic word. Its statement rests on its own truth. This truth is called beauty. Beauty is a fateful gift of the essence of truth [*Geschick des Wesens der Wahrheit*], and here truth means the disclosure of what keeps itself concealed. The beautiful is not what pleases, but what falls within that fateful gift of truth [*Geschick der Wahrheit*] . . . What is stated poetically, and what is stated in thought, are never identical [*das Gleiche*]; but there are times when they are the same [*das Selbe*].[29]

Heidegger identifies the origin of the poetic word's intrinsic value in its beauty, which is part of the philosophical quest for truth as unconcealed concealment. The importance of the "poetic statement" stems from its position at the center of (Heidegger's) philosophy but also from its historical specificity. The sameness of poetry and philosophy is grounded in the differences of their forms.

This trajectory of Heidegger's argument allows then for a decisive conclusion: Hölderlin's poetic word, which chronologically precedes Heidegger's philosophy, leads an afterlife in the philosopher's thought, but in a way that upsets any notion of hierarchical or temporal linearity. First, the poetic word—being more than mere ornamental quotation—claims the right to its own truth, a truth that is equiprimordial with concern for *Alētheia*. Second, by pointing out that his thinking leads the way in a discussion about the relationship between poetry and thought, Heidegger turns the temporal and

---

28. Heidegger, *What Is Called Thinking?* (1968), 12. For the German original, see: Heidegger, *Was heisst Denken?* (1954).

29. Heidegger, *What Is Called Thinking?*, 19–20.

historical succession upside down and claims that the result (his thinking) is in fact the premise (the impact of Hölderlin's work). At the same time, however, it is on the philosopher's way *toward* thinking that he hears "a word of poesy" and follows the aesthetic call—a call that ultimately leads him on a physical trip to Greece. In that sense, afterlife indicates that poetry lives on in philosophy and vice versa. The travel journals, instead of being documents of a reiterative process of thinking, draw on the incompleteness of discourses, the necessity of fragments, and the mutual supplementation of poetry and philosophy.[30]

Before we continue, let us use Heidegger's endeavor to navigate between discourses and describe their interrelation as an excuse to take a brief detour through Jacques Derrida's 1967 critique of the logocentrism of Western metaphysics in *Of Grammatology*, wherein the idea of the logic of supplementation occupies an important place. Drawing on Heidegger, Derrida rejects the focus of Western philosophy on presence or that which *is*. In linguistic terms, he repudiates the obsession with speech and promotes concepts that have traditionally been perceived as secondary to the spoken word, most important among them writing and text. Derrida's venture is not least a rejection of the idea of an origin or a transcendental signified to which signifiers are subject and to which they refer in the fashion of a quasi-optional supplement. Derrida's decisive move is to privilege what has been neglected precisely because of its supplementary character. A feature of textuality itself, the supplement, as Derrida understands it, is inherently paradoxical. "The concept of the supplement," he writes, "harbors within itself two significations whose cohabitation is as strange as it is necessary. The supplement adds itself, it is a surplus, a plenitude enriching another plenitude . . . But the supplement supplements. It adds only to replace. It intervenes or insinuates itself in-the-place-of; if it fills, it is as one fills a void."[31] Set against this deconstructionist backdrop, Heidegger's approach shows how poetry and philosophy supplement each other between lack and excess—a process that ultimately obliterates the origin of the dynamic of supplementation and renders indiscernible which discourse carries greater authority.

Flexible forms of poetry and thinking appear in a realm of discontinuous transition, one that—to repeat Heidegger's words—will turn out to be

---

30. My interpretation of the relationship between the two works as mutual supplementation goes further than that of Müller-Funk, who understands it as mutual comments; see Müller-Funk, *Die Dichter der Philosophen*, 19.

31. Derrida, *On Grammatology*, 144–45.

"a possibly very long sojourn."[32] In his travel journals, "sojourn" is a state of dwelling in which the rapidly advancing world-time of the industrial age is suspended.[33] Sojourns happen among ruins, when those born (too) late take it upon themselves to do the work of supplementation. In this constellation, sojourn emerges as a temporal entity that is identical neither with Heidegger's life-time nor with the time of the world, but instead comprises characteristics of the first and stands in contrast to the second. Sojourn is a concept that points to a limited time period, to a temporal sequence or an interruption in the course of world-time.

Heidegger's travels to Greece reveal just how precarious the various meanings of Being and just how delicate the significance of existence and human history are. They emerge in situations of decay, against the backdrop of temporal limitations and crises of continuity. But just as these instants of disintegration display the fragility of our lives and the mutability of the worldly context in which they evolve, they are also moments of possibility. Out of the supplementation and transformation of forms emanates an afterlife of discourses poised to make up for historical and anthropological deficiencies and ensure the survival of the intellectual ruins of the past.

Freud's Disturbance of Memory

The way in which Heidegger arrives at profound musings about the discursive force of antiquity's ruins from his reluctant encounter with Greece is unique in its detail. In terms of the underlying configuration, however, it is not unprecedented. In what follows, we go back in time to the year 1904 to join Sigmund Freud on a trip to Athens, which he described in a letter written to Romain Rolland more than thirty years later. The journey will serve as the context for yet another reflection on a similar dynamic of discursive innovation and afterlife that Heidegger would later engage against the backdrop of tensions between life-time and world-time. As will be shown, what both thinkers have in common is an incentive for discursive transformation that is not primarily visual; in other words, their visual experiences are subject to an elaborate discursive framework before they even take place. Before we accompany Freud on this next adventure, let us first take a look at the role of archaeology and ruins in one of Freud's studies on hysteria and the late work

---

32. Heidegger, *Contributions to Philosophy (Of the Event)*, 6–7.

33. At the beginning of *Sojourns*, Heidegger talks about the world he lives in as a "human world that races along the borders of self-destruction" ("eine[] Menschenwelt, die am Rande der Selbstzerstörung entlang rast"), (*SJ*, 4; *HG*, 215).

Civilization and Its Discontents (*Das Unbehagen in der Kultur*), published in 1930. They will prepare the ground for an assessment of what is specific about his encounter with *Greek* ruins. The goal is to uncover the textuality that ruins manifest that in some cases accounts for the continuity of time, meaning making, and the discourses in which they appear. In others, it triggers fundamental reexaminations and renewal.

Throughout Freud's work, the comparison between archaeology and the practice of psychoanalysis is a recurring rhetorical strategy and a correspondence that he deemed enlightening like no other. In "Delusion and Dream in Wilhelm Jensen's 'Gradiva'" ("Der Wahn und die Träume in W. Jensens 'Gradiva'"), published in 1907, Freud explicitly states that "there is no better analogy for repression, which at the same time makes inaccessible and conserves something psychic, than the burial which was the fate of Pompeii, and from which the city was able to arise again through work with the spade."[34] Just as an archaeologist uncovers earlier stages of human history by digging vertically into its buried layers, the psychoanalyst digs into the past history of the human soul and exposes the "mental antiquities" (*seelische Altertümer*) that populate the foreign regions of the unconscious.[35] Freud's remark varies a theme that he introduced in 1905 in "Fragment of an Analysis of a Case of Hysteria" ("Bruchstück einer Hysterie-Analyse"), wherein he speaks of "discoverers" who "bring to the light of the day after their long burial the priceless though mutilated relics of antiquity."[36]

In her reading of Freud's 1905 study, Julia Hell shows that there are good reasons why the quality of the relationship between the archaeological metaphor and the analyst's method ought to be described as visual. Freud seeks to explain how symptoms can give some indication of the cause of hysteria by inviting his readers to follow a thought experiment in which an explorer comes across architectural remains in an unfamiliar environment and has two options to approach them: either interpret what meets the eye or "uncover what is buried." If the explorer chooses to examine what is hidden underneath the debris, the stones will speak like symptoms by indicating what they used to be when they were part of a whole.[37] Hell argues that ruins "take shape as the effects of a visual trajectory . . . All Freud's archeologist needs

---

34. Freud, "Delusion and Dream in Wilhelm Jensen's 'Gradiva'" (1999), 40.
35. Freud, *Interpretation of Dreams (First Part)* (1999), 549.
36. Freud, "Fragment of an Analysis of a Case of Hysteria" (1999), 12. See also Hell, *Conquest of Ruins*, 21.
37. Freud, "Fragment of an Analysis of a Case of Hysteria," 192.

to do is look, look and read," for what the explorer sees explains itself. The "essence" of Freud's analogy between archaeology and psychoanalysis, Hell concludes, is therefore "empiricism, the unmediated apprehension and comprehension of the world through vision."[38]

While Freud's work on hysteria lends itself to a visually informed juxtaposition of the unconscious and ruins, the comparison has lost its air of self-explanatory obviousness when Freud reiterates it in *Civilization and Its Discontents*. He is now eager to prove that our imagination and means of visual representation (*anschauliche Darstellung*) are not suited to shed light on the life of the mental organism. In his text, Freud once again sends an archaeologically versed traveler on an imaginary tour of discovery, this time in Rome. And while the knowledgeable visitor finds ruinous traces of the ancient metropolis scattered across the modern cityscape, Freud points out that the landscape of the unconscious itself bears no ruins. As if all of Rome's architectural history were intact and present in one space, nothing perishes and everything persists in the subconscious. The past and the present coexist in perfect, incorruptible integrity: "Now let us, by a flight of imagination, suppose that Rome is not a human habitation but a psychical entity with a similarly long and copious past—an entity, that is to say, in which nothing that has once come into existence will have passed away and all the earlier phases of development continue to exist alongside the latest one."[39] Freud acknowledges, however, that assuming this kind of far-reaching simultaneity of the nonsimultaneous and translating it into spatial terms pushes the boundaries of the imaginable. Hell states that for the present and the past to come into view at once, a specific skill is required—namely, a "scopic mastery" that allows for the utmost flexibility of the gaze, apt to smoothly shift between perspectives.[40]

In what follows, I pursue a different aspect of Freud's "archaeology of the soul" by focusing not on the visual challenge but on the uncertain self-evidence of the alliance between the unconscious and ruins. Freud's trip to Greece and the epistolary travelogue he writes years later, to which I shall now turn, reveal that the visual experience on the Acropolis does not require a skilled and agile observer but rather one who has a discursive framework at one's disposal, a grand gesture or form that lends the encounter sense, purpose, and structure. As we will see, the form capable of elucidating the events in Athens is the Oedipal conflict. In the temporally intricate constellation of

---

38. Hell, *Conquest of Ruins*, 22–23.
39. Freud, *Civilization and Its Discontents*, 69.
40. Hell, *Conquest of Ruins*, 135.

distorted memory triggered by the experience of decay and told in retrospect, the question is how a core piece of Freud's thinking shapes the textuality that ruins manifest and how it is, in turn, affected by it.

Freud wrote his aforementioned open letter to Rolland on the occasion of the novelist's seventieth birthday and framed it as a deficient substitute for a worthier sign of admiration that he felt incapable of creating.[41] Ten years Rolland's senior, Freud claimed that the "powers of production" were failing him at his age. The self-analysis he decided to perform instead was based on the recurring memory of a mysterious mental process that he had experienced and left unanalyzed "a generation ago." As Freud apologetically forewarned the addressee, it required "more attention to some events in my private life than they would otherwise deserve" (*SE*, 239).

In the fall of 1904, Freud and his younger brother visited the Acropolis on their annual trip to the Mediterranean. The siblings had ended up in Athens somewhat accidentally. Initially headed to Corfu, they abandoned their original destination at the last minute due to an acquaintance's recommendation to avoid the heat of the island and spend their short holidays in the Greek capital. With only a few hours left before the departure of the boat from Trieste and in strangely "depressed spirits," they had first ruminated on the manifold reasons why a journey to Athens might be ill advised (*SE*, 240). But when it was time to embark, they tacitly agreed in an inexplicable mutual change of heart that the trip was the right thing to do. "Such behavior, it must be confessed, was most strange," Freud writes. "Later on, we recognized that we had accepted the suggestion that we should go to Athens instead of Corfu instantly and most readily. But, if so, why had we . . . foreseen nothing but obstacles and difficulties?" (*SE*, 240).

The similarities between the circumstances of Freud's and Heidegger's travels to Greece are obvious. The same purpose is met with a variety of ultimately ineffective arguments as to why it should not be pursued. Compared to Heidegger's long-term reluctance, the Freud brothers' afternoon-long indecision does evoke an impression of coquetry rather than agony, but the premises for the eventual journey are closely related. They both have to do with the status and perception of reality. Freud, for his part, even though he does not understand the reasons at the time, is aware that even the short hesitation is

---

41. Freud, "New Introductory Lectures on Psycho-Analysis and Other Works," in *The Standard Edition of the Complete Psychological Works of Sigmund Freud*, vol. 12 (1964, hereafter cited as *SE*), 239–48. For the German original, see Freud, "Brief an Romain Rolland (Eine Erinnerungsstörung auf der Akropolis)" (1978), 250–57.

significant. He will wonder for years why the time before the departure from Italy was so unpleasant.

In both Freud's letter and Heidegger's account, Greece is the site of a key moment in their respective travel experiences that would not only expand the limits set by the journey but also affect their intellectual personae. Whereas Heidegger's entire undertaking is consciously geared toward the moment of truth and reassurance in Delos, and *Alētheia* and discursive transformation in Athens, Freud finds himself exposed on the Acropolis to an unpremeditated instant of amazement that "this really *does* exist, just as we learnt at school" (*SE*, 241). In the course of his belated interpretation of this spontaneous and bewildering reaction when faced with the ruins of antiquity, Freud draws a connection between his surprise and his gloomy mood in Trieste. He reads both incidents as "expression[s] of incredulity," at the sudden prospect, called forth in Italy, of seeing Athens and at the actual sighting of a place thought to be beyond his reach. Yet what should have been a manifestation of joy about a unique occasion came in "distorted . . . disguise" and confused the beholder (*SE*, 243). In retrospect, Freud found his doubts about "a piece of reality"—namely, his unexpected presence in Athens—"doubly displaced." They were "shifted back into the past," and they were "transposed" from Freud's "relation to the Acropolis onto the very existence of the Acropolis" (*SE*, 243). As a result, the marveling disbelief of the grown-up traveler regarding his current situation was transformed into a skepticism he had allegedly felt as a boy who questioned what he was taught at school. In his letter, Freud explains these shifts as coping strategies in the light of a "feeling of derealization" (*Entfremdungsgefühl*) that is itself a defense mechanism: "The whole psychical situation, which . . . is so difficult to describe, can be satisfactorily cleared up by assuming that at the time [meaning: on the Acropolis] I had (or might have had) a momentary feeling: "*What I see here is not real*" . . . the phenomena of derealization . . . all serve the purpose of defense; they aim at keeping something away from the ego" (*SE*, 244–45). In other words, derealization depends on a distortion of the past. Freud terms his experience among the ruins a "disturbance of memory" (*Erinnerungsstörung*) that leads to false assumptions about his doubts as a boy: "It is not true that in my schooldays I ever doubted the real existence of Athens. I only doubted whether I should ever see Athens" (*SE*, 246).[42]

---

42. The degree to which Freud potentially manipulated the narrative he created for Rolland to fit his analysis, rather than the other way around, can be guessed from the postcard to his wife Martha from September 4, 1904. Freud describes his visit to the Acropolis as well as the fact that he went to see the ruins anything but unprepared for an extraordinary encoun-

Like Heidegger, Freud struggles to determine the status of the reality he faces once he physically arrives in Greece, and he activates the full force of his interpretive skills to understand the emotional and circumstantial conditions of the events he failed to grasp in the moment. But unlike the philosopher, Freud does not seem to agonize over the key piece of his psychoanalytic theory. To the contrary, his letter swiftly turns to the Oedipal conflict to explain reality's distorted appearance. Freud understands the tensions to which he found himself exposed on his journey as being rooted in his childhood and the living conditions of his birth family. On the one hand, the wish to travel that he felt as a young man appears to him as an expression of the urge to escape the economic limitations of his youth. The fulfillment of this wish is linked to a certain sense of euphoria for having achieved the unexpected. "I might that day on the Acropolis have said to my brother: '. . . here we are, in Athens, and standing on the Acropolis! We really *have* gone a long way!' " On the other hand, the unpleasant mood in Trieste and the initial temporally displaced negation of the reality of the Acropolis are, according to Freud, a manifestation of guilt. "There was something about it that was wrong," Freud writes, "that from earliest times had been forbidden. It was something to do with a child's criticism of his father, with the undervaluation which took the place of overvaluation of earlier childhood" (*SE*, 247). The son, thus Freud's conclusion, felt guilty for having exceeded his father, who was neither able to travel nor—for educational reasons—interested in the Acropolis as a destination. "The very theme of Athens and the Acropolis in itself contained evidence of the son's superiority. Our father . . . had had no secondary education, and Athens could not have meant much to him" (*SE*, 247).

Freud's birthday present to Rolland—just like Heidegger's birthday present to his wife—displays a singular combination of set pieces of a biographical narrative, the reflection on intellectual work, and a reference to the broader context of a transgenerational tension. Freud's account crossfades periods of his personal life—boyhood, the time of the journey, and the time when he wrote the letter—and increases the already considerable complexity of their mutual impact by embedding them in the desires of the educated early twentieth-century upper middle class. Life-time appears as a layering of temporal dimensions and—similar to Heidegger's notion of the sojourn—as a disruption or deceleration of world-time. In other words, time concepts converge on the Acropolis. The past anticipation of a doubted reality and the retrospective insight into

---

ter: he specifically claims that he was wearing his best shirt. See Freud, *Unser Herz zeigt nach Süden* (2007).

the actual existence of the same, now present, reality coincide. The discourse that Freud establishes in view of the debris is one that confirms the afterlife of the past by staging its belated understanding. If we consider the symbolic realm of Freud's archaeological approach to the human psyche, it is fair to say that the remains appear as a reminder that the past will always come back to haunt us because at least its ruins are destined to survive. Furthermore, ruins are an affirmation of the distance that lies between those born (too) late—to use Heidegger's term—and the generation of their fathers, both in terms of the passage of time and, as in Freud's particular situation, because the cultural significance of the Acropolis is not obvious to fathers and sons alike.

To reiterate my point: the appropriate interpretation of the experience in Athens and the function of ruins depends on an already existing discourse. Just as Heidegger's trip ultimately revolved around the first and second beginning of philosophy and the meaning of Being, Freud thinks and argues within the paradigm of the Oedipal conflict that he first proposed in 1899 in *The Interpretation of Dreams*. Yet it appears that the Oedipal conflict is not open to supplementation or even transformation, as is the case with the form of Heidegger's thinking that supplements and is supplemented by poesy. Freud's feeling of unproductivity—he states in his letter that he feels like "an impoverished creature, who has 'seen better days'" (*SE*, 239)—does not seem to jeopardize the confidence in his main claim. Instead, the moment of weakness is also a moment of reassurance: the lack of inspiration is used as an excuse to once more fully display the virtue of the Oedipal conflict.[43] With reference to Derrida, one could say that Freud's thinking is anchored in an original discourse. However, if we take seriously what Freud tells Rolland—namely, that writing about himself (and the issues with his father) functions as a substitute, which is used for lack of a better and more appropriate topic to write about on the occasion of a friend's birthday—then his principal concept loses some of its comprehensive, next to metaphysical validity. Seen as a surrogate, the Oedipal conflict fills a void and turns into its own supplement. As such, it is itself not only open to the work of supplementation and change but also prone to the new manifestations typical of the afterlife of forms. Freud did not realize a radically new form, but he used the Oedipal conflict as a lens that would allow him to understand what he saw in Athens. In turn, the Oedipal conflict entered a new constellation with the discourse about the ruins of

---

43. A similar argument was made by Françoise Meltzer in her to-date unpublished manuscript "Rome and Athens: Freud among the Ruins." Meltzer's focus lies on Freud ignoring the sculpture of Athena in Athens, a neglect that she links to his fear of destabilizing the plausibility of the Oedipal.

the Acropolis that was already part of Freud's archaeological understanding of the subconscious.

As different as they may be in their details, both Heidegger's and Freud's Grecian travels reveal the intrinsic affiliation between ruins, forms of thinking and writing, their potential for change and stability that draw on concepts of supplementation, and the complexities of time. Tied to the "staging" of this interplay between the components is an emphasis on the nonlinearity of temporal movements, the instability of meaning, and the tentative character of all forms. But at the same time, notions of "afterlife" mediate between continuous and discontinuous processes. They make transitions between forms and shifts between levels of reality thinkable.

2

Afterlife:
Hans Blumenberg and Walter Benjamin

In this chapter, I assess the theoretical perspectives on decay, afterlife, and form and their relation with life-time and world-time as developed by two twentieth-century German philosophers, Hans Blumenberg and Walter Benjamin. Their positions productively reframe Martin Heidegger's and Sigmund Freud's accounts from chapter 1 while simultaneously putting them into perspective. The examination of how and why ruins manifest a specific textuality that impacts temporal, semantic, and historical concepts and paradigms is subject to terminological refinement.

Blumenberg and the Question of Life-Time and World-Time

After the failure of the last German military offensive of World War II in the Ardennes in 1944, Adolf Hitler reportedly told one of his adjutants, Nicolaus von Below, "We will never surrender. We may go down, but we will take a world [*eine Welt*] with us."[1] It took Below almost forty years to reveal this remark by his superior to the public. Hans Blumenberg, in his book *Lebenszeit und Weltzeit* (*Life-Time and World-Time*), first published in 1986, suggests that the delayed "confession" was due to the traumatic effect of the last of Hitler's "monstrosities" (*Ungeheuerlichkeiten*): the delusional attempt to give his life-time the superhuman magnitude of world-time. Drawing on Freud, Blumenberg speaks of Hitler's "absolute narcissism," which made him think

---

1. Quoted in Blumenberg, *Lebenszeit und Weltzeit* (2001; hereafter cited as *LW*), 80: "Wir kapitulieren nicht, niemals. Wir können untergehen, aber wir werden eine Welt mitnehmen." To date, there is no English translation of *Lebenszeit und Weltzeit*, and thus all translations for this source are mine.

of his individual life-time as the ultimate measure of all things, the criterion that lent meaning to world-historical time. Blumenberg submits that extreme narcissists assume that once they die, the world ceases to exist. They thrive in times of war, when political actions require urgency, and therefore life-time and world-time approximate each other. The fast sequence of events creates the illusion that everything of importance is about to happen while one is alive to witness it. Quoting the historian Sebastian Haffner, Blumenberg concludes that this is the reason why in wartime Hitler was politically happy (*LW*, 81).

The first part of this chapter locates Blumenberg's thoughts on life-time and world-time included somewhat casually in chapter 1 in the context of his philosophy and especially the anthropological trajectory his work assumed in later years. This examination entails the question regarding the underlying concepts of "life" and "world" that Blumenberg furnished with a temporal and historical index and staged in clear contradistinction to each other. As we shall see, having a world and dealing with life are two human endeavors that require skills and means for dealing with an overwhelming reality—a goal that Blumenberg shares with Heidegger and Freud. For all three thinkers, forms—whether they are exclusively textual or not—are involved in the mediation between reality and the subject that faces it. In Blumenberg's case, they specifically serve as a source of comfort.[2] Blumenberg speaks of cultural forms of significance that come in the shape of myths, stories, artworks, and rhetorical figures. They are flexible, are open to supplementation, and, as I shall explain, always appear in a state of transformation. While Blumenberg is not interested in ruins per se, his theory does pay attention to the mutability of forms and their cultural function. Above all, he offers an examination of how forms balance out the tensions between life-time and world-time. Many of the discourses about ruins considered in this book are, at their core, an attempt at coming to terms with the imposition that world-time poses for life-time.

Blumenberg's thoughts on Hitler's madness and his active political and personal self-sabotage are placed in the second part of *Lebenszeit und Weltzeit*, putting power-sociological emphasis on the time relations at stake. They follow a mythical and philosophical examination of the concepts life-time and world-time, and they are included in a broadly conceived reflection on the evolution of astronomy since antiquity. Blumenberg starts out with the observation that the discovery of the vastness of the cosmic space in the early

---

2. I discuss the aspect of consolation in the later section on Benjamin in this chapter.

modern period required remeasurement of the time that was needed to traverse it. To the contemporaries of the sixteenth-century astronomic reform he attributes a newly gained sense of the "width of the temporal horizon" (*Weite des Zeithorizonts*) that came at the cost of a growing gap between life-time and world-time. In other words, Blumenberg has no doubt that this experience of dissociation is modern or, more precisely, postmedieval. In his estimation, the "medieval consciousness" fundamentally lacked generosity (*Grosszügigkeit*) in dealing with the future. Long-term planning was prevented by the eschatological expectation of the imminent end of time and especially the coincidence of this event with the conclusion of one's own dwelling on earth (*LW*, 115).[3] The Middle Ages appear like a period of transition between a mythical prehistory—when life-time and world-time were identical—and a modern notion of their divide, one that reaches an uncanny, pathological level in modernity's political fanaticisms.[4]

At the beginning of the second part of *Lebenszeit und Weltzeit*, entitled "Öffnung der Zeitschere" ("Opening of the Time Gap"), Blumenberg draws an analogy between the biblical myth of the loss of paradise and what the German phenomenologist Edmund Husserl called "life-world" (*Lebenswelt*). In both states, the paradisiac as well as the "life-worldly," life-time and world-time are congruent with each other, and those within these states are unconscious of themselves and their surroundings. Once the step out of paradise or the life-world is taken, consciousness sets in. Blumenberg uses the myth to equate the beginning of human awareness with the expulsion from the Garden of Eden, when death, the limitation of life-time, was introduced as a sin-induced punishment. Yet he argues, in a surprising interpretation of a biblical passage in the book of Revelation in which the devil is characterized as acting under time pressure, that the "density" of time (*die Enge der Zeit*)

---

3. In his 1979 essay "'Erfahrungsraum' und 'Erwartungshoizont'" ("'Space of Experience' and 'Horizon of Expectation'"), Reinhart Koselleck raises the issue of dissociation—or lack thereof—in premodern times with respect to the relationship between experience and expectation which, in his view, is subject to a fundamental change in the second half of the seventeenth century: "As long as the Christian doctrine of the Final Days set an immovable limit to the horizon of expectation (roughly speaking, until the mid-seventeenth century), the future remained bound to the past. Biblical revelation and Church administration had limited the tension between experience and expectation in such a way that it was not possible for them to break apart [*auseinanderklaffen*]." See Koselleck, *Futures Past* (2004), 264.

4. The common thread running through Blumenberg's work on these eras and themes is the concern with phenomenology that he developed in his extensive engagement with Edmund Husserl and Martin Heidegger.

is not the aftermath of evil but its source.[5] Human malice stems from the postlapsarian insight that finite creatures have infinite desires. Their spite is fueled by a sense of being deprived of the world-time that will be available to others (*LW*, 71–71). Blumenberg's critical reading of Husserl puts emphasis on the observation that simultaneously being *within* the life-world and *knowing* about it is impossible.[6] In *The Crisis of European Sciences and Transcendental Phenomenology* (first published in German in 1936), Husserl characterized the life-world as a "realm of original self-evidences" (*ein Universum vorgegebener Selbstverständlichkeiten*).[7] What he had in mind was a prescientific and prephilosophical stage of human consciousness that was in alignment with the world. "Life-world" can be understood as a zone of suspended references, in which perceptual expectations cannot be disappointed because there is no concept of that which lies beyond the life-world.[8] In other words, what can be referenced is present, accessible to the senses: "That which is self-evidently given is, in perception, experienced as 'the thing itself,' in immediate presence, or in memory, remembered as the thing itself; and in every other manner of intuition is a presentation of the thing itself."[9] Husserl's life-world is a tool, meant to overcome a fundamental, technology-induced disconnect between humankind and science by giving the latter the chance to revisit its own foundations. In Blumenberg's reinterpretation, it is an enclave of ignorance (*Enklave der Unwissenheit*) and therefore of an archaic sense of homelike belonging (*archaische Heimatlichkeit*), of security and contentment with the world (*Weltbehagen*; *LW*, 55–56).

Yet Blumenberg dismisses this prestage—according to Husserl, the basis of modern science—as an abstraction. He argues that there is no such thing as a "sphere of constant presence" without a notion of that which is absent, because life constantly points beyond itself.[10] Furthermore, he claims that

---

5. See Revelation 12:12 in Coogan, Brettler, and Newsome, *New Oxford Annotated Bible*: "Rejoice then, you heavens and those who dwell in them! But woe to the earth and the sea, for the devil has come down to you with great wrath, because he knows that his time is short!"

6. For the following remarks on Blumenberg's reading of Husserl, see Heidenreich, *Mensch und Moderne bei Hans Blumenberg*, 111–15. For Blumenberg's concept of *Lebenswelt*, see Sommer, "Lebenswelt," 160–70.

7. Husserl, *The Crisis of European Sciences and Transcendental Phenomenology* (1970), 167. For an annotated version of the German original, see Husserl, *Die Krise der europäischen Wissenschaft und die transzendentale Phänomenologie* (2012).

8. Blumenberg calls "a world that keeps its promises" an "amusement park" (*Erlebnispark*; *LW*, 49).

9. Husserl, *Crisis of European Sciences*, 167.

10. Quoted phrase translated from Heidenreich, *Mensch und Moderne bei Hans Blumenberg*, 113: "Eine Sphäre ständiger Anwesenheit."

Husserl's life-world is not suitable as a conceptional foundation from a phenomenological point of view because it cannot be phenomenologically reduced.[11] Put otherwise: the life-world-experience cannot be described "from within."[12] Describing it from without, however, annihilates it. Blumenberg's conclusion is that the awakening of time-conditioned consciousness always coincides with a departure from the life-world. The moment it is left behind,[13] when—with the separation of life-time and world-time—consciousness emancipates itself and history begins, then the struggle of positioning one's life vis-à-vis the world starts as well (*LW*, 71–76). Against the provocation and "humiliation" inflicted on humans by an indifferent world—a world that has time in abundance, of which, as Blumenberg puts it, it "boasts to life"—they activate strategies of time saving. In extreme cases they find comfort in the fantasy that even though they are bound to die, no world will be left to survive them and mock their mortality (*LW*, 78).

Here, as in other works, Blumenberg's philosophy proves to be deeply concerned with anthropological questions. From his engagement with Husserl and Heidegger emerges a phenomenology that focuses on mortality and the conditions of human existence and survival, yet unlike his predecessors, Blumenberg does not shy away from decidedly anthropological methods.[14] At the core of his concern, Blumenberg detects the fundamental paradox of time, the tension that stems from the experience that "nothing is so much our own as time, and yet so utterly beyond our grasp" (*Zeit ist das am meisten Unsrige und doch am wenigsten Verfügbare*; *LW*, 74). Blumenberg's multidimensional approach—which employs and combines mythological, philosophical, and scientific points of view—above all does justice to the complexity of the problem at hand and to the diversity of possible strategies to address it. However, it also shines a light on some of this philosopher's most daring concepts.

---

11. In phenomenological terms, the life-world cannot be bracketed by epoche, which is, however, a suspension of judgment about the outside world that is necessary in order to approach the essence of things.

12. Blumenberg calls the attempt to do so the "life-world misunderstanding" (*LW*, 23); see the title of the first chapter of *Lebenszeit und Weltzeit*. As Heidenreich puts it, Blumenberg insists that the world cannot be thought of as nonexistent in a meaningful way (Heidenreich, *Mensch und Moderne bei Hans Blumenberg*, 114).

13. In fact, Blumenberg considers the life-world a state that we have always already left (*LW*, 54).

14. This is evident in Blumenberg's interest in Arnold Gehlen. For Husserl's and Heidegger's skepticism toward anthropology, see Heidenreich, *Mensch und Moderne bei Hans Blumenberg*, 33.

The most influential among them is undoubtedly Blumenberg's notion of an "absolutism of reality" (*Absolutismus der Wirklichkeit*) that he set forth in *Work on Myth* (*Arbeit am Mythos*, 1979).[15] Blumenberg argues that humanity's cultural project began when men—coping with a "lack of adaptation" to their environment (*WM*, 4)—started developing strategies to face an overwhelmingly incomprehensible world that caused them "existential anxiety" (*Lebensangst*; *WM*, 6). Heavily drawing on Heidegger, he puts emphasis on the necessity to rationalize anxiety into fear.[16] This rationalization can occur neither through experience nor knowledge, but only by way of "devices [*Kunstgriffe*] like that of the substitution of the familiar for the unfamiliar, of explanations for the inexplicable" (*WM*, 5). In other words, fear is directed at and can be controlled through objects and practices that introduce a distance between the subject and that which frightens it, while anxiety is undirected and indeterminate. In that sense, culture in its entirety can be considered a coping strategy, which makes the encounter with reality endurable.[17] The primal forms of self-defensive distancing from the "terror" of reality, however, are names, metaphors, and myths, Blumenberg asserts: "What has become identifiable by means of a name is raised out of its unfamiliarity by means of metaphor and is made accessible, in terms of its significance, by telling stories" (*WM*, 6). All three forms mediate between humans and the absolute unknown by way of images and language, or—as Blumenberg phrases it—through the force of "imaginative entities" (*imaginative Instanzen*; *WM*, 6).[18] The skill to use these entities to create a bearable, manageable world for oneself is what Blumenberg terms "the art of living" (*Lebenskunst*). Instead of comprehensive meaning, it produces forms of significance, concise cultural modes—and Blumenberg explicitly includes aesthetic objects—that emerge "from the diffuse surrounding field of probabilities" (*WM*, 69). "To have a world," Blumenberg states, "is always the result of an art" (*einer Kunst*); an art, one might add, in the sense of a skill, capable of reducing the absoluteness of the absolutism of reality (*WM*, 7).

---

15. For the following discussion, see Blumenberg, *Work on Myth* (1985; hereafter cited as *WM*), especially the first chapter.

16. Heidegger deals with the difference in *Being and Time* (2001; hereafter cited as *BT*), paragraphs 30 and 40, pp. 179–82, 228–35.

17. Heidenreich, *Mensch und Moderne bei Hans Blumenberg*, 56.

18. Wallace translates *Instanzen* as "authorities." I prefer the term *entities* to emphasize that people put objects between themselves and the "absolutism of reality." For the project of language as a distancing strategy, see also Blumenberg, *Paradigms for a Metaphorology* (2010), published first in German as *Paradigmen zu einer Metaphorologie* (1997).

Blumenberg revisits the notion of "having a world" in *Lebenszeit und Weltzeit*, here relating it to human perception of time. In the context of this later book, coping with the indifference of the world—or, as we may now call it, the "absolutism of reality"—can only succeed against the backdrop of a "world-horizon" (*Welthorizont*), which puts the significance of individual lives into perspective. In reference to Hitler's comment on the defeat in the Ardennes and his delusion that the temporal horizon of his own life coincided with the limit that the world-horizon imposed on time, Blumenberg writes, "Hitler had no world. This is why he uses the term with the indefinite article [*a* world, *eine Welt*]" (*LW*, 84). By implication, living—the ability to create and shape a world and stake out its possibilities—must have been an art that Hitler did not master.

The juxtaposition of two of Blumenberg's core concepts allows for the conclusion that the absolutism of reality besets humans outside the life-world and comes in the form of world-time.[19] The birth of consciousness carries with it the insight of the subject into its contingency, and it exposes the individual's anxiety about "*Being-in-the-world as such*" (*BT*, 230; italics in the original). The idea of "having a world" introduces objects and practices into the equation. They are elements of an "art of living" that refers to the world and makes it intelligible and sufferable by using signs and symbols—or, in our terminology, by using forms. Above all, the art of living acknowledges the world's existence and makes concessions to the prevailing influence of its continuity.

It is a conspicuous feature of Blumenberg reception that opinions about the philosopher's significance are deeply divided. His extensive work—unique in style, rich in material, and overall a document of a relentless reading activity—has earned him the title of an intellectual historian and occasionally led to the labeling of his writings as literature. In some cases, this categorization has prevented him from being taken seriously as a philosopher in his own right, and yet by the same token, Blumenberg has also been dubbed the most important philosopher of the twentieth century. Even then, there are major differences among his supporters about how to assess some of the philosopher's

---

19. As Frantz Josef Wetz has pointed out, the concept of life-world is almost diametrically opposed to the idea of an absolutism of reality. Blumenberg associates life-world with a realm of unspoiled, desirable immediacy to things, from which—as the biblical myth indicates—humans have been expelled against their wish. Once again, he argues with Husserl against Husserl when he reinterprets the phenomenologist's position that life-world is a domain that philosophers—for the sake of an objective, observational point of view—leave behind deliberately. See Wetz, *Hans Blumenberg: Zur Einführung*, 132, 137.

core topics, most significantly—with regard to the anthropological focus of the later work—Blumenberg's perspective on humankind's relationship with meaning (*Sinn*) as it is shaped by their attitude toward reality.[20] The discrepancies have implications for the often bemoaned inaccessibility of Blumenberg's writings as well as their enormous hermeneutic productivity.[21]

Even though the ambiguity inherent in much of Blumenberg's work is generally matched by its creative potential, it remains a challenge to make sense of the fact that an oeuvre that is as historical in nature as Blumenberg's philosophical anthropology simultaneously reckons with anthropological constants and universals that can neither be historicized nor attributed the systematic vigor of genuinely philosophical theories. This suggests that in order to tease out the full epistemological weight of Blumenberg's ideas, one has to navigate between the abstraction of anthropological constants and the concreteness of historical processes.

Decay and Afterlife builds on Blumenberg's notion of "forms of significance" and "imaginative entities," the use of which is essential to the art of living and which in turn provides subjects with a world, a livable relation to reality. The semiotic, semantic, and temporal nature of this connection between the living being and the "world-horizon" to which it seeks to relate is the focus of each of the discourses about ruins explored in the previous and subsequent pages. On the one hand, my observations corroborate Blumenberg's insight that forms of significance constantly change. Being supplemented and transformed is one of their decisive features. They are always already a reception of what has gone before.[22] Yet instead of focusing on the facilitating and mediating function of forms, I proceed on the assumption that forms not only arbitrate between lives and worlds but also establish, shape, and change them, while concurrently being exposed to their influence. It is in this sense that forms are historical and temporal and that they provide "otherwise unobtainable knowledge."[23] What forms represent is as much a question of the temporalities proper to them as it is one of the time perceptions of the cultural-historical context.

---

20. Heidenreich, *Mensch und Moderne bei Hans Blumenberg*, 12–14.

21. They also have implications for the perception of Blumenberg's existentialism as politically conservative. See Habel, "Die Eskalation der Zeit," n.p.

22. See Blumenberg, "Wirklichkeitsbegriff und Wirkungspotential des Mythos" (1971), 28.

23. Gamper and Hühn, "Einleitung," 14. The authors refer to Adorno's concept of form in the *Aesthetic Theory* as a generator of new knowledge ("Form als artikulierter Inhalt erzeugt eine anders nicht zu erreichende Erkenntnis"). As I will show, Blumenberg's thinking includes the idea of afterlife in a reception-aesthetical sense.

On the other hand, the challenges of reality not only require flexible forms but also a concept that explains how forms and signs persist. As indicated in the introduction, *afterlife* is one such concept suitable for capturing change in persistence and persistence in change. The following final section of this second chapter uncovers the roots of my understanding of *afterlife* in Walter Benjamin's work. To this end, I first explore the role of mortality that Georg Simmel introduced to the life-philosophical discussion and tied to the function of forms by describing death as "form-defining" and, paradoxically, a producer of "more life." Benjamin draws on these ideas when he studies the role of forms in historical processes and the way in which such processes are connected to the course of life and guided by the prospect of death. Placing Benjamin in dialogue with Heidegger, Freud, and Blumenberg in the subsequent step reveals that for all four thinkers the concept of life depends on their specific perception of the limitations imposed by death. At the same time, the particularities of Benjamin's life-philosophical reflections and his form-specific notion of history are brought to the foreground. Benjamin develops out of his understanding of the baroque in *The Origin of German Tragic Drama* an argument that emphasizes the reciprocity of ruins and forms and pictures history as meaningful only in the stages of its decline and the inconspicuousness of its debris. In other words, Benjamin's thoughts add to the theoretical positions examined thus far by perceiving reality as decidedly historical. As a consequence, coping with reality means dealing with history, and dealing with history is the equivalent of coming to terms with its shattered forms.

Walter Benjamin and the Question of Afterlife

There comes a risk with every scholarly recourse—and this book is no exception—to Walter Benjamin's work. Germanist and comparatist Daniel Weidner has identified this risk as the tendency to perceive Benjamin's ideas as broadly applicable terminologies.[24] On a similar note, the philosopher Eli Friedlander pointed out the common understanding of Benjamin's writings as a "vast array of brilliant and idiosyncratic insights," suitable for "the most varied interpretations and appropriations."[25] Both scholars agree that Benjamin's work has been selectively used and sometimes exploited in ways that often lacked real interest in the complexities of the author's thinking. Their assessments

---

24. Weidner, "Fort-, Über-, Nachleben" (2011), 177. For a modified English-language version of this text, see Weidner, "Life After Life" (2012).

25. Friedlander, *Walter Benjamin: A Philosophical Portrait*, 1.

of the reasons and consequences, however, are different. Friedlander states that this reception—intrigued by the simultaneously self-evident and obscure and, above all, "unclassifiable" nature of Benjamin's images and concepts—has failed to "engage the rigor of [his] thought." In other words, it refused to recognize Benjamin's positions as genuinely philosophical.[26] Weidner, on the other hand, detects a widespread failure to acknowledge the nonconceptuality in much of Benjamin's writing. But, despite this fundamental discrepancy, each intervention implicitly calls on those who extract their interpretive tools from Benjamin's work to justify their decision and—if nothing else—relate it to the legitimate demand for a comprehensive appreciation of Benjamin's literary and philosophical approach.

In accordance with this appeal, the following considerations try to maximize the validity of the abstract and concrete, historical, and conceptual qualities of *afterlife* by simultaneously anchoring the term in historical semantics and discourses and displacing it into a new discursive environment. Affected but not limited by the context of its origin, the term can unfold novel facets of its meaning.

In philosophical and literary contexts, there is hardly much controversy about the significance Benjamin attributed to a reevaluation of history.[27] This purpose is most salient in his last work, "On the Concept of History," which he wrote in Parisian exile shortly before his death in 1940; it was published posthumously in 1942.[28] The text—composed in a situation of imminent political and existential threat—is an effort to formulate the conditions for a critical perception of the past.[29] Against historicism's method of sympathetic intuition (*Einfühlung*) into bygone events and the concatenation of seemingly objective facts into an absolute causality of history, Benjamin invokes historiography as an act of construction that blasts (*heraussprengen*) the "past charged with now-time . . . out of the continuum of history" (CH, 14). This instant of "dialectical destabilization" is what Benjamin calls the "tiger's leap"

---

26. Friedlander, *Walter Benjamin*, 1–2.

27. According to Lutz Niethammer, those who completely missed the debate and with it a chance to rethink history are—of all people—the historians. See Niethammer, *Posthistoire*, 141.

28. See Benjamin, "Über den Begriff der Geschichte" (1980; hereafter cited as BG), 701. For the English version, see Benjamin, "On the Concept of History" (2006; hereafter cited as CH), 395. In the text citations, the accompanying number indicates the number of the respective thesis rather than the page number.

29. Jeanne Marie Gagnebin points out that the moment of production is a moment of crisis and urgency that demands the recipient's commitment and does not allow for an attitude of hermeneutic indifference. Gagnebin, "'Über den Begriff der Geschichte,'" 285–86.

(CH, 14). It reveals "the true image of the past" that "flits by" elusively if the present "does not recognize itself as intended in that image" (CH, 5). Its potential to disturb historical "conformism" is revolutionary and messianic at once because the leap disrupts the narrative of dominant historiography and produces the wish for a different kind of temporality (CH, 6).[30] The break in the official historical narrative that Benjamin propagates—the rewriting of the story told by victors—coincides with a turn to history's margins and its unacknowledged debris (CH, 9).

Adding to this perspective while simultaneously reframing it, Weidner states that Benjamin's reconsideration of history includes an attempt to rethink historical meaning as a relationship between life and afterlife.[31] "Afterlife" is a "figure of thought" (*Denkfigur*) that Benjamin employs to reach a twofold goal: (1) it allows him to draw on the terminology and semantics of the contemporary discourses that evolve around *life*, and (2) it permits him to exceed these very discourses rhetorically rather than conceptually. The modification of a specific use of language—such as metaphors, terminological operations, and conceptual constellations (*Begriffskonstellationen*)—sparks cultural, philosophical, and political reconsiderations.[32]

Early twentieth-century discourses across the humanities employed the word *afterlife* (*Nachleben*) in a largely nonterminological, albeit sometimes programmatic, fashion. Established in the field of classics as a descriptor for issues concerning reception history, *afterlife* referred to life in such a way that historical work could be perceived as something other than reconstruction—namely, as an act of reviving the past and rendering it relevant for the present.[33] The German *Nachleben*, which is a verb-derived noun, could then assume the double meaning of something past living on, and something past being relived (as in the German *nacherleben*).[34] In Wilhelm Dilthey's historical hermeneutics, which—around the turn of the twentieth century—sought to distinguish human sciences (*Geisteswissenschaften*) from natural sciences (*Naturwissenschaften*), history is a "life-nexus" (*Zusammenhang des Lebens*)

---

30. Gagnebin, "'Über den Begriff der Geschichte,'" 284, 293.
31. Weidner, "Life After Life."
32. Weidner, "Fort-, Über-, Nachleben," 163, 177–78. In the subsequent pages, I closely follow Weidner's approach to Benjamin's understanding of *afterlife* while simultaneously expanding his argument with respect to my focus.
33. Refer back to the introduction for a brief assessment of the discussion around Aby Warburg's understanding of *Nachleben*.
34. Weidner, "Fort-, Über-, Nachleben," 163–65. Weidner mentions Otto Immisch's *Das Nachleben der Antike* of 1919 as an example and points out the two options of *Antike* being an objective or subjective genitive.

or "productive nexus" (*Wirkungszusammenhang*) that is interpreted, experienced, and relived by an individual. This nexus finds its most immediate expression in autobiographical works (*Selbstbiographie*) that integrate "the parts of the life of mankind . . . into a whole."[35] The crux of the matter is, in short, that life—understood as a combination of experience and interpretation—was considered a universal point of reference for historical as well as aesthetic or philosophical reasoning. According to Weidner, the human sciences of the time could therefore rightly be labeled "life sciences" (*Lebenswissenschaften*). However, the coherence of the various sciences brought together under this label was, at the same time, precarious, and the term *life* was itself semantically unstable. A critical moment ensued when the philosopher and sociologist Georg Simmel—who in his earlier years had addressed many of the same concerns that occupied Dilthey—took a turn in his late work toward an understanding of life that included life's opposite.[36]

Drawing on ideas that he had explored in the 1911 essay "Der Begriff und die Tragödie der Kultur" ("The Concept and Tragedy of Culture"), Simmel developed the argument that life was "more-life" and "more-than-life" in "Lebensanschauung" ("The View of Life"), a text that Simmel referred to as his "testament" in a letter to the philosopher Hermann Graf Keyserling and that he released for publication shortly before his death in 1918.[37] As I will discuss in more detail in chapter 9, Simmel sets up in his earlier work a model that situates the idea of culture between the antagonistic forces of a continuously flowing stream of individual life and the static forms of its objective expressions. The process of cultivation—in Simmel's eyes, a process of questioning and challenging "the natural facticity of the world"—is, at its core, tragic, because life, in order to become concrete and real, is forced into cultural forms that can never fully contain it: "The paradox of culture is that the subjective life, which we feel in its continual flowing and which pushes of its own volition

---

35. Dilthey, *Formation of the Historical World in the Human Sciences* (2002), 219. For the German original, first published in 1910, see Dilthey, "Der Aufbau der geschichtlichen Welt in den Geisteswissenschaften" (1927), 198.

36. Weidner, "Fort-, Über-, Nachleben," 165. Simmel's *Probleme der Geschichtsphilosophie* (*The Problems of a History of Philosophy*) from 1892 is an example of his engagement with questions regarding the contemporary discourse on the differences between human and natural sciences and the role of hermeneutics in historical science (*Geschichtswissenschaft*). Simmel never directly quoted Dilthey; see Jung, *Georg Simmel: Zur Einführung*, 98.

37. See Simmel, "Der Begriff und die Tragödie der Kultur" (1996), 385–416; Simmel, "Concept and Tragedy of Culture" (1997), 55–75; Simmel, "Lebensanschauung" (1999), 209–425; Simmel, *View of Life: Four Metaphysical Essays* (2010). For the letter to Keyserling, see Simmel, "Briefe 1912–1918" (2008), 928.

towards its inner perfection, cannot, viewed from the idea of culture, achieve that perfection on its own, but only by way of those self-sufficient crystalized structures which have now become quite alien to its form [*jene, ihm jetzt ganz formfremd gewordene . . . Gebilde*]."[38] In "Lebensanschauung" Simmel builds on this thought when he writes that life as life "needs form" while at the same time "as life it needs more than a given form." And he continues:

> Something else is also there, something inexpressible, indefinable, that we feel of every life as such: that it is more than every assignable content; that it swings out beyond every content, regarding it not only from the inside out (as is the nature of the logical content statement) but likewise from without, from what is beyond it . . . Thus the dimension is suggested into which life transcends itself when it is not only more-life [*Mehr-Leben*], but more-than-life [*Mehr-als-Leben*]. This is always the case when we call ourselves creative.[39]

To this transgressive quality of life, which materializes in ever new forms and in a constant movement of life reaching beyond itself, Simmel adds death as yet another boundary waiting to be crossed.[40] He suggests that death is "fully inflexible for our consciousness" (because we know *that* it will inevitably happen) and "fully fluid" (because we don't know *when* it will happen). Between these two kinds of awareness about death, the forms of life take shape, and it is in that sense that death is "unconditionally form-defining" for life. Surprisingly, life assists its "form-giver" by trying to escape from it:

> Every step of life appears . . . as positively and a priori formed by death, which is a real element of life . . . This forming is codetermined . . . by the *aversion* to death . . . by the fact that . . . all our . . . ways of behavior . . . are an instinctive or conscious flight from death. Life, which we consume in order to bring us closer to death, we consume in order to flee it.[41]

This ultimately means that "more-life" is being produced in the face of that which is "more-than-life," or "the other" of life, or its inherent, antithetical driving force. Simmel regarded it as one of the "colossal paradoxes" of Christianity that it had deprived death of its "life-inherent quality" by employing a notion of afterlife that was built on the idea of life's eternal continuity "beyond

---

38. Simmel, "Concept and Tragedy of Culture," 55–58, 74.
39. Simmel, *View of Life*, 15.
40. Weidner, "Fort-, Über-, Nachleben," 166.
41. Simmel, *View of Life*, 70.

the form-boundary of its end."[42] In "Lebensanschauung" the contours of the paradox become clear: for Simmel, "life" is a universal category only because it includes its opposite.[43] Separated from death, it loses this comprehensive validity that Christianity intended to emphasize in the first place.

Including life's antithesis in an emerging twentieth-century philosophy of life, however, was an intellectual as well as rhetorical difficulty to which the contemporary discourses had to respond.[44] One of the thinkers who accepted the challenge was Simmel's student and admirer Walter Benjamin.

Walter Benjamin's attitude toward the philosophy of life (*Lebensphilosophie*) was ambivalent and seems to have changed considerably over the course of his writing career. In his later work—particularly in the 1939 essay "Über einige Motive bei Baudelaire" ("Some Motifs in Baudelaire")—Benjamin took a critical stand as to how *Lebensphilosophie* dealt with the question of experience. The argument he makes is aesthetic in essence. By comparing the cultural impact of lyric poetry in his own time with the popular success that Baudelaire achieved with his 1857 volume *Les Fleurs du Mal* (*Flowers of Evil*), Benjamin observes that, at the beginning of the twentieth century, the conditions for the reception of lyric poetry have become less favorable. The genre, he notes, has lost its rapport with the experience of the reader. In an effort to understand the reasons for this shift, Benjamin finds that since the late 1800s, philosophy has typically been preoccupied with the pursuit of what it considered to be "'true' experience" (*"wahre" Erfahrung*). The various attempts to achieve this kind of authenticity are what Benjamin subsumes under the term *Lebensphilosophie* and associates with a common problem: life-philosophical ventures derive their categories from poetry, nature, and myth and tend to neglect the historical-material aspects of *Erfahrung*—in other words, the reality of "man's life in society." Benjamin's radical conclusion is that a line of historical-material detachment leads from Dilthey's 1907 work *Das Erlebnis und die Dichtung* (*Poetry and Experience*) to Ludwig Klages and Carl Gustav Jung, and ultimately culminates in fascism.[45] *Erlebnis*, Dilthey's term to denote true experience—the creation of which is the domain of the poet (thus the title *Poetry and Experience*), who deploys it

---

42. Simmel, *View of Life*, 68. Simmel does not use the term *afterlife* in this context, but he speaks of "otherworldly existence."
43. Weidner, "Fort-, Über-, Nachleben," 167.
44. Weidner, "Fort-, Über-, Nachleben," 167.
45. See Benjamin, "Some Motifs in Baudelaire" (1973), 110. For the German version, see Benjamin, "Über einige Motive bei Baudelaire" (1991), 608.

against an authenticity-deprived industrial age—becomes Benjamin's word for human self-estrangement (*Selbstentfremdung*).⁴⁶ Benjamin's usage stands in opposition to true—that is to say, historical—*Erfahrung*.⁴⁷

In light of this late text, one might be surprised to find that sixteen years earlier, in "The Task of the Translator," Benjamin spoke of historicity using Dilthey's life-philosophical terminology in an affirmative way.⁴⁸ This initial interconnection of what would eventually become incompatible concepts was closely tied to Benjamin's thoughts on the relationship between an original work of literature and its translation. His assessment evolves ex negativo from an evaluation of what poetry (*Dichtung*) and translation are not. Most important, he contends that their significance lies neither in a communicative function (*Mitteilung*) nor in the assertions (*Aussagen*) they make; in other words, the essential quality of poetry and translation does not derive from their content. Instead, Benjamin foregrounds the idea that translation is a "form," ascribing it an aspect of autonomy that usually pertains to the original.⁴⁹ However, the form-being of translation, the way in which it exceeds mere imitation, repetition, and dependence on what came before, can only be understood in reference to the original. "To comprehend [translation] as a form," Benjamin writes, "one must go back to the original, for the laws governing the translation, lie within the original, contained in the issue of its translatability [*Übersetzbarkeit*]." And he concludes: "If translation is a form, translatability must be an essential feature of certain works" (TT, 254; AÜ, 10). That is to say, if works are translated, the translation follows from their structure. The translation becomes the place in which aspects of the original's inherent significance can manifest themselves. Or, as the philosopher Samuel Weber put it, "The original can only be itself by becoming something different."⁵⁰ At first glance, it seems obvious that Benjamin's reasoning emphasizes the reciprocity between the original and the translation. After all, he characterizes their relationship as "the most intimate connection" (*nächster Zusammenhang*).⁵¹ And yet, there is a paradoxical twist in Benjamin's argu-

---

46. Benjamin, "Über einige Motive bei Baudelaire," 681.
47. Weidmann, *Flanerie, Sammlung, Spiel*, 67–69.
48. For the discussion of this work, see Benjamin, "The Task of the Translator" (2002, hereafter cited as TT), 253–63; Benjamin, "Die Aufgabe des Übersetzers" (1972, hereafter cited as AÜ), 9–21.
49. See Weber, *Benjamin's -abilities*, 56–57. Weber traces the "autonomy" of Benjamin's form back to Immanuel Kant.
50. Weber, *Benjamin's -abilities*, 61.
51. The English "the most intimate connection" is Samuel Weber's translation. The Harvard edition translates the phrase as "the closest relationship."

ment: complementary to the claim of closeness is the insistence that translations arise from the original without bearing any meaning for it. Benjamin compares this to "the manifestations of life" (*die Äusserungen des Lebens*) that are intimately related to "the living" (*das Lebendige*) from which they derive but for which they are of no relevance. Nevertheless, the relationship is, in both cases, natural (*natürlich*) or, as Benjamin—following Dilthey's example— formulates it, a "life-nexus" (*Zusammenhang des Lebens*; AÜ, 10). This life-nexus is historical insofar as life can be ascribed not only to something that possesses organic corporeality but also to everything that has history (*allem demjenigen, wovon es Geschichte gibt*). In Benjamin's understanding, life and history are associated in an "entirely unmetaphorical" sense (TT, 254). He leaves no doubt that, with regard to works of art and literature, they have to be conceived as analogous: "The history of the great works of art tells us about their descent from prior models [*kennt ihre Deszendenz aus den Quellen*], their realization [*Gestaltung*] in the time of the artist, and what in principle should be their eternal afterlife [*Fortleben*] in succeeding generations" (TT, 255; AÜ, 11). In other words, what generates the history of an artwork is the coalescence of three temporal dimensions and phenomena: its past origin, its present formation, and its future afterlife or—in a literal translation of the German *Fortleben*—its potentially eternal "living on."[52]

Originals thus live on in translations, and translatability is an indicator of a text's historicity.[53] In an earlier passage of the essay, Benjamin uses *Überleben* (survival)—another derivative of the verb *leben* (to live)—to indicate that the life-nexus between work and translation is essentially a matter of going beyond life: "A translation issues from the original—not so much from its life as from its afterlife [*Überleben*]" (TT, 254; AÜ, 10). In his explanation of *Fortleben* (living on), Benjamin draws attention to the transformative and regenerative forces of translations vis-à-vis the life of the original: "For in its afterlife [*Fortleben*]—which could not be called that if it were not a transformation and a renewal of something living [*des Lebendigen*]—the original undergoes a change" (TT, 256; AÜ, 12). Benjamin calls this change a "maturing process" or, literally, an "after-ripening" (*Nachreife*) that—if it is continuous—leads to a work's fame (*Ruhm*). And it is here, in the age of fame, that the paradoxical relationship between originals and translations takes full effect. For the translations that emerge now—without signifying anything for the original—help it unfold its meaning: "In them [the translations of the age of

---

52. Samuel Weber has noted that *Fortleben* carries the connotation of "living away" and therefore points to a movement beyond mere life. See Weber, *Benjamin's -abilities*, 67.

53. For a similar thought, see Weidner, "Fort-, Über-, Nachleben," 168.

fame] the life of the originals attains its latest, continually renewed, and most complete unfolding" (TT, 255).

Daniel Weidner made a point of predicating Benjaminian literary fame on the death of a work's author. He argues that poetic immortality in the sense of *Fort-* and *Überleben* is not mere continuance of a tradition but continuance *after* death, if not *through* death. To Weidner, the connection between fame and transience is decisive for Benjamin's notion of afterlife (*Nachleben*) and an element that distinguishes his understanding from that of other early twentieth-century discourses.[54] Interestingly, the term *Nachleben*, which Benjamin's contemporaries favored, does not appear in "The Task of the Translator." Benjamin brings it up in other works, such as the *Arcades Project*, spanning 1927–1940, and his 1937 essay on the Marxist scholar Eduard Fuchs.[55] Both texts couple *Nachleben* with historical understanding, using almost the same wording. The *Arcades Project* further relates history and afterlife to the notion of fame: "Historical 'understanding' is to be grasped, in principle, as an afterlife of that which is understood; and what has been recognized in the analysis of the 'afterlife of works,' in the analysis of 'fame,' is therefore to be considered the foundation of history in general."[56] The motifs of fame and history clearly establish a connection between *Fortleben, Überleben, Nachleben,* and the texts in which the notions—in Weidner's terminology, the "figures"—are developed. However, it is important to acknowledge that, in "The Task of the Translator," the focus seems to lie in the significance of "living-on" and "survival." It remains to be seen what exactly this means for Benjamin's project of a reconsideration of history.

Benjamin's engagement with the status of works of art and literature in relation to life and history can be sharpened if we return to the other theoretical positions considered here. A look back at *Lebenszeit und Weltzeit* shows that the idea of fame, with which Benjamin explains the concept of history, allows Blumenberg to clarify what he means by *world*. His remarks on Hitler's lack of a world are accompanied by the observation that Hitler did not have the term *fame* at his disposal. "To think of fame, to speak of fame," Blumenberg writes, "depends on the continuance of the world."[57] He thus gestures to-

---

54. Weidner, "Fort-, Über-, Nachleben," 170.

55. See Benjamin, *Arcades Project* (2002), and, for the German version, Benjamin, "Das Passagen-Werk" (1991); Benjamin, "Eduard Fuchs: Collector and Historian" (1975), 27–58; Benjamin, "Eduard Fuchs, der Sammler und der Historiker" (1991), 465–505.

56. Benjamin, *Arcades Project*, 460.

57. Translation by Nicholls, *Myth and the Human Sciences*, 238.

ward a historical continuity in the course of which historical greatness—and Blumenberg also speaks of immortality—can be achieved (*LW*, 84). The juxtaposition of his approach with Benjamin's ultimately makes the decidedly historical characteristics of Blumenberg's *world* apparent.

To claim a direct reception-historical relation between the two thinkers in this matter, however, would be an overstatement of the actual attention Blumenberg paid to Benjamin's work. Overall, there are only a few explicit mentions of the older philosopher by the younger.[58] Even the Benjamin revival that stirred the intellectual community of the 1960s seems to have left only scarce traces in Blumenberg's work.[59] Consequently, the comparison is of primarily systematic and conceptual nature and requires the caveat that it combines two disparate intellectual cultures. In this sense, there are similarities in the difference between Blumenberg and Benjamin—not only in terms of the function of fame for the conceptualization of history and the world but also with regard to the significance attributed by the two authors to life and form.

As I discussed in some detail in the first part of this chapter, Blumenberg's understanding of *life* is grounded in Husserl's phenomenological category of *Lebenswelt* (life-world), the preconscious state before history. Leaving this realm goes together with a break between life and world and an awareness of their temporal disparities that entails the necessity of forms. One could say that the contrasting dynamics of divergence and mediation shape the relation between life, world, and form. Blumenberg's anthropological perspective accounts for an emphasis on human survival. Those who live on have found form-supported ways of dealing with reality, which is essentially the reality of impending death and our fear of it.

Despite Blumenberg's clearly mediation-centered understanding of forms, his thinking includes the notion of their afterlife. For Blumenberg, forms live on in aesthetic reception. Metaphors or myths survive in new shapes, which carry elements of the old form but simultaneously surpass it. Some forms outlive the conclusion of the cultural period in which their world-explaining power was at its height. An example is the persistence of myths in postmythical times. It suggests that even under the condition of what might be called modern rationality, mythical perception and explanation of the world is a human desideratum.

---

58. Most extensively in Blumenberg's *Matthäuspassion* (*The Saint Matthew Passion*), in the context of a discussion of messianism. See Blumenberg, *Matthäuspassion* (1988).

59. See Köhn, "Hans Blumenberg liest Walter Benjamin," 87, 98.

The reason for this has to be sought in the human need for consolation. In *Beschreibung des Menschen* (2006; *Description of Humankind*), Blumenberg paradoxically argues that—in light of mortality and the arbitrariness of existence—humans yearn for solace but are, at the same time, inconsolable. With this claim, Blumenberg reaffirms his pivotal proposition that humans are biologically deficient beings (*Mängelwesen*) and exist *in spite* of their constitutive vulnerability. Consolation is a strategy of survival "in the midst of the negation," as Blumenberg puts it. In other words, it is an instrument that renders the unbearable contingency of reality bearable and enables humans to live on (*was Weiterleben . . . möglich macht*).[60] Forms are effective tools of consolation. The idea of their afterlife opens a space between memory and reception, preservation and transformation, which has been described as programmatic for Blumenberg's philosophy. It allows for an approach to history that saves what is savable but is willing to let go of what is lost.[61]

The divergence between life and world—especially if we consider the latter in its historical nature—underlies Blumenberg's approach to forms, their function, and their afterlife. The exact opposite seems to be true for Benjamin. As already noted, there exists a close affinity between life and history in his work, which prompted him to state that everything historical possesses life and brings Samuel Weber to ask why Benjamin took the trouble to bring up the concept of life if all he meant was, in fact, history. Weber's answer demarcates the place of death in Benjamin's historical thinking and implicitly draws a line back to Blumenberg. "The history that emerges out of this discussion of 'life,' 'afterlife,' 'living-on' is a history that is mindful of mortality," Weber writes. "What marks this vision of history is precisely its subjugation to death, what Benjamin calls its *Todverfallenheit*." The consequence for forms—which "The Task of the Translator" exposed as translations (and vice versa)—is that, under the condition of *Todverfallenheit*, they become what Weber called a "strange kind of hybrid," teetering on the brink between survival and transience, ever ready to carry the original into the next stage of its afterlife, the next phase of its history, while enduring in their own finitude; for unlike originals, Benjamin regards translations as not translatable (AÜ, 150).[62]

With the idea of life's *Todverfallenheit*, or literally life that is falling toward death, Benjamin is certainly not at odds with the philosophical context around 1900, and the manifold attempts—those of Freud, Heidegger, and

---

60. Blumenberg, *Beschreibung des Menschen*, 633.

61. Looked at from this angle, it comes as no surprise that Blumenberg has been called—in the same breath as Aby Warburg—a theoretician of *Nachleben* by Moxter, "Trost" (2014), 337–49.

62. Weber, *Benjamin's -abilities*, 63–68. See also Hirsch, "Die Aufgabe des Übersetzers," 612.

Blumenberg included—to identify death as an integral part of life. In *Being and Time*, for example, Heidegger defined the meaning of *Verfallenheit* (fallenness, subjugation) with respect to *Dasein* (Being) and its relation to the world (*Welt*) in the sense of social and cultural norms: "Dasein has, in the first instance, fallen away [*abgefallen*] from itself as an authentic potentiality for Being its Self, and has fallen into the world [*an die Welt verfallen*]. Fallenness into the 'world' means an absorption in Being-with-one-another, in so far as the latter is guided by idle talk [*Gerede*], curiosity and ambiguity" (*BT*, 220).[63] A later passage indicates that authenticity and affirmation of *Dasein*—which are prevented by *Dasein*'s focus on the world as its main concern—become possible under the condition of "Being-towards-death" (*Sein zum Tode*), the successful acceptance of death, not only as the end of life but as the event that determines the space within which Being chooses its possibilities (*BT*, 305).

For the present argumentation, it is most significant that Heidegger had paved the way for the notion of *Verfallenheit* as early as 1921/22, when—in his lecture series *Phänomenologische Interpretationen zu Aristoteles* (*Phenomenological Interpretations of Aristotle*)—he introduced the term *Ruinanz* (ruinance) to describe factical (*faktisch*) everyday life as a movement.[64] Specified as downfall—*Sturz* in German, which is Heidegger's translation of the Latin *ruina*, a term that emphasizes the process of disintegration rather than the decayed object—*Ruinanz* denotes the (falling) movement of life away from itself and toward the world to which it is exposed (*dass der Sturz im Sein des faktischen Lebens jeweils es seiner Welt aus-setzt*; GA 61, 131; *PI*, 142).[65] Like Blumenberg, Heidegger draws attention to a division: between authentic *Dasein*, on the one hand, and the distraction from authenticity by the world, on the other. A distinctive feature of "ruinant" life is that it lacks historical time. "Ruinance takes time away," Heidegger writes, "i.e. it seeks to abolish the historiological [*das Historische*] from facticity. The ruinance of factical life possesses this sense of actualization [*Vollzugssinn*]: abolition of time" (*PI*, 104). In other words, ruinance deprives *Dasein* of temporal and historical authenticity or—if we once again look forward to *Being and Time*—it suppresses life's self-awareness as temporal and historical, its knowledge about finitude, and our acceptance of death: our "ownmost possibility" (*BT*, 295). Yet this denial of mortality stands in opposition to what Heidegger calls the "counter-ruinant"

---

63. Bracketed *abgefallen* in the original. Other bracketed additions are mine.

64. See Heidegger, *Phänomenologische Interpretationen zu Aristoteles*, in *Gesamtausgabe* (1985; hereafter cited as *GA*), 131. For the English translation, see Heidegger, *Phenomenological Interpretations of Aristotle* (2009; hereafter cited as *PI*).

65. See the "Introduction" and my remarks on the etymology of *ruina*.

(*gegenruinant*) movement of philosophical interpretation. The pursuit of *Dasein*'s authenticity and its philosophical explication happen within ruinance, but their movement simultaneously resists the downward trajectory (*Sturz*) of life, "counter-ruinantly" (*GA* 61; *PI*, 153). Heidegger's concept of ruinance seems to suggest that philosophical understanding of Being itself—the thinking that opens up the meaning of Being and that, in my reading of *Sojourns*, I called *form*—essentially consists in an anticipation of death and (in contrast to Blumenberg, for whom death takes the role of an obstacle that triggers the anthropological imperative to overcome it) an acknowledgment of loss and finitude.[66] Like Benjamin, Heidegger ties this acknowledgment to a concept of life's historicity.

Even a cursory glance at Freud's work reveals his preoccupation with much the same challenges that busied both Benjamin and Heidegger—at least as far as the issue of mortality is concerned. The question of an interconnection between life and death is most explicitly addressed in his 1920 work *Jenseits des Lustprinzips* (*Beyond the Pleasure Principle*). Based on the observation that some individuals show a compulsion to repeat unpleasant or traumatic experiences, Freud speculated about a death drive that he considered to be aimed at life's return to the inorganic state of its origins. Arguing teleologically and retrospectively at the same time, he noted, "If we are to take it as truth that knows no exception that everything living dies for *internal* reasons—becomes inorganic once again—then we shall be compelled to say that 'the aim of all life is death' and, looking backwards, that 'inanimate things existed before living ones.'"[67] Yet the drives that are aimed towards death are opposed by the life drives, notably the sex drives. According to Freud, both types are conservative, trying to bring back previous states of "living substance."[68] The death drives, however, seek to reestablish the inorganic by taking the shortest possible route to the end, while the life drives—which are, in fact, headed toward the same goal—pause and take detours and suspend the ending by retaining life. Freud spoke of a "vacillating rhythm" in which "one group of instincts rushes forward so as to reach the final aim of life as swiftly as possible; but when a particular stage in the advance has been reached, the other

---

66. This is the position of Hans Ruin in his analysis of Heidegger's *Phenomenological Interpretations*; see Ruin, "Thinking in Ruins," 30. One conclusion that must be drawn from Heidegger's lecture is that forms are counterruinant. As I will show subsequently, I do not share this position.

67. Freud, *Beyond the Pleasure Principle* (1995), 32; emphasis in the original.

68. Freud, *Beyond the Pleasure Principle*, 34.

group jerks back to a certain point to make a fresh start and so prolong the journey."[69]

Beyond the Pleasure Principle has been read as a turning point for Freud on the basis of which he initiated, around 1920, his realignment of psychoanalysis to give it a more pronounced focus on cultural issues.[70] Fifteen years later, he would formulate the connection explicitly: "I perceived ever more clearly that the events of human history, the interactions between human nature, cultural development and the precipitates of primeval experience ... are no more than a reflection of the dynamic conflicts between the ego, the id and the super-ego, which psycho-analysis studies in the individual—are the very same processes repeated upon a wider stage."[71] With this projection of psychoanalytical categories from the realm of internal human life onto that of external cultural-historical life, Freud brings his own speculation about a life/world relationship into play. Most important, the historicization and culturalization of the drive theory adapts the temporal rhythm of striving and lingering for the "historical stage" and thereby defies any dictate of teleology. Retrospect, delay, anticipation, and deferred action (*Nachträglichkeit*) are the dominant movements in and of time that preclude any suspicion of linearity and—by simultaneously claiming their unity and their divide—uphold the tension between life and death.

Seen against the backdrop of liminal time and space between life, death, and the notion of an afterlife of forms in the case of Blumenberg and Heidegger (that is, if we include Heidegger's understanding of Hölderlin's poetry), the singular scope and the unique methodological avail of Benjamin's account must be underscored. At first glance, the four thinkers' similarities seem to outweigh their differences by far. Not only are their assessments comparable but so are their time concepts. Benjamin's focus on anachronisms, temporal leaps and breaks, the simultaneity of the nonsimultaneous, and anticipations and belatedness are elements of Heidegger's, Freud's, and Blumenberg's reasoning as well. Yet despite the convincing arguments that could be made both against and in favor of Benjamin's independence, I would like to draw attention to two aspects that clearly distinguish Benjamin's approach and shed new light on decay and afterlife and especially the historicity that emerges from their interaction.

The first distinction is that none of the other three thinkers puts comparable emphasis on the hybrid nature of forms and their significance for a

---

69. Freud, *Beyond the Pleasure Principle*, 35.
70. Weigel, "Jenseits des Todestriebs," 41–57.
71. Freud, "Autobiographical Study" (1995), 72.

concept of history that is based on the acknowledgment of demise and the concurrent will to preserve. The second distinction—and this is closely related to the first point—is that only Benjamin associates his observations with the historical period of the baroque, which guides his reflections on forms and finitude. A juxtaposition of "The Task of the Translator" and *The Origin of German Tragic Drama*, the texts in which he dealt with these two issues, reveals Benjamin's unique position and illuminates the difficult figure of "life after life."

The Origin of German Tragic Drama is dedicated to a study of baroque allegory. In response to the dominance of idealist aesthetics and its preference for the suprahistorical characteristics of the symbol, Benjamin rehabilitates allegory as a poetic device and a form of art. In his reading, the early modern drama—set against the concrete backdrop of the disastrous Thirty Years' War that ravaged Europe between 1618 and 1648—exposes "history as the history of the suffering of the world" and stages it as ruin, "significant only in the stations of its decline [*Verfall*]."[72] This baroque insight into the significance of finitude and mortality, which manifests itself in what Benjamin called a "baroque cult of the ruin," is present in the world of thought as allegory—or, to use the wording of the frequently quoted passage, "allegories are in the realm of thoughts what ruins are in the realm of things" (*OGD*, 178). The meaning of history, as it were, derives from its shattered forms beyond beauty and totality. It emerges from allegories and ruins and their defective fragmentariness that points toward *Todverfallenheit* and is significant precisely in this subjugation to death.[73] At the same time, in addition to this "appreciation of the transience of things," allegory works toward rescuing them "for eternity" (*OGD*, 223). The background for this thought is the idea that the origin of allegory lies in medieval Christianity, which faced the remains of antiquity just as the baroque is confronted with the ruins of the Thirty Years' War. According to Benjamin, the Middle Ages saved antiquity's "theological essences

---

72. This is Samuel Weber's translation of the passage from Benjamin's *The Origin of German Tragic Drama* (1998; hereafter cited as *OGD*), see Weber, *Benjamin's -abilities*, 68. The English translation by John Osborne, which seems to focus on Benjamin's religious metaphors, states that "the baroque, secular explanation of history as the Passion of the world; its importance resides solely in the stations of its decline" (*OGD*, 166). The German *Verfall*, which both Weber and Osborne translate as "decline" could be translated more accurately as "decay," which puts an emphasis on the fragments and shattered pieces on which allegorists ruminate. For the original, see Benjamin, *Ursprung des deutschen Trauerspiels* (1991), 343.

73. Benjamin explicitly claimed that finitude and meaning belong together when he wrote, "The greater the significance, the greater the subjection to death [*Soviel Bedeutung, soviel Todverfallenheit*]" (*OGD*, 166).

[*theologische Wesenheiten*]" by insisting on allegory, which "established itself most permanently where transitoriness and eternity confronted each other most closely" (*OGD*, 223–24). In the space in between, signification happens. Benjamin's decisive step was to no longer locate the production of meaning in symbols but rather in the dialectical figures of decay and retention.[74] Baroque poets were identified as allegorists whose melancholic gaze turned ruins and debris into "highly significant [*hochbedeutend*] fragments" that Benjamin labeled "the finest [*edel*] material in baroque creation" (*OGD*, 178).

The situation of the baroque German tragic drama has been compared to the one at stake in the "Task of the Translator." Weber established the connection by invoking the irreducible finitude that translations share with allegories and ruins.[75] One way to make sense of the comparison is by harking back to Benjamin's argument that translations are of no significance for the original and at the same time responsible for the actualization of its possibilities. They oscillate, so to speak, between a work's state of decay and its proper realization. This simultaneity of development and disintegration is an essential aspect of a translation's form-being and constitutes the tension in which afterlives unfold. Forms emerge as finite, inherently fragmented and decayed entities that are just as ephemeral as they are concrete and open to the attribution of new meaning. It is a result of this process that the vicinity of translations to allegories and ruins becomes fully visible. On the one hand, determined by their finitude and decadence, all three appear as the stuff of change and signification, historical by way of mortality. On the other hand, they all entertain a relationship with eternity in the ambiguous sense that Benjamin delineated: in the sense of continuous transmission to the point of a work's fame that also carries religious and theological implications, pointing even beyond earthly life.

For all these reasons, translations, allegories, and ruins can be subsumed under the common term *form*, which turns out to be essentially hybrid, including items from the realms of thought (allegories), matter (ruins), and cultural practices (translations). Such a broad understanding of form makes possible one rather far-reaching conclusion for the interpretation of ruins: if ruins are forms and forms by definition unite material and conceptual characteristics, and furthermore if forms are ruins that enable afterlives through transformation and decline, then this profound reciprocity suggests that the ruins encountered by the protagonists of this book are more than just motifs, more than mere catalysts for processes of formation. They are conceptually

74. Ruin, "Thinking in Ruins," 25.
75. Weber, *Benjamin's –abilities*, 68.

related to the changing and surviving forms that emerge when life and world, in the face of decay, enter a constellation.[76]

Benjamin's understanding of forms has to be considered in close connection with his thoughts on the relationship between life and history, original and translation, ruin and allegory, and, above all, the role of mortality. Mortality appears as the common denominator of all the philosophical and theoretical works discussed here, and it will serve as the center of many of the discourses about ruins examined on the following pages. For Heidegger, Blumenberg, and Benjamin—and, in a more general sense, for Freud, too—only the awareness of death enables life and history; mortality is the link between the two.

Benjamin takes this reasoning one step further. His argument gives center stage to forms and—partly deriving their characteristics from an actual historical context—declares them essential for any concept of historicity that is based on the acceptance of mortality. The explicit historical embedding is the main difference between Benjamin and Georg Simmel, who with his life-philosophical observations puts comparable weight on forms but—similar to Freud in his analysis of drives—draws largely cultural-theoretical conclusions. In contrast, Benjamin relates history and forms by showing that forms are inherently fragile, and he claims that this fundamental finitude of forms has never been more manifest than in the baroque period, with its cult of the ruin and the rumination on fragments as a constant reminder of death and the vanity of earthly matters.

Seen in this way, Benjamin's focus on broken forms is more than a counterstatement to idealist aesthetics and more than a rehabilitation of allegory or a reevaluation of modernity. To be sure, it is all this as well. But most of all, it is a manifestation of history's relation to life and its origin in forms. Benjamin's attention on the baroque uncovers that from its ruins and remains arises a concept of history that—against the backdrop of a decades-long war—implicates life and its transience and reaffirms, at the same time, that there is life after life: that life emerges from the forms of decay and that in these forms we can catch a glimpse of eternity.

---

76. In a certain sense, the "fate" of Heidegger's term *ruinance* is an example of the gravitation of ruins/forms toward materiality and conceptuality at once. The strictly conceptual use of the term to describe a movement away from the acceptance of mortality disappears from Heidegger's work after the *Phenomenological Investigations*, and ruins will reemerge again in Heidegger's late work. Seemingly nothing but the concrete setting for the philosopher's *Sojourns*, they are at the center of the reconfiguration of his philosophical discourse.

The following readings of discourses about ruins will put this theoretical frame to work. These case studies will linger on the complexities of time and the beauty of forms; they will ruminate over the shattered pieces of reality and dig through the layers of history. From this vertical movement of the readers' eyes a narrative will emerge that tells of how things fall apart, of how they change shape or survive, or else break all over again.

11
The Propitious Moment

3

Petrarch and the View of Rome

Differamus que restant in proximum diem . . .

Let us put off what remains until another day . . .
FRANCESCO PETRARCA

Picking Up Pieces: Vaucluse, Rome, and the Politics of the Fruitful Moment

It was August 1352 when, from the district Vaucluse in Southern France, a number of letters reached Francesco Nelli, secretary to bishop Angelo Acciaioli I and prior of the Chiesa dei Santi Apostoli in Florence, in short succession. The sender was Petrarch, whom Nelli had befriended two years earlier. In the self-chosen solitude of his retreat at the river Sorgue, the poet had been working on several literary projects for the past months. Yet the letter of August 10 indicates that his work did not proceed smoothly. Petrarch complains to Nelli that various obligations imposed upon him all too frequent travels, giving him the uneasy sense of being everywhere and nowhere at once: "I am constantly in motion amidst incessant noise, and am simultaneously here, elsewhere, and, therefore, nowhere—a common malady in those who continually move around" (*LFM*, 13:6).[1]

In Vaucluse, Petrarch mainly tried to recover some of the focus that he had lost during a recent stay in Avignon. The city, to which Petrarch returned regularly, was contradictorily subject to the poet's publicly proclaimed hatred. He despised the noise and the depravity of "Babylon," as he scornfully called the residency of the exiled papal court and the place where he had spent a good portion of his life. Petrarch was born in 1304 in Arezzo, Italy. His father Pietro di Parenzo, a supporter of the pope in the power struggle between the Roman Catholic Church and the Holy Roman emperor, brought his wife Eletta Canigiani to the Tuscan town after he was forced to leave the city-state of Florence in 1302. Francesco was aged eight, his younger brother, Gherardo, five, when the family moved to Avignon, where Pietro hoped to

---

1. Petrarca, *Letters on Familiar Matters* (2014; hereafter cited as *LFM*, with book and letter number). For the Latin original and an Italian translation, see Petrarca, *Le Familiari* (1974).

find work as a lawyer. His oldest son's aversion for Avignon had political reasons, and they were tied to an unswerving belief in the exclusive legitimacy of Rome's universal imperial power. Seeing that power restored, including the return of the papacy to the Eternal City, was one of Petrarch's paramount goals. When, in the mid-fourteenth century, the Rome-born notary Cola di Rienzo initiated his attempt to revive the Roman Republic and a government of the people by revolting against the nobility, the poet was enthusiastic. "Petrarch had been the private friend, perhaps the secret counsellor, of Rienzi: his writings breathe the most ardent spirit of patriotism and joy," the British historian Edward Gibbon reported in *The History of the Decline and Fall of the Roman Empire*, a six-volume work first published from 1776 to 1789. "All respect for the pope, all gratitude for the Colonna, was lost in the superior duties of a Roman citizen."[2] The scope of Petrarch's actual influence on Cola is unclear, but there can be no doubt that they both shared the same dream of Rome's resurrection. As Gibbon indicates, Petrarch's sense of a common cause was strong enough for him to abandon old loyalties. Petrarch did not hesitate to break with Cardinal Giovanni Colonna, his friend and patron of many years, whose family had become one of the main targets of Cola's antiaristocratic campaign. It was only when Cola's despotic ambitions prevailed and he could no longer disguise his intention to betray the interests of his followers that Petrarch started to back out of the ideological engagement. In 1347, he called off a trip to Rome when he heard of Cola's unruly behavior and went to Parma instead. Petrarch wrote to Cola and explained his reasons:

> After I left your court, a number of letters from friends followed my departure in which the questionable turn of your affairs . . . reached me. They say that you do not love the people as you used to . . . Things will always go as eternal law decrees. I cannot change them, but I can flee from them. You have therefore freed me from a considerable task: I was hastening to you with all my heart, but I am changing direction. (*LFM*, 7:7)

The great difficulty of this process for Petrarch is evidenced by his enduring hope, which informs even this apparent rejection of the self-declared "tribune of the people," that the reports he received from Rome might be inaccurate: "But perhaps what I am saying may be false. Would that it were really so; for never would I more willingly have been wrong" (*LFM*, 7:7).[3] At the same

---

2. Gibbon, *History of the Decline and Fall of the Roman Empire* (1802), 343.
3. For this and the details of Cola's story, see Celenza, *Petrarch: Everywhere a Wanderer*, 76–83.

time, Petrarch's confidence in Rome's recovery and his firm advocacy for the city started to crumble. Turning his back on Cola meant parting with Rome as well: "For a long time farewell to you . . . , dear Rome; if what I hear is true I would rather visit the Indians or the Garamantes" (*LFM*, 7:7).

The August 10 letter to Nelli revisits the topic of Cola's triumphs and failures. It is, therefore, simultaneously a comment on Petrarch's own political trajectory, which he combines with thoughts about the nature of his work and the virtue of poetry—in other words, a poetics in miniature. In what follows, I start from a reading of the letter's insights into specifically Petrarchan thoughts on the state of the world, his own life as well as the forms suited to establish a connection with reality. I first examine how Vaucluse and Rome are set up as semiotically and semantically significant places between fiction and reality. In several digressions, I tie the relevancy of both locations to the textual and historical contexts. I then turn my attention to two famous letters that Petrarch wrote after his first and second visit to the Eternal City. I show that—under the impression of the sight of Rome's ruins—Petrarch reflected on the city's magnificent past but, against the backdrop of semiotic and semantic fragility, struggled to grasp Rome's greatness poetically. Unlike those scholars who have seen Petrarch's reluctance to give the discourse about ruins a textual form as prudent hesitation on the threshold between the premodern and the modern,[4] I understand Petrarch as a proponent of kairos, the right point in time when the mediation between the conditions of one's individual life and the world succeeds by the agency of forms. However, Petrarch's writings—rather than documenting the attainment of the propitious moment—speak of its delicacy and elusiveness. The narrational circling around the opportune occasion is therefore a strategy that foregrounds figures of delay, suspension, time pressure, and privation. This seems to imply

---

4. These positions reaffirm historical periodization to which even the most careful studies of Petrarch occasionally resort when explaining the poet's comprehensive impact on Western culture. For instance, Andrew Hui in his comprehensive and instructive study of Renaissance ruins is well aware of the perils of periodization but cannot—or does not want to—fully avoid them when he reiterates Petrarch's scholarly oft-cited status as a vanguard of historicism and the modern self. See: Hui, *Poetics of Ruins in Renaissance Literature*, 61, 89. A similar observation applies with respect to the monumental and groundbreaking study of Petrarch as a European intellectual of the fourteenth century, by Karlheinz Stierle; see Stierle, *Francesco Petrarca: Ein Intellektueller*. Stierle seems somewhat undecided as to whether he wants to emphasize that Petrarch was the embodiment of a radically new world, which was neither antique nor modern but a hitherto unknown category, or whether he wants to draw attention to the idea that Petrarch was responsible for the implementation of the most consequential demarcation line between the Middle Ages and the modern period. Both options presuppose the premise of periodization.

that the right form that can ensure the survival of intellectual ruins from the past has yet to be found.

With a nod to Jacques Derrida's philosophy of writing, which states that written signifiers permanently defer textual meaning because the thing they *re*-present is never *present*, the German Romance scholar Karlheinz Stierle conceives the structure of postponement in Petrarch's texts as a deferral of the production of a complete work. He essentially claims that for Petrarch—whom he considers the first major fragmentist before the Romantics—fragmentariness is a "primary experience," derived from his direct encounter with ruined Rome.[5] Put in our terms, Petrarch knows of no such thing as a complete form and nevertheless holds it up as the coveted ideal.[6] Stierle's assessment—above all, his association of Petrarch's poetics of postponement with the experience of ruins—is of fundamental importance for my approach. This importance notwithstanding, my analysis has a different focus. I examine both the relation between the "right form" and the "right time" and the means with which Petrarch seeks to grasp their significance. The propitious moment in which I am interested is a moment of historical, biographical, and poetic possibility. I ask how Petrarch understands and creates this possibility and, most important, why he also tries to avoid it. In this context, I will turn to Petrarch's poem *Trionfi* (*Triumphs*) in the last part of this chapter. A long-term project like many others of Petrarch's works, the *Triumphs* are an example of how the poet tried to mediate the concept of the right time with that of the right form. The perspective on kairos that Petrarch develops here will reveal uncharted aspects of his historical significance.

The valley of Vaucluse where Petrarch had purchased a small cottage shortly after a much-anticipated first visit to Rome in 1337 was dubbed, by the poet—in spite of its vicinity to Avignon—his "most delightful transalpine solitude."[7] The epigrammatic praise of the secluded spot in a 1351 letter to Philippe de

---

5. Stierle, *Francesco Petrarca: Ein Intellektueller*, 272, 427, 525–30, 808. Without mentioning Stierle, Hui makes a similar point when, with respect to Renaissance humanism, he speaks of an "aesthetics of the unfinished" that finds its predecessor in Petrarch, who collected *vestigia* (traces) of a lost past. See Hui, *Poetics of Ruins in Renaissance Literature*, 6. The difference from Stierle lies in the reverse temporal focus. While Stierle seems more interested in the "not yet," Hui emphasizes the "no longer."

6. John Freccero also measures Petrarch's distance between signs and signifiers, in Augustinian/Neoplatonic terms; see Freccero, "Fig Tree and Laurel," 34–40.

7. The note *Transalpina solitudo mea iocundissima* was added by Petrarch to his copy of Pliny's *Historia Naturalis* next to a drawing of a heron eating a fish. In the background, a narrow path leads up a rocklike hill to a church at the top. A river seems to spring from the rock.

Cabassole, bishop of Cavaillon and seigneur of Vaucluse, is at once an indulgence in the site's unique natural beauty and its staging as the birthplace of Petrarch's poetic persona. Here, all the threads of his life converge and result in poetic productivity:

> Valle locus Clausa toto mihi nullus in orbe
> Gratior aut studiis aptior ora meis.
> Valle puer Clausa fueram iuvenemque reversum
> Fovit in aprico vallis amena sinu.
> Valle vir in Clausa meliores dulciter annos
> Exegi et vite candida fila mee.
> Valle senex Clausa supremum ducere tempus
> Et Clausa cupio, te duce, Valle mori.

No place in the world is dearer to me than the Vale Enclosed, and none more favorable for my toils. In my boyhood I visited the Vale Enclosed, and in my youth, when I returned, the lovely valley cherished me in its sunny bosom. In my manhood I spent my best years sweetly in the Vale Enclosed, while the threads of my life were white. In my old age I desire to live out in the Vale Enclosed my allotted time, and in the Enclosed Vale, under thy guidance, to die. (*LFM*, 11:4)

Vaucluse would never lose, in Petrarch's descriptions, this air of a location bound up with destiny. Yet earlier correspondences with Luca Cristiani (Olimpio), a close friend from Petrarch's college years in Bologna, evince that the reasons for the significance of the remote valley were more complex than the epigram might suggest.

There was one instance in which Petrarch's treasured "port in stormy moments" failed to provide the required shelter, and the experience haunted the poet (*LFM*, 13:6). He reports to Olimpio in 1349 that in the solitary landscape he tried in vain to hide from "that youthful fire which raged within me for so many years" (*LFM*, 8:3). Even though these allusions remain somewhat vague, there is no doubt that Petrarch is talking about the consequences of his encounter with Laura, the addressee and subject of his love lyrics in *Rerum vulgarium fragmenta* (*Fragments of Vernacular Matters*, sometimes called *Rime Sparse—Shattered Rhymes*—and, since the sixteenth century, *Canzoniere*), a collection of 366 Italian poems that the author himself arranged over many years.[8] According to a note that Petrarch inserted into the flyleaf

---

8. The collection consists of 317 sonnets, 29 canzones, 9 sestinas, 7 ballads, and 4 madrigals—a total of 366 poems. For the Italian text and an English verse translation, see Petrarca, *The "Canzoniere," or "Rerum Vulgarium Fragmenta"* (1996; hereafter cited as *RVF*). Numbers in the text citations represent poem and line number.

of the Ambrosian Virgil codex, the most famous among the many precious manuscripts in his possession, he met Laura for the first time as a young man: "Laura, illustrious through her own virtues and long famed through my verses, first appeared to my eyes in my youth, in the year of our Lord 1327, on the sixth day of April, in the church of St. Clare in Avignon, at matins."[9] In rough chronological order, part 1 of the *Fragmenta* is dedicated to the time between the *innamoramento* (falling in love), the first glimpse of the forever unattainable beloved and her death in 1348—which, according to Petrarch, also occurred on the sixth of April.[10] The second part, starting at poem 264 of 366, documents the poet's mourning of her loss. As Teodolinda Barolini pointed out, this division was Petrarch's intention but could not always satisfy editorial needs for transparent narrative orders. The headings that some editors added spelled out the respective content of the two sections (*In vita di madonna Laura*/*During the Life of Lady Laura*; *In morte di madonna Laura*/*After the Death of Lady Laura*) and were meant to remedy what Barolini calls "the tenuous and opaque love story that the poems do not narrate so much as conjure and suggest."[11]

The long-standing and ongoing scholarly debate about the authenticity of Laura's historical existence seems to be partly motivated by a similar desire to avoid ambiguity. In 1525, the editor and commentator of Petrarch's poetry, Alessandro Vellutello, provoked a veritable investigative furor when he claimed that he had solved the mystery of Laura's identity.[12] On the other end of the spectrum, there are those interpreters who focus on the poetic character of the *Fragmenta* for which they deem Laura's historicity per se irrelevant.[13] Drawing attention to the homophony between Laura's name and the Italian (*l'aura*) and Latin (*aura*) terms for "breath," "air," "breeze," or "gleam," both Stierle and Peter Hainsworth have argued that with Laura a

---

9. Wilkins, *Life of Petrarch* (1961), 77. For the Latin text, see De Nolhac, *Pétrarque et l'humanisme*, 286–87: "Laurea, propriis uirtutibus illustris et meis longum celebrate carminibus, primum oculis meis apparuit sub primum adolescentie mee tempus, anno Domini m° iij^c xxviij die vj° mensis Aprilis in ecclesia sancta Clare Auin. hora matutina."

10. Petrarch manipulated the April 6 date—understood by all his early readers as the miraculous coincidence of Laura's appearance and her death on Good Friday—to make history conform to his truth. April 6, 1327, actually fell on a Monday. See Martinelli, "Feria sexta aprilis: La data sacra del Canzoniere del Petrarca," 449–89; Dutschke, "The Anniversary Poems in Petrarca's *Canzoniere*," 83–101.

11. For this point as well as a critical guide to the *Fragmenta* in combination with a reflection on the significance of time, see Barolini, "Self in the Labyrinth of Time" (2009), 34.

12. See Rushworth, *Petrarch and the Literary Culture of Nineteenth-Century France*, 17.

13. For example Weinrich, *On Borrowed Time*, 22.

"poetic dialectic of absence and presence" (Stierle), something "insubstantial and empty, or, alternatively . . . something . . . vital" (Hainsworth) is at stake. Building on this thought, Barolini reads the multifaceted name as a poetic device, which—in bringing out Laura's transience and concreteness, her evanescence and tangibility—promotes the one principal theme of the *Fragmenta*, anticipated by the title: that "the self [is] subjected to multiplicity" and dispersion, "caught in the flux of time and change."[14]

The question whether Laura was real, an invention, or a cypher for the spirit of imagination and creativity need not be answered here.[15] In the context of Petrarch's letter to Olimpio, her poetic function is evident. The ferocity of Petrarch's passion that not even Vaucluse could calm is the condition and the price he had to pay to be able to "sing" at all: "Thus, the flames in my heart spread through my bones and filled those valleys and skies with a mournful, but, as some called it, pleasant tune. From all of this emerged those vernacular songs of my youthful labors" (*LFM*, 8:3).[16] In that sense, Vaucluse continued, on the one hand, to be—even under the extreme circumstances of Petrarch's *innamoramento*—a concrete geographical space of poetic possibility. On the other hand, in much the same fashion in which he upset the reader's assessment of Laura's status, Petrarch offered, in the epistle to his friend, an alternative view of the valley:

> But if I might boast to you . . . without sounding as though I were bragging, I ask you this: aside from the peacefulness of the mountains and of the fountain and of the woods, what of any moment has happened in that place that could be considered, if not more outstanding, certainly more noteworthy than my residing there? I may even dare suggest that for many people that place is known as much for my name as for its certainly extraordinary spring. (*LFM*, 8:3)

Petrarch maintains that the one who confers true significance on Vaucluse is the poet. The place is as much his invention as it is a beautiful spot in the South of France.

Rather than dismissing as hubris Petrarch's claim that he 'invented' Vaucluse, Enrico Fenzi interpreted the "confession" to Olimpio as an indicator that the

---

14. Stierle, *Francesco Petrarca: Ein Intellektueller*, 653; Hainsworth, *Petrarch the Poet* (1988), 135; Barolini, "Self in the Labyrinth of Time," 37–38. Poem 5 of *RVF* is an example of Petrarch's play on this ambiguousness of Laura's name that he repeatedly implies but never states outright.

15. Petrarch's correspondences show that even his contemporaries suspected that Laura was to be interpreted as a fictional character and that Petrarch took some delight in playing with their bewilderment. See Stierle, *Francesco Petrarca: Ein Intellektueller*, 508–12.

16. Petrarch clearly invokes the medieval courtly paradigm of service and reward, in which the lady's refusal to grant the poet the reward of her love fuels his creative capacity.

poet's ideas on the concept of *patria*—the notion of home and birthplace—were about to change. Fenzi suggests that Petrarch's obsession with Italy as well as his belief in the inalterability of the country's status as his "native land" and of its political and religious authority were on the verge of being replaced by a flexible concept of origin and belonging, which the individual was free to construct and choose.[17] Yet three years after his note to Olimpio, Petrarch writes to Nelli:

> Here [in Vaucluse] I have acquired two small gardens perfectly suited to my skills and taste. To attempt a description for you would be too long. In short, I believe that no similar spot exists in all the world, and, to confess my unmanly fickleness, I regret only that it is not in Italy . . . I assure you that I could perhaps settle here, except that it is so far from Italy and so near Avignon. Why should I conceal my two weaknesses? My love of Italy charms and tempts me, my hatred of Avignon stings and revolts me. (*LFM*, 13:8)

Judging by this passage, the perfect location, which Petrarch imagines for himself, could not be more concrete. Viewed together with the event of Petrarch's permanent return to Italy in 1353, it appears to thoroughly refute Fenzi's point that Petrarch's understanding of the significance of a place was largely undetermined or symbolic. However, there are two important regards in which Fenzi's assessment proves to be accurate. For one, even though Petrarch left Vaucluse and, in a very real sense, moved to his native country, he did not settle in Rome, the city that, in his perception, had hitherto carried all the weight of historical and political legitimacy. Petrarch decided to go to Milan—a move that, at the time, equaled a commitment to a new vision of Italy, with the Lombardic city-states as the center of political power. Fenzi's other insight was that Petrarch's Vaucluse, instead of being just a geographical place of exceptional value, combined aspects of poetic, biographical, historical, and political importance. Vaucluse was a melting pot in which life, world, and form converged.

Petrarch's August 10 letter to Nelli is unique in that it combines this topological potential of the semantically highly charged French resort with the conceptual and historical scope of Rome, the poet's "place of all places," equal parts real and phantasmagorical.[18] Writing from Vaucluse, Petrarch casts a light on recent events that evolved around Cola di Rienzo, bringing back memories of political hope and disillusionment that were closely tied to the Eternal City,

---

17. Fenzi, "Petrarca e l'esilio," 386.
18. Stierle, *Francesco Petrarca: Ein Intellektueller*, 263.

the melting pot of secular and spiritual dominance and a semiotic benchmark for any attempt to explain the way of the world. Together with the conceptual and historical scope of both localities, Petrarch also brings the strong but rare forces of poetry and—as we have already seen—his personal writing situation into view. "What I intend to write today," he tells his friend, "you will find set forth in this letter: poetry, a divine gift granted to few, has begun nowadays to be dishonored, not to say profaned and prostituted. Never in Athens or in Rome, never in the days of Homer and Virgil, was there so much discussion as in this age on the banks of the Rhone; yet never was there a time or a place when in my opinion so little was understood about it" (*LFM*, 13:6). To make his argument about the decline of poetic skills among contemporaries, Petrarch takes an unexpected detour and first reports to Nelli how in Avignon he witnessed Cola's extradition to Pope Clement VI. "Recently there came to the Curia Nicola di Lorenzo—I should not say that he came but that he was led there captive—once a truly feared tribune of the city of Rome yet now the most miserable of men" (*LFM*, 13:6). Cola, whose megalomaniacal ambitions had cost him the support of the pope shortly after his power grab in 1347, was forced to leave Rome and hide in a monastery for two years. In 1350, he was ready for a comeback. Cola went to Prague, where he hoped to win the emperor Charles IV's support for yet another attempt to achieve his political goals in Rome and Italy. But instead, Charles imprisoned him and later delivered him to Clement. Petrarch writes:

> While he might have died with great glory on the Capitoline, he instead suffered imprisonment in Bohemia and shortly afterward in Limoges, to his shame and that of the Roman name, and even to that of the republic . . . He who filled evil men throughout the world with terror and fear, he who gave good men the most joyful hope and expectation, entered the Curia humble and despised. He who was once accompanied by the entire Roman populace . . . was unhappily walking hither and yon, accompanied by two guards, through a crowd eager to see the face of the man whose name was recently so celebrated. Moreover, he had been sent by the Roman king to the Roman pontiff. What an astonishing affair! (*LFM*, 13:6)

Rome's name, intimately linked to Cola by a common destiny, runs like a refrain through the passage. Notably shaken by the sight of the disgraced "tribune" but unsure whether he deserves pity, Petrarch looks back at his own role in the "affair." "How involved my pen was in praising and advising him is better known than I would perhaps wish," he admits to Nelli. "I loved his virtue, I praised his aims, I admired his spirit. I rejoiced with Italy, and I foresaw the sovereignty of the Holy City and peace throughout the entire world" (*LFM*, 13:6).

Petrarch ultimately came to understand Cola's downfall as a chain of missed opportunities that made a prediction of the course of events fundamentally impossible: "Unaccustomed as I am to being a prophet, I indeed wish that he [Cola] had not tried to be one ... If then he had exercised only his clemency against the country's murderers, he could have kept them alive ... I recall having written him ... about this; had he paid attention to it, the affairs of state would now be quite different and today Rome would not be enslaved nor he a captive" (*LFM*, 13:6). Yet while, in Petrarch's opinion, Cola deserved to be condemned for the disastrous outcome of his misled endeavors, public opinion denounced him for all the wrong reasons: "Only one charge is directed against him, and if he is condemned for it, he will, at least for me, be not infamous but worthy of eternal glory. The crime is that he dared to have wanted the republic safe and free, and to have all matters dealing with the Roman Empire and Roman power dealt with in Rome" (*LFM*, 13:6). Whether or not Cola would be punished was still undecided when Petrarch penned his letter, and it was precisely the uncertainty of the situation that caused the poet to launch into an argument about poetry.

The transition between the political and the poetological part of the epistle is clearly marked as a passage from serious matters to more entertaining ones. Petrarch explicitly announces that, after the sad story of Cola's misfortunes, he intends to make Nelli laugh. The source of potential amusement is the rumor that Cola's single hope to be rescued from his precarious condition is his reputation as an exceptional poet. As Petrarch points out somewhat disparagingly, the advocates of the "tribune" reiterated Cicero's famous defense of his teacher when they contended that "it is terrible to punish a man dedicated to such sacred studies." Petrarch then indulges in praising the Muses for their immense power, strong enough to save a man from death. Yet the deep irony of his joy over the unexpected honor bestowed on poetry and Cola's sudden luck becomes clear, at the latest, when Petrarch reminds Nelli that, despite being well-read and eloquent, Cola never composed a single poem. "I wanted to tell you this," he concludes, "so that you may grieve at the ill fortune of the former defender of the republic, that you may rejoice over his unexpected release, that you may with me become equally indignant and amused about the reason for that release" (*LFM*, 13:6).

Petrarch's deliberations reveal the degree to which he considered political and poetic matters to be intertwined. In his remarks on Cola, he critiques a lack of aesthetic judgment, taste, and knowledge that he observed, in his time, even among the most illustrious men of church and state. He is astonished to find that these men do not know "even the first and most general principles of an art in which we know the masters of the world at one time exercised their lofty talents with passion and constancy despite their involvement in public affairs" (*LFM*, 13:6). In that sense, the bottom line of Petrarch's letter that "the poets are far fewer" than generally assumed concurrently indicates that, politically speaking, the true "masters of the world" are very rare as well.

The dream of a revived and rebuilt Rome that, with Cola's "assistance," turned into the nightmare of the city's eternal ruin certainly left its mark on what many scholars have called Petrarch's "poetics of the fragment." The letter to Nelli contains explicit references to the brokenness of Petrarch's poetic forms. At the very outset he states, "Here [in Vaucluse] I am awaiting . . . the end of autumn . . . In the meantime, then, lest my rural sojourn be wasted, I am gathering fragments of past meditations in order to add something each day to my major works, if possible, or to complete some minor ones." Halfway through his report about Cola's miserable arrival in Avignon, Petrarch apologizes to Nelli for his fragmented, frequently interrupted report, admitting that his emotions are preventing him from writing coherently (*LFM*, 13:6).

Indeed, the entire collection of the *Epistolae Familiares* (the *Familiar Letters*), which were prepared by Petrarch and included the August letter to Nelli, must—like the *Canzoniere*, which in all probability is the result of the same impulse—be regarded as an effort to gather and compile the dispersed pieces of a manifold work, while facing the pressure of a limited lifetime and the uncertainties of a capricious fate. The dedicatory letter to his friend Ludwig van Kempen (Socrates), starts with the perplexed question, "What are we to do now, dear brother?" Petrarch writes against the backdrop of the devastation the plague brought in 1348 and describes his growing desire to come to terms with the personal losses he has suffered.[19] He finds a "great number of writings of different kinds that lie scattered and neglected throughout my house," poems and letters that piled up during a restless life that never allowed him to permanently settle (*LFM*, 1:1). And while, looking through the countless papers, he initially feels entertained by his own creations, Petrarch soon realizes that he wants to find an efficient way to deal with them, because

> the recollection of the brevity of life overcame me. I feared indeed an ambush, for what is more fleeting, I ask, than life, and what more determined than death? I reflected on the foundation that I had established, on what remained my labors and on lingering years. It seemed indeed madness, to have undertaken so many long and demanding works in such a brief and indefinite period of time, and to have directed my talents which would hardly suffice for limited undertakings to so great a variety of writings. (*LFM*, 1:1)

---

19. These losses included Laura, who, according to Petrarch, died of the plague.

The letter to Socrates is programmatic. It tells the story of Petrarch's toils and sets the tone for the collection that follows. At first sight, the main theme seems to be a wish for unity that the author, buried in the fragments of his life's work, struggles to achieve. The ideal of the coherent form and fear of distortion hover over the revisions that Petrarch confesses to have made to the letters: "The deformity of the collection could be easily discerned though it was hidden in individual letters." Therefore, redundancies had to be eliminated and verbosity reduced. What troubled Petrarch the most, however, was that the chronological order of the letters seemed to reveal a deterioration of his style that, in turn, pointed to a weakness of mind and character: "I am ashamed of a life fallen into excessive softness. The very order of my letters will testify to this." The confusion he experiences has to do with the disarray of temporal relations: "Could it be that I was a man in my youth and a youth in my old age? Unfortunate and cursed perversity!" Petrarch discloses that his initial plan had been to "change the order or to make entirely unavailable . . . those letters which I now condemn" (*LFM*, 1:1).

In the letter to Socrates, the mutual impact of time and form and their exceedingly ambivalent affiliation becomes all too clear. To begin with, the initial decision to gather the fragments of continuous creation is in itself a measure taken in light of limited lifetime and impending death. Petrarch then complicates the issue by implying that linear time opposes the intended unity of form—a problem, which only a manipulation of the chronological order can solve. Then again, it appears that unity of form may simply be an unattainable goal, mainly because of the congruence between life-time and time of the form—or as Petrarch formulates, "For me writing and living are the same thing" (*LFM*, 1:1). The volume, into which he condenses the pieces of a lifelong conversation with his friends, he calls—despite the simultaneous claim of integrity—a "reduced form" (*quod recolligo et in libri formam redigo*) of what began in his youth and will only end in death.

On various levels, the *Epistolae Familiares* convey a strong sense of there being—"in the flux of time and change," to use Barolini's expression again—something that could be called the fruitful moment. It emerges as an instant of historical, biographical, and poetic possibility when the awareness of mortality or lack of time meets broken or dispersed forms. The beginnings of both letters—the one to Socrates and the one to Nelli—contain laments over the brevity of time and the proximity of death, and they are juxtaposed with remarks about the fragments of Petrarch's work that he is about to compile. They prepare, against the backdrop of personal lifetime, the ground for the moment when the continuity of history—inextricably linked to Rome's fate—emerges as an option.

Yet kairos is hard to capture. Cola's story is essentially an account of missed political opportunities; and when Petrarch depicts himself with Horace's words as one who will rise "fearless" from the ruins "if the world slips into destruction," he does so with the caveat that it "remains to be seen" how he will "fare in the trials of life" (*LFM*, 1:1). The appropriate point in time eludes.[20] What can be grasped, however, are the constellations in Petrarch's work that spark visions of the propitious moment: forms that live on, the world that continues and life that persists. What can be observed are the poetic and rhetorical strategies he developed that circle around the phantasm that constantly evades. For Petrarch, the potentiality of the propitious moment was tied to this approach, and it was tied to places: to the beauty and security of Vaucluse and to Rome's exposed and broken majesty.

Form Suspended: Petrarch Visits the Ruins

Ferdinand Gregorovius, the nineteenth-century German historiographer whose work we will look at more closely in chapter 5, summarized the significance of the relationship between life, world, and form with respect to Petrarch in a few trenchant sentences. A short chapter of his monumental *Geschichte der Stadt Rom im Mittelalter* (*History of the City of Rome in the Middle Ages*) depicts Petrarch as a personality whose life was most tightly bound to the fate of Italy and particularly Rome. He appears as someone who, through his writings, documented the historical events of his time and added "a streak of personal life" (*einen Zug persönlichen Lebens*) to the history of the eternal city.[21] Gregorovius speaks of an "ardent desire" (*heisse Sehnsucht*) that drove Petrarch toward the place whose heroes, monuments, and artists had populated his imagination since childhood. The poet's own present appeared to him only "in the forms of the Roman world" (*in den Formen der römischen Welt*; *GSRM*, 2:670).

In the face of such great expectations, the actual encounter with the site of his longings could have easily ended in disappointment for Petrarch. When he visited the city for the first time in 1337, he was well aware that he would find "but a reflection of ancient Rome" (*LFM*, 2:9). Worried that the city's desolate state would inevitably spoil the image that Petrarch had, based on extensive readings, created for himself, Cardinal Giovanni Colonna had advised against

---

20. The end of the *Secretum* where Franciscus postpones his own conversion shows that this is a recurring motif in Petrarch's work.

21. Gregorovius, *Geschichte der Stadt Rom im Mittelalter* (1988; hereafter cited as *GSRM*), 2:669–75. Numbers in citations refer to volume and page number.

the trip, and it seems that Petrarch indeed postponed his journey more than once. But unlike Martin Heidegger, for whom most of his first visit to Greece was a confirmation that reality and readings are incompatible, Petrarch apparently found that his experience was not at odds with what he had gathered from books. In a letter from Rome, Petrarch let Colonna know that all his misgivings were unfounded: "Reality I am happy to say diminished nothing and instead increased everything. In truth Rome is greater, and greater are its ruins [*reliquie*] than I imagined" (*LFM*, 2:14). The short letter does not go into the details of this greatness. But the use of the word *reliquie*, or *relics*, for the remnants seen by Petrarch might give us an idea of the sublime nature of the experience.[22]

Thus, Petrarch took the trip without much delay. What he did postpone, however, was an elaborate description of his impressions of Rome. In fact, his inability to write about what he had seen was the first thing he mentioned to Colonna: "You thought that I would be writing something truly great once I had arrived in Rome. Perhaps what I shall be writing later will be great. For the present I know not where to start, overwhelmed as I am by the wonder of so many things [*miraculo rerum tantarum*] and by the greatness of my astonishment [*stuporis mole*]" (*LFM*, 2:14). Apparently, although Rome did not fail its beholder in terms of the deep effect it had on his *aisthesis*, his perception, Petrarch could not easily turn this experience into written or aesthetic form. The right moment for this step was yet to come.

Four years later, in 1341, Petrarch returned to Rome for the occasion of his crowning as poet laureate. As we learn from a letter to Colonna, the poet had received an invitation from the Roman senate the very day the chancellor of the University of Paris asked him to accept the same honor in Europe's cultural capital. "The affair does indeed seem almost incredible [*res pene incredibilis videtur*]," Petrarch tells the cardinal. "I entertain grave doubts in my mind, being driven on the one side by the charm of novelty [*novitatis gratia*], and on the other by reverence for antiquity [*reverentia vetustatis*]." Finally, he asks Colonna for advice: "Help my fluctuating mind with your counsel" (*LFM*, 4:4). The "affair" was, however, far less surprising than Petrarch made it sound. His correspondence with the theologian Dionigi di Borgo San Sepolcro, whose high standing with Robert of Anjou was used by Petrarch to gain the attention and support of the king of Naples, reveals that

---

22. I have already mentioned, in the introduction, Heckscher's comments on this aspect: see Heckscher, *Die Romruinen*, 26–27. For a short comment on Petrarch's first impression of Rome, see Mayer, "Impressions of Rome," 165–66. Mayer calls Petrarch "truly ruin-minded" because he recognizes grandeur in rubble.

he had carefully planned the course of events that ultimately led to the reception of the laurel wreath on the Capitoline. The move to revive a rite that, in the fourteenth century, appeared somewhat outdated seems to have been as much a conscious attempt to satisfy an inclination toward vanity as it was a serious endeavor to establish continuity with antiquity and restore some of Rome's cultural-political aura.[23] This time, Cardinal Colonna advised in favor of a journey to the Eternal City.

During the same visit, Petrarch explored Rome with the Dominican monk Fra Giovanni Colonna. The letter to his companion in which Petrarch later recalled their wanderings around the ruinscapes would become an important document for those readers who tried to demonstrate—implicitly or explicitly—the poet's modernity.[24] There are two mutually related central arguments that are frequently cited to support this claim. Broadly speaking, one is temporal and historical, the other one is related to poetics and possibilities of self-expression. Elaborating on the first point, one could say that Petrarch's gaze upon ruined Rome has been seen as the moment when—in the face of ruins and in contrast to a medieval notion of continuous time—temporal discontinuity was introduced to historical reflection. Theodor Mommsen famously called Petrarch "the first modern man," who, in his letter to Fra Colonna, drew a demarcation line between ancient and modern history.[25] In a different way and without mentioning Petrarch's modernity directly, Aleida Assmann declares that the ruins Petrarch sees (and reads) in Rome and "stages" in his letter are memorial sites or fragments of a lost life-nexus—in other words, material signs of discontinuity. A new cultural memory can emerge from the remains if the sites of destruction are embedded in narratives that explain their origin and meaning. Considered in this way, modernity becomes a sort of compromise between the continuity and discontinuity of history.[26] With respect to the second argument, the assumption is usually that a coincidence exists between Petrarch's work—his poetics, his archival

---

23. Stierle, *Francesco Petrarca: Ein Intellektueller*, 349–54. Stierle considers Petrarch's plan to be part of his self-fashioning through "grand gestures." See also Emmerson, *Key Figures in Medieval Europe*, 520, and Petrarch's letter to Cardinal Giacomo Colonna (*LFM*, 4:6) in which, with respect to the crowning, he states that vanity is the nature of man.

24. The letter was probably revised in 1341; see Wilkins, *Petrarch's Correspondence* (1960), 59.

25. Mommsen, "Petrarch's Conception of the 'Dark Ages,'" 106–29. Mommsen's thoughts stand in the same tradition as those of Burckhardt, *Civilization of the Renaissance in Italy*. See also Cassirer, *Individual and the Cosmos in Renaissance Philosophy*. Both Burckhardt and Cassirer focus on Petrarch as the discoverer of landscape and on his letter to Dionigi about the ascent of Mount Ventoux.

26. Assmann, *Erinnerungsräume*, 309.

and editorial activity of gathering dispersed fragments—and the poet's idea of the self, which, shattered and fragmented as it often appeared to critics, is deemed to have anticipated the modern self.[27] In what follows, I will draw on the observation that Petrarch establishes a specific relation between continuity and discontinuity that has to do with the brokenness of his forms, yet without reiterating the claim of his modernity.

Petrarch begins his letter with a digression. Rome and the walks with Fra Colonna are invoked merely in half a sentence—"We used to walk widely by ourselves throughout Rome"—before the poet launches into a discussion of antique philosophy and the search for truth. Speaking in the capacity of a Christian thinker, Petrarch claims that he possesses the right standard to distinguish between suitable and inappropriate strands of thought, and he calls on his Christian audience to always make their belief the point of reference for any reception of "philosophical, poetic, or historical writings." The argument closes with a peculiar remark that touches on genre characteristics of the epistle: "I have said these things at random [*incidenter*] as far as they seem to befit a letter of this type" (*LFM*, 6:2).

The next paragraph returns the focus to the setting and the movement of the interlocutors: "We used to wander together in that great city." Wherever they set foot, they become caught up in a piece of history that requires to be thought through and talked about. In this manner, Petrarch takes his readers on a tour de force through the entirety of Rome's turbulent history, from the city's mythological origins to the time of the kings, to the epoch of empire and on to the period of the Christian martyrs. The description of their suffering is also the moment when Petrarch pauses again, this time to note the imbalance between the necessary shortness of his letter and the unfathomable magnitude of Roman history: "But where shall I end? Can I really describe everything in this short letter? Indeed, if I could it would not be proper." Those who might think that all of Roman history fits in a single letter are, to Petrarch's chagrin, the Roman citizens themselves: "Sadly do I say that nowhere is Rome

---

27. See, e.g., Freccero, "Fig Tree and Laurel," 34–40; Barolini, "Making of a Lyric Sequence" (1989), 1–38; Mazzotta, "*Canzoniere* and the Language of the Self" (1978), 271–96; Dotti, *Petrarca e la scoperta della coscienza moderna*, 15–26; Stierle, *Francesco Petrarca: Ein Intellektueller*, 525. See also Blumenberg, *Legitimacy of the Modern Age* (1983), in which Blumenberg interprets Petrarch's ascent of Mount Ventoux as a moment of sea change in which the poet turns his gaze away from God and toward the world at his feet, thereby generating a new awareness of the world and the position of the individual in it. Gur Zak points out that Petrarch's focus on fragmentation (and exile) has led to critics' perception of him not only as modern but also as the "embodiment of the postmodern self"; see Zak, *Petrarch's Humanism and the Care of the Self*, 9. Gregorovius regarded Petrarch's way of treating Roman history as "modern humanity" (*GSRM*, 2:671).

less known than in Rome"; and Petrarch adds the line that contributed to the letter's status as a founding document of the Renaissance, symbolized by the rebirth of Rome in all its glorious, antique majesty: "For who can doubt that Rome would rise again instantly if she began to know herself?"[28] However, this thought is interrupted as well and a solution to the problem postponed: "This is a complaint to be dealt with at another time" (*LFM*, 6:2).

On their tour through the city, the two friends finally reach the Baths of Diocletian, where they rest on the rooftop of the building, the ruins in plain view: "And as in our travels through the remains of a broken city [*menia fracte urbis*], there too, as we sat, the remnants of the ruins [*ruinarum fragmenta*] lay before our eyes ... Our conversation was concerned largely with history which we seem to have divided among us, I being more expert in the ancient ... you in recent times" (*LFM*, 6:2). Finally, their conversation turns to moral philosophy and the origin of the arts. In his reading of the passage, Stierle noted that the term *fragment*, understood as the trigger of the friendly dialogue, acquires the meaning "piece" in an emphatic sense, signifying a part that evokes the whole. In this case, it is ruins that evoke the entirety of history, thereby allowing the idea of eternal, timeless Rome to rise from the debris.[29]

I would like to suggest a different interpretation by shifting the attention to the strangely pleonastic expression *ruinarum fragmenta* (remnants of the ruins) and the semiotic side of Rome's precarious status. The question is why Petrarch emphasizes that there is a part of the part, a fragment of the ruin, that initiates the conversation about all of history. One answer would be that Petrarch is suggesting that, conceptually, the ruins are the whole. They are what is being evoked by the fragments, what can be contemplated and gazed at. They are a semiotic point of reference, a form, an aesthetic object. However, these forms are broken, semiotically and semantically unstable, open for senselessness or the attribution of meaning but, above all, for discursive deliberations. This view indicates that even though ruined Rome functioned as a place of aesthetic admiration, its status as a semiotic realm that can be described or used as a backdrop for acts of signification is problematic. Throughout the entire letter, Petrarch hints at this issue and blends it with the question of time. When he digresses from the actual topic, when he admits that the digression happened "at random," when he thinks about how his short letter and the long history of Rome coincide, when he imagines the conditions under which Rome would resurge but suspends all further reflection, the poet is—in

---

28. See Hui, *Poetics of Ruins in Renaissance Literature*, 111, wherin Hui speaks of the letter as the Renaissance's "founding manifesto" and a "rallying cry for rebirth."

29. Stierle, *Francesco Petrarca: Ein Intellektueller*, 267.

each case—struggling with the semiotic challenges that the Eternal City poses. His thoughts circle around temporal conflicts, the validity of contingency and duration; time and again he follows the impulse to wait for kairos, the right moment, while he simultaneously produces text in the meantime.

Nowhere is this impetus more pronounced than in the closing passages of the epistle, where Petrarch finally mentions his reason for composing it. Giovanni Colonna apparently asked him to put in writing his thoughts on the origin of the arts that he had shared with his friend while overlooking the ruinscape. Yet Petrarch sees himself incapable of fulfilling Fra Colonna's wish:

> Give me back that place, that idle mood, that day, that attention of yours, that particular vein of my talent and I could do what I did then. But all things are changed [*Sed mutata sunt omnia*]: the place is not present, the day has passed, the idle mood is gone, and instead of your face, I look upon silent words ... The subject is clearly not a small one, this letter is already too long [*abunde crevit*], and we have not yet started, though the end of this day is at hand [*nondum cepimus et diei huius extremum est*]. Let us put off what remains until another day [*differamus que restant in proximum diem*]. (LFM, 6:2)

Petrarch's reasoning has been understood as a lament of the lost presence of kairos.[30] Some critics have noted that, with the act of writing the letter, the poet had, in fact, already complied with his friend's request that he pretended to refuse.[31] In my reading, I insist on the relation of this thought to the core of Petrarch's poetics at which lies the argument that the right moment for formation has not passed but is, instead, indefinitely deferred. On the basis of a semiotic realm that lies in ruins, formation is an intricate but ongoing endeavor.

Even in cases in which Petrarch's complicated relationship with Rome seems to have found an adequate poetic form, the issue of kairos and the difficulty of building upon ruins shines through. An example is poem 53 of the *Rerum vulgarium fragmenta*, a canzone usually called "Spirito gentil" ("Noble spirit") after its opening line. The noble spirit that the lyric *I* (*io*) addresses, and from whom it expects guidance for Rome's return to its "old way of life," has been identified with Cola di Rienzo:[32]

---

30. For example, by Zak, *Petrarch's Humanism and the Care of the Self*, 3.
31. Stierle, *Francesco Petrarca: Ein Intellektueller*, 269.
32. There are conflicting opinions about when the poem was written. One assumption has been that Petrarch composed it shortly after his first visit to Rome; see, e.g., Celenza, *Petrarch: Everywhere a Wanderer*, 64. If Cola was indeed the poem's addressee (see, e.g., Hennigfeld, *Der ruinierte Körper*, 158), this would potentially date the composition to a later time. Petrarch met Cola in 1343 in Avignon. However, the last stanza of the poem implies that the lyric *I* has never met the "noble spirit" but has only heard of him (see the quotation from the poem at the end of this section).

> Spirito gentil che quelle membra reggi
> dentro a le qua' peregrinando alberga
> un signor valoroso accorto e saggio:
> poi che se' giunto a l'onorata verga
> colla qual Roma et suoi erranti correggi
> et la richiami al suo antiquo viaggio
> io parlo a te...

Noble spirit, you who informs those members / inside of which there dwells in pilgrimage / a lord of valor who is keen and wise: / now that you have achieved the honored staff / with which you guide Rome and its erring people / and call her back to her old way of life / to you I speak... (*RVF*, 53:1–7)

This hopeful tone of the first stanza is immediately met by an expression of helpless desperation in the face of Italy's and Rome's miserable situation and the unlikelihood of change. The passage is tied to the notion of a missed opportunity:

> Che s'aspetti non so, né che s'agogni
> Italia, che suoi guai non par che senta,
> vecchia, oziosa e lenta;
> dormirà sempre et non fia chi la svegli?
> Le man l'avess' io avolto entro' capegli!

For what Italy waits or yearns I know not, / for she does not appear to feel her woes— / she's idle, slow and old; / will no one wake her, will she sleep for ever? / If only I could grab her by the hair! (*RVF*, 53:10–14)

From the very beginning, the poem is torn between confidence and despair. Long descriptions of civil unrest and human suffering are interrupted by calls on the spirit to ease Italy's and Rome's pain. Declarations of belief in possibilities alternate with overt resentment toward the unworthy contemporaries to whom the task of improvement has been entrusted:

> Non spero che giamai dal pigro sonno
> mova la testa per chiamar ch' uom facia...
> ma non senza destino alle tue braccia...
> è or commesso il nostro capo Roma...
>
> Ahi nova gente oltra misura altera,
> Irreverente a tanta et a tal madre!
> Tu marito, tu padre...

I have no hope she'll ever move her head / In sluggish sleep, loud as the shouts may be.../ but destiny now places in your arms... / the head of all of us, the city Rome. / Ah, you newcomers haughty beyond limits, / irreverent to a mother great as she! / Be husband, be her father... (*RVF*, 53:15–20; 80–82)

Finally, the engagement with the past reveals that what the future might hold can only be considered in terms of a reparation of what has been broken and of what is now an all-encompassing ruin. The reinstallation of semantic and semiotic power literally stands on shaky ground:

> L'antiche mura ch' anchor teme et ama
> et trema 'l mondo, quando si rimembra
> del tempo andato e 'n dietro si rivolve,
> e i sassi dove fur chiuse le membra
> di ta' che non saranno senza fama,
> se l' universo pria non si dissolve,
> et tutto quel ch' una ruina involve,
> per te spera saldar ogni suo vitio.

The ancient walls which all the world still fears / and loves and trembles, every time it thinks / of turning back to look at those past times, / recalling those tombstones which hold the bodies / of men who will not be without great fame / until our universe dissolves away, / and everything involving this one ruin, / through you they hope to mend all of the faults. (*RVF*, 53:29–36)

The overall uncertainty of Rome's future is heightened because no one knows when it will arrive. The final verses of "Spirito gentil" are a reminder that the right time to reinstate the appropriate form for the revival of Rome's authority is not yet here. Petrarch's Rome poem is not that form. Instead, it is a humble plea—not for authority but for mercy:

> Sopra 'l monte Tarpeio, canzon, vedrai
> un chavalier ch' Italia tutta onora,
> pensoso più d'altrui che di se stesso.
> Digli: "Un che non ti vide anchor da presso,
> se non come per fama uom s' innamora,
> dice che Roma ogniora . . .
> ti chier mercé da tutti sette I colli."

Upon Tarpeian Mount, my song, you'll see / a knight to whom all Italy pays honor, / who thinks of others more than of himself. / Tell him: "One who's not seen you yet up close, / but only as one falls in love through fame, / says Rome keeps begging you . . . / from all her seven hills to show her mercy." (*RVF*, 53:99–106)

The Brevity of Time: Petrarch's Letters to Pope Urban V

In 1353, Petrarch decided to return to Italy. His friend Lelius received a long letter that contained all the motives for the poet's departure from France and explained his intention to settle in Rome. Petrarch frames his move as a surrender to a long-felt sense of displacement and the desire to find a final home. Once associated with Vaucluse, the dignity of the livable site, where the dots of life connected and the thought of the end of time resembled a pleasant anticipation of arrival, was assigned to the city on the banks of the Tiber:

> There is no place I would rather dwell than in Rome, and I would have remained there forever had my destiny allowed. No eloquence could express how highly I esteem those glorious remnants [*fragmenta*] of the queen city, those magnificent ruins and the many impressive signs of her virtue [*ruinasque magnificas et vestigia . . . virtutum*] . . . It is in that very city—I would like to be able to say half ruined [*dicere vellem posse semiruta*]—that I would prefer to spend now even more eagerly than is usual whatever remains of my life. (*LFM*, 15:8)

But Petrarch's Roman plans remained merely a dream that never came to fruition. Upon his relocation to Italy, Petrarch went to Milan and—to the dismay of famous friends such as Giovanni Boccaccio, who accused him of opportunism and greed—entered the service of the despotic archbishop Giovanni Visconti.[33]

More favorable critics of the poet's choices underscored Petrarch's pragmatic sense for the political moment of the early 1350s in which the realization of democratic ideas called for a unification of the northern Italian city-states; among them, Milan was the most potent player. Petrarch's considerations were not solely political, though. According to Stierle, the realignment of the political focus went hand in glove with an orientation toward the vernacular that became Petrarch's new poetic medium and the language of his most ambitious project, the *Rerum vulgarium fragmenta*. Viewed in this light, Milan would have been the new center of a cultural-political effort to foster a sense of community that could rightly be characterized as "Italian."[34]

How comprehensive Petrarch's plan was—how thoroughly he understood the signs of the times and the extent to which his turn toward Milan was, in fact, a genuine attempt to seize and shape the historical present—is difficult to determine. Even though he did not end up living in Rome, he never abandoned his support for the city and tirelessly beseeched both the emperor and the pope to return. This commitment seems to contradict the theory of Petrarch's slow but steady detachment from a Rome-centered worldview.

Petrarch himself made a strong case against the hypothesis of estrangement in his 1366 letter to Pope Urban V.[35] The document is lengthy, comprising the

---

33. Caferro, *Petrarch's War*, 45.
34. Stierle, *Francesco Petrarca: Ein Intellektueller*, 519.
35. For a discussion of Petrarch's letters to Urban V, see also Stierle, *Francesco Petrarca: Ein Intellektueller*, 464–67.

entire seventh book of the poet's collection of *Letters of Old Age* (*Rerum senilium libri*). Petrarch initially takes some time to introduce himself as someone who has always had the ear of important political and religious figures. He highlights his extraordinary skills as an "observer of outstanding men," who have to prove true greatness to qualify for his praise. Petrarch had heard encouraging reports about Urban V, but he was hesitant to join those voices that extolled the new pontiff because he desired to wait for truly singular deeds, worthy of admiration.[36] At this point, Petrarch's tone changes. The wait, he complains with undisguised displeasure, has been too long. "I waited for you for a full three years," the poet tells the pope. "Now, as you see, the fourth year is coming around and the days are passing, and still nothing is being done." Petrarch announces that, "among so many flatterers," he will be Urban's "one critic" and demands that "our pastor" fulfill his "essential and uppermost" duty and "lead the flock back to its own original fold" (*LOA*, 7:1).[37]

Petrarch stages Urban's return to Rome as the sole matter of pressing urgency, which the pope has wantonly neglected. In a cascade of mordant rhetorical questions and quotations from the biblical book of Lamentations that mourn the destruction of Jerusalem, he paints a vivid picture of Rome's pitiful condition and the pontiff's responsibility to reinstate his "bride" as the center of Christianity:

> Everything indeed goes well in Avignon . . . But tell me, I beg you, in the meantime how is your bride doing? Who is the consul that governs her? Who is the general that defends her? . . . She is sick, helpless, widowed, wretched, lonely; and clothed in widows weeds she cries all day and night, singing those prophetic words: "How lonely she sits, the once crowded city!" . . . Her houses are in ruins and her walls tottering, her churches are collapsing [*iacent domus, labant moenia, templa ruunt*] . . . How can you . . . merciful Father . . . how *can* you, I say, sleep peacefully under gilded coffered ceilings on the bank of the Rhone when the Lateran lies in ruins [*Lateranum humi iacet*] . . . and when what had recently been the church of the Apostles is now a ruin and a shapeless heap of stones [*iam ruina est, informisque lapidum aceruus*]? (*LOA*, 7:1)

Again, as in the letters from Rome, Petrarch hesitates to apply meaning to Rome's ruins. Yet this time, not even the unspecific allusion to the rapport between greatness and decay is at hand. The letter seems to focus less on the indexicality of ruins than on the materiality of the actual fracture. There is

---

36. In light of Petrarch's experience with Cola di Rienzo, one has to suspect that the poet had become wary of premature enthusiasm.

37. Petrarca, *Letters of Old Age* (1992; hereafter cited as *LOA*, with book and letter number). For the Latin text, see Petrarca, "Epistolae de rebus senilibus" (1581), 811–27.

no sign of an aesthetic experience or the evocation of the whole by the fragment. History is not a matter of synopsis from a privileged point of view or a question of memory, triggered by architectural remnants. Instead, the emphasis on the here and now of the material disintegration evokes a concept of extreme temporal scarcity that guides the historical "negotiations" Petrarch conducts with the pope. The question that brings the two aspects together is a blatant provocation of the pontiff: "What therefore is being done? Why the delay [*Quid procrastinatur*]? Whence this hesitation [*Vnde ista cunctatio*]? . . . What are you waiting for [*Quid expectas*]? For everything to go to ruin and plunder [*ut cuncta depereant, uastenturque*]? I ask, has not everything been plundered enough already [*Parum ne autem . . . iam uastata omnia*]?" Petrarch leaves no doubt that there is a right time for Urban to act and that the time is now. Throughout the entire epistle, he repeatedly insists on his claim and occasionally makes the plea sound like a threat: "But if you overlook it [*negligis*; the return to Rome], or if you delay it [*differis*], and meanwhile the allotted time slips by [*datumque interim tempus elabitur*], believe me you will regret it then and you will blame yourself when grief will be useless and regret too late [*poenitentia sera erit*]." He even discloses his suspicion that there is a strategy behind the pope's hesitation: "Or through such long delay [*tantis expectationibus*], are you trying to appear forced to do what you ought to have willingly done long ago [*quod pridem volens facere debuisti*]?" (*LOA*, 7:1).

Approximately one year after he received Petrarch's letter, Pope Urban V left Avignon and returned to Rome. The extent to which he was influenced by Petrarch's persuasive powers cannot be ascertained. But unlike the supplicant—who, despite all his efforts to establish Rome as the place of kairos, never took the final step to settle there—Urban decided not to waste any more time. Petrarch followed up with another letter in which he profusely applauded the pontiff's choice and pressed him to stay true to his purpose and restore the damaged city:

> Use all the power of your holy talent to repair what has been torn apart [*sparsa recolligas*], set up what has toppled [*lapsa erigas*], reform what has been spoiled [*deformata reformes*], buttress what has been shaky [*nutantia firmes*], restore what has been used up [*consumpta restaures*]. A wise man does not abandon his destroyed home [*euersam domum*], but rebuilds and restores it [*attollit ac reficit*] . . . I admit you have a shattered city [*urbem conquassatam*], but still holy and venerable to the human race . . . the mother of cities, capital of the world, stronghold of the faith. (*LOA*, 9:1)

Yet when Urban invited him to Rome, Petrarch activated all his procrastinatory skills and made long-winded excuses to justify the postponement of the trip. As if working against his own goals, he once again avoided the city that, in his writings, bore all the significance of the appropriate time and place.[38] Kairos that should have done away with the fragments and brought a restauration of the intact form would lapse unused. The coincidence of the right time and the right form never materialized. Despite Petrarch's appeals, the pope left Rome for Avignon in 1370, and the poet's own notion of historical, biographical, and poetic possibility remained unalterably bound to broken forms.

Stierle has argued that, by eventually accepting Rome's downfall as the event that inflicted an unsurmountable break on the course of history, Petrarch left the medieval historiographical concept of the *translatio imperii* behind. The idea that empires supersede each other in linear succession and thereby transmit their historical legitimacy was replaced by the awareness of the ineluctable discontinuity of time.[39] Petrarch's long-term project *Trionfi*, which nevertheless adheres to the desire for duration and continuity, seems to be the poetic acknowledgment of this truth. The last part of the poem, the "Triumphus eternitatis" ("Triumph of Eternity"), also clearly attests to the potential postponement of the propitious moment of historical, biographical, and poetic possibility to timeless eternity.

Glory and the Postponement of the Propitious Moment: *Trionfi*

"Your heart," Petrarch told Pope Urban V in his first letter to the pontiff, "will never be content until you are with your flock in Rome ... a greater glory [*gloria*], which will endure for ever and ever, will accrue to you from this than from any deeds that have been done ... throughout the centuries" (*LOA*, 7:1). Glory that leads to fame, which—as Petrarch states to the pope—results from political action, was something the poet sought to achieve through his work. In *De vita solitaria* (*On the Solitary Life*), Petrarch notes that one of his reasons for having withdrawn to the solitude of Vaucluse was his desire, by way of quiet thinking and writing, to leave something to the memory of those who would come after him. In doing so, he hoped to halt the march of days and extend this very short life-time.[40]

---

38. In a similar manner, Petrarch avoids a trip to Jerusalem but nevertheless writes a travel guide.

39. Stierle, *Francesco Petrarca: Ein Intellektueller*, 726.

40. For the Latin text, see Petrarca, *Opere latine* (1975), 544: "aliquid meditando et scribendo nostri memoriam posteris relinquere, atque ita dierum fugam sister et hoc brevissimum vite tempus extendere."

These remarks show that Petrarch was aware of the provocation posed by an ongoing world-time to the limitations of life-time. His wish for fame can be seen as the impulse of someone who possesses "world," or the equivalent of a historical perspective, as Hans Blumenberg put it. In Walter Benjamin's terms, fame itself as the afterlife of works is the basis of a history that is not oblivious to mortality. In the face of death, works ripen to the age of fame where they live on as forms.

If we take seriously both the future glory and fame that Petrarch envisages for the pope along with his own desire for renown, then the title *Trionfi*, which he gave his long poem, is programmatic. It refers to the acts of outbidding, excelling, and surpassing—of oneself as well as others, on a structural as well as thematic plane.[41] Against the backdrop of Petrarch's struggle with the problems of time and form, the promise of the *Trionfi* lies in their ability to overcome the elusiveness of one and the brokenness of the other.[42] The triumph entails that this work will ripen and come to fruition and that it will live on as an intact form.

In a letter to Giovanni Boccaccio, written in the mid-1360s, Petrarch—in the course of discussing the possibilities of the "just invented, still new" use of the vernacular—mentions that he "undertook a great work in that style [*magnum eo in genere opus*]" that eventually turned into something like a failed "construction project":

> Having laid, as it were, the foundations of that edifice [*aedificii fundamentis*], I gathered the cement and stone and wood . . . I finally came to realize that it was a waste of effort to build on soft mud and shifting sand, and that I and my work would be torn to shreds by the hands of the mob [*meque et laborem meum inter vulgi manus laceratum iri*] . . . I halted and changed my mind. (*LOA*, 5:2)

Scholarship has long assumed that Petrarch is referring to the *Trionfi*, which he wrote in the Tuscan language and continued to supplement and revise over a period of more than thirty years.[43] The ambitious undertaking seems

---

41. Stierle speaks of the title as a sign of self-surpassing (*Zeichen der Selbstüberbietung*). Stierle, *Francesco Petrarca: Ein Intellektueller*, 663.

42. It poses a problem that the English translations of *gloria* and *fama* often seem reversed. In other words, the Latin *gloria* is sometimes translated with the English *fame* and the Latin *fama* with the English *glory*. However, this interchangeability is important for my argument because both terms imply that a work can live on beyond the time of its composition and—if we follow Daniel Weidner—beyond the author's death.

43. Bosco, *Francesco Petrarca*, 216.

to be unfinished.⁴⁴ Apposite to the metaphors of the aforementioned passage from *Letters of Old Age* (*LOA*, 5:2), Stierle called the poem an "impressive ruin [*eindrucksvolle Ruine*]" that, building on a "specifically 'medieval' understanding of continuity," never attained the poetic coherency intended by the author.⁴⁵ If we take this to be accurate, then the structural ambitions on display in the *Trionfi* could be interpreted—at least for the time being—as an attempt to remedy a formerly accepted discontinuity of time and history that Petrarch based on the experience of ruined Rome.

The *Trionfi* are not least an attempt to overcome the powerful model Dante had established with his work, particularly the *Commedia*.⁴⁶ In his correspondence with Boccaccio, Petrarch offers ample evidence of how torn he was between admiration and rejection of his predecessor. On the one hand, a signal of conscious affiliation with the *Commedia* on a formal plane is the use of the vernacular and the *terza rima*. And even the eponymous *Triumphs*—invoking the triumphal procession of victorious Roman commander's into Rome—was prefigured in Dante's masterpiece.⁴⁷ On the other hand, there is no lack of indications that Petrarch was eager to dissociate himself from the paragon. Without mentioning Dante by name, he declared to Boccaccio that he wanted "no guide who leads me, not one who binds me to him, one who leaves me to use my own sight, judgement and freedom; I do not want him to forbid me to step where I wish to go beyond him in some things [*preterire aliqua*], to attempt the inaccessible [*inaccessa tentare*]" (*LFM*, 22:2).⁴⁸

Petrarch's dilemma was obvious even when, on the surface, it took the shape of a firm rebuttal of those who accused him of disdain for Dante. In a response to a now lost letter from Boccaccio, who seems to have implied the addressee's envy by apologizing for praising the author of the *Commedia*, Petrarch vehemently denied any such suspicion as baseless:

> You ask pardon . . . for seeming to praise unduly a fellow countrymen of ours . . . as though . . . that praise for him or for anyone else would detract

---

44. For an analysis of the genesis of the *Trionfi* and the work's textual instability, see Eisner, "Petrarch Reading Boccaccio," 131–46.

45. Stierle, *Francesco Petrarca: Ein Intellektueller*, 663. This also means that the *Trionfi* are not—like the *Rerum vulgarium fragmenta*—a work made up of fragments. The fragmentary character is inadvertent, so to speak. For a similar argument, see Finotti, "Poem of Memory," 63.

46. Martin Eisner has pointed out that the focus on Dante's significance for Petrarch's *Trionfi* has distracted from other important influences and particularly Boccaccio's *Amorosa visione*. See Eisner, "Petrarch Reading Boccaccio," 132–34.

47. Stierle, *Francesco Petrarca: Ein Intellektueller*, 663–64.

48. See Cachey, "Between Petrarch and Dante," 25. Cachey refers to Marco Ariani, who identified the "inaccessible" with the *Trionfi*.

from my personal glory [*mee laudis*]. You assert that, whatever you say about him, if closely examined, redounds to my glory [*in meam gloriam verti*] . . . Hence nothing in your apologetic letter disturbed me except that I am still so little understood by you . . . Believe me, nothing is so foreign and no curse more unknown to me than envy. (*LFM*, 21:15)

In the same epistle, a few paragraphs later, Petrarch elaborates on the question of glory that resounds in these first sentences of his response to Boccaccio (the terms used are *laus* and *gloria*). He narrates how Dante, a Florentine native, became friends with his father after both were exiled from Florence. But unlike Pietro di Parenzo, who proceeded to France to protect his family, Dante stayed in Italy and "resisted" by "devoting himself all the more vigorously to his literary pursuits, neglecting all else and desirous only of glory [*omnium negligens soliusque fame cupidus*]." "In this," Petrarch continues, "I can scarcely admire and praise him too highly when nothing—not the injustice suffered at the hands of his fellow citizens, not exile, poverty, or the stings of envy, not his wife's love or his devotion to his children—diverted him from his course once he embarked upon it" (*LFM*, 15). In spite of Petrarch expressing his approval of Dante's unapologetic determination, there are indicators that his remarks contain an implicit critique and are, overall, an attempt to diminish the other poet's literary achievements. Especially the hidden allusion to Dante's condemnation of Ulysses for his pursuit of adventure in canto 26 of the *Inferno* has not gone unnoticed. Petrarch seems to imitate the tone of Ulysses's account of his sole obsession with seeing and knowing the world and thereby to underlay his approval of Dante's singlemindedness with a harsh rejection of his ethical standards.[49] What is more—as Zygmunt Barański argued—Petrarch reinforces this criticism of Dante's moral integrity by relating his wish for fame and glory to the poet's use of the vernacular. The *volgare*, Petrarch points out somewhat scornfully, made Dante popular among the ignorant masses, which is not necessarily to be considered an honor:

> This [the ignorance of the masses] was not the least of my reasons for abandoning his style of composition [i.e., the *volgare*, or vernacular] to which I devoted myself as a young man . . . I had no hope, then, that the tongues or

---

49. For an examination of this relation as well as of the significance of Ulysses for Petrarch's view of Dante in general, see Cachey, "Between Petrarch and Dante," 26–27; and Barański, "Petrarch, Dante, Cavalcanti," 78. The passage from the *Inferno* in the Hollanders' English translation reads: "Not tenderness for a son, nor filial duty / toward my aged father, nor the love I owed / Penelope that would have made her glad, could overcome the fervor that was mine / to gain experience of the world / and learn about man's vices, and his worth" (Dante, *Inferno* 26.94–99).

minds of the rabble would be any more flexible or kind to my works than they were to those whom habit and favor had made popular in the theater and public squares ... I fully realize how little the esteem of the ignorant multitude carries weight with learned men. (*LFM*, 21:15)

As a result, Dante appears not only as the embodiment of debatable ethics but also as an advocate of questionable poetic choices. In Petrarch's view, this representation ultimately proves that his status as an exceptional poet has been grossly overestimated by literary critics.[50] Petrarch insinuates that persistence rather than brilliance is responsible for Dante's popularity and mentions other gifted writers who unfortunately lack his sense of purpose: "Many other great talents ... would be distracted by the least disturbance" (*LFM*, 21:15). Finally, Petrarch compares Dante's sole focus on the vernacular to his own versatility that allowed him to playfully exercise his skills in that lower art before advancing to higher grounds:

> I too was devoted to the same kind of writing in the vernacular [*vulgari eloquio ingenium exercebam*]; I considered nothing more elegant and had yet to learn to look higher [*altius aspirare didiceram*] ... How true can it be that I am envious of a man who devoted his entire life to those things that were only the flower and first fruits of my youth? How, when what was for him, if not his only occupation, surely his principal one, was for me mere sport, a pastime, a mental exercise [*michi iocus atque solatium fuerit et ingenii rudimentum*]? (*LFM*, 21:15)

Even if to some readers Petrarch's critical view of Dante in his letter to Boccaccio might appear considerably less obvious than, for example, Zygmunt Barański suggests, the observation that the reference brings out the tensions in Petrarch's conception of the vernacular and in his notion of fame is indisputable. Fascinated by both, Petrarch rejects and embraces them in rhetorically elaborate fashion, which renders the *Trionfi*—a poem written in the *volgare* that deals with the topic of fame and glory—an ambivalent enterprise from the outset.

The *Trionfi* begin with a return of the lyric *I* to what appears to be Vaucluse. The poet, absorbed and pained by sweet and sad thoughts of the day when he

---

50. Barański, "Petrarch, Dante, Cavalcanti," 78–79. Barański notes the same criticism with respect to Dante in Petrarch's *Rerum vulgarium fragmenta* and the *Trionfi*. Justin Steinberg discusses the letter quoted here (*LFM*, 21:15) and one from *Letters of Old Age* (*LOA*, 5:2) with a focus on Petrarch's observations about the circulation of vernacular literature and his concern with textual corruption in Steinberg, "Dante *Estravagante*, Petrarch *Disperso*, and the Other Woman," 263–89.

first set eyes on Laura and all his sufferings began, is suddenly carried away by a vision and finds that he has been led back to the "enclosed place [*al chiuso loco*]." The subjective tone of the first verses, which anticipate the poem's focus on the experience and, most of all, the memories of the lyric *I*, has often been understood as an intentional divergence from the beginning of Dante's *Commedia*, which opens with a more universal perspective on the life not of one, but of many. In lieu of Dante's progression toward his transcendental destiny, Petrarch's lyric *I* dwells on the past and his remembrance of earthly matters:[51]

> Al tempo che rinova i mie' sospiri
> per la dolce memoria di quel giorno
> che fu principio a sí lunghi martiri,
> già il Sole al Toro l'uno e l'altro corno
> scaldava, e la fanciulla di Titone
> correa gelata al suo usato soggiorno.
>
> Amor, gli sdegni e 'l pianto, e la stagione
> ricondotto m'aveano al chiuso loco
> ov'ogni fascio il cor lasso ripone.
>
> The season when my sighing is renewed
> Had come, stirring the memory of that day
> Whereon my love and suffering began.
> The sun was warming one and the other horn
> Of Taurus, and Tithonus' youthful bride
> Sped in the coolness to her wonted station;
>
> Springtime and love and scorn and tearfulness
> Again had brought me to that Vale Enclosed
> Where from my heart its heavy burdens fall.
> ("Triumphus cupidinis," 1.1–9)[52]

In the soothing remoteness of the solitary valley, the poet falls asleep on the grass. In his dream, he sees a "leader, conquering and supreme," riding a triumphal car like a Roman emperor (*pur com'un di color che 'n Campidoglio / triumphal carro a gran gloria conduce*). The "leader" is Cupid, as a shadow explains to the lyric *I*, and he spearheads an endless procession of famous lovers. The poet, qualified by his own suffering from an undying but

---

51. See, e.g., Finotti, "Poem of Memory," 4–65.
52. For the Italian original, see Petrarca, *Trionfi, Rime estravaganti, Codice degli abbozzi* (1996). For the English translation, see Petrarca, *Triumphs of Petrarch* (1962). Numbers in the parenthetical citations correspond to part and line numbers of the triumph.

unattainable love, joins the ranks of the sorrowful who are subject to the triumphant leader.

Cupid's defeat of those who love is the first of a sequence of six triumphs, each containing a "vast allegorical spectacle" and surpassing the one that went before.[53] In the "Triumphus pudicitie" ("Triumph of Chastity"), the god of love is forced to surrender to the virtuous who resist him. The one whose purity is unmatched is the poet's beloved. But while she comes out of the battle with Amor unscathed, she is vanquished by death in the "Triumphus mortis" ("Triumph of Death"). It takes place on the sixth of April, the same day on which the poet was first bound by his love for Laura: *L'ora prima era, il dí sesto d'aprile, / che già mi strinse, et or, lasso, mi sciolse* ("April the sixth, it was, and the first hour, / When I was bound—and now, alas, set free!"; "Triumphus mortis," 1.133–35).[54] Grief over transience and loss and the awareness that all earthly things are vain dominate the first part of this triumph. Yet the poet is offered unexpected solace by Laura, who talks to him from a delightful afterlife and assures him of the love that she always felt but never let break the law of honor. She asserts that, even though she refused to give him the reward for which he longed, his service utterly pleased her. In a truly medieval manner, the denial appears as that which fueled the poet's productivity. His songs in turn lent fame and glory to the name of the beloved woman: *e piacemi il bel nome, se vero odo, / che lunge e presso co tuo dir m'acquisti* ("And pleasure the fair name thy poetry / Hath won for me, I ween, both near and far"; "Triumphus mortis," 2.130–31).

It therefore seems like a natural consequence that fame conquers death in the "Triumphus fame" ("Triumph of Fame"). Stierle spoke of an "aesthetic monotony of enumeration" (*ästhetische Monotonie der Aufzählung*) with respect to Petrarch's endless list of Roman, antique, Jewish, and Christian heroes that take part in the triumphal procession and are supplemented with a catalog of celebrated philosophers, historiographers, and poets. They are so many that the poet loses track of the order in which they appear. It seems as if the founding pillar of fame, the ability to remember—which will be fully consumed in the "Triumphus temporis" ("Triumph of Time")—were starting to crumble. The excess of triumphs over triumphs becomes impossible to control.[55]

Transience, life's brevity, and the ruin of the world are the themes that dominate the fifth triumph of time over fame. It starts with a monologue

---

53. Mazzotta, *Worlds of Petrarch*, 99.

54. I have already mentioned Petrarch's note on the flyleaf of his Ambrosian Virgil codex, where he specifies the date of his first encounter with Laura and the date of her death, claiming that both happened on the sixth of April. The *Canzoniere* brings up April 6 in poems 211 and 336.

55. Stierle, *Francesco Petrarca: Ein Intellektueller*, 675–79.

by the envious sun, who questions precisely the one characteristic of fame that—if, once again, we follow Blumenberg and Benjamin—is its most important trait: the capability to grow and ripen after death.

> E se fama mortal morendo cresce,
> che spegner si devea in breve, veggio
> nostra eccellenzia al fine; onde m'incresce.

If mortal fame, that soon should fade away, / Increases after death, then I foresee / Our excellence at an end, wherefor I grieve. ("Triumphus temporis," 1.10–12)

Yet fame relies on the memory of those who perform memorable deeds, and memory fades if time passes too quickly for humans to follow its course. Thus, the sun, which is initially opposed by historians and poets (*istorico o poeta*), accelerates time and leaves the lyric *I*, whose thoughts and tongue are too slow to catch up, in a state of bewilderment and fear. The moment of terror is also a moment of insight. As if looking into a mirror, the poet clearly recognizes his own mortality and that of the world, and he surrounds his self-imposed memento mori with a host of motifs of earthly vanity:

> Stamani era un fanciullo et or son vecchio.
>
> Che piú d'un giorno è la vita mortale?
> Nubil' e brev' e freddo e pien di noia,
> che pò bella parer, ma nulla vale.
>
> Qui l'umana speranza e qui la gioia,
> qui ' miseri mortali alzan la testa,
> e nesun sa quanto si viva o moia.
>
> Veggio or la fuga del mio viver presta,
> anzi di tutti, e nel fuggir del Sole,
> la ruina del mondo manifesta.

This morn I was a child, and now I'm old. / What more is this our life than a single day, / Cloudy and cold and short and filled with grief, / That hath no value, fair though it may seem? / Within this life men set their hope and joy / And raise their heads in miserable pride, / Yet no man knoweth when his life will end. / And now I see how fleeting is my life— / Nay more, the life of all—and in the flight / Of the Sun the manifest ruin of the world. ("Triumphus temporis," 1.60–66)

Time is avaricious, rapacious, deadly; it interrupts (*interrompe*) everything mortal; it "conquers all, triumphs over names and the world!" (*Cosí 'l Tempo triumfa i nomi e 'l mondo!*); and it consumes the propitious moment and, with it, the possibility of the right form. After all—as Fabio Finotti argued—the "Triumph of Time" also marks a critical moment of poetic self-doubt in which Petrarch contemplates whether he himself has failed as a poet:[56]

> Segui' già le speranze e 'l van desio;
> or ho dinanzi a gli occhi un chiaro specchio
> ov'io veggio me stesso e 'l fallir mio . . .

I followed then my hopes and vain desires, / But now with mine own eyes I see myself / As in a mirror, and my wanderings . . . ("Triumphus temporis," 1.55–57)[57]

If, at this point, the sequence of triumphs had reached its goal, the poem would have ended with the final abrogation of kairos. Life and the world would have fallen prey to the greediness of all-consuming time, and forms would have lost their afterlife in fame. The living memories of historians and poets would have been obliterated. The end of history would have been declared and, with it, the end of poetry, leaving the last word to ruin. This kind of ending would have suggested that the successive suspension of triumphs indicates a linear progression toward a climax that concludes a temporal and historical development.

Petrarch's inclusion of a sixth triumph foregrounds the extent of the conflict that he faced as a result of the tension between the continuity and discontinuity of time and history and between the brokenness and integrity of forms. There are indicators that, in the *Trionfi*, the teleological aspect is complemented by affirmations, grounded in the work's memorial character, of time's discontinuity. Finotti pointed out the circular structure that the act of remembering establishes. The initial experience of the lyric *I* takes him back in time and allows him to see what has already happened as a future event. Figures that appeared in one triumph emerge again in the next and provoke the uncanny awareness that "what seemed cancelled returns."[58] In short, the temporal structure that was revealed by Petrarch's political stands, his historical reflections, and his thoughts on the human condition returns, once again, in the poetic form of the *Trionfi* and against the poet's own structural intention. Remembering, lingering, pausing, interrupting, returning, repeating are the dynamics of postponement that delay the propitious moment of historical, biographical, and poetic possibility and lend the poem its fragmented,

---

56. Finotti, "Poem of Memory," 77.

57. *Failure* is the more appropriate translation of *fallir* than *wanderings*.

58. Finotti, "Poem of Memory," 76. Finotti mentions other elements of circularity—for instance, Petrarch's use of sources that require a "vertical" rather than "horizontal" reading.

ruinous character and an air of incompleteness. Seen in this light, there are cracks in the continuity even before the "Triumph of Time" causes the ultimate break.

Yet postponing kairos is not the same as letting go of it. In the case of the *Trionfi*, letting go of kairos at the end of time would have meant abandoning a poetic concept that was attached to the ideal of the intact form and that Petrarch intended to realize with his poem. This shows that even if Petrarch's goal was to achieve continuity and integrity, the discontinuity of postponed kairos was, in fact, what kept this goal within reach. The delay was, in other words, what made history possible. Petrarch therefore faced the problem of having to hold on to kairos of historical, biographical, and poetic possibility within the realm of eternity. He wrote the "Triumphus eternitatis" ("Triumph of Eternity") shortly before his death. It would be his last work and would sketch out the paradox of what it potentially meant to realize kairos outside of time.

In the midst of the turbulent current of time, the lyric *I* turns to its own heart, asking for guidance: *In che ti fidi?* ("Whom do you trust?"; "Triumphus eternitatis," 1.3; translation mine). The heart answers that it trusts the Lord, who has never failed those who believe in him. It admits to having delayed its renunciation of the deceptive world for all too long. And yet, "divine mercy never comes too late" (*Ma tarde non fur mai grazie divine*; "Triumphus eternitatis," 1.13). In these first verses of the last triumph, the order of time and the significance of the right moment are at stake. Missed by humans and seized by God, kairos contains an element of the ahistorical and atemporal.

As the poet continues to contemplate the goal of earthly matters that heaven frequently transforms and changes, he seems to behold a new world rising in the distance, in an immobile and eternal age (*veder mi parve un mondo / novo, in etate immobile ed eternal*; "I at last beheld / A world made new and changeless eternal"; "Triumphus eternitatis," 1.20–22). In this world, time has come to a halt. It is no longer divided into the past and the future, but it instead rests in an eternal, absolute present that unifies what used to be dispersed:

> Non sarà piú diviso a poco a poco,
> ma tutto inseme, e non piú state o verno,
> ma morto il tempo, e variato il loco.

No more will time be broken into bits, / No summer now, now winter: all will be / As one, time dead, and all the world transformed. ("Triumphus eternitatis," 1.76–78)

Then, unexpectedly, the poet returns to the topic of fame. In the new world that he imagines, fame and beauty will be restored to the deceased who were once truly famous and whose beauty was uncorrupted. This time, however, the state of perfection will last:

> e quei che fama meritaron chiara,
> che 'l Tempo spense, e i be' visi leggiadri,
> che 'mpallidir fe' 'l Tempo e Morte amara,
>
> l'oblivion, gli aspetti oscuri et adri,
> piú che mai bei tornando, lascieranno
> a morte impetuosa, a' giorni ladri:
>
> ne l'età piú fiorita e verde avranno
> con immortal bellezza eterna fama.

And those who merited illustrious fame / That time had quenched, and countenances fair / Made pale by Time and bitter Death, / Becoming still more beauteous than before / Will leave to raging Death and thieving Time / Oblivion, and aspects dark and sad. / In the full flower of youth they shall possess / Immortal beauty and eternal fame. ("Triumphus eternitatis," 1.127–34)

There is one who will rise in the bloom of her youth, more beautiful than all the others who await their transformation. She possesses the poet's heart and has always been at the heart of his work. In these last verses, Laura is resurrected as the reason for the poet's fame and the substance of his poetry:

> Ma inanzi a tutte ch'a rifar si vanno,
> è quella che piangendo il mondo chiama
> con la mia lingua e con la stanca penna.

Before them all, who go to be made new, / Is she for whom the world is weeping still, / Calling her with my tongue and weary pen. ("Triumphus eternitatis," 1.136–37)

At the end of his work and his days, the poet returns to her whom he has cherished throughout his entire life as the source of his poetic force. The moment of remembrance is at once a moment of imaginative projection of Laura, who will appear again in her *bel velo* (beautiful veil), her immaculate shape.[59] The coming of this state, however, lies in an undetermined future. When it will be and if it will happen is not for the poet to know:

---

59. This seems in conflict with the "resolution" to the *Rerum Vulgarium Fragmenta*, where the poetic *I* seems to sacrifice the idol of Laura entirely.

> Quando ciò fia, no 'l so: se fu soppressa
> tanta credenza a' piú fidi compagni,
> a sí alto segreto chi s'appressa?

When this shall be, I know not; not to those / Who were His trusted comrades was the hour / Of death made known: who then may seek to know? ("Triumphus eternitatis," 1.102–5)

Based on Petrarch's experience with ruined Rome and his many attempts to overcome the fragile historical and semiotic status of the decayed city and its impact on his poetics, realizing kairos could only mean that the intact form had to be restored at the right time. However, as we have seen, this seemingly obvious inference is precluded because Petrarch missed every opportunity to seize the propitious moment. This failure to do so allowed for the conclusion that not the fulfillment of kairos but rather its delay is the vital temporal operation that creates the historical, biographical, and poetic possibilities.

By ultimately placing kairos, which was expected to bring unity and the realization of the beautiful form in timeless eternity, Petrarch on the one hand made sure that the propitious moment would persist but that it would never be realized. On the other hand, Petrarch once more turned his attention to fame. The invocation of this concept in the last triumph introduced a profoundly historical (and poetic) concept into an ahistorical and atemporal setting.[60] If we avoid the immediate assumption that Petrarch changed his perspective and wanted to delineate the enduring quality of fame and glory, we have to draw the opposite conclusion: Petrarch meant to emphasize that even eternity cannot escape from history. What this means by implication can hardly be overstated: kairos can never be realized as long as we are caught in history, which—as humans and mortals—we inevitably are and always will be.[61] In the end, Petrarch clearly saw that we are left only with the shattered forms of our existence, our poetry, our world, but that it is from there that new lives, new worlds, and new forms may occasionally arise. Their goal is not to hasten toward completion. All they do is hesitate, return, linger, falter, remember. And sometimes, they spark a moment of ephemeral, imperfect beauty.

---

60. For a similar observation and a different conclusion, see Finotti, "Poem of Memory," 84.

61. The comparison with Dante seems to further elucidate the nature of Petrarch's concerns. For Dante, the importance of the generative coincidence between the Pax Romana under Augustus and the birth of Jesus was huge, amounting to the idea of the "fullness of time"; see Kantorowicz, "Man-Centered Kingship," 451–95. Petrarch's focus seems to be more cultural and secular, not preoccupied with providential Christian history.

4

Poliphilo and the Dream of Ruins

> In this decayed hole among the mountains
> In the faint moonlight, the grass is singing
>
> T. S. ELIOT, *The Waste Land*

The *Hypnerotomachia Poliphili*, an allegorical romance about Poliphilo's quest for his unobtainable beloved, Polia, first appeared in print in 1499 with the Venetian printer and publisher Aldus Manutius.[1] The sponsor of this undertaking, the Venetian jurist Leonardo Grassi, dedicated the book to the Duke of Urbino, Guidobaldo di Montefeltre. One of the Grassi brothers had fought under Guidobaldo's command in the wars between Florence and Pisa and enjoyed great favor from the duke. The *Hypnerotomachia* is a token of Grassi's gratitude. In his dedication, he models the duke as the ideal recipient of the book and the *Hypnerotomachia*, in turn, as the ideal gift. It is a perfect match for which the presenter and the presentee are equally responsible. The duke, as Grassi states, is a lover of literature and a connoisseur, who only needed someone attentive enough to recognize this literary inclination in a man of politics—and naturally, the jurist claims this role for himself. Grassi makes a point of juxtaposing his own endeavor as a discoverer of Guidobaldo's true passion, his willingness to invest money in the edition of the book, and the accomplishments of his brother, who put his life on the line for the duke. He thereby associates the gifts of life and literature, which appear as equally valuable.[2]

---

1. This chapter is a revised version of an article that was first published with Brepols and translated from German by Jake Fraser. See Prica, "Lingering" (2018).

2. I follow Marco Ariani and Mino Gabriele's two-volume edition of the *Hypnerotomachia*: Colonna, *Hypnerotomachia Poliphili* (1988; hereafter cited as *HP*, with volume and page number). I also use the single-volume English translation by Jocelyn Godwin: Colonna, *Hypnerotomachia Poliphili: The Strife of Love* (1999; hereafter cited as *SL*, with page number). In the Latin quotations, *v* has been rendered according to phonetic value, as *u*, and *&* as *et*.

Yet the part that Grassi imagined for the duke was not just that of a passive addressee. Guidobaldo—much like Martin Heidegger four hundred years later—probably experienced the ambiguous benefit of a gift that was, at the same time, a burden. For Grassi assigned to him the responsibility of a patron as well as of a parent to the "orphaned" *Hypnerotomachia*, whose author was unknown: "We commit it [the book] to your present patronage so that it may flourish boldly under your name" (*SL*, 2).

The question of authorship is among the most hotly contested and persistently unsolvable problems in scholarship on the *Hypnerotomachia*. Much of the debate revolved around the work's thirty-eight chapter initials that form an acrostic that refers to a certain Franciscus Columna who loved someone called Polia: POLIAM FRATER FRANCISCUS COLUMNA PERAMAVIT (Brother Francesco Colonna loved Polia exceedingly). On the basis of this statement and the book's concluding remarks, which mention location (Treviso) and time (1467) of the composition, interpreters speculated about potential authors.[3]

The acrostic was verifiably decoded as early as the beginning of the sixteenth century, yet Grassi was likely not aware of it. His eagerness to use the Duke of Urbino's name as a sort of quality seal on a work that was anything but unproblematic seems to suggest that his gesture was at least partly a makeshift solution resulting from a lack of alternatives. It is evident from the dedication that Grassi wants to promote and protect the expensive undertaking that the *Hypnerotomachia* was, and he therefore expresses great admiration for the author. But he also gives readers a first taste of the difficulties that they are about to face. The biggest and most conspicuous problem that he brings up is the language—a mélange of Latin, the vernacular, and occasional Greek. Even the title is hard to decode. *Hypnerotomachia* is

---

3. The most popular suggestions were that Colonna was a Venetian Dominican father called Francesco Colonna or a Roman nobleman from the house of Colonna. Neither of the theories regarding authorship could be proven. Additional, equally speculative theories link the author to Lorenzo de' Medici and Leon Battista Alberti, see *HP*, 2:lxiii–xc; and Schmidt, *Untersuchungen zu den Architekturekphrasen in der "Hypnerotomachia Poliphili."* For a comprehensive study of the presumed biographical background of Colonna, see Casella and Pozzi, *Francesco Colonna: Biografia e opere*. A critical response can be found in *HP*, 2:lxv–lxxi; see also Calvesi, *La Pugna d'amore in sogno di Francesco Colonna romano*. In connection with the dedicatory and introductory portions of the novel, one finds both immediately before and after the actual novel a dispute (attributed to the Latin poet Andrea Marone) between an "I" and the muse about who is hiding behind the name Poliphilo. Ariani and Gabriele interpret the muse's answer *Nolumus agnosci* as an anagram for *Columna gnosius* (*HP*, 2:495n3). For the interpretation of *per* as *exceedingly* in the translated phrase, I credit Stewart, *Ruins Lesson*.

probably a combination of the Greek terms for sleep (ὕπνος; *hýpnos*), love (ἔρως; *érōs*), and strife (μάχη; *máchē*), which is why it has commonly—and incompletely—been translated as *Strife of Love in a Dream*. Determined to advocate for the work, Grassi first offers the peculiar explanation that the writer produced this linguistic hybrid to prove his diligence. The other reason the jurist states, with the unmistakable goal of flattering the duke, is that it is aimed only at the most intellectually capable and educated among potential readers. They have to be equipped with the most agile mind to understand a work that is made up of poetry, philosophy, and refined speech (*SL*, 3).[4] However, he quickly adds that the book's figures, images, and agreeable narrative form compensate for all the difficulties and make even the most complex lessons it intends to teach accessible (*HP*, 1:2).

Leonardo Grassi's introductory address offers topoi typical of engaged apologetics, and it testifies to his infallible sense for the problems that his print project would pose. Ten years after the publication of the book, Grassi would only have managed to sell a small segment of the print run.[5] Prominent scholars whom he had hoped to win over with his flattery of great minds criticized and even mocked the work—mostly for its hermetic linguistic form, just as Grassi had anticipated. Fifty years later, the first French translation of the *Hypnerotomachia* that was neither particularly true to its source nor concerned with completeness was a huge success, proving once again that the original was unreadable for most who tried.[6] In contrast, the book's 172 woodcuts were broadly received and appreciated as artworks that preserved the treasures of antique culture. In the course of their reception in the early Renaissance, they were ascribed to some of the best-known Venetian artists.[7] Albrecht Dürer was one of the few buyers of the first edition of the book and in all probability more interested in the illustrations than the text.[8]

---

4. In this context, poetry has to be understood as part of the *ars rhetorica* (art of rhetoric); see *HP*, 2:492n21.

5. See Casella and Pozzi, *Francesco Colonna: Biografia e opere* 2:153, doc. 140; and the reference in Schmidt, *Untersuchungen zu den Architekturekphrasen in der "Hypnerotomachia Poliphili,"* 101.

6. Schmidt, *Untersuchungen zu den Architekturekphrasen in der "Hypnerotomachia Poliphili,"* 12–13.

7. Most attributions have been disproven. One exception is Benedetto Bordon. See Oechslin, "Traum, Liebe, Kampf," 83–84.

8. See Casella and Pozzi, *Francesco Colonna: Biografia e opere*, 1:97–101, on the entry showing Dürer's possession in the copy possessed by the Staatsbibliothek München, and on the reception of the woodcuts. On the reception of the images, as well as a partially critical response to Casella and Pozzi, see Schmidt, *Untersuchungen zu den Architekturekphrasen in der "Hypnerotomachia Poliphili,"* 15.

Despite harboring no illusions about the accessibility of the *Hypnerotomachia*, Grassi did not recommend that recipients renounce the text. For him, it was the combination of text and images that provided what he thought was at the core of the work: a unique and all-encompassing kind of knowledge about nature and the past, worthy of preservation and transmission (*HP*, 1:2).

The *Hypnerotomachia* has rightly been read as a text that explores the relationship between the main character and antiquity, on the one hand, and the past more generally, on the other. The two books tell the story of the dreaming lover Poliphilo, who follows Polia through unknown landscapes, past ruins from antiquity and fantastic architectonic structures. His journey, undertaken both alone and in the company of nymphs, finally ends in the Temple of Venus, where Poliphilo meets Polia and is then united with her on the island of Kythira. Their union, however, is not meant to last. Polia, who in the second book retells the events from her own perspective, disappears after a final embrace with her lover, and we later learn that she has died. In terms of its literal meaning, the *Hypnerotomachia* is a book of lost love, and, as Poliphilo's name and that of his beloved Polia indicate, his love for her extends to—or is an allegory of—many things.[9] Among those things, architecture so clearly takes center stage that it has earned the text the reputation of a landmark in architectonic writing.[10] It has not been lost on scholarship that Poliphilo's approach to architecture is eroticized. The buildings and structures he encounters are objects of desire that he yearns to touch and absorb through his longing gaze. The wish for immediate contact with the material, however, is paired with reflections about the origin and the past of the constructions in front of the beholder's eyes, many of which are ruins. Relating love and antiquity, Andrew Hui described Poliphilo's perception of ruins as being driven by an erotic desire for the lost (antique) past.[11] If, with Hui's perspective in mind, we look back at Panofsky's statement in the introduction to this book that the Renaissance grieves over the dead body of antiquity—in contrast to the Middle Ages, which galvanizes it—we would have to assume that Poliphilo's dream can be understood as a sort of eroticized grieving process over the past that eludes him.[12]

---

9. The combination of πολλοί (*polloi*) and φίλος (*philos*) that makes up the name Poliphilo indicates that he is a friend (lover) of many things. Polia, as in the Greek word for *many* (πολλά), is the object of love and friendship.

10. See Stewering, "Architectural Representations in the *Hypnerotomachia Poliphili* (Aldus Manutius 1499)," 6–25, who counts Poliphilo—in her terms the Master of Polifilo—among "painter-architects like "Francesco di Giorgio Martini, Leonardo and Raphel" (21).

11. Hui, *Poetics of Ruins in Renaissance Literature*, 133.

12. Panofsky, *Renaissance and Renascences in Western Art*, 113.

Without denying the distinctness and significance of the sense of loss and desire that shapes the *Hypnerotomachia*, I will, in the following reading, turn to a different problem that is no less fundamental and provides a new, more pronouncedly hermeneutic and narratological angle from which to analyze the function of ruins in text and images. My thesis is that the *Hypnerotomachia* adheres to an ideal of love and antiquity that is timeless, static, and conservatory. This everlasting ideal is contrasted—as the book's lengthy title indicates—with the transience of human life: *Hypnerotomachia Poliphili, ubi humana omnia non nisi somnium esse docet, atque obiter plurima scitu sane quam digna commemorate* (HP, 1:1). While dreaming, thus we learn, Poliphilo teaches that everything human is nothing but a dream. Yet at the same time, he reminds the reader of much knowledge of great worth. In other words, the preservation of a dead body of knowledge about the past, accessible only to memory but timelessly valuable, is connected to a certain tendency to disavow the value of life. Taking my cues from this beginning, I will show that the ruins contradict the impositions of timeless ideals, which they imbue with history. Ruins are the sites of the propitious moment in which the dreamer establishes narrative continuity with the past and the future. As we will see, this process is a corrective for a specific mode of interpretation. While Poliphilo's gaze lingers on objects, reading and analyzing them so as to ultimately obsess over their stupendousness, he is unable to leave the cycle of intent admiration; ruins introduce an "active gesture of inquiry" into the story—or, what we might also wish to call, its discursivity.[13] It is as a result of this gesture that Poliphilo ultimately acquires a different kind of knowledge than the one promised by the title. The knowledge he gains is an insight into the dynamic of continuity and the postponement of death. Therefore, despite being framed by motifs of death and vanity—the dream at the beginning and an epitaph to the dead Polia at the end of the romance—the *Hypnerotomachia* is ultimately a stubborn affirmation of life, the bitterness that comes with the loss of antiquity notwithstanding.

Labyrinth and Dream

Before the story of Poliphilo's somnambulant journey can begin, the *Hypnerotomachia* already makes a point of emphasizing the importance of the act of lingering by guiding the readers into mysterious spaces. In a Latin elegy and

---

13. For this definition of the act of lingering as an "active gesture of inquiry" in a different context, see Vogl, *On Tarrying*, 13. Giorgio Agamben noted a dynamic of *festina lente* (make haste slowly) in the *Hypnerotomachia*; see Agamben, "Dream of Language," 46–47.

an Italian prose text, an anonymous voice addresses the recipients, providing them with a sort of manual for a selective reception of the book.[14] Those who do not like love stories, the instructions read, should focus on the structure of the story. Those who care little for structure will take pleasure from style and language or else from the geometry that the story includes; if none of this sounds appealing, they can entertain themselves by deciphering the characters and symbols with which the text is replete (*HP*, 1:3). A list-like summary of the plot follows, which even explains how the two volumes of the book are related.

The entire elegy appears like a blurb for the romance's diverse forms of representation. The quintessential form, however, is the labyrinth, because, as the elegy states, it can comprise "the whole of human life" (*tota vita hominum*; *SL*, 4; *HP*, 1:4). The editors of the Italian edition of the *Hypnerotomachia*, Marco Ariani and Mino Gabriele, understand this remark as a way for the writer to authorize an allegorical approach to the text, whose function is to bring light into the darkness of the labyrinth—that of life and that of the story. In a similar manner, they also interpret the epitaph to the dead Polia at the conclusion of the text, and the dedication to the living Polia at the beginning of the *Hypnerotomachia*, as indicators that the entire fiction is based on the distinction between historical and symbolic registers. Polia, we read in the epitaph, lives better now that she is dead (*Polia, quae vivis mortua, sed melius*; *HP*, 1:466) because she lives on—as a textual fantasy, so to speak—in Poliphilo's wise words (*Tedum Poliphilo somno iacet obrutus alto, / Pervigilare facit docta per ora virum*; *HP*, 1:8). And these words that *are* the romance are dedicated to her as a living person at the beginning of the fiction.[15]

The labyrinth sustains a relation to the dream from the title. The dream too relates to human life in its totality (*humana omnia non nisi somnium*); and just as the labyrinth is described as dark, the dream produces indistinct, enigmatic images that warrant interpretation. In this regard, the reference to dream and labyrinth points to the allegorical sense of the text and invites a hermeneutics that does it justice.[16]

If we take the spatial implications of the labyrinth seriously, then the readers of the *Hypnerotomachia*, as the elegy imagines them, are recipients who

---

14. Ariani and Gabriele agree with Casella and Pozzi in their assessment that the elegy was written by the author of the *Hypnerotomachia*. See *HP*, 2:493n5.

15. *HP*, 2:489–500n1. Models for this form are Dante and Petrarch.

16. Ariani and Gabriele understand the passage about the labyrinth as an authorization of an allegorical reading of the entire book; see *HP*, 2:494n1. The address to the reader in prose vernacular takes up both the motif of the labyrinth and the plot summary, but it takes the perspective of Poliphilo.

try to orient themselves in the labyrinth of the text or, by way of analogy, in the maze that is human life. They are required to continually change direction and to linger, at the same time, in a circumscribed space. Their movement is equal parts teleological—insofar as it is geared toward finding the exit or the center—and potentially circular, repetitive, and misleading. The readers share these properties with the dream movement of the sleeping Poliphilo. His first somnambulic steps at the beginning of book one lead him into a thick forest, where he promptly loses his way.[17] In the impenetrability of the thicket, which Poliphilo immediately compares to the labyrinth of the Minotaur (*HP*, 1:15), all actions are characterized by their lack of direction. Even his lamenting sighs miss their mark and are, instead, thrown back by Echo. Between fearful hesitation and anxious hurry, every impulse dissolves into a crippling indecisiveness, which finally spreads over Poliphilo's thoughts as well and compels them towards the unknown potential horrors and dangers to his life (*HP*, 1:14–15).

Yet Poliphilo is not only an obsessive dreamer. The depiction of the sleepless protagonist hours before the dream show him to be a brooder, tormenting himself as he continues to agonize over the same object: his unrequited love for Polia. "I sighed and wept for my importunate and unsuccessful love," we read, "thinking over point by point the nature of unmatched affection, and how best to love someone who does not love in return" (*SL*, 12). Like the affects this desperate yearning produces, Poliphilo's pondering has no real point of reference. In the end, the aimless thoughts that poison his waking hours intrude into his dream world as well (*HP*, 1:12).

With his exit out of the woods, Poliphilo appears to have found a provisional direction for his further actions: he wants to quench his unbearable thirst. But when the dream presents him with everything he desires—a clearing, a spring, fresh water—he allows himself to be distracted by a heavenly voice that captures his heart and his desire.[18] The original activity is interrupted, deferred, and for a time replaced by another, which again gives the protagonist a goal and again leads him astray. For the source of the music eludes him whenever he nears it. The senseless efforts to find it exhaust him and he lies down under an oak tree, where he quarrels with fate and ultimately comes to interpret his situation as the cruel postponement of a wel-

---

17. Dante's *Divina Commedia* was obviously model and source for the *Hypnerotomachia*. The entire first book is structured according to Dante's work. See Stewering, "Architectural Representations in the *Hypnerotomachia Poliphili*," 6–25.

18. For the motif of thirst for love and music as comfort for the lovesick, see *HP*, 2:534n4, 537–38n4.

come death. In a state of mindless indifference, Poliphilo finally falls asleep again, this time within his dream (*HP*, 1:19).

The model applied in the *Hypnerotomachia* to the sleep and dreams of Poliphilo follows a long tradition of interpretation and classification of dreams. The key figure for the conception of dreams in the Middle Ages was Macrobius. In his theory, the intensity of sleep is related to the dreams' visionary quality. Light sleep is accompanied by nightmares (*insomnia*). However, since they are closely related to one's experience in a waking state, they have no meaning for the prediction of the future. One of Macrobius's examples is the distress of a lover who, uncertain about the feelings of his beloved, is driven to bad dreams. Contrasted with this are *somnia*, mysterious dream images that emerge in deep sleep and bear truth about the future but require interpretation.[19]

Following this schema, the transition from the first to the second dream narrative in the *Hypnerotomachia* is a qualitative leap. The moment when Poliphilo falls asleep is described twice with exactly the same participial construction, the first time as sweet (*quella parte . . . da uno dolce somno opressa*; *HP*, 1:12) and the second time as deep (*fui di eminente somno opresso*; *HP*, 1:19). The horrible visions of the first stage disappear almost as soon as Poliphilo drifts off into sleep again. As we will see, his attention is subsequently captured by wondrous objects that astonish him and that he cannot immediately understand. Just like the true content of the prophetic dream images that emerge in deep sleep, the meaning of the things Poliphilo sees is only accessible through interpretation.

The *Hypnerotomachia*'s manifest immersion in tradition justifies a reading that takes the Macrobian distinctions into account. However, they cannot be the only basis for analysis. The striking motivic and argumentative similarities between narrative and metanarrative components at the beginning of the *Hypnerotomachia* that include even the framing text passages suggest that structural criteria deserve just as much attention as the content. For instance, the structural perspective points to a concern of the romance with textual interpretation rather than the degree of truthfulness in dreams. It implies that those who want to explore the labyrinth of human life are forced to linger. As a method of interpretation, thus the bottom line of the romance's beginning, lingering can be obsessive, an endlessly circling movement that appears to persist, in a kind of petrification, in the now. Against this background,

---

19. Macrobius, *Macrobii Ambrosii Theodosii Commentariorum in Somnium Scipionis libri duo*; Hüttig, *Macrobius im Mittelalter*; Schedler, *Die Philosophie des Macrobius*; Reck, "Traum," 171–201; Ussani, *Insomnia*, 118; Probst and Wetz, "Traum," 1461–73.

one could say that Poliphilo's first dream depicts the failure of interpretation. Looking forward to the second dream, the question is how interpretation can succeed.[20]

Ruins

In his descent into slumber, Poliphilo escapes the dark forest and finds himself in a cheerful hilly region covered with all manner of plants. He walks to the edge of a valley between two high mountains. In the valley, he spots a tower and a building (*una grande fabrica*), which he identifies from a distance as antique structures (*opera et structura antiquaria*). Driven by a suspicion of the significance of what he sees, Poliphilo hurries toward them (*la quale cosa de intuito accortamente existimando dignissima*). The closer he gets, the larger the construct appears to him and the more his desire to admire it grows (*di mirarla multiplicantise el disio*). It finally turns out to be an enormous obelisk built upon a huge, pyramid-like block of stone (*una vasta congerie di petre*; *HP*, 1:22).[21]

Poliphilo's wish to not merely see but admire the object that gradually reveals itself to him as he approaches has hermeneutic (and aesthetic) implications. While only the actual structure in its enormity evokes the affect of astonished admiration, Poliphilo's wish prefigures a typically contingent aesthetic effect. His expectation exposes his later experience as premeditated. In other words, the anticipation of a spontaneous reaction turns the following observation and description of classical architecture into an act of interpretation. The emphasis does not lie on the overpowering visual surprise but on the discursive embedding of the experience that precedes even the experience itself. This role of the discourse is to be kept in mind as I examine, in what follows, two architectural ekphrases that are narrated from Poliphilo's point of view and placed at either end of the second dream. The first ekphrasis deals with the pyramid and the obelisk that I have mentioned previously. The second is included in Poliphilo's visit to the temple of the unhappy lovers. The two passages are related to each other by the prominence they give to the representation of ruins.

---

20. In her study of the text, Olimpia Pelosi focuses on the dream world as a particular kind of space. Here, what counts is not so much reason—in the sense of a means of interpretation—as participation in the symbols. See Pelosi, *Il sogno di Polifilo*, 19. It is not entirely clear what this participation consists in.

21. The text speaks of a heap of stones. The reader learns later that it has the shape of a pyramid.

In her work on the architectural ekphrases of the *Hypnerotomachia Poliphili*, Dorothea Schmidt has emphasized the erratic status of these passages.[22] Her main criticism is that the extensive descriptions are overloaded with information that seems to serve no other purpose than to demonstrate the learnedness of the author. They stick out from the narrative flow because, according to Schmidt, they are not allegorized like the rest of the story, and one is left to speculate about their meaning.[23] With this observation, Schmidt implicitly asks about the narrative function of the ekphrases. I will take up her question as a counterpoint to the majority of scholarship that focused on the ekphrastic display of theoretical architectural knowledge by the author.[24]

Poliphilo's examination of pyramid and obelisk takes its time. His curious gaze observes, marvels, discovers, deliberates, and reflects, while moving from detail to detail. Poliphilo walks upon the pyramid, lingers with its material, its proportions, the decorative elements, the incorporation of the entire construct into the surrounding landscape, and then attempts to imagine the costs and the amount of labor, organization, and skill the construction required (*HP*, 1:20–30). His attention is centered on the immense size of the structure and the difficulty to grasp and describe it. The time and effort that Poliphilo nonetheless puts into the undertaking appears to be aimed at demonstrating the essential incomparability of this bold example of architectonic art (*tanta insolentia di arte aedificatoria*; *HP*, 1:22): "The height of this obelisk far exceeded the summits of the flanking mountains, and would have, so I thought, even if they had been famous Olympus, the Caucasus, or Mount Cyllene" (*SL*, 22). Neither the baths of Hadrian nor the obelisks of the Vatican, Alexandria, or Babylon—the hyperbolic praise continues—neither the Labyrinth at Lemnos nor the Mausoleum of Ninos compares to the magnificent object. The Egyptians were not capable of such invention and neither was Dimokrates, who wanted to build Alexander the Great a city on Mount Athos. No time has ever conceived of and much less seen anything similar (*Ne unque in alcuno saeculo, ne viso, ne excogitato tale*; *HP*, 1:25–30).

Poliphilo's excitement in the face of the sheer perfection of the construction is accompanied both by a praise of past times and a somewhat pessimistic view of the present. The artists of antiquity are called sacred fathers

---

22. Schmidt is primarily interested in the Temple of Venus, which is not the object of my concern here, as ruins play no particular role in its description.

23. Schmidt, *Untersuchungen zu den Architekturekphrasen in der "Hypnerotomachia Poliphili,"* 15.

24. For example, Borsi, *Polifilio Architetto*; Oechslin, "Traum, Liebe, Kampf," 83–84; in the broader sense of "architecture," see Kretzulesco-Quaranta, *Les jardins du songe*, on the influence of the *Hypnerotomachia* on European gardens.

(*sancti patri antiqui artifice*) who have taken all virtue and skill into the grave with them, leaving nothing behind for the moderns (*HP*, 1:42). The moderns follow neither the law of symmetry nor that of proportion but nonetheless boast that they are architects. The loss of the worthy masters of architecture has led to a loss of architectonic terminology, and Poliphilo blames his own inability to capture in words the beauty he sees on a lack of vocabulary. Finally, architecture is praised as the most noble creation of the Roman Empire, whose downfall through ignorance and barbarism can only be lamented (*HP*, 1:31). In the face of such aggrandizement of the past, Hanno-Walter Kruft spoke of a "backwards-facing utopia," which he understood as part of a new sense for architecture that the *Hypnerotomachia* helped establish at the end of the fifteenth century.[25] In what follows, I will relate Kruft's thought to the narrative function of the ekphrases. For the context of the *Hypnerotomachia*, one has to ask precisely how such a utopia comes into existence and what its actual objective is.

From the beginning, ruins play a central role in the work's description of ancient structures and their uniqueness.[26] In one of the first depictions, Poliphilo's astonishment is caused by the contrast between the fragmentation of the structure, on the one hand, and its massive size, on the other (*la crassitudine de questa fragmentata et semiruta structura*; *HP*, 1:22). Many elements are only partially destroyed; others are reduced to their mere material. They appear as formless rubble overgrown with plants, allowing no insight into their former state. Thus Poliphilo, confronted with a marble-covered area, assumes that it was either a hippodrome, a colonnade, or an alley (*HP*, 1:32). Wherever architecture is intact to the extent that the original purpose can be guessed, a space opens up for the observer's imagination. The effect of the intact structures must have been overpowering, Poliphilo presumes, when even the remainders of antiquity are capable of producing such admiration (*HP*, 1:59). In this manner, ruins are indicators of past perfection, and their prominence in the text can be understood as a symptom of a backward-facing utopia in Kruft's sense.

However, ruins are also breaks and discontinuities in a kind of continuum of the ideal. They disrupt the view of that which is intact and even of the artwork as such when, for example, they draw the viewer's attention away from art and toward nature (*HP*, 1:22–23). Ruins literally impede the observation of the

---

25. Kruft, *Geschichte der Architektur-Theorie*, 68.

26. Although the *Hypnerotomachia* is a favorite reference for research on ruins, scholars have rarely asked about their function for the narration as a whole. Sabine Forero-Mendoza takes a few steps in this direction; see Forero-Mendoza, *Le temps des ruines*, 102–5.

whole when Poliphilo, in the course of his wide-ranging inspection of the site, must climb over and maneuver around them to get an unencumbered view of the structure (*uno agere di ruine scando di grande fracture*; HP, 1:35). And finally, ruins are the location where Poliphilo, frightened by the approach of a dragon, breaks off his investigation and returns to his journey (HP, 1:61).

At the core of the first ekphrasis lies a fantasy of completeness that the ruins disturb. They introduce time and glimpses of the outside world into the atemporal, ideal totality of the work of art. This claim might seem surprising in a context that draws on antiquity. The atemporality that characterizes the obelisk passage is easily demonstrable, however. First of all, the sequence is located within the macrostructure of a dream narrative, which begins and ends with a description of the emergent dawn, thereby appearing to condense all the events into a single moment (HP, 2:501n2). The ekphrasis sticks out as an erratic block in the terrain of Poliphilo's wanderings; the author lingers there—from the perspective of narrative strategy far longer than necessary—without advancing the plot at all. Finally, within this framework, antiquity is in no way understood as historical, even though the text repeatedly insists on the antique nature of the building. The product of antiquity is compared with numerous (semi)mythical examples, whose role is not to contextualize historically the majesty of Poliphilo's sights but rather to confirm them in their general validity and absoluteness. Only the ruins introduce the disruptive knowledge about the present's before and after, implying with their state of decay that there used to be an intact structure and that the present building will be subject to transformation. The ruins are a medium in which the past is related to the future and historical time can be grasped.[27]

Even beyond their significance for the role of history within the *Hypnerotomachia*, ruins affect the narrative. They incorporate the somewhat isolated ekphrasis back into the romance by bridging the gap to the love story. It is remarkable that Polia is mentioned only a single time in the entire ekphrasis. Poliphilo thinks of her in just that moment in which the sight of the classical structure overwhelms him. He declares that her image always occupies his thoughts, but that he is now for once entirely absorbed in the view of the building that fills his gaze entirely. He then proceeds to describe the architecture further, without mentioning Polia again (HP, 1:31). From this hermetic situation, the ruins offer a possibility of departure and a way to continue the narrative. For it is among the ruins that Poliphilo is threatened by a dragon and that he concurrently realizes how doomed his entire existence is: "I heard a sound in the ruins like the breaking of bones and the cracking of branches.

27. For this concept of history, see Koselleck, *Futures Past*.

FIGURE 1. Poliphilo among the ruins in *Hypnerotomachia Poliphili* (Venice: Aldus Manutius, 1499). Woodcut. Photograph courtesy of Boston Public Library.

I stood stock still, my delightful recreation shattered . . . I heard the deafening hiss of a giant serpent . . . Oh how wretched and cruel was my fate!" (*SL*, 61). Yet he rejects the brief thought of a welcome end and replaces it with the desire for life in which a future union with Polia is possible:

> Although I naturally did not think of hateful death as pleasant in the least, I reckoned that at this moment it would be welcome. But try as I would, I could not wish for it, as I tried to face it firmly in my uncertain, unhappy and timorous life. Ah, how I resisted the dissociation of my spirit! I rejected death, refused its advantages and regretted its noxious presence. For I was incensed when I thought of how I might die without any consummation of my immense love. (*SL*, 63–64)

In this context, the two woodcuts to which the described passage refers deserve attention. They both show ruins or architectural fragments. The first image is located before the text passage in which Poliphilo first sees the obelisk (figure 1). In the foreground of the image, one can see a number of architectural fragments, a torso, a column base, and a capital. They are placed in

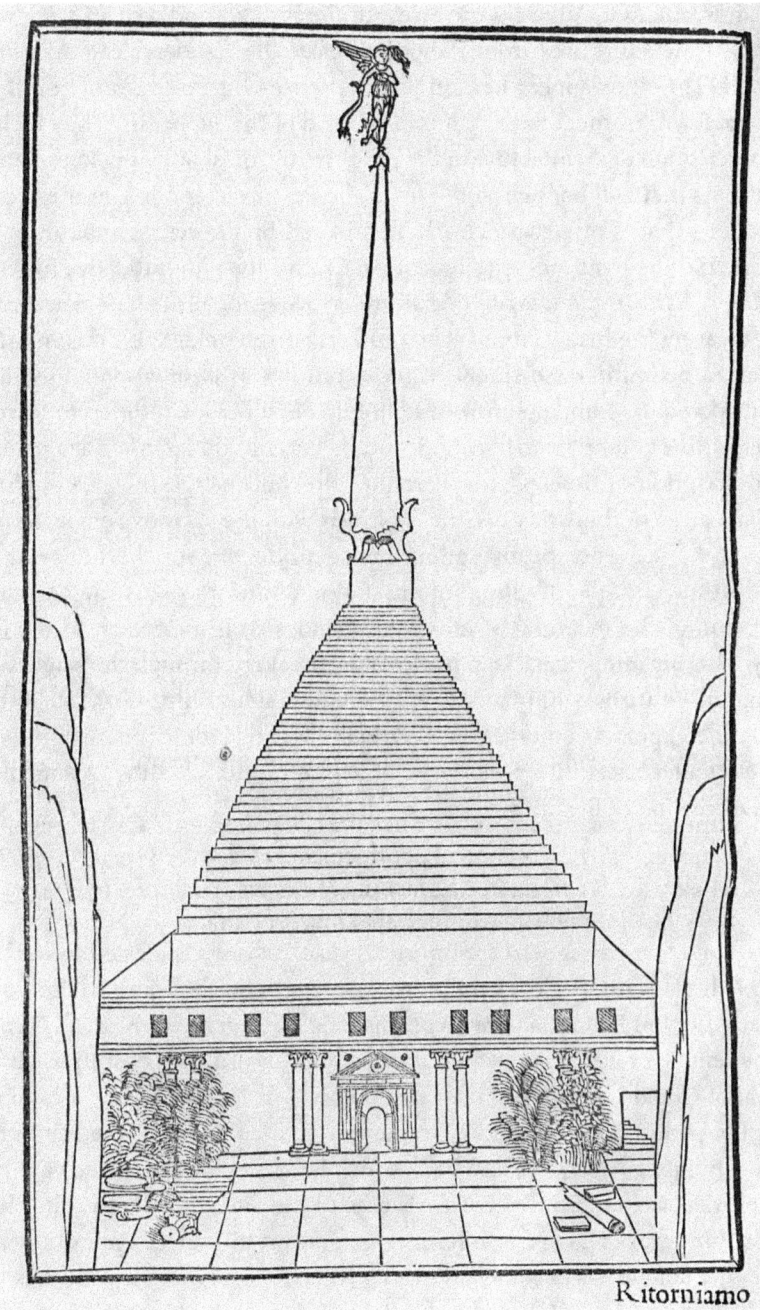

FIGURE 2. The pyramid in *Hypnerotomachia Poliphili* (Venice: Aldus Manutius, 1499). Woodcut. Photograph courtesy of Boston Public Library.

the landscape that Poliphilo traverses. In the background we can see a wolf, which in the story flees from Poliphilo before the wanderer can take flight himself. The ruins appear here in just the sense of narrative function that I described with respect to the ruins at the end of the ekphrasis. They include the description of architecture in the narrative by foreshadowing in the image the events that will happen in the text. The destroyed column in the second woodcut—that is otherwise clearly dominated by the representation of the obelisk and the pyramid—has less of a narrative than an indicative function (figure 2). Within the image, the ruin refers to the obelisk's before and after, thus creating the historicity of that which is represented. With this in mind, Dorothea Schmidt's assessment of the ekphrases as isolated entities can be reconsidered. In comparison with Poliphilo's first dream, a different form of lingering is at stake in the second one. It initially threatens to stagnate in the description of timeless, ideal architecture, but then it links, through the medialization of time in ruins, the ekphrasis with the narrative environment, making the text's perspective on antiquity productive for the future of the story. In the end, the dwelling interpretation of a work of art merges into a revelation of the meaning of life that coincides with the return to the love story. This meaning consists in living on by breaking through the stagnation. Living on, in turn, is only possible as a temporal and historical act. In that sense, the ekphrasis emerges—beyond all allegorization of its parts—as an aspect of allegorical interpretation that deploys historical time as a medium for the creation of meaning.

The (Hi)Story of Love

The second text passage that prominently displays ruins is located toward the end of the narration told from Poliphilo's perspective and just before Polia's narrative within Poliphilo's dream begins. The lovers have been ritually united in the temple of Venus. Together, they set out toward the coast to await the arrival of Cupido, who is to take them on his boat to Kythira, the location of their final (physical) unification. On the way, they come across the ruins of an ancient building (*veterrimo aedificio*), which Polia identifies as the Polyandrion Temple dedicated to Pluto.[28] Formerly a luxurious site of the Pluto cult, where lovers came from all over to offer sacrifice meant to protect against an early death, the temple has become a decaying ruin, a mass grave for countless victims of unhappy love (*HP*, 1:236–38). Poliphilo considers himself wonderfully educated through Polia's eloquent narration but is, in the next moment, entirely

---

28. The Greek πολυάνδριον (*polyandrion*) means "communal burial site."

captivated by her beauty. What follows is an ekphrasis of her face and body. Poliphilo's curiosity, his way of focusing on details, and his dedication to the object are similar to the description of the building in the first ekphrasis. However, the emphasis lies on Poliphilo's astonishment and admiration, as well as his physical reaction to what he sees. The sight fans the flames of his desire until he can no longer bear it. His thoughts are directed obsessively toward fulfillment. Poliphilo is saved from this state of utmost inner strife by Polia's suggestion that he take a closer look at the temple, while she plans to remain behind to watch out for Cupido. Aware of Poliphilo's enthusiasm for works of antiquity, she encourages him to set out immediately on a sightseeing trip of the temple (*le antiquarie ope[re] ad te summamente piaceno di vedere*; HP, 1:239–42).

From here onward, Poliphilo channels his entire inappropriate desire into the attentive exploration of the temple.[29] His activity is one of decryption. He derives hypotheses from the remaining evidence and interprets fragments with respect to the whole that they used to be. Poliphilo's first reaction upon catching sight of the temple is the assumption of its original grandeur and majesty, and he deduces from remnants of stone tribunes the former location of graves (HP, 1:242). In contrast to the first ekphrasis, Poliphilo strictly *reads* fragments. This effort culminates in the nearly excessive reading of the epitaphs of deceased lovers and their stories of hardship and misery (figure 3). Poliphilo lingers with these stories, occasionally unable to completely understand their content as a result of the dilapidated state of the gravestones and ornaments (HP, 1:252–71).[30]

In light of the first ekphrasis, what seems particularly surprising here is that this text passage too, despite its thematic relevance to the love story—which is, after all the *Hypnerotomachia*'s primary narrative strand—nonetheless gives the impression of an isolated narrative unit. To be sure, observation, which played a decisive role in the first ekphrasis, recedes into the background and gives way to the process of reading. Yet Poliphilo seems to draw from the sad tales a pleasure similar to that which he drew from the unusual obelisk. Again and again we read that Poliphilo turns with great enjoyment from one work to the next, and his pleasure seems to rise simultaneously with the number of objects he sees (HP, 1:256). All of Poliphilo's efforts are directed toward the accumulation of things for his visual curiosity. His discoveries produce the desire for more discoveries (HP, 1:260). This is a manner of lingering that

---

29. For this passage, see Martine Furno's detailed analysis of the treatment of antiquity in the *Hypnerotomachia*: Furno, *Une "Fantasie" sur l'antique*.

30. The inscriptions on the broken tablet and the base of the vase read: "Hail, viewer, and weep, I pray. An unhappy queen, madly loving a wondering guest, alas, with an unfortunate gift," and "Nothing is more sure than death" (SL, 469).

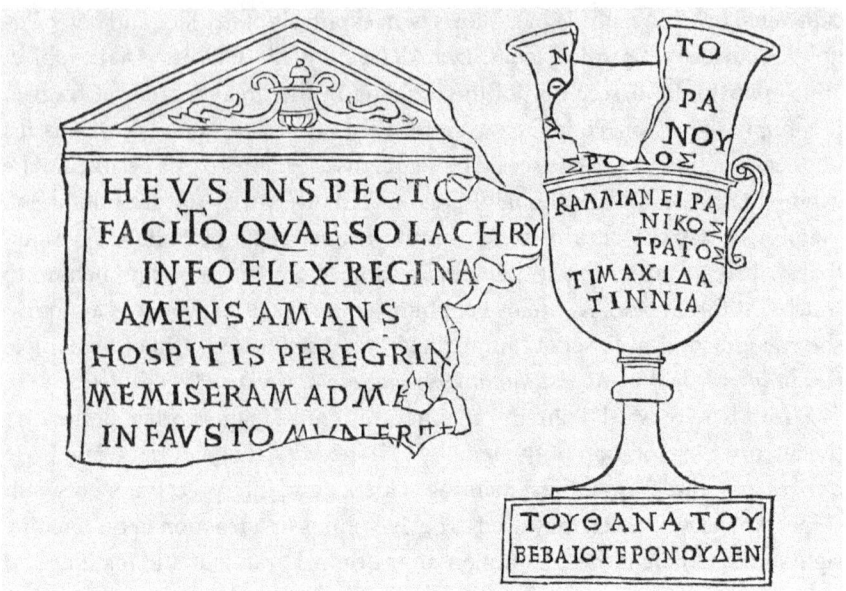

FIGURE 3. Fragments in the ruined temple of deceased lovers seen by Poliphilo in *Hypnerotomachia Poliphili* (Venice: Aldus Manutius, 1499). Woodcut. Photograph courtesy of Boston Public Library.

accumulates narrations without having consequences, however, for the continuation of Poliphilo's own story.

Poliphilo's curiosity peaks when he reaches the story of the abduction and rape of Proserpine. Seen on a half-destroyed mural painting, Poliphilo is first annoyed that he cannot marvel at the work in its totality. But when the scope of what he reads forces its way into his consciousness, a horrible thought occurs to him. The fate of Proserpine causes him to revert back from "archaeologist" to lover, linking his own story with the one that he has just read in the ruins. His expedition into the ruins of the past, Poliphilo realizes, has drawn him away from Polia's side and exposed her to the risk of abduction. Propelled by sudden fear, Poliphilo swiftly turns away from what he calls his noble and meaningful search, his praiseworthy pilgrimage and learned respite (*lasciando tanto incoepto nobile, et praeclara inquisitione et laudabunda lustratione, et virtuoso solacio*). And despite Poliphilo's evident anxiety, one senses in this formulation a certain regret because he has to interrupt his tour through antiquity. Panicked, Poliphilo runs through brush and pathless ruins (*avie ruine*) back to the shore, finally reaching Polia half dead (*non tuto vivo ma semi mortuo*). Under her care, life flows back into his limbs (*HP*, 1:272–74).

The ruins passage, as becomes clear at its conclusion, outfits Poliphilo and Polia's love with a history, and it introduces into Poliphilo's desire—previously fixed on visual triggers and untimely fulfillment—the moment of kairos, which lies in the future. To that end, the narrative lingers with the past torments of lovers, which must be read from the ruins and interpreted in order to deploy the full scope of their effects. It is telling that the majority of stories that Poliphilo reads refer to historical figures, even if the final story, which contributes to Poliphilo's disenchantment, is a myth. At stake in this scene is the growth of knowledge through interpretation, which Poliphilo achieves. As in the first ekphrasis, ruins are linked to time and history. However, now the focus has shifted. The first instance showed that an idealized antiquity only acquires a proper meaning and function after being equipped with a temporal and historical index. The focus of the second example, however, lies on the manner of the reception of antiquity through the medium of ruins—and thus upon a process of reading in which the reader ultimately comes to realize the historicity of his own (hi)story. He learns, so to speak, how the ruins of the past survive. At the point when Poliphilo recognizes the connection between the decrypted fate on the epitaph and his own destiny, that destiny finds a continuation; its conclusion, along with that of Poliphilo's life, is deferred, postponed to the right moment.

The *Hypnerotomachia Poliphili*, long scorned in its reception as an inaccessible riddle, had an impact on the second half of the fifteenth century unparalleled in the context of the reception of antiquity.[31] In that sense, Grassi's wish to pass on knowledge was fulfilled, although less in the intermedial sense he suggested than with respect to the images.

The basic tension that the *Hypnerotomachia* displays is that of how to make sense of the narrative of life in the face of a lost ideal. The gesture of lingering as a mode of gaining insight into both, the ideal that was lost with antiquity and human life as a labyrinthian and dreamlike mystery, has a tendency to lose direction and hover and brood time and again over the same objects. In this setting, ruins break the spell of hermetic closedness. They introduce history into timelessness and, by breaking the stagnation of the lingering standstill of interpretation, they open up the narrative toward a new understanding of the value of life. In this new form of allegorical interpretation lies the *Hypnerotomachia*'s potential that ultimately turned it into a key novel of the late fifteenth century. Its significance derives not so much from it being a reverence to antiquity, but rather a manifesto of hermeneutic transformation.

31. Forero-Mendoza, *Le temps des ruines*, 102–15.

III

Living On

5

Ferdinand Gregorovius, Hildebert of Lavardin, and the Rupture of Continuity

Diese grosse Arbeit ist mein wahrhaftes Leben.

This great work is my real life.
FERDINAND GREGOROVIUS

On January 19, 1861, the German historiographer Ferdinand Gregorovius (1821–1891) noted in his journal:

> The world stands in arms . . . The reaction continues in Naples; Sicily is in revolt . . . The moderates still hope that Garibaldi will allow himself to be dissuaded from his mad expedition to Venetia . . . To-day is my fortieth birthday. It seems sad to pass this Rubicon of man's estate [*Mir wurde es schwer, diesen Rubikon des männlichen Alters zu überschreiten*]. I went to the Lateran, drank a glass of wine at the Osteria, on the ruins of the Baths of Trajan [*auf den Trümmern der Bäder Trajans*], and found there the first almond tree in bloom; this was my only well-wisher . . . Have described to-day the capture of Rome by Robert Guiscard.[1]

At the time, Gregorovius, who was originally from Neidenburg in East Prussia, had been living in Rome, the place in which he had chosen to establish himself as an independent writer, for nearly a decade. Here he started to work on the *History of the City of Rome in the Middle Ages* (*Geschichte der Stadt Rom im Mittelalter*), a venture that took him almost twenty years to finish. Gregorovius's *Roman Journals*, in which he documented his entire stay in the Eternal City between 1852 and 1874, allow us some insight into the evolution of this monumental project and its relation to the upheaval in contemporary Italian politics that the German expatriate came to witness more or

---

1. Quotations from the original German are taken from Gregorovius, *Römische Tagebücher 1852–1889* (1991; hereafter cited as *RT*), 122. For the English translation, see Gregorovius, *The Roman Journals 1852–1874* (1907; hereafter cited as *RJ*), 121. In subsequent citations I will indicate the page number from the German as well as the English version.

less involuntarily.[2] In 1852, the Risorgimento, the Italian national unification movement, had already laid claim to many of the sovereign principalities and regions of the Apennine peninsula that would later be consolidated into the kingdom of Italy. Rome, however, was an exception. Gregorovius's first encounter with the city coincided with a peculiar moment of political stalemate and a resulting delicate social equilibrium. After a long period of economic and political decline in the wake of the unsettling experiences of the French Revolution and the European revolutions of 1848, the Papal States—with the help of French troops and supported by a small group of papal administrators and Rome's nobility—had abolished previously implemented reforms and reestablished prerevolutionary conditions. Neither the Roman bourgeoisie nor the rural population constituted an opposition to these developments that reinforced old power relations (*RT*, 22–25). Kruft and Völkel argue that Gregorovius, who as a liberal was deeply disappointed with the failure of the 1848 revolution in his native East Prussia, hoped to escape from politics altogether by replacing the political shipwreck at home with the political vacuum in Rome. Yet the early 1860s brought the breakthrough of the unification movement with parts of the Papal States falling to the kingdom of Sardinia. An attempt by the Italian general Giuseppe Garibaldi to capture Rome failed in 1867 but—as *The Roman Journals* documents—the events seem to have startled Gregorovius out of his slumber of oblivion and given his historical observations a more political angle (*RT*, 30–37).[3] A journal entry from May 1859 shows that to him the progression of his work on the history of Rome and the turmoil of the Risorgimento were intimately connected and that both were related to life in the sense of Gregorovius's personal existence (*Dasein*):[4]

> On April 29 the *Allgemeine Zeitung* announced the first volume of my *History of the City of Rome in the Middle Ages*. Its appearance thus coincides with what in all probability is the revolution that will transform Italy; and in what

---

2. For an overview of the genesis and the historical context of *The Roman Journals*, see the introduction to the German edition by its editors Hanno-Walter Kruft and Markus Völkel (*RT*, 9–40), on which I heavily draw for the following remarks. Both Kruft and Völkel's edition (*RT*) and Annie Hamilton's English translation (*RJ*) are based on Friedrich Althaus's second edition of the *Römische Tagebücher* from 1893. The original manuscript that Gregorovius had bequeathed to his friend Althaus is lost. What Kruft and Völkel found in Gregorovius's literary estate and added to their edition instead is a journal that he kept from 1875 to 1889 (*RT*, 15).

3. The journal entries from October 1867 report the events around Garibaldi's invasion and his arrest. Gregorovius wrote an essay about the same topic, "Krieg der Freischaren um Rom" ("War of the Volunteer Corps for Rome"), his only piece on contemporary history.

4. In their introduction, Kruft and Völkel point out that Gregorovius generally favors "historical parallelism" as a means of historical interpretation (*RT*, 37).

time will fall its end?—as yet impossible to foresee [*in welche Zeit wird wohl ihr nicht abzusehendes Ende fallen?*]. Shall I be permitted to finish this great task? I am excited; the very foundations of my life's purpose laid with great difficulty and as yet scarcely solid, totter beneath me [*Ich bin aufgeregt: unter mir wanken die kaum mit grosser Mühe gelegten Fundamente meines Daseins*]. (RT, 79; RJ, 56)

According to the passage, life's continuity depends on the ground on which it stands: Gregorovius's history of Rome, which he called his "real life" (*wahrhaftes Leben*; RT, 130; RJ, 134) and which occupied a specific position in the course of world-historical events. In Gregorovius's description, world, life, and form seem to overlap.

Something similar is at stake in the historiographer's birthday entry. The mention of revolutionary machinations precedes a melancholy account of what for the author at age forty was the crossing of a biographical threshold. This time, instead of standing on metaphorically shaky ground, Gregorovius finds himself sitting on the actual ruins of the Baths of Trajan, drinking a toast to himself. The scene is reminiscent of Petrarch's repose on the ruins of the Baths of Diocletian but lacking the outlook on Rome's ruinscape and into history. Gregorovius's focus rests on himself and his lonely celebration; his gaze is directed at the immediate surroundings. The reference to the *History of the City of Rome in the Middle Ages* occurs in only one laconic sentence and is completely free of the explicit pathos in the earlier description of the forthcoming publication. Even in the journal entry in which Gregorovius documented historical upheaval coinciding with his fortieth birthday, world and form are just as closely intertwined. For if we spell out what Gregorovius implies, then we can glean from the 1861 note that Gregorovius's birthday—which he concluded gloomily and encumbered with thoughts about life's transience—coincided with the composition of a passage in the *History of the City of Rome* that depicts the terrible misfortune Rome suffered at the hands of the Norman conqueror Robert Guiscard, Duke of Apulia, Calabria, and Sicily, in 1084.[5]

The devastation of the city by Guiscard followed an episode of the Investiture Controversy. In his long-standing feud with Pope Gregory VII over the right to install high-ranking ecclesiastics, King Henry IV had appointed Wibert of Ravenna as Pope Clement III in 1080. Four years later, the king and his antipope entered Rome, their access enabled by Romans who had started

---

5. For a detailed history of the Norman expansion in southern Italy and Guiscard's role, see Loud, *Age of Robert Guiscard*.

to defect to Henry.⁶ Clement III was recognized as the legitimate pontiff, and he crowned Henry emperor of the Romans in turn. In the meantime, Gregory refused to surrender. He had entrenched himself in Castle Sant'Angelo when his vassal Robert Guiscard came to his rescue.⁷ Gregorovius's grim portrayal of the horrors following Guiscard's arrival gives an example of what he had in mind when he claimed that his writing was an attempt to combine historiography and artistic representation:⁸

> The unhappy city, however, which was surrendered to his [Guiscard's] soldiers for plunder, became the scene of more than Vandal horrors [*mehr als vandalischer Greuel*] ... The city fought valiantly but in vain; the despair of the people of Rome was stifled in blood and flames, for, in order to save himself, Robert had set fire to a portion of the city. When both flames and the tumult of battle had subsided, Rome lay a heap of smoking ashes before Gregory's eyes; burnt churches, streets in ruins, the dead bodies of Romans formed a thousand accusers against him [*waren tausend Ankläger gegen ihn*].⁹

In a gesture worthy of Scipio's historiographers (recall the account that opened the introduction to this book), Rome's chronicler imagines Gregory's reaction to the utter devastation of his residence, but unlike Polybios or Appian, Gregorovius is much more hesitant to concede feelings of regret or worry to the pope. He depicts Gregory VII as a tool of fate whose active endorsement of Guiscard's atrocities is difficult to assess but whose involvement in the ruin of Rome is undeniable:

---

6. Cowdrey, *Pope Gregory VII*, 228–29.

7. Ullman, *Short History of the Papacy in the Middle Ages*, 104, gives a slightly different account than Gregorovius, who focuses on Rome's fall. Ullman describes how the Normans managed to drive Henry and his troops from Rome, but the devastation they left in their wake prompted insurgencies among the population and eventually forced Guiscard to leave Rome and take Pope Gregory with him.

8. See *RT*, 9. Kruft and Völkel quote from a letter Gregorovius wrote to his editor Cotta in 1858 in which he dissociates himself from the German historian Leopold Ranke: "Ich bin nicht Schüler Herrn Rankes ... Ich suche Forschung und künstlerische Darstellung zu vereinigen und wünsche auch, dass man mir zugäbe, die Kunst des Erzählens zu besitzen" (I am not Mr. Ranke's student ... I seek to combine research and artistic representation and I hope to be recognized for mastering the art of narration); translation mine. Kruft and Völkel even claim that Gregorovius self-identified as a poet and writer in the first place and as a historian in the second.

9. Translation slightly modified. For the four-volume German original, introduced in chapter 3, see *GSRM*, 2:107–108. For the English translation, see the eight-volume edition Gregorovius, *History of the City of Rome in the Middle Ages* (1894–1902; hereafter cited as *HCRM*), 4.1:246. Subsequent citations of these two works include volume and page number from the German version and volume number (and in the case of volume 4, additional part number) and page number from the English version.

The brutal fury of the victors satisfied itself for some days in robbery and murder, until the Romans, a cord and a naked sword round their necks, threw themselves at the feet of the duke . . . The sack of Rome remains a dark stain on Gregory's history, more so than on that of Guiscard. It was Nemesis that compelled the Pope, however hesitatingly and reluctantly, to gaze upon the flames of Rome. Was not Gregory VII in the burning city (and it burned on his account) as terrible a man of destiny as Napoleon calmly riding over bloody fields of battle? . . . Not one of [his] contemporaries has recorded that he made any attempt to save Rome from the sack or ever shed a tear of compassion for the fall. (*GSRM*, 2:108; *HCRM*, 4.1:247–48; translation modified)

The tears that Gregory neglected to cry were shed—at least figuratively—about two decades later by the French bishop Hildebert of Lavardin (c. 1056–1133). He likely visited Rome around 1100 and composed two poems in elegiacs shortly after his stay in the eternal, now infinitely miserable city.[10] Following the account about Guiscard's deeds, Gregorovius—in an effort to make up for Gregory's lack of empathy with an example of someone who sympathized with the defeated—quotes the entire first poem, which he calls Hildebert's "touching lament over the ruins of Rome [*seine rührende Klage über die Ruinen Roms*]" (*GSRM*, 2:108; *HCRM*, 4.1:248).

In light of Gregorovius's identification with his work on Rome's history and the documented chronology of his writing progress, the coincidence between his bemoaning of mercilessly passing life-time and the narration of Hildebert's grief over the collapse of Rome and thus over the discontinuities in world-time is remarkable. Proceeding from this focal passage, this chapter will show that Hildebert and Gregorovius—each in their specific manner—examine the possibilities of living on in the face of evident rupture and discontinuity. Their works reveal that life and its continuance depend on life's relation to the world, and that the relation to the world is established by forms. From the point of view of Walter Benjamin's considerations, one could say that in the works of the German historiographer and the French bishop, history's relation to life and life's origin in forms is once again at stake. Additionally, Hildebert's poetic forms, in particular, will reveal that "having a world" and relating to it rely on semiotic operations that build up and represent this very world in the first place. Put another way, this chapter explicitly supplements the historical dimension of what the term *world* denotes by querying its semiotic characteristics. It is, at the same time, an examination of the semiotic aspects of the textuality that ruins manifest.

---

10. Gibson, "Hildebert of Lavardin on the Monuments of Rome," 131.

Rather than an anticipated or belated form of humanism that has been attributed to Hildebert and Gregorovius, respectively, it is the way in which they conceptualize life's continuation that ascribes to them their rightful place within the history of ideas. While Hildebert's notion of life has a Christian index and combines spiritual and historical criteria of continuity, Gregorovius searches for ways to negotiate the experience of discontinuity historically. As he shows in a surprising interpretative move, historical time emerges from life-time, which is mediated through form.

Christian Life: Hildebert of Lavardin's Rome Poems

When in 1938 Wilhelm Heckscher included Hildebert of Lavardin's two Rome poems in an essay on Roman relics in medieval settings, he felt it adequate to identify them as "often discussed."[11] Since that time, scholarly attention on the bishop's work has been unrelenting, and many a study starts with an apology for resuming an inquiry into such thoroughly explored territory.[12]

The interest in Hildebert's writings, however, is not a phenomenon of the twentieth and twenty-first centuries. It is a curious circumstance that the ecclesiastic—who despite his occasional opposition to worldly power, had a successful career as bishop of Le Mans and later archbishop of Tours—seems to have always been better known for his achievements as a writer than for his attainments within the Roman Catholic Church.[13] Until the late Middle Ages, authors modeled their literary artifacts on his stylistically sophisticated texts that drew on the poetic form and diction of the classical Latin past.[14] The Rome elegies are the most famous examples in a large corpus of poems that deal with questions of liturgy, the Bible, holy Christian figures, and theological topics.[15] Some of them enjoyed widespread recognition among Hildebert's contemporaries and their popularity was only surpassed by that of the sermons and epistles. The French cleric Peter of Blois (c. 1130–c. 1211) was

---

11. Heckscher, "Relics of Pagan Antiquity" (1938), 207.

12. See, e.g., Smolak, "Beobachtungen zu den Rom-Elegien Hildeberts von Lavardin," 371.

13. This was pointed out in a review by Ziolkowski, "*Hildebertus Cenomannensis episcopus: Carmina minora* by Hildebertus, A. Brian Scott," 203–5.

14. Czapla, "Zur Topik und Faktur postantiker Romgedichte," 144.

15. Peter von Moos has pointed out that the term *elegy* is a misnomer that is owed to the later reception of the poems and its nostalgia for ruins. He counts the poems among the panegyric genre of city praise. See Von Moos, "Homo creans in den Romgedichten Hildeberts von Lavardin" (2019), 177.

a vocal admirer of his fellow countryman's perfectly formed letters and used them as templates for his own correspondences.[16] In 1889 the German classicist Eduard Norden pointed out Hildebert's influence when it came to historical dynamics of anticipation and retention. In a reading of the Rome poems, he stated, on the one hand, that Hildebert's gaze upon the ruins was affected by the same "sentimental longing" (*sentimentale Sehnsucht*) that—in the eyes of many—would become Petrarch's signature feature. On the other hand, he hypothesized that because of the bishop's "unmeasured" (*ungemessen*) fame among contemporaries and posterity, he was responsible for the classicist tendency in Latin poetry in twelfth- and thirteenth-century France that enabled the sustained interest in Roman poets such as Tibullus and Propertius.[17]

There are two major milestones in the reception history of Hildebert's work that deserve to be mentioned here. One is A. Brian Scott's edition of Hildebert's shorter poems, the *Carmina minora*, which in 1969 replaced the flawed version of Migne's *Patrologia Latina* as the standard text for Hildebert studies. Scott's main endeavor was to identify among a vast number of manuscripts those that contained material that could reliably be credited to the bishop.[18] The other landmark is Peter von Moos's comprehensive monograph *Hildebert von Lavardin (1056–113): Humanitas an der Schwelle des höfischen Zeitalters* (*Hildebert of Lavardin [1056–1133]: Humanitas on the Threshold of the Courtly Era*) from 1965. The study is mainly concerned with Hildebert's humanism that von Moos intended to substantiate as a compromise between antique and Christian thought.[19] Scott acknowledged this effort as a corrective to some scholarly voices that—one-sidedly focused on the bishop's taste for classical literature and culture—considered Hildebert's poetry to be "an early manifestation of the humanism of the Italian renaissance."[20] One of the famous representatives of this view is Jacob Burckhardt, who detected a

---

16. Cotts, *Clerical Dilemma*, 74–75.

17. Norden, *Die antike Kunstprosa*, 723–24.

18. Czapla, "Zur Topik und Faktur postantiker Romgedichte," 44. I use A. Brian Scott's 2001 second edition of the *Carmina minora*, which offers a reprint of the 1969 edition with some corrections and additions and a supplementary bibliography: Hildebertus, *Hildebertus Cenomanensis Episcopus, Carmina minora* (hereafter cited as *CM*, with poem and line numbers). For a review of the second edition, see Ziolkowski, "*Hildebertus Cenomannensis episcopus, Carmina minora* by Hildebertus, A. Brian Scott," 203–5. Scott has laid out his criteria for the selection of what he thought were authentic manuscripts in Scott, "Poems of Hildebert of Le Mans," 42–83.

19. Von Moos, *Hildebert von Lavardin (1056–1133)*.

20. For this and a critical appraisal of von Moos's book, see Scott, "Peter von Moos, 'Hildebert von Lavardin 1056–1133,'" 187.

form of "humanist enthusiasm" (*humanistische Begeisterung*) in Hildebert's Rome poems.[21]

Others have criticized von Moos's core thesis that Hildebert tried to reconcile two diametrically opposed worldviews—a positive vision of humankind, based on a Stoic ideal of political and social harmony, and Christian pessimism, grounded in the premise of earthly vanity—as being too particular and too general at once.[22] Von Moos specifically emphasized this assumption with respect to the Rome poems, and even though more recent studies on the elegies tend to increasingly concentrate on philological matters in the narrower sense—for instance, the question of Hildebert's classical sources—von Moos's approach and his concern with humanism remain a dominant perspective in research.[23]

In Scott's edition, the two poems on the city of Rome are numbered 36 and 38.[24] There has been some controversy about whether or not they should be regarded as directly related compositions.[25] The prevailing scholarly opinion, however, sees the poems as two positions in a dialogue, as allocution and response, apostrophe and prosopopeia, or—in one way or another—as an antithesis, which is a suggestion that I will interrogate later in this chapter.[26]

Spoken from the perspective of the lyric *I*, the nineteen couplets of the first poem are directed at broken (*fracta*) and intact (*integra*) Rome. The city's former grandeur is blended in with the present ruin, and lament and admiration, even of the fracture, balance each other:

> Par tibi, Roma, nihil cum sis prope tota ruina.
> quam magni fueris integra, fracta doces.
> longa tuos fastus etas destruxit, et arces
> Cesaris et superum templa palude iacent.

---

21. Quoted in Von Moos, *Hildebert von Lavardin (1056–1133)*, 242.

22. Tilliette, "Tamquam lapides vivi," 363.

23. See, e.g., Gibson, "Hildebert of Lavardin on the Monuments of Rome," 131–78.

24. This nonsequential numbering is because of their separation in the manuscript that Scott used, see the preface to the 1969 edition of the poems, xxxiii–xxxiv.

25. In one essay, von Moos seems to raise doubts that the poems belong together; Von Moos, "Par tibi, Roma, nihil" (1979), 120. Yet in his monograph, he treats the poems as corresponding parts of a pair and states as much: Von Moos, "Homo creans in den Romgedichten Hildeberts von Lavardin," 173. On the same page of the monograph, however, he points out that the poems have also been transmitted separately and read as independent works.

26. On the poems as dialogue, see Von Moos, "Homo creans in den Romgedichten Hildeberts von Lavardin," 173. On the poems as antithesis, see Tilliette, "Tamquam lapides vivi," 361–62; Smolak, "Beobachtungen zu den Rom-Elegien Hildeberts von Lavardin," 377; Michel, "Rome chez Hildebert de Lavardin," 197.

GREGOROVIUS, HILDEBERT, AND THE RUPTURE OF CONTINUITY 141

> Nothing is equal to you, Rome, although you are almost entirely a ruin. Broken, you teach how much you were worth when you were whole. Long years have destroyed your pride, and the citadels of Caesar and the temples of the gods lie sunk in marshes. (*CM*, 36:1–4)[27]

From this image of destruction, in which past splendor shines through the ashes and the rubble, Hildebert moves to invoking the reasons for Rome's incomparable success. He depicts a unique coalescence of prudent warfare, the wise use of laws, economic prosperity, benevolence from gods and strangers, and even a geographical advantage that founded and helped preserve the city's unmatched power. The whole world—thus Hildebert finishes his thought—contributed to Rome's wealth. Leaders gave their treasures, fates their favor, and artists their expertise:

> quem gladii regum, quem provida iura senatus,
> quem superi rerum constituere caput;
> quem magis optavit cum crimine solus habere
> Cesar, quam socius et pius esse socer.
> qui crescens studiis tribus hostes, crimen, amicos,
> vi domuit, secuit legibus, emit ope.
> in quem, dum fieret, vigilavit cura priorum,
> iuvit opus pietas hospitis, unda locum.
> materiem, fabros, expensas axis uterque
> misit, se muris obtulit ipse locus.
> expendere duces thesauros, fata favorem,
> artifices studium, totus et orbis opes.

> The swords of kings, the wise laws of the senate, the gods established it to be the head of the world. Caesar preferred to possess it alone through crime, rather than to share it, and to be a pious father-in-law. As it grew through three qualities, it tamed its enemies through force, it cut back crime through the laws, and bought friends through wealth. As long as it was coming into being, the care of ancestors watched over it, the piety of a stranger helped the task, and the sea helped the place. Both sides of the world sent materials, craftsmen and contributions, the very place offered itself for building the walls. Leaders spent their treasures, the Fates spent their goodwill, artists spent their expertise, and the whole world spent its wealth. (*CM*, 36:7–18)

---

27. Here, as in my paraphrases of the poems, I use the English translation by Gibson, "Hildebert of Lavardin on the Monuments of Rome," 131–78.

And yet:

> urbs cecidit, de qua si quicquam dicere dignum
> moliar, hoc potero dicere "Roma fuit."
> non tamen annorum series, non flamma nec ensis
> ad plenum potuit hoc abolere decus.
> tantum restat adhuc, tantum ruit, ut neque pars stans
> equari possit, diruta nec refici.

The city has fallen, about which, if I were to try to say anything worthy, I will be able to say this: "It was Rome." But not the sequence of years, not fire and not the sword could destroy this splendour in full. So much still remains, so much is fallen, that neither could the part that stands be equalled, nor could the part that is destroyed be repaired. (*CM*, 36:19–24)

Within the rhetorical logic of the poem, the fall of the city comes as a shock after the elaborate description of Rome's achievements and wealth, leaving the lyric *I* at a loss for appropriately dignified words (*si quicquam dicere dignum moliar*), only capable of acknowledging the simple fact that "Rome was" (*Roma fuit*). However, as Bruce Gibson has argued, this claim of linguistic inadequacy and limited means of expression forms a stark contrast to the tradition in which the phrase *Roma fuit* stands. Because of its relatively frequent use in classical literary tradition, the short sentence alludes to a whole range of intertextual meanings that Hildebert's rhetorical strategy conceals.[28] In other words, while he contends that the pronouncement says little, it is extraordinarily telling in its brevity. Here, as in the following lines, the bishop intends to navigate the intricate juxtaposition of greatness and ruin and—as the inconsistencies of line twenty suggest—not without difficulty.

For us to better comprehend what Hildebert is trying to come to terms with, a comparison between the medieval perspective and the discourses around ruins and grandeur that I sketched out in the introduction to this book is in order. There we saw that the Romantics—and, if we accept Karlheinz Stierle's reading, Petrarch—build their understanding of the relation between decay and magnificence on the contrast set up by present fragmentation and former integrity. Ruins point beyond themselves toward a glorious past, and, within that deictic space, imagination can operate. However, chapter 3 has already exposed the complications of this basic premise with respect to Petrarch by carving out the poet's struggle with Rome's semiotic fragility. In a similar way, the challenges that Hildebert faces in his elegy on Rome arise

---

28. Gibson, "Hildebert of Lavardin on the Monuments of Rome," 138. Gibson mentions its use by Lucan, Livy, Propertius, Virgil, Ovid, and Tacitus.

from the uncertain semiotic status of the eternal city. Yet this time the question is not how poetic form can grow out of devastation. Instead, the bishop seems to reinforce the abeyance by avoiding a clear distinction between the signs that *indicate* grandness (ruins) and those that *represent* it (intact buildings). Rome's glory is neither failing nor thriving. The destruction is neither comprehensive nor negligible.

What this lack of distinction entails can be grasped heuristically with a sideways look at George Spencer-Brown's approach to logic and epistemology. In the *Laws of Form* (1969) the mathematician introduces a formal calculus to describe observation as a basic act of cognition. The operation of the observer is twofold: he draws a distinction, and he indicates one side of the distinction as currently relevant. In Spencer-Brown's terminology, the observer differentiates between marked and unmarked states.[29] This approach was taken up and modified by Niklas Luhmann, who in his systems theory linked it to the production of meaning in acts of communication. According to Luhmann, meaning emerges from the difference between marked and unmarked sides of a distinction—in other words, from the difference between actuality and potentiality. That which is realized in a situation of communication only bears meaning with respect to unrealized possibilities. Yet only the marked, indicated side of a distinction is open to further differentiations and acts of communication.[30]

Spencer-Brown and Luhmann both understand the complementary processes of distinction and indication as epistemological procedures in the first place. I would like to suggest that in the case of Hildebert they are creative and hermeneutic procedures as well; their lack is an obstacle for creative production and interpretation. Put in semiotic terms, the adjacency of grandeur and ruin that Hildebert depicts appears to level out differences between symbols and signs. Without these differentiations, indication in the sense of a production of meaning that is open to interpretation becomes ambiguous or obsolete. This is particularly evident in the ensuing lines of the poem where Rome's regeneration is declared impossible:

> confer opes marmorque novum superumque favorem,
> artificum vigilent in nova facta manus,
> non tamen aut fieri par stanti machina muro,
> aut restaurari sola ruina potest.

---

29. Spencer-Brown, *Laws of Form*, 1: "We take as given the idea of distinction and the idea of indication, and [] we cannot make an indication without drawing a distinction."
30. Luhmann, *Social Systems*, 93.

> Bring wealth and new marble and the favour of the gods, let the hands of artists be wakeful at their new works, but the crane cannot be made equal to the wall that is standing, nor can the deserted ruin be restored. (*CM*, 36:25–28)

The status quo is effectively unchangeable. The lack of distinction offers no point of reference on which indication or signification can draw.[31]

Hildebert then turns to enhancing the emphasis on Rome's splendor once again by pointing out that not even godly power could diminish its man-made resplendence, and he finally refines that very thought by taking it in a markedly aesthetic direction:

> cura hominum potuit tantam componere Romam,
> quantam non potuit solvere cura deum.
> hic superum formas superi mirantur et ipsi,
> et cupiunt fictis vultibus esse pares,
> non potuit Natura deos hoc ore creare,
> quo miranda deum signa creavit homo.
> vultus adest his numinibus, potiusque coluntur
> artificum studio quam deitate sua.

> The diligence of men could fashion a Rome so great that the diligence of the gods could not destroy it. Here, even the gods themselves admire the images of the gods, and they desire to be equal to their crafted expressions. Nature could not create gods with these countenances, with which man has created the statues of the gods that must be admired. These gods are helped by their expression, and they are worshipped more for the skill of the craftsmen than for their own divinity. (*CM*, 36:29–36)

Von Moos has noted that framing the concept of perfection as a purely human achievement is not an unusual occurrence in Hildebert's work. Furthermore, the notion that art is not just mimetic but able to surpass nature in beauty had circulated in Christian thought since late antiquity. However, what in von Moos's estimation is unique to Hildebert is his emphasis on the idea that art contains the reasons for its value in itself. Circumventing gods or nature, Hildebert identifies art as the direct source of Rome's greatness and a

---

31. In a different understanding of the ruin and in reference to Georg Simmel's essay "The Ruin," von Moos has pointed out that *carmen* 36 is not about fragmentation but about the ruin as a new (aesthetic) whole; see Von Moos, "Homo creans in den Romgedichten Hildeberts von Lavardin," 180–81; cf. Simmel, "Die Ruine" (1996). While I would like to emphasize the semiotic uncertainty instead of the ruinous integrity, I agree with von Moos's assessment that Hildebert is not trying to express contempt for the world or lament over the vanity of human existence, but that instead his goal is to reflect on the possibilities of living on.

cause for divine aspiration and envy.³² The work establishes the world, and it remains to be shown how.

The contrast between human skills and godly potency has been understood as a sort of structural climax to an overall antithetically organized text. The first poem itself was considered to be the thesis to another antithesis represented by the second poem. With respect to *carmen* 36 there is, indeed, much evidence for it being based on antipodes. Ruin and integrity, splendor and debris, the past and the present, men and gods are juxtaposed on several levels of the composition, from content to syntax and vocabulary. Contrasting adjectives and verbs (*integra–fracta; stantem–cecidisse; restat–ruit; equari–refici*) express the dynamics of buildup and breakdown, and they are intertwined with each other through chiasms (*quam magis fueris integra, fracta doces*) and parallelisms (*et stantem tremuit, et cecidisse dolet; tantum restat / tantum ruit; cura hominum potuit tantam componere Romam, / quantam non potuit solver cura deum*). Hildebert underlines his insistent lingering on Rome's glory by way of anaphoras at the beginning of each clause in lines 7–9 (*quem gladii–quem iura–quem superi–quem Cesar*) and thereby augments the contradistinction to the inevitable, yet in the argumentative course of the poem surprising, fall in line 19 (*urbs cecidit*).³³

In *S/Z*, the French semiotician Roland Barthes in 1970 introduced the antithesis as the most stable rhetorical device around which the semantic meaning of narrative texts is usually organized. In Barthes's understanding, the antithesis "consecrates" the eternal division between two terms that are independently meaningful and therefore inexpiable. At the same time, however, the opposites that the antithesis brings face-to-face like "two fully armed warriors" are an "alliance of words" in which the antagonism is reconciled. This rhetorical figure of reconciliation is the paradox. Barthes characterizes it as a "passage through the wall of the antithesis," and, in that sense, the paradox is always a transgression of a classification and therefore the breach of a taboo.³⁴ As a figure of "mutual encroachment" of two terms, it "outplays meaning and engenders horror."³⁵

If, with respect to *carmen* 36, we take Barthes's structuralist analysis as a heuristic to illuminate the problem at stake, then the lack of distinction

---

32. To support his point about art emancipating itself from mimesis, von Moos mentions Emperor Theodosius I and the late antique poet Prudentius as examples; see Von Moos, *Hildebert von Lavardin (1056–1133)*, 252–53.

33. See Czapla, "Zur Topik und Faktur postantiker Romgedichte," 154.

34. Barthes, *S/Z* (1990), 26–27.

35. Barthes states this in his 1973 essay on Poe's *Valdemar* wherein he analyzes the transition between life and death; see Barthes, "Textual Analysis of Poe's *Valdemar*" (1988), 182.

between ruin and splendor in Hildebert's elegy could be reinterpreted as the reconciliation of two opposites in the paradoxical figure of magnificent decay.[36] The conclusion would have to be that, by joining the two sides of the division, the paradox keeps the specific implications of each in limbo and obscures possible points of departure for signification. The production of meaning would end there, dissolved in simultaneous praise and lament, had Hildebert not written a second poem about Rome—this time from the perspective of the city itself—and had Barthes neglected to elaborate on his understanding of the paradox.[37]

Gregorovius dignified Hildebert's grief over the ruins of Rome by quoting *carmen* 36 in full, but he did not honor the second poem with the same exhaustive treatment. In his history of Rome he personified the city as the "unfortunate sibyl" and paraphrased the speech she gives about her "conversion"—from a place of the eagle to a realm of the cross, from a subject of Caesar to a follower of Peter and from a dweller on earth to an inhabitant of heaven—in two sentences (*GSRM*, 2:109; *HCRM*, 4.1:250). Gregorovius assumed that Hildebert—alarmed by the "pagan emotions" that Rome had aroused in him—tried to obliterate his weakness with a poetic image of consolation, intended to thwart the hopeless grief of the earlier depiction.

Carmen 38 begins with a female-personified Rome recounting her former pleasure in vain divinities (*Dum simulacra mihi, dum numina vana placerent*; *CM*, 38:1) and the fall of the things that used to make her great as soon as she abolished false idols. Special emphasis lies on the assertion that now that Rome has fallen, she scarcely remembers herself:

> vix scio que fuerim, vix Rome Roma recordor,
> vix sinit occasus vel meminisse mei.
>
> I scarcely know who I was, scarcely do I Rome remember Rome,
> scarcely does my fall allow me even to remember myself. (*CM*, 38:7–8)

In an escalation of the notion of opposites, the antitheses that follow this thought contain no sense of "adversative confinement." In other words, unlike the first poem, which fostered the idea that Rome is great *despite* its devastation, the second poem predicates that the decay—or rather, Rome's overall lowliness—is what *makes* it not just great but grander:

---

36. I abstract from Barthes's analysis, which refers to a narrative text, not a poem.

37. Since Percy Ernst Schramm's 1929 examination of the Rome poems, there has been consensus over the last two lines of *carmen* 36 being a later addition, see Schramm, *Kaiser, Rom und Renovatio*, 300.

> gratior hec iactura mihi successibus illis:
> maior sum pauper divite, stante iacens.
> plus aquilis vexilla crucis, plus Cesare Petrus,
> plus cunctis ducibus vulgus inerme dedit.

> This loss is more pleasing to me than those successes: as a pauper, I am greater than when I was rich, prostrate I am greater than I was when I stood tall. The standards of the cross are more than my eagles, Peter is more than Caesar, a defenseless crowd gave more than all the leaders. (CM, 38:9–12)

In line 11, the cross, which as the dominant signifier shapes the entire second poem, is mentioned for the first time. More precisely, it is the standards or banners of the cross, the *vexilla crucis*, that the personified city commends. As a sign of military power, unity, and belonging, a banner is what makes a combatant group recognizable, its intentions visible. Semiotically speaking, a standard is a potent vanguard that points beyond itself to a content of broader significance. This function of the term *vexillum*, denoting a part that indicates the whole, connects it to a second, closely related meaning that stems from a concrete use. It appears in the hymn *Vexilla regis*, which was composed by the late antique bishop Venantius Fortunatus (c. 530–609) and first sung in a procession in which fragments of the true Cross of Jerusalem—a gift from the Byzantine emperor Justin II to the Frankish princess Radegunda—were carried from the French town of Tours to Poitiers. It later became part of the Roman liturgy, and it accompanied, as a crucial element of the observance of Good Friday, the delivery of the Eucharist to the high altar. The hymn begins by referring to the fragments as the standards of the king, the *vexilla regis* that step forward (*prodeunt*), presumably to the front of the procession. The following stanzas praise the mystery of the cross, the symbol of suffering and triumph, the figure of life and death.[38] Yet the fragments are also more than indicators. The parts of the so-called True Cross that travel between places are venerated as relics. They are tangible "remains" that carry the power of the intact object. Shortly after Helena, Emperor Constantine's mother, claimed to have found the True Cross on a pilgrimage to the Holy Land in 326, splinters of the cross started to circulate throughout the Roman Empire. The saying went that they were so numerous, they could have paved the streets of Rome.[39]

Kurt Smolak noted with some excitement that Hildebert's second Rome poem is unique in that it includes a hymn to the cross, making use of the

---

38. Gibson, "Hildebert of Lavardin on the Monuments of Rome," 146. See this source also for the reference to Venantius's hymn.

39. Kohl, *Die Macht der Dinge*, 49.

typical panegyric function of anaphoras and polyptota of the term *crux* (cross). He points out that the paradoxes established by the poem are an expression of the folly of the cross, the *stultitia crucis* about which Saint Paul taught the Corinthians (1 Cor. 18).[40] And indeed: taking advantage of much the same paradox that in Venantius's hymn pertains to the cross, Hildebert's poem proceeds to assert that Rome's real—that is, nonearthly—strength stems from her brokenness. Physically and politically ruined, she is now spiritually mighty:

> stans domui terras, infernum diruta pulso;
> corpora stans, animas fracta iacensque rego.
> tunc misere plebi, modo principibus tenebrarum
> impero: tunc urbes, nunc mea regna polus.
> ... ruit alta senatus
> gloria, rocumbunt templa, theatra iacent,
> rostra vacant, edicta silent.

When I stood, I tamed the earth, destroyed, I beat down the underworld; when I stood I ruled bodies, broken and prostrate I rule souls. Then I ruled over the wretched plebeians, now I rule over the lords of the shades; then cities were my kingdom, now it is heaven ... the lofty glory of the senate has fallen, the temples have collapsed, the theatres lie low, the rostra are empty, the edicts are silent. (*CM*, 38:13–21)

The last fifteen lines ultimately juxtapose decline and the cross. The semiotic vacancy that the collapsing signs of empire leave is ultimately filled by the symbol of salvation, the point of reference for those who hope that life will continue after the fall of worldly authority:

> ista iacent ne forte meus spem ponat in illis
> civis, et evacuet spemque bonumque crucis.
> crux edes alias, alios promittit honores,
> militibus tribuens regna superna suis.
> sub cruce rex servit, sed liber; lege tenetur,
> sed diadema gerens; iussa tremit, sed amat.

Those things lie low so that my citizen may not perchance place his hope in them, and cast out the hope and good of the cross. The cross promises other homes, other honours, granting heavenly realms to its soldiers. Under the cross serves the king, but he is free; he is kept in place by the law, but he wears the crown; he trembles at the commands he receives, but he loves them. (*CM*, 38:25–30)

---

40. Smolak, "Beobachtungen zu den Rom-Elegien Hildeberts von Lavardin," 374.

In the end, Rome concludes that neither her emperors nor her senators, neither her soldiers nor her orators, who conquered the earth in her name, could ever achieve what the cross enabled: the possession of heaven (*crux dedit una polum*; *CM*, 38:36).

Carmen 38 is deeply rooted in the common Christian idea that Christian life is fully realized in the lowliness of the cross. What is surprising is the way in which Hildebert emphasizes the semiotic properties of the cross and its ability to break through the paradoxical reconciliation of opposites that made up the notion of magnificent decay and thwarted any further production of meaning. The novel semiotic order weaves a new network of significations, the equivalent of a new world to which life can refer. The cross that, with respect to *carmen* 36, guides the antithetical disposition of the second poem is—at least for Hildebert's addressees—the quintessence of life that has vanquished death and decay. Representing physical agony and its spiritual defeat, the cross is a symbol that is atemporal and subject to temporality at once.

At this point one could contend with some justification that even if *carmen* 38 solves the problem of a semiotically deadlocked situation in poem 36, it is itself another paradox and must—according to the logic of my argument—result in similar stagnation. This objection would be undeniable if it were not for another singularity of Hildebert's elegy, which leads directly back to Roland Barthes's reflections on the paradox. To make the connection, we have to consider in greater detail that in the second poem, Rome speaks from the perspective of the lyric *I*. While her praise of the cross fulfills the genre expectations that one might ascribe to a hymn, the memory of her imperial past lends her speech a narrative streak that utilizes the rough chronological order of "before" and "after" and a dynamic of outbidding that contrasts the two, implying a progression from one to the other.

The narration that the poem suggests is ultimately the characteristic that links it to Barthes. In wrapping up his thoughts on the antithesis and the paradox, Barthes states that the one who induces or supports the transgression in which the two aspects of the antithesis can be reconciled is the narrator. Her body is the site in which the opposites are "brought together" as a "composite substance." In other words, the narrator embodies the paradox. She is a supplement or an excess with respect to a discourse that the antithesis—as Barthes puts it—has already rhetorically "saturated." To use the familiar terminology again, the narrator breaks a taboo by disrupting the antithetical "harmony." It is by way of this excess, Barthes concludes, "that something can be told and the narrative begin."[41]

---

41. Barthes, *S/Z*, 28.

If with respect to the second poem we take the broken urban body of the narrator Rome as the site of the excess, then *carmen* 38 is not the end of signification caused by the paradox, as is the case in *carmen* 36. Instead, it is the place where a "world" of semiotic relations is newly established and a fresh (hi)story of continuing life begins—for Christians in general and for Hildebert as a Christian poet and theologian in particular.

Ever since Gregorovius made his statement about *carmen* 38 being an expression of Hildebert's regret, the seemingly irreconcilable ideological gap between the two Rome poems has received broad attention. Von Moos places it in a long tradition, initiated by Ambrose, that contrasted antique and Christian Rome, but he concedes that within a medieval context the kind of enthusiasm for the former that Hildebert displays is rather unusual.[42] In explaining the differences, von Moos strikes a psychological chord by claiming that the bishop felt conflicted and torn between nostalgia for an idealized antique past and latent disappointment about the Christian present that, in his perception, had lost some of its vigor. Admiration for the "old culture" seemed to get in the way of the still fairly new faith. *Carmen* 38 expressed a compromise in which the poet gave preference to the higher, heavenly principle because—despite wishing otherwise—he did not believe that reality offers the conditions for simultaneously worldly and spiritual fulfillment. Von Moos further supports this claim by pointing out that throughout his entire work, Hildebert shows little interest in salvation-historical temporality and only rarely refers to the end times or the last eon—which according to medieval historical thinking would have been his own—before Christ's second coming. He asserts that in accordance with many Christians who lived in the Gallo-Roman end phase, Hildebert nurtured a pessimistic attitude toward his own decadent time.[43] From this point of view, it might indeed look as if the ruins of *carmen* 36 were indicative of a historical awareness of the final stages in a teleological process that Hildebert—in an atypical gesture—replaced with the nontemporality of the otherworldly reign of the cross.

However, the semiotic perspective reveals that something else is at stake. After the collapse of Rome in the first poem, Hildebert establishes a new semiotic and semantic order. First, building a semiotic network in the sense of an "entirety of significations" means keeping a world-reference for individual human existence. Second, keeping a world-reference amounts to preserving a

---

42. Von Moos, *Hildebert von Lavardin (1056–1133)*, 241.
43. Von Moos, *Hildebert von Lavardin (1056–1133)*, 257. This position has been criticized by Tilliette, "Tamquam lapides vivi," 363.

historical point of view. The symbol of the cross, even though interpretations notoriously focus on its spiritual meaning, is a sign of paradoxical symbiosis between the essential aspect of Jesus's historical life and his function as the resurrected savior and provider of new spiritual life. Furthermore, it marks a new historical period, which is a revaluation of all values and at the same time a continuation of the Roman Empire that, with the destruction of Rome, and true to the idea of a translation of empire, gasps one last time in magnificent decay before it passes on its power.

The Melancholy of Living On

"L'hypothèse de Ferdinand Gregorovius ... ne semble guère fondée" (The hypothesis of Ferdinand Gregorovius seems completely unfounded), Jean-Yves Tilliette wrote about the historiographer's comment on Hildebert's *carmen* 38. Tilliette refers to a specific reading that claims that Gregorovius thought of the first poem as an early work while he considered the second poem to be Hildebert's revocation of a youthful gaffe.[44] Yet the German text is not unambiguous. Gregorovius, who mentions explicitly that Hildebert puts words in Rome's mouth, making her a self-declared convert from idolatry to Christianity, uses the temporal adverbs *noch* (still) and *nun* (now) to express Rome's state of mind "then" and "now": "'When I still [*noch*]', for so he [Hildebert] caused the unfortunate sibyl to speak, 'when I still took pleasure in idols, my army, my people and my marble magnificence were my pride ... but now [*nun*], I have exchanged the eagle for the cross'" (*GSRM*, 2:109; *HCRM*, 4.1:250). Gregorovius does not decide, however, whether this declaration reflects Hildebert's opinion and therefore refers to his progression from youth to maturity. If we nevertheless accept Tilliette's interpretation, then we also have to acknowledge that Gregorovius's supposition was not as misguided as Tilliette thought. At the very least, the historiographer recognized that for the bishop the transition from the first to the second poem was a question of how to live on. In Gregorovius's labeling of *carmen* 38 as Hildebert's self-consolation, Hans Blumenberg's idea of forms being essentially forms of solace resounds and lends an element of redemption to the idea of life's continuance.[45]

---

44. Tilliette, "Tamquam lapides vivi," 362.

45. However, while Blumenberg understands forms as making up for a fundamentally human biological deficiency, in Gregorovius' eyes Hildebert compensates for a moral and ultimately aesthetic shortcoming.

In many ways, the problem of living on was Gregorovius's concern as well. As we have already seen, the *History of the City of Rome in the Middle Ages*—in Gregorovius's understanding a chronicle of the past and an artwork at once—was the form that the historian explicitly identified with his life. Seen in this light, it reflects on both the work and the life that he constantly sought reassurance for the feasibility and practicability of his project. The sense that the undertaking was risky, subject to circumstance, prone to interruptions, and potentially even doomed to fail was ingrained in Gregorovius's self-perception from the very start of the research and writing process. In a journal entry from October 3, 1854, he reports:

> I propose to write the history of the city of Rome in the Middle Ages. For this work, it seems to me that I require a special gift, or better, a commission from Jupiter Capitolinus himself. I conceived the thought, struck by the view of the city as seen from the bridge leading to the island of S. Bartholomew. I must undertake something great, something that will lend a purpose to my life [*Ich muss etwas Grosses unternehmen, was meinem Leben Inhalt gäbe*]. I imparted the idea to Dr. Braun, secretary to the Archaeological Institute. He listened attentively and then said, "It is an attempt in which anyone must fail" [*Dies ist ein Versuch, an dem jeder scheitern muss*]. (RT, 53; RJ, 16)

The intimate connection between life, world, and form—to which *The Roman Journals* as a sort of mise en abyme of the constellation adds complexity and self-reflexive potential—necessitates the assumption that Gregorovius's oft-expressed concern for the beginning, the continuation, and the conclusion of his main work is, at the same time, a preoccupation with how and under which circumstances his life can continue and endure.[46] Writing on and living on become synonymous.

Yet even though Gregorovius juxtaposes his own birthday on the ruins of Rome and Hildebert's lament over the decayed city and despite the similarity in emphasis that both thinkers put on the notion of life, their concepts of what it means to live on are quite different. Aside from the obvious divergence in textual genre, Gregorovius's approach lacks Hildebert's reevaluation of cultural parameters. In the face of discontinuity, Gregorovius's attention does not seem to lie on drastic sea change. In the introduction to his German edition of the *History of the City of Rome in the Middle Ages*, Waldemar Kampf describes the

---

46. By *constellation* I am referring to the multilayered arrangement of texts, arguments, and temporal dimensions. While the *History of the City of Rome* is a chronicle of the past and explicitly identified as Gregorovius's life, *The Roman Journals*, a text that we might call a chronicle of the present, is a report about the progress of Gregorovius's work and a comment on his life—a life in which he produces the text that in turn he calls his real life, and so on.

author as a conservative voice within the history of ideas. According to Kampf, the political events of 1848 led to a breakthrough of realism with all its side effects: the emergence of the masses and the repression of the individual, the rise of empirical science and the devaluation of idealism's philosophical systems, the focus on the state and political events and the increasing alienation from cultural-historical considerations. Together with Jacob Burckhardt, Kampf counts Gregorovius among those historians who, intellectually deeply rooted in the second half of the eighteenth and the first half of the nineteenth centuries, concentrate their analytical energy on the human condition rather than the political life of the young nation-states. This emphasis meant that rather than disavowing the prerevolutionary conditions, thinkers with a cultural-historical focus sought to see links and coherences between the past and the present.[47]

It is therefore perhaps not surprising that, although Gregorovius chose to cover Rome's fate from its first fall in 410 to the Sack of Rome in 1527, telling Rome's story from decay to decay, he insisted that ruins do not just mark ruptures and breaks but have a history of their own.[48] Bringing the distinction between antiquity and Christianity into play, Gregorovius states that "the ruins of antiquity survived . . . [They] have their place in this History as well as the Church and the Papacy" (*GSRM*, 1:52; *HCRM*, 1:115). The argument that leads to this conclusion initially seems to imply that discontinuity is the actual signature of the relationship between antiquity and Christianity. "[A]t the beginning of the fifth century," Gregorovius writes in the very first book of the *History of Rome*, "all these splendid buildings of the Romans [*diese erhabenen Bauwerke der Römer*], closed, deserted, despised, dishonoured [*verlassen, verschlossen, verachtet und ungeehrt*], had become mere lifeless pomp made up of dead stones [*tote Pracht von totem Stein*]. Christianity had acquired possession of the immense city, but remained utterly powerless [*unvermögend*] to absorb the unfathomable inheritance of the fathers into its new life [*dieses unermessliche Erbe der Väter in sein neues Leben aufzunehmen*]" (*GSRM*, 1:51; *HCRM*, 1:114, translation modified). The passage reads like a comment on Hildebert's two Rome poems. New Christian life—thus the unmistakable proposition—has cut ties with the pagan past by thoroughly renouncing "a perfectly developed civilization." Only occasionally does Christianity make selective and in itself fragmentary use of the antique remains, by adopting "a solitary temple, a group of columns, or a few blocks of marble." Nevertheless,

---

47. Kampf's comment can be found in *GSRM*, 4:9–15.

48. With the inclusion of the Sack of Rome, Gregorovius established yet another relation between the past and contemporary Italian politics by framing his study with an event that in the sixteenth century put a preliminary end to Italy's early hopes for independence.

Gregorovius ultimately finds that "the Rome of antiquity was not completely severed from the new Rome. The Christian city rose within its ancient predecessor and harmonized with it, pagan and Christian elements blending together." In the end, Rome is a unique example of a city's double antique and Christian nature (*GSRM*, 1:51–52; *HCRM*, 1:114–15).

This position is decidedly different from Hildebert's, which overcomes the disconnect between antique and Christian Rome in a leap of semiotic virtuosity, making use of the potential of the paradox and conceptualizing life as continuing beyond historical rupture but in completely new—that is to say, Christian—form. In comparison, Gregorovius seems to offer a semiotic compromise, which in light of conflicting antique and Christian cultural paradigms includes antique fragments in Christianity's material culture as a form of *spolia* (reused matter), and they are signs that, despite their fragmentariness and because of their material tangibility, are apt to account for continuity with the past. Gregorovius's focus does not rely on a reevaluation of cultural values and a reconfiguration of symbols and signs, but it counts, instead, on forms of gradual transition. This emphasis indicates a specific understanding of history that suggests that if continuity is at stake, continuity is also the solution. It further means that Gregorovius rejects what, in Hildebert's strategy, emerged as an element of sudden solace and redemption. Living on is not a matter of salvation but of historical progression that, instead of suspending the present's relation with the past, works toward carefully preserving it.

For Gregorovius, one way to emphasize continuity was to display historiographical—and, as was his ambition, artistic—textual production as a grieving process that connected the living with the dead and anticipated death from within life. In March 1856, Gregorovius seems to have suffered a breakdown, caused by his work on the history of Rome. On Easter Sunday he notes:

> On February 24 [I] was obliged to give up my work in the library, because I had lost the necessary energy. I have since spent a gloomy month. Such are the consequences of overwork. March and April are dismal months for me, since the best has passed away [*da ist mir das Beste hinweggestorben*]. On the 16th I made my will and set my affairs in order. The *History of the City of Rome* stands over me in the night like some far-off star [*wie ein fernes Gestirn*]. Should fate allow me to finish it, no suffering in the world would be too great for me resolutely to endure. (*RT*, 60; *RJ*, 25)

His first encounter with Italy was a time spent in deep depression, following the death of a friend:

> I had previously imagined that all the inspiring influences of my life would expand in Italy, awaking within me a wealth of new ideas; but my mind

remained dormant, and this state of blank inertion troubled me [*dieser öde Zustand machte mich sehr unglücklich*]. I doubted whether I was capable of producing anything that would live [*Ich verzweifelte daran, dass in mir noch etws Zukunftsvolles lebte*]. I almost despaired of my future [*Ich gab mich fast verloren*]. (*RT*, 44; *RJ*, 2)

At the same time, grief appears to have impaired the flux of Gregorovius's creativity, compromised his confidence in the course of continuing life-time, and cast doubt on the possibility of a livable future. It is not until the journal entries of later years that, for all of Gregorovius's self-centered introspection and withdrawal from the world, there is simultaneous evidence of a difficult but continuous creative process. The Rome project advanced even if it did so slowly and intermittently.

The key to an understanding of this apparent contradiction lies in an often made comparison between Gregorovius's decision to take on the task of documenting the history of Rome in the Middle Ages and Edward Gibbon's resolution to record the decline of the city, which he later extended to a history of the fall of the Roman Empire. In fact, Gregorovius himself suggested the connection. "I am reading Gibbon again," he noted in his journal. "His work . . . was inspired by Rome. To him the idea came on the Capitol, to me . . . on S. Bartolomeo, in sight of Trastevere and the Imperial palaces. I no longer remember the date" (*RT*, 59; *RJ*, 25). Gibbon's moment of inspiration has been recounted by the historian in his autobiography. He talks about an almost religiously solemn experience among the ruins of the Capitol when the layers of time overlapped to inspire a work about the destruction of "the solid fabric of Roman greatness."[49] Gibbon recounts, "It was at Rome, on the fifteenth of October, 1764, as I sat musing amidst the ruins of the Capitol, while the barefooted fryars were singing Vespers in the temple of Jupiter, that the idea of writing the decline and fall of the City first started to my mind." Gibbon goes on to speak of the unique effect that Rome had on his imagination, simultaneously kindling and satisfying his enthusiasm and curbing his curiosity for "meaner objects."[50] Christopher Woodward called Gibbon's *Decline and Fall* "one of the most optimistic books ever written." He highlights the historian's "Enlightenment optimism," his confidence in progress toward perfection, and his belief that humankind would never again fall back into barbarism. Rise and fall, thus his conviction, was not a necessary, endless cycle.[51]

---

49. Gibbon, *History of the Decline and Fall of the Roman Empire* (1802), 3.
50. Gibbon, *Autobiographies* (1986), 302.
51. Woodward, *In Ruins*, 188–89. See also Hell, "Imperial Ruin Gazers," 172.

In contrast, and even though the setting in which he made up his mind to venture on the Rome project is reminiscent of the one that his older colleague depicted, Gregorovius's moment of initiation into his work is contextualized very differently. He embeds the passage in two accounts about death: of the German painter Riepenhausen, whom he visited on his deathbed, and of Corsini, a former Roman senator, whose burial he witnessed. In this "deadly" setting, Rome appears as "the demon with whom I struggle; should I issue victorious from the contest—that is to say, should I overcome this omnipotent and universal being (*Weltwesen*) and make her a subject of exhaustive inquiry and artistic treatment for myself—then shall I also be a triumphator" (*RT*, 61; *RJ*, 28). At this early point in the writing process, Gregorovius implies that he viewed Rome as an aesthetic challenge that is intertwined with accounts of death. More than twenty years later, in a comment on the stubborn refusal of the Romans to grant him, the foreign historiographer of their city, citizenship, Gregorovius laid out that "work" to him had never been about earning someone's gratitude or their reward but that his relationship with work had always been personal and artistic (*künstlerisch*). To Rome's chronicler, scientific matter (*wissenschaftlicher Stoff*) was only significant if it served as material for the formative idea (*die gestaltende Idee*). The History of the City of Rome, Gregorovius concludes, could not have taken shape if it hadn't been for that day on the bridge Quatro Capi, when the enchanting, ideal image of Rome was suddenly reflected inside of him (*wenn nicht . . . auf der Brücke Quattro Capi das bezaubernde Idealbild Roms sich in meinem Innern abgespiegelt hätte*; *RT*, 61).[52] As Kampf stated, more than anything, Gregorovius's opus magnum was the result of artistic intuition (*GSRM*, 4:15).

Traditionally, the kind of grief that not only allows for artistic intuition but is rather the very source of creativity has been called *melancholy*. Aristotle's opening question in book 30 of *Problemata Physica* (953a)—where he asks why it is "that all those who have become eminent in philosophy or politics or poetry or the arts are clearly of an antrabilious [melancholic] temperament"—combines for the first time "the concepts of excellence and extraordinariness . . . with melancholia."[53] Ever since, the juxtaposition of melancholy and the force of imagination, the correlation of genius, knowledge, prophetic ability, and a fragile physical and mental state have been persistent motifs in Western culture. The eager medieval followers of the Greek physician Galen's humoral pathology further reinforced the association between

---

52. To my knowledge, there is no English translation of this part of the journal.
53. First quotation from Aristotle, "Problemata Physica" (1984). Second quotation from Földenyi, *Melancholy: Melankólia*, 7. Aristotelian authorship of the text is not verified.

melancholy and illness by insisting on an imbalance of the complexion of the melancholic's bodily fluids—mostly a preponderance of black bile—and the influence of Saturn, the star of melancholy that governs thoughts of death and desperation over the passing of time.[54] This medical explanation was blended with the theological paradigm of acedia, the indolence of the heart, a condition that originally described the debilitated mental state of a hermit who was subject to sensual temptation. This specific kind of passivity was linked to a lack of confidence that salvation was guaranteed, which then could lead to the deadly sin of desperation. Walter Benjamin would later make the same argument with respect to the baroque German tragic drama, when he spoke of the disappearance of eschatology (*Ausfall der Eschatologie*) in early modern times. Furthermore, the Middle Ages focused on the simultaneous hubris and vanity of the melancholic's intellectual endeavors. As the literary critic László Földenyi put it, for the medieval understanding, "[a] melancholic racks his brain over *unnecessary* things," and anything that is unnecessary is excessive with respect to the wholeness and flawlessness of God-made existence and therefore a disruption and an insult to the infallibility of the creator. Földenyi expands on this thought by drawing the conclusion that if melancholics reflected on the unnecessary, they ultimately speculated about *nothing*, joining the concepts of excess and lack, which unsettled the order of the universe and upset the closed medieval cosmos.[55] In the so-called early modern period, the term *melancholy* underwent a significant semantic transformation that originated mainly from poetic texts. Such works by the Italian philosopher Marsilio Ficino (1433–1499) marked a shift from an understanding of melancholy as a pathological character trait or a habit to that of melancholy as a temporary state of mind. Robert Burton termed the latter in the *Anatomy of Melancholy* (1621) "transitory melancholy which goes and comes upon every small occasion of sorrow, need, sickness, trouble, grief, passion, or perturbation of the mind."[56] Melancholy could now be perceived as a "subjective mood" that affected individuals occasionally and boosted their poetic and intellectual ability. It became the signature feature of artists and scholars and an indicator of their creative genius and knowledge.[57] The Enlightenment stigmatized the melancholic—and simultaneously the power of imagination that most

---

54. Klibansky, Panofsky, and Saxl, *Saturn and Melancholy*.

55. Földenyi, *Melancholy: Melankólia*, 58.

56. Burton, *The Anatomy of Melancholy* ([1621] 2001), pt. 1, sec. 1, mem. I, subs. 5, p. 143. With respect to the significance of Ficino's work, see Wagner-Egelhaaf, *Die Melancholie der Literatur*, 42–61.

57. Klibansky, Panofsky, and Saxl, *Saturn and Melancholy*, 217–18; Valk, *Melancholie im Werk Goethes*, 32.

pronouncedly defined him—as the stereotypical obstacle for the natural order of reason. The melancholic's self-sufficient withdrawal from the world and the often dangerous proximity of his condition to madness were considered provocations to the functioning of society.[58] Hartmut Böhme has deemed this denunciation of the melancholic to be the ultimate break between the aesthetic and the social realm that could never be truly reversed.[59] Romanticism inherited it, rendering its melancholics nostalgic, deeply solitary figures "at the boundary of human possibilities."[60] Böhme explicitly mentions the failed revolution of 1848 as the event that sealed the fate of the artist, who thenceforward was restricted to the subcultural sphere.[61]

On a more semiotic and discourse-theoretical note, Martina Wagner-Egelhaaf has carved out in her study *Die Melancholie der Literatur* (*The Melancholy of Literature*) that at the core of melancholy lies an experience of fundamental imbalance and disorder, which she ultimately interprets as a crisis of signification.[62] Walter Benjamin stated as much when he called the baroque melancholic a "brooder over signs" (*Grübler über Zeichen*) who allegorizes the world to compensate for its lack of a metaphysical point of reference, its absence of meaning.[63] Deprived of a metaphysical vantage point, things appear to the melancholic gaze as isolated fragments or ruins of an overarching, now unavailable complex of meaning.[64] The melancholic is reduced to pondering the sheer materiality of these scattered signs, and he is pained by their ambiguity, opacity, and arbitrariness, which he cannot decipher. In other words, melancholy is an expression of semiotic and semantic disturbance that points to something unspeakable and unrepresentable.[65]

In Gregorovius's work, diverse elements of tradition have merged to create a unique kind of melancholy that is beholden to the extraordinary closeness between life and form, and this relationship shapes the author's understanding of history. Gregorovius is isolated and nostalgic for the past like the Romantic ruin gazers of his time who sought hidden grandeur in the debris; his work is informed by a sense of immanence, the materiality of history and the

---

58. Schings, *Melancholie und Aufklärung* (1977), 47.
59. Böhme, "Kritik der Melancholie und Melancholie der Kritik" (1988), 264.
60. Földenyi, *Melancholy: Melankólia*, 206.
61. Böhme, "Kritik der Melancholie und Melancholie der Kritik," 264.
62. Wagner-Egelhaaf, *Die Melancholie der Literatur*, 162.
63. Benjamin, *Ursprung des deutschen Trauerspiels* (1991), 370.
64. Wagner-Egelhaaf, *Die Melancholie der Literatur*, 185.
65. See Horn, *Trauer schreiben*, 27. In Walter Benjamin's *Origin of German Tragic Drama*, allegory emerges as the figure that voids signs of their signification and provides them with new meaning.

signs of decay and mortality; the creativity he claims is constantly threatened by fear of failure, brought about by the transience of life and the disorder of the contemporary moment. Most evidently in contradistinction to Hildebert's spiritual renewal, which uses the potential of the paradox to transform antique ruin into Christian life and transliterates potential stagnation into semiotic and poetic productivity, Gregorovius's main work appears first and foremost as semiotically precarious, but it does not end in melancholy excess.[66] Its unrealized conclusion and the incompleteness of its form point directly to death but do not use the awareness of mortality as a semiotic turning point. On June 10, 1866, Gregorovius notes in *The Roman Journals*, "A severe chill, which I caught at Albano, left me good for nothing for a fortnight . . . I wanted to save this work from the ruin that we are about to encounter [*Aus dem Ruin, dem wir entgegentreiben, wollte ich diese Arbeit retten*]. I have begun to write chapter vii [of the *History of the City of Rome*]" (*RT*, 208; *RJ*, 252, translation modified).

Gregorovius's melancholy clearly has a retarding effect. The desire for closure and completion is oddly intertwined with a tendency to wait and linger, to blame the overwhelming magnitude of the process of formation and the dependency of the work on life and world for the recurring stagnation. This repeated delay warrants the question as to whether melancholy is ultimately a strategy that allows Gregorovius to postpone the ending of his work in order to gain life-time. The historiographer's journal entry from November 13, 1870, suggests that such a strategy is in the realm of possibility:

> My labours ended, Rome withers for me. I walk through the streets, follow the traces of my passion and enthusiasm, which I feel no longer, and it seems to me as if all those monuments which I investigated so eagerly, now looked down on me ghost-like and dead . . . to leave Rome means for me to take leave of my true life [*Rom verlassen heisst für mich von meinem wahren Leben Abschied nehmen*]. (*RT*, 298; *RJ*, 389)

One year later, however, the paradigm has shifted. In December, Gregorovius is on the verge of completing the *History of the City of Rome in the Middle Ages*. And while he admits that the fulfillment of his life's project makes him painfully aware of mortality, it seems that at this point the anxiety of finitude no longer applies to his work, which has turned into something bigger than life:[67]

---

66. I hereby do not want to argue that Hildebert was a melancholic but that he reconfigured the melancholic excess that Földenyi defined as the *skandalon* for medieval thought and turned it into a semiotics of redemption.

67. I assume that Gregorovius in the following quote speaks not only about the city of Rome but also about his work.

> When I have written the concluding survey, I shall have put the final touches to my life's work. This alters my attitude to Rome. I sever myself from Rome, which for me is becoming the legend of my little life [*Ich löse mich von Rom ab, welches für mich zur Legende meines kleinen Lebens wird*]. Nothing else can so painfully bring home to me the transient nature and instability of human things. (*RT*, 316; *RJ*, 417, translation modified)

The *History* takes the form of a legend, a piece of writing between historical fact and aesthetic invention that surpasses the limits of individual human existence and acquires universal significance. In the aesthetic form of the legend, Gregorovius's *History* enables a continuance of life-time as world-time. "I can say of myself," Gregorovius states in his final entry, "[that] I created that which did not exist; I threw light on eleven dark centuries in the city and gave the Romans the history of their Middle Ages. This is my monument here. I can therefore go away with a mind at ease. I could also willingly remain. But a self-conscious feeling struggles against the idea of surviving myself here in loneliness [*mich hier in Einsamkeit zu überleben*] and growing old in Rome, where everything is becoming new and transformed" (*RT*, 343; *RJ*, 458, translation modified). In Gregorovius's thinking, world-time is continuous time. In contradistinction to the turmoil of the world in which Gregorovius lives as well as the commotion of Hildebert's medieval semiotic adventure, Gregorovius's historical concept is not one of twists and turns. It draws on melancholy that glues the past to the present and the future; it slows down the pace of "the history of the world [that] rushes along with steam-like force" and ensures that history remains conscious of mortality (*RT*, 302; *RJ*, 396). But for all its decelerating powers, melancholy does not indicate the end of history. Melancholy brings to the fore that world-time has to be conceptualized as emerging from a slowly fading life-time and that the mediating force is what Gregorovius liked to see as aesthetic form.

On a late December day in 1872, Gregorovius summarized twenty years of labor in a passage that finally gave his project closure and his melancholy a cautious, hesitatingly optimistic streak of happiness:

> With 1872 closes a period of twenty years of life in Rome. I look back with satisfaction on this long space of time, during which, amid troubles indescribable, I have worked my way upwards to the light. My life's task is ended, and my work at the same time has been recognized by the City of Rome as worthy of its subject. Never have I felt myself so free or so happy. (*RT*, 328; *RJ*, 436)

Gregorovius and Hildebert, each in their respective historical moment, deal with the problem of living on in the face of discontinuity. Hildebert, even though he keeps with the medieval context from which he argues and leaves the final word to Christianity and salvation, ultimately sketches out a semiotics rather than an eschatology of living on, and he does so neither theologically nor philosophically but poetically. Gregorovius insists on the concept of continuity in a historical environment that bases itself on disruption and, antithetically to a century that moves away from the individual and turns toward crowds and masses, asserts that world-time is essentially aesthetically mediated life-time.

The next chapter turns to the seventeenth century and the problem of living on in Martin Opitz's translation of Seneca's tragedy *Troades*. In a period that, according to stereotype, was characterized by melancholy brooding over signs related to death, Opitz will uncover a possibility of living on enabled by the form of the translation.

6

Lucius Annaeus Seneca, Martin Opitz, and the Overcoming of Vanity

Die Welt kostet Zeit.

The world costs time.
HANS BLUMENBERG

"The devil knows that he has little time [*Der Teufel weiss, dass er wenig Zeit hat*]," Hans Blumenberg noted at the beginning of the second part of *Lebenszeit und Weltzeit* (*LW*, 71), quoting the biblical book of Revelation (Rev. 12:12). With this, he put in mythological terms what he would relate to the historical experience of world-time anxiety, the fear that life-time was too short to achieve anything of historical and political significance. Using the example of Hitler, Blumenberg highlighted the abhorrent consequences of this angst when it befalls a narcissistic personality with the power and the ambition to enforce the convergence of life-time and world-time. The "brevity of time" was "the source of evil [*Enge der Zeit ist die Wurzel des Bösen*]" (*LW*, 71), and the paragon of evil was the proclamation of total war and the purposeful maintenance of a temporal state of emergency in which world-time could be reduced to a single life-time.[1]

The following pages turn away from the perpetrators and turn to those left behind after a war has destroyed their world. This chapter explores the Stoic philosopher Seneca's tragedy *Troades*, which he composed around 54 CE, and the German poet Martin Opitz's translation of this work (*Trojanerinnen*) that he wrote in 1625, the seventh year of the Thirty Years' War. Emphasizing the triad of life, world, and form, but arguing from distinct historical points of view, Seneca and Opitz draw disparate conclusions from the loss and decay that surface in the mythology of the Trojan War.

With respect to Seneca's work, my main claim is that the problem with which he wrestles is not the shortness of life in contrast to the temporal abundance of the world but, on the contrary, ongoing life-time in the face of a

---

1. See chapter 2 on Hans Blumenberg and Walter Benjamin.

vanishing world and decreasing world-time. As I will show, Seneca's Troy is fashioned pronouncedly as a network of signs that makes up the Trojan women's world and the point of reference for their lives. The city's ruin deprives their lives of meaning. One could say that in a surprising fit of desperation, Seneca replaced the typically Stoic concern about how to lead a good life with the Trojan women's burning question about how to live at all. In his treatise on the shortness of life (*De brevitate vitae*), Seneca had argued that individual life is long enough if life-time is not wasted on vain purposes.[2] In *Troades*, however, life-time seems unduly long.

If for Seneca the main problem surrounding the mythology of Troy is an excess of life-time that has lost its capacity to signify, Opitz reinstates a signifying power through framing the relation between translation and original. With Opitz's work, translation as form comes into play. In simultaneous proximity to and distance from the original, it unfolds its transformative force in the Benjaminian sense: comprehensible only against the background of the source, the translation brings to the fore some of the inherent significance of the original, which in turn means that the original lives on in the form of the translation. The philological details of Opitz's *Trojanerinnen* and, most important, the paratexts that frame it reveal how the translator—in dialogue with his own situation as a witness of the Thirty Years' War—develops modes of reckoning with the experience of war-related vanity. In these paratextual spaces, Opitz reinstates semiotic points of reference that Seneca's *Troades* had lost: in the preface to the reader, the dedication to the literary scholar August Buchner, and the notes to his translation, for example.

"Campus ubi Troja fuit": Seneca's *Troades*

Seneca's play opens with the Trojan queen Hecuba mourning over the ruins of Troy.[3] The city is shaken to its foundations, the pillars and protecting walls have collapsed. Consuming fire, rubble, ashes, and finally the pillaging of the

---

2. Cooper, *Pursuits of Wisdom*, 144–225. Cooper lays out how Stoicism understood good life as a matter of order in the sense of living in harmony with the cosmos. – On the concept of the good in Stoicism, also see Pfau, *Minding the Modern*, 87–88. – It has been a subject of extensive discussion how Seneca's tragedies relate to his philosophy with advocates for both an understanding that saw the plays as case studies for Seneca's philosophy (e.g., Staley, *Seneca and the Idea of Tragedy*) and interpretations that focused on tragic aspects of his philosophy (e.g., Harst, "Germany and the Netherlands: Tragic Seneca in Scholarship and on Stage," 149–73). For an English translation of *De brevitate vitae*, see Seneca, *On the Shortness of Life* (2005).

3. In the section head, "Campus ubi Troja fuit" translates as "A field where Troy once stood." These words are spoken by Aeneas in the third book of Virgil's *Aeneid*.

defeated city are the motifs that shape the image of total destruction. Troy lies in ruins, and even these last signs of former greatness are going up in smoke above the battlefield. The Phrygian leaders have been murdered or have died in battle—Prince Hector at the hands of the Greek hero Achilles and King Priam at the hands of Achilles's son Pyrrhus—and the surviving Trojan women are about to be distributed among the victorious Greeks and dispersed as prisoners into their respective domains. Hecuba calls on gods, humans, and even the ruined city itself to witness that Troy's fate has been foretold, but that the Trojans, deaf to prophecy, did not listen. The queen's invocation is like a flash of consciousness and reveals a sudden awareness that this outcome was not inevitable. But the moment passes and Hecuba breaks off her mourning for Troy when she realizes that she is confronted by a fate that has already befallen her people: "I call the gods to witness (hostile though they are to me), and the ashes of my country ... all disasters that have happened ... I Hecuba saw first while great with child, and I voiced my fears. I was a futile prophetess before Cassandra."[4] Toward the end of her opening speech, when she addresses the chorus of her fellow prisoners, Hecuba shifts the focus of mourning away from the ruins of Troy and toward the trauma that has afflicted the Trojan women taken as slaves by Greek warriors. In the face of their calamity, her own lingering age appears as inadequately persistent (*vivax senectus*):

> But why, lingering old age [*vivax senectus*], lament the downfall of a city that is overthrown? Ill-fated one, face these fresh griefs; Troy by now is an old distress [*vetus malum*] ... Yet this [the destruction of Troy] is not enough for the gods above: even now the urn is casting lots, selecting a master for the daughters and daughters-in-law of Priam, and I shall follow—see, a worthless prize! One man betroths Hector's wife to himself, another hopes for Helenus' wife, another for Antenor's; there is even someone who desires your bridal bed, Cassandra. (*TW*, 147)

The women's fate appears as the ultimate misfortune that dwarfs Hector's and Priam's violent deaths. As a consequence, the Trojan king and prince are only transitional objects of grief:

HECUBA: Faithful companions of my fall, unbind your hair ... Let your old griefs return once more, but outdo the usual style of mourning: it is Hector we mourn for [*Hectora flemus*].

---

4. For the Latin text and the English translation, see Seneca, *Trojan Women*, in *Tragedies* (2018), 142–45 (hereafter cited as *TW*, with page number).

CHORUS: We have all unbound our hair . . . Hands, be violent, strike my breasts with mighty blows! I am not satisfied with the usual sound: it is Hector we mourn for [*Hectora flemus*].

HECUBA: Turn your mourning: pour out your tears for Priam now; this suffices for Hector.

CHORUS: Receive our mourning, king of Phrygia; receive our tears, twice-captured old man.

HECUBA: Turn your tears elsewhere: my Priam's death is not to be pitied, women of Troy . . . his neck will never bear the yoke of the Greeks in defeat. (*TW*, 152–55)

The portrayal of Hector's and Priam's downfall gives us an idea of the reason for Hecuba's insistence that the women's destiny is the real tragedy. Hector, who is mourned first, appears as personified Troy; his body is equated with urban spaces and architectural signs. The prince's last day is the day when the city ceases to resist and Troy is turned into a ruin: "Pillar [*columen*] of our country, delayer of doom, you were a defense for weary Phrygians, you were a wall [*murus*], and by your shoulders she stood buttressed for ten years; with you she fell [*tecum cecidit*] and Hector's last day was his country's also" (*TW*, 152–53). King Priam, in the words of the chorus, takes "everything" (*omnia*), with him when he dies, and he is considered blessed for this reason: "Blessed [*felix*] is Priam; Blessed are all who, dying in war, have taken with them their whole lost world [*omnia secum consumpta tulit*]" (*TW*, 154–57). For the chorus, both Hector and Priam are fortunate to no longer live after the decline of Troy. The chorus imagines them happily united in Elysium. Their blessed state is clearly not that of a successful reduction of world-time to the dimensions of life-time, but it originates instead in the grace of not having to live on after the end of everything—a grace of which the Trojan women are deprived.

How is one to understand the end of "everything"? It is the end of a world (and this is indeed how John G. Fitch renders this phrase in his 2018 translation). Against the backdrop of Hecuba's thoughts on appropriate and inappropriate grief, it is possible to specify with greater accuracy precisely what this world—the things that disappear with the dead and the decayed—entails. For one, the world is an assembly of intact urban architecture. The signs of Troy's integrity—such as pillars and walls—are metaphorically transposed onto Hector's body. Comparisons and analogies—for example, between the heroes of Troy and their city and narratives like Hecuba's retrospect that evokes Troy's former greatness—establish the city not only as a semiotic network but as a world in the sense of a social space with its own constellation of power and gender relations and a particular order of communal life. After the city's collapse, the abandoned women find themselves in a situation of utter contingency in which the order of signs is dissolved and social cohesion lost. The ultimate expression of their isolation and alienation from what used to be their world is that the lot determines their final destination.

That the loss of "everything" is a loss of semiotic and social relations and contexts that are tied to the city of Troy becomes visible in the following scene where the perspective shifts to the Greek camp. It seems at first that not only the relation between the Trojans and their city is a relation of world-reference, but that this is also true of the relation between Troy and its archenemy. The beginning of the second act is dominated by the indirect presence of the fallen Achilles who, temporarily resurrected from the dead, claims the reward for his achievements in the Trojan War in exchange for his countrymen's safe passage home:

> Go on, you idlers, carry away the honors owed to my hands, launch your ungrateful ships—to travel through my seas! It cost Greece no small price to appease Achilles' wrath, and it will cost her dear. Let Polyxena, betrothed to my ashes, be sacrificed by Pyrrhus' hand and quench my tomb's thirst. (*TW*, 157–59)

On behalf of his father, Pyrrhus insists that the Greeks grant Achilles's wish that Polyxena be sacrificed. In a heated debate with Agamemnon, Pyrrhus delivers a painstaking list of the wars Achilles has fought, only to conclude that the one against Troy would have sufficed to merit him the highest possible honors. Pyrrhus's reasoning in support of his father's cruel demand suggests that even from the point of view of the conquerors, represented by their greatest hero, Troy is the point of reference with which semiotic and semantic relations rise and fall.

Yet this view of Troy is put into perspective by other protagonists on the Greek side. Agamemnon, instead of fully acknowledging Achilles's achievements, teaches Pyrrhus a lesson in moderation and restraint. In Stoic terms, the general cautions Achilles's hotheaded son against the arrogance of the victor who ignores the vicissitudes of fortune that tend to turn abruptly and crush the supposedly lucky when they least expect it.[5] Regretful of the destruction of Troy, Agamemnon wants to preserve whatever signs of life remain: "I wanted the Phrygians beaten down and defeated; but as for being ruined and leveled to the ground [*ruere et aequari solo*], I would actually have prevented it . . . Whatever can survive [*superesse*] of Troy, let it remain [*maneat*]" (*TW*, 164–65).

---

5. For a thorough analysis of the Stoic elements in Agamemnon's argument, see Ortiz Delgado, "La moderación de las pasiones o indicios de estoicismo en las *Troyanas* de Séneca," 196–99.

Initially, Agamemnon's argument against Pyrrhus looks like an intervention against unnecessary cruelty and an expression of compassion for the Trojans. But the Stoic background and the semiotic circumstances allow for an alternative reading. The general's assumption that life still lingers in the ruins is, at the same time, a rejection of the idea that Troy fell with Achilles (and vice versa) and that the city's condition is the point of reference for Greek world- and life-time. The Stoic concept of self-preservation lies at the bottom of the general's fear that wrongdoing will come back to haunt him. In that sense, by emphasizing that the Greek world did not disappear with Troy, Agamemnon primarily promotes the persistence of Greek instead of Trojan life. Even Pyrrhus himself brings up an aspect of Achilles's death that dissociates it from the end of Troy, for he suggests that his father was meant to avoid the war altogether and grow old in peace: "Though bidden to run away from war, to draw out a sedentary life in lengthy old age [*longa sedens aevum senecta ducere*], and to outdo the years of the old man of Pylos, he ... confessed himself a man by taking up arms" (*TW*, 160–61). By pointing out his father's missed chance for a long life, Pyrrhus refers to what Blumenberg called the "insult" of ongoing world-time for a much shorter life-time. The persistence of Hecuba's age in the queen's opening monologue, which makes her endure life even though her world is gone, is diametrically opposed to the unrealized length of Achilles's life-time despite the continuance of the world. In short: There is considerable evidence that for the Greeks, life goes on after Troy and that now, after the war, a world exists where future (Greek) life will take place. After all, the whole conflict about Achilles's request centers on the conditions of the Greeks' return home. And while Agamemnon's pity attempts to veil that one world can survive only at the expense of the other, the verdict of the seer Calchas at the end of the scene finally spells out that Troy has to be erased without a trace. Not only does Calchas approve Achilles's right to Polyxena, but, in the name of the gods, he also demands the sacrifice of Hector's son Astyanax. The last male descendant of the Trojan royal dynasty seems to disturb the dynamic of loss and gain that determines the Greek-Trojan relationship, and he therefore has to be eliminated.

At first sight, Astyanax's existence seems to disprove that Priam takes everything with him when he dies. From the perspective of Odysseus, who in act 3 calls on Hector's wife Andromache to surrender the boy whom she has hidden in his father's grave, Troy will only be defeated and the Greeks safe when the future Hector (*futurus Hector*, i.e., Astyanax) is no longer alive: "Nervous trust in uncertain peace will always possess the Danaans, always fear at their back will force them to glance around and not allow them to disarm, as long as your son, Andromache, gives heart to the defeated Phrygians" (*TW*, 189).

While he is the Greek's last threat, Astyanax is designated by Andromache the Trojan's last hope: "O son, true descendant of a great father, one hope for the Phrygians and only hope for our ruined house [*spes una Phrygibus, unica afflictae domus*]" (*TW*, 183). However, a closer look shows that Astyanax, the apparently powerful promise of Troy's potential resurrection from the rubble, is embedded in a surprisingly weak network of signs. For one, the dead Hector is presented as an ideal against which Astyanax is measured. Like a revenant that evokes all the horrors of new Trojan power but is, at the same time, ghostly and unreal, Astyanax has a spectral and vague semiotic quality about him. He is simultaneously identical with Hector and different from him. When Odysseus inquires into Astyanax's whereabouts, Andromache—using the term *omnia* (everything) again—suggests that, with respect to the whole of Troy, Astyanax is only a part: "Where is Hector? Where are all Phrygians? Where is Priam? You look for the one, I look for my world [*unum quaeris: ego quaero omnia*]" (*TW*, 190–91). It is the princess's intention to downplay the threat her son poses for the Greeks and divert their attention from him. However, the way she phrases her answer to Odysseus also points to Astyanax's fragmentary character and a certain feebleness of his symbolic significance.

In a sense, Astyanax has been an outlier ever since he was born in an untimely manner, or as Andromache puts it: "O child born too late for the Phrygians, but too soon for your mother" (*TW*, 183). And there are further indicators that he is unreliable as a symbolic bearer of hope. Andromache recounts a frightening dream in which Hector commands her to save their son. But the clarity of the assignment is cast in doubt by the very frame of the dream and the description of Hector as a delusive shadow that fades in Andromache's arms when she awakes. What is more, Hector appears to regret that Astyanax is still alive and some of Troy therefore intact. He harshly rebukes Andromache not for lack of hope but once more for misdirected grief: "Leave off weeping. Are you lamenting Troy's fall? I wish she were completely fallen!" (*TW*, 179–81).

The connection between Astyanax and justified hope for the city is established explicitly only by Andromache, but even then with a gesture of hesitation and insecurity. In the face of overwhelming evidence for Troy's ill fate, her bold wish that Astyanax may be the one to avenge and rebuild the city, collect and protect its dispersed peoples, and return to the Trojans their land and their name shrinks to a modest plea for bare life. She disqualifies as hubris what Blumenberg called "infinite wishes" for a world-reference and settles for finite life-time and meaningless existence:

> Will that time come, that happy day, when you as defender and champion of Trojan soil will set up a resurgent Pergamum, bring home its citizens scattered

in exile, and give the country and the Phrygians back their own name? But remembering my lot I fear such grand prayers. Let us live: this is enough for prisoners [*quod captis sat est: vivamus*]. (*TW*, 182–83)

Ultimately, Astyanax is neither an embodiment of his city like Hector or Priam nor a reintroducer of "world" and its time. He confirms that at this point there is no world-time in the wake of ruined Troy and its fallen heroes, no hope that could be more than a form of nostalgia. Having life-time means nothing if there is no world-time to which it could be related. In that sense, the desperate rhetorical question that Andromache asks Odysseus after the discovery of Astyanax's hiding place is not only an expression of motherly love and conscientiousness toward Hector but also a judgment on the semiotic power of a literary figure: "Shall these ruins of a city reduced to ashes be quickened by this child? Shall these hands raise up Troy? Troy has no hopes, if she has such as these" (*TW*, 207).

Trojan hopelessness—caused by the loss of a world, unsettled for a brief moment but finally perpetuated by the unfulfilled expectations directed at Astyanax—is supplemented and confirmed when, toward the end of the tragedy, a messenger reports to Hecuba and Andromache that Polyxena and Astyanax have died. He recounts how a large group of Greeks gathered to see Astyanax leap from the only tower still standing in Troy and Polyxena being executed by Pyrrhus on Achilles's tomb. From hills and trees, remains of walls, burned roofs, and grave mounds, the audience watched, as in a theater (*theatri more*), the last act of the fall of Troy. Given the indebtedness of *Troades* to Stoic doctrine,[6] Astyanax's attitude of fearless pride in the hour of his death and the account of his jump as a voluntary act warrant the consideration of the scene as a portrayal not only of Stoic calm and serenity—a posture that Polyxena's quiet awaiting of the deadly strike suggests—but of suicide:

> The boy's steps did not lag as he made his way to the high walls. When he stood forward on the top of the tower, he turned his alert gaze this way and that, fearless in spirit . . . the boy grasped by the enemy's hand was fiercely proud . . . Of the whole crowd, he did not weep who was wept for . . . he leaped down of his own accord, into the midst of Priam's kingdom. (*TW*, 235)

Stoicism held that suicide was permissible if it served a common cause or if, conversely, continuing one's life did not.[7] Understood as suicide, Astyanax's

---

6. Trinacty, "Senecan Tragedy," 29–40, argues in favor of an understanding of Seneca's tragedies as philosophical. Astyanax and Polyxena are mentioned as examples of "Stoic resolve in the face of death" (36).

7. Irvine, *Guide to the Good Life*, 197–201.

death would emphasize what the semiotic point of view reveals: as a bearer of signs and world that could sustain the survivors' hope, he is of no avail to the Trojans. Like the buildings that constituted the city, Astyanax's body is finally crushed and scattered and turned into a ruin: "The features of that illustrious form, his face and those noble traces of his father, were disfigured as his weight hit the ground below. His neck was broken by the impact against stone, the skull split with the entire brain forced out. He lies a shapeless corpse" (*TW*, 237).

It is a disturbing afterthought that the unspeakable horror of the children's deaths is matched by the brutality that surrounds it. It pushes the boundaries of Seneca's often-noted self-conscious use of theatrical metaphors in which life appears as a tragedy and all the world as a stage.[8] In this instance, the Greeks play the role of spectators in the tragedy of world-dissolution: In contrast to the isolation of the Trojan women among the ruins of their world, the Greeks gaze at the spectacle in which the last Trojan descendants play the leading part. The Greeks thereby establish a theatrical community, a social context that implies world-reference. The semiotic consolidation of the Greek world is tinged with cruelty, occurring precisely at the moment in which all reference points for the Trojan world have been dissolved, rendered shapeless, like the broken corpse of Astyanax.

Against this background, the second appearance of the chorus after Agamemnon and Pyrrhus's dispute poses a major epistemological, narratological, dramatic, and hermeneutic challenge. The choral ode insists on the finality of death, a claim that stands in contradistinction to the end of the first act, wherein the chorus talks about Priam's and Hector's otherworldly Elysian joys:

> Is it futile to yield the soul to death? Are the wretched faced with further life [*restat miseris vivere longius*]? . . . All that is known to the rising or setting sun, all that is laved by Ocean with its blue waters twice approaching and twice fleeing, time will seize at the pace of Pegasus . . . Arrived at the pools that bind the gods' oaths, you no longer exist at all . . . After death is nothing [*nihil*]; death itself is nothing [*nihil*], the finishing line of a swiftly run circuit. Let the greedy drop hopes; the anxious, fears: greedy time and Chaos devour us [*Tempus nos avidum devorat et chaos*]. (*TW*, 176–77)

The passage is unmistakably another condensed literary examination of an aspect of Stoic philosophy; this time, immanence and the improbability of afterlife are at stake. Nevertheless, the scene caused confusion and released

---

8. See Littlewood, "Theater and Theatricality in Seneca's World," 161–73. For an examination of the metaphor of "world theater" with respect to stage entrances and exits, see Wild, "'They haver their exits and their entrances,'" 89–131.

an element of speculative energy among Seneca scholars who tried to come to terms with the play's structural and thematic inconsistencies that the choruses seemed to epitomize.[9]

One contentious debate concerned the speakers of the second choral ode. The classicist Andreas Heil claimed that the chorus had to be identified with the Greeks, an assertion that—as he was well aware—set him apart from the majority of Seneca scholars.[10] Heil mainly focused on Andromache's criticism of the grieving Trojan women at the beginning of act 3:

> Sad crowd of Phrygian women, why tear your hair, beat your breasts in sorrow and drench your cheeks with floods of tears? Our past sufferings were trivial, if these sufferings deserve tears... I would have followed my husband by now, if this one (indicating Astyanax) did not hold me... [he] prolongs my ordeal. (*TW*, 179)

He stated that the princess's comment is comprehensible only as an answer to the first appearance of the chorus and its mourning of the fall of Troy and not as a response to the second choral ode, which directly precedes it. Heil's other reason to introduce a Greek chorus was the failure of the second choral ode to respond to Kalcha's announcement of Astyanax's and Polyxena's impending executions—an omission that Heil considered irreconcilable with the position of the Trojan women. Yet to make sense of his own belief that it was the Greeks who pondered the comfort of death's finality after the complete obliteration of the Trojans had been predicted, Heil was forced to make numerous assumptions about the staging of the tragedy that he ultimately struggled to support.[11] In what follows, I will show that a reading of the second choral ode that stays closer to the text reveals unexpected facets of the complex passage and allows insights into its function.

---

9. See, e.g., Zwierlein, *Die Rezitationsdramen Senecas*; Fantham, *Seneca's "Troades"*; Scherer, "Zur Funktion des zweiten Chorlieds der *Troades* des Seneca," 572–78. That Seneca's philosophical argument is not consistent throughout his work has been pointed out with respect to the second choral ode by Rosanna Marino; see Marino, "Il secondo coro delle *Troades* e il destino dell'anima dopo la morte," 57–73.

10. Heil, *Die dramatische Zeit in Senecas Tragödien*. Heil's argument mainly emerges from a discussion of an essay by William Owen; see Owen, "Time and Event in Seneca's *Troades*," 118–37.

11. Heil's argumentation is thorough and supported by evidence from the manuscripts. However, its persuasiveness is limited because he can only speculate about crucial elements of his concept, as for example whether or not the chorus was present onstage or received its information about the situation in the Greek camp and among the Trojans offstage. See Heil, *Die dramatische Zeit in Senecas Tragödien*, 130, 159.

The first noteworthy observation is that almost every sentence from the second choral ode can be applied to either the Greeks or the Trojan women, or both. The introductory remarks—"Are the wretched faced with further life [*restat miseris vivere longius*]? . . . All that is known . . . time will seize at the pace of Pegasus"—cohere with the situation of the Trojan women if the supposition is that they are cursed to stay behind after everything (*omnia*) is gone and therefore hope for their own swift end. Considered from the perspective of their enemies, the sentence bears an aspect of consolation. Understood as the reaction of the war-weary Greeks when they hear of Achilles's postmortal reappearance that could potentially suck them back into the cycle of endless war, the expression of certainty about death's reliable finality gives them solace. The same applies to the thoughts on nothingness: "After death is nothing; death itself is nothing, the finishing line of a swiftly run circuit." Spoken by the Greeks, these ideas express potential comfort. Spoken by the Trojan women and related to their wish to die, the "nothingness" that follows death and the "nothingness" of death itself correspond to "everything" that disappears with Priam. In that sense, death is an empty point of reference that in turn refers to nothing.

The last sentence to be considered here speaks of greedy time and chaos: "Let the greedy drop hopes; the anxious, fears: greedy time and Chaos devour us [*Tempus nos avidum devorat et chaos*]." While, at first sight, the mention of the eager and the anxious seems to include both the Trojans and the Greeks, a closer look suggests that the Trojans should be excluded from both cases because greed and anxiety require a frame of reference that allows for hope or fear. Such a frame is missing on the Trojan side. However, there is also the personal pronoun of the first-person plural (*nos*/us) that deserves attention. Grammatically speaking, it can serve either to denote the collective of the eager and the anxious or it can be understood as a third entity that shares the fate of the other two—namely, to be consumed entirely. A similar problem emerges with respect to the grammatical subject. In addition to leaving open who is being devoured, the Latin text leaves open who does the devouring. The possibilities are either time by itself or time together with chaos—that is, formless primeval matter. The first case sets up chaos as a direct object, falling prey to time in exactly the same manner as the collective of the chorus. The second option assumes that time and chaos cooperate in the endeavor to consume their objects.

Tradition supports the first reading and thus the emphasis on the greediness of time.[12] Yet this interpretation is by no means indisputable, and it can seem

---

12. For the topos of greedy time, see Koerner, "Mortification of the Image," 85. Koerner refers to Ovid's *Metamorphoses*, Martin Luther's sermon on Christ's ascension from 1527, and the etymological relation between *mors* (death) und *morsus* (bite).

entirely implausible, depending on how one translates the Latin/Greek *chaos*.[13] Its weaker meanings such as "abyss," "darkness," or "obscurity" suggest that a world exists as a point reference but that, consumed by time, it is about to come to an end. Consequently, the sentence reflects the situation of the Greeks. But if one supposes that by *chaos* Seneca means "primeval matter out of which the orderly cosmos was built," a different picture emerges. Against the backdrop of the loss of world that the Trojans have suffered, there are good reasons to consider *chaos* as a sort of worldlessness in the sense of unformed matter that is distinctive from the state before and after the world.[14] It offers no points of reference for the creation of meaning or a reason to live on.

In contradistinction to those scholars who understand Seneca's work as an exercise in constancy and perseverance, I claim that at the root of Seneca's historical thinking on display in *Troades* lies a rejection of the concept of continuity. The tragedy erases the Virgilian idea of an enduring empire that the Trojan refugee and progenitor of Rome, Aeneas, preserves. In this way, the aspect of "fearless indifference" in the face of nothingness or even the hope for a "happy continuation of life" take a backseat.[15] Looking forward to the Seneca reception in the so-called baroque era, the Stoic's emphasis of an extreme form of *vanitas* (vanity, nothingness) becomes a conspicuous feature of the text instead. Throughout the play, Seneca uses *vanitas* and its derivatives (even if scarcely), which will evolve into key terms of baroque spirituality, art, and poetry; each time the concept appears, it refers to deceptive, opaque, and instable signs and the time lost trying to decipher them or apply them to an object.[16]

---

13. See Kurdzialek, "Chaos," 980. Kurdzialek points out that in Stoic understanding, chaos is characterized by indeterminacy, formlessness, and disarray—in other words, by the same traits that apply to Plato's concept of a primary, orderless mass. See also Plato, *Timaeus*, 33, 30a.

14. It supports this reading that there are editions of *Troades*—and Martin Opitz used one of them by Petrus Scriverius—that inserted a comma before "et chaos." This solution adds a third option to the possible translations—namely, that time consumes us, which results in chaos (translatable as: Time devours us, and then: chaos). Opitz did not exploit this possibility for his translation.

15. The two aspects have been pointed out by Stroh, "Troas," 447.

16. See, e.g., *TW*, 196–97, where Agamemnon argues against Pyrrhus that "sceptered power" is "anything but a name overlaid with false glitter [*vano fulgore*]"; in the second choral ode (*TW*, 206–7), the chorus states that our spirit disappears as smoke fades [*ut . . . fumus . . . vanescit . . . spiritus*]; in *TW*, 238–39, Ulysses responds to Andromache, who accused him of being a coward, with the words, "The courage of Ulysses is known well enough to the Danaans, and too well to the Phrygians. There is no leisure to waste the day in empty words [*non vacat vanis diem conterere verbis*]: the fleet is weighing anchor."

If Seneca's tragedy implicitly refuses the Virgilian emphasis on the transfer and continuity of empire, perhaps this is because—as an inhabitant of Caligula's, Claudius's, and Nero's Rome—the philosopher perceived the Eternal City as a ruin that could not be restored.[17] However, there lies a certain irony in the fact that in order to express this thought, Seneca heavily draws on literary tradition: on Euripides's plays *Hecuba* and *Troades*, Ovid's *Metamorphoses*, and Virgil's *Aeneid*, among other texts.[18] Yet this ambiguity reflects on a larger scale the ambiguity that lurks in the semiotic and even grammatical details of his work. Such an ambiguity will allow Opitz the opportunity to align himself with Seneca and simultaneously to differ from him, even within the formal boundaries of a translation. The similarities and differences in emphasis to which I will now turn can only be understood adequately if they are considered as the result of an aesthetic as well as a historical reflection.

Tampering with Time: Martin Opitz's *Trojan Women*

The reception of Seneca's work among Roman writers, thinkers, and rhetoricians was mixed, to say the least. Reserved, somewhat cautious acknowledgments of his style and philosophical position coexisted with straightforward rejection or even disregard. The tide turned with the growing influence of Christianity. The appearance of Seneca's brother Gallio as Saint Paul's advocate against the Jews in the Acts of the Apostles (18:12–17) and a fourth-century forged correspondence between Saint Paul and Seneca himself document the high esteem in which the Stoic was held in Christian circles and the extent to which he was considered an authoritative figure for the young religion. In *De anima* 20, the church father Tertullian famously claimed him for the Christian cause: "Seneca saepe noster" (Seneca is often one of us), and the poet and Christian apologist Lactantius characterized him as the most astute of all the Stoics ("omnium Stoicorum acutissimus") because of the perceived proximity of his thinking to Christian ideas.[19]

These positive reactions were not limited to Seneca's moral-philosophical writings. His tragedies—the only surviving tragic works of Roman antiquity—received broad recognition throughout the entire Roman Empire. They influenced late antique grammarians and poets such as Prudentius and Sidonius

---

17. See Albrecht, *History of Roman Literature*, 1161; for this question in relation to the problem of dating the *Troades*, see Seneca, *Troades* (2001), 8–9.

18. For a discussion of Seneca's sources, see Calder, "Originality in Seneca's *Troades*," 75–82.

19. Albrecht, *History of Roman Literature*, 1194–95; Tertullianus, *De anima*; Lactantius, *Divinarum institutionum libri septem*, passage 8.23.

and the philosopher Boethius, whose *Consolatio Philosophiae* contains formal allusions to the dramas. Boethius's treatise also names Seneca—who was ordered by Emperor Nero to kill himself—alongside Socrates as an example of philosophical martyrdom. As we approach the so-called Middle Ages, however, this picture changes. The German classicist Winfried Trillitzsch pointed out that even in the centuries immediately after Seneca's death, his readers—only vaguely aware of the existence of Seneca the Older—started to mistakenly attribute the father's rhetorical texts to the son. Instead of distinguishing between the older rhetorician and the younger philosopher and dramatist, the divide was made between Seneca the rhetorician and moral philosopher—along with his perceived Christian attitude—and Seneca the pagan author of the tragedies. As one might expect, the early Middle Ages had great appreciation for the former while the tragedies had faded into oblivion. They started to reappear sporadically during the Carolingian Renaissance, with references to the works occurring in poems, grammar books, and chronicles. More opportunities for the reception of Seneca's tragedies were made possible in the eleventh and twelfth centuries by the codex *Etruscus Laurentianus* 37.13, which marked the beginning of the manuscript tradition and by the heavily copied so-called *A* text.[20] In the twelfth century, Seneca's dramas were used in classrooms and as a source of maxims. But it would not be until the fourteenth century that the tragedies were properly rediscovered. Starting in Italy, the late Middle Ages constituted the period in which Seneca's influence on European tragic style started to gain momentum. The first play of the early Renaissance that imitated the classical Roman style was Albertino Mussato's Latin drama *Ecerinis* from 1315.[21]

The *editio princeps*, or first printed edition, of Seneca's tragedies appeared in Ferrara in 1484. It was followed almost immediately by a German edition and enthusiastic interest from German humanists—most prominently Conrad Celtis—and reformers such as Philipp Melanchthon, who appreciated the moral benefit of the dramas. Nevertheless, the authorship of the tragedies and the reconciliation of *Seneca philosophus* and *Seneca tragicus* remained much-discussed issues throughout the subsequent centuries. While the Paduan prehumanist circle around Mussato had correctly ascribed Seneca's dramas and the moral-philosophical writings to one and the same person, Petrarch, who had been an avid Seneca reader in his youth, revived doubts about the Stoic's

---

20. Rouse, "The *A* Text of Seneca's Tragedies," 93–121.
21. Trillitzsch, "Seneca tragicus," 120–36; Albrecht, *History of Roman Literature*, 1194–96; Ferri, "Transmission," 45–49.

authorship of the former.²² The discussion did not cease until the seventeenth century, and it left its mark on the Seneca editions that, by the so-called baroque era, had become abundant.²³ The Stoic's work and, most of all, the perceived tensions between philological style and philosophical substance occupied the minds of such thinkers as the Flemish humanist Justus Lipsius and the Dutch poets and scholars Daniel Heinsius, Hugo Grotius, and Joseph Justus Scaliger.²⁴ Their influence on German poets—most important, on Martin Opitz and Andreas Gryphius—resulted in an unprecedented Seneca revival in baroque German tragic drama.²⁵

When Martin Opitz (1597–1639) translated Seneca's *Troades* in 1625, Germany was seven years into a political, social, and religious strife that involved most of Europe and would leave the Habsburg Empire in ruins. Contemporary historians have called the Thirty Years' War "Europe's tragedy," "European catastrophe," or "German trauma."²⁶ For Martin Opitz, who was born in Bunzlau in Silesia and died from the plague before the end of the war, it was most likely all of the above—or at least this is what we can gather from his works. Opitz did not comment politically on the events of his lifetime, but his poems, translations, prose works, and poetics contain countless allusions to his disastrous present, and they are abound with war-related motifs.²⁷

In *Ex bello ars*, Nicola Kaminski suggests that Opitz's 1624 *Buch von der deutschen Poeterey* (*Book of German Poetics*)—a text widely regarded as having revolutionized German poetic composition and earned Opitz the title of "founder of German literature"—did not emerge from an appreciation of the beautiful and idyllic or from a care for literature and language but from Moritz of Orange's army reform. Kaminski claims that the rhythms of the military lockstep resound in Opitz's poetic meters.²⁸ According to Kaminski, Opitz conducted a religiously motivated military campaign through trans-

---

22. Trillitzsch, "Seneca tragicus," 120–36.

23. Harst, "Germany and the Netherlands," 154, mentions the editions by Martín Delrío (1576), Justus Lipsius (1588), Daniel Heinsius and Joseph Scaliger (1611), Thomas Farnabius (1613), Petrus Scriverius (1621), and Johann Friedrich Gronovius (1661).

24. Harst, "Germany and the Netherlands," 155.

25. Trillitzsch, "Seneca tragicus," 120–36.

26. "Europe's tragedy" is used by Wilson, *Thirty Years War*. "European catastrophe" (*europäische Katastrophe*) and "German trauma" (*deutsches Trauma*) are used by Münkler, *Der Dreissigjährige Krieg*.

27. See Becker-Cantarino, "Opitz und der Dreissigjährige Krieg," 38–52. The most obvious example are Opitz's poems *Trostgedichte in Widerwertigkeit des Krieges* (*Poems of Consolation in the Adversities of War*) from 1633.

28. Moritz of Orange popularized the lockstep, and it finally helped him succeed in the decades-long Dutch revolt (1568–1648) against Roman Catholic Habsburg.

lation with the goal of occupying foreign territory (other languages) and populating it with German words, meters, and subjects. Part of this undertaking was the use of the Alexandrine verse—a meter that Opitz popularized and applied to translate the iambic trimeters and anapests of *Troades*, as well as other texts—but with a German accentuation. In other words, for Opitz, the Thirty Years' War was a source of art.[29]

Kaminski's ideas are innovative because she detects an aesthetic paradigm where others—as I will show in this section of the chapter—have seen Opitz's attempt to apply Seneca's Stoicism in a situation of crisis as a mere moral and genre-related operation. However, with respect to *Troades*, her argument reaches the limits of its own metaphor. For Opitz, even though his is the first translation of a Seneca tragedy into the German language, does not colonize the original as if in a military campaign. Underneath the surface of a seemingly neo-Stoic approach, Opitz transforms his source in a semiotic and temporal sense. The result is an overcoming of the *vanitas* to which Seneca surrendered, not by means of a reverence for Seneca's philosophical project but by way of structural changes. Almost in passing, Opitz contradicts the common stereotype that the baroque is a time of inescapable vanity and the omnipresence of death. His work turns out to be an exercise not in enduring life but in continuing a life that is free to set a purpose for itself.

Martin Opitz twice points out the analogy between the situation of the Trojan women and the situation of Germany in the Thirty Years' War: first in the dedication of his Seneca translation to August Buchner, and then in the preface to the reader. In the dedication to Buchner, who appears to have encouraged the translation, Opitz embeds the comparison in a complex combination of aesthetic arguments, on the one hand, and historical and power-political considerations, on the other. Such arguments reveal an idiosyncratic approach to the concept of time. Opitz describes how he went on a journey in Silesia and, having nothing better to do and being unable to remain idle, started to work on a translation of *Troades*. Surprised by how little effort this undertaking required, he decided to translate the whole tragedy. Opitz insists on the significance of time in this context by pointing out how he started his work in a situation of leisure and abundance of time and how, somewhat contradictorily, the translation was finished in the shortest time possible:

> And since I could not find anything else to do and because I am incapable of leisure, I tried to translate the almost divine beginning of *Troades*—compared to which there is nothing more brilliant in that genre—into our language and

---

29. Kaminski, *Ex bello ars oder Ursprung der "Deutschen Poeterey."*

meter . . . In any case, because of the ease with which I handled most of it, this lovely folly [*amabilis haec insania*] teased me and I thought that I would achieve something worthwhile if I started work on the entire tragedy, particularly because my distance from my books did not allow that I dedicate myself to more important studies . . . Incidentally, I dedicated them [the *Trojanerinnen*] to you, most learned man, because I could—if an excuse were necessary—make plausible on your, an eyewitness's, word how I dedicated to this cause only few hours, virtually doing something else simultaneously.[30]

This passage allows for two possible interpretations. One option is that the lack of time that Opitz is so eager to emphasize is an admission of aesthetic deficiency. The other possible reading suggests that the opposite is true and the time deficit is a benchmark of aesthetic virtuosity.[31] The easiness of the task that Opitz faced might underline the resulting similarity between the highly praised original and the translation or, where facility is associated with lack of care, it could be an excuse for the disparity between the two. Whichever option seems more likely, the important point is that in both cases Opitz relates the question of artistic performance to a reflection on time: one whereby a temporal compression is foregrounded in the production of art either to elevate or excuse the quality of the product.

Moreover, time is the category that connects aesthetics, history, and power-political considerations. Opitz characterizes the war as a situation in which the accelerated loss of education and culture require urgent counterefforts, which he tried to provide by offering a quick publication of the German *Troades*. Opitz explicitly states that the translation—understood as an educational and cultural project—is politically significant because it has an impact on the foundation and the stability of the state. This ultimately means that the aesthetic act, which was accomplished under the condition of time

---

30. All translations mine. See the Latin text in Opitz, *Gesammelte Werke* (1979; hereafter cited as OGW), 429; German translation in Opitz, *Lateinische Werke* (2011; hereafter *LA*), 50–51: "Cumque, ut sum otii impatiens, aliud cum agerem non occurreret, divinum plane Troadum initium quoque nihil extat in hoc genere luculentius, in nostrum sermonem numerosque convertere conatus sum . . . me certe ob facilitatem qua pleraque illius mihi exciderant, amabilis haec insania lusit, ut operae pretium me me facturum crederem, si tragoediae universae manus admoverem, cumpraesertim haec a libellis meis absentia studiis gravioribus incumbere me non pateretur . . . Ceterum tibi illas propterea inscripsimus, Vir eruditissime, quod, sive aliqua excusatione opus est, tua μάρτυρος αὐτόπτου fide probare satis possim, quam sine omni cura et fere aliud agendo huic rei paucas horas dederim."

31. For the devaluation or, on the contrary, the praise of *Troades* in the so-called baroque, see Schings, "Seneca-Rezeption und Theorie der Tragödie" (1974), 523.

pressure—according to Blumenberg *the* war-specific time concept—enables historical and political continuity:

> I would have postponed the publication if... I did not assume that it is also desired by those whose influence and benevolence we trust, with respect to which we rightly disregard some uncultured minds. The enemies of the Muses and any kind of education may resentfully acknowledge that even in these dreadful adversities of the civil wars there are still very significant and great men, who cultivate and protect the renown of our sciences without which states do not seem to stand on solid enough ground.[32]

The reference to "our (female) prisoners of war" (*captivae nostrae*) finally brings home how inextricably Seneca's literary product and the present historical situation, the historical and mythological past, and Opitz's translation become blurred together:

> May our (female) prisoners of war have the courage to step out into the free air and publicly, before everyone's eyes, show through their example that this evil is not new, that most powerful cities, entire kingdoms and provinces are being destroyed and razed to the ground. They may also share with us their former remedy against the pain, however it may have looked: a fate that others have suffered before us and now so many are suffering with us can be endured with greater equanimity.[33]

The possessive pronoun of the first-person plural and the use of the present tense in combination with the mention of the suffering women make it difficult to distinguish—at least in the first sentence—between temporal and historical dimensions or forms of representation. The Thirty Years' War, Seneca's Rome, the fate of Troy, and Opitz's translation coalesce with the explicit goal of alleviating the pain of an unpredictable future.

The prologue to the reader, the second text passage that frames Opitz's translation, has a focus similar to that of the dedication to Buchner, but—now

---

32. OGW, 428, *LA*, 51: "De editione haesissem, nisi... eos etiam ita velle suspicari non ita diu potuerim, quorum auctoritate et benevolentia freti plebeias quasdam mente jure non moramur. Sciant et invideant hostes Musarum omnisque humanitatis, supresse etiamnum in his bellorum civilium quantumvis atrocissimis calamitatibus summos maximosque viros, qui literarum nostrarum, sine quibus ne res quidem publicae constare satis videntur, gloriam mirum in modum fovent ac tuentur."

33. OGW, 428, *LA*, 51: "Commitant itaque sese libero aeri captivae nostrae suoque exemplo publice et in oculis omnium ostendant non esse novum hoc malum, urbes validissimas integraque regna et provincias exscindi funditus et vastari. Doceant nos quoque suum ullud doloris qualecumque remedium: moderatius ferri sorte eam posse, quam et alii ante nos passi sunt et nunc tam multi nobiscum patiunt."

addressing a broader and German-speaking audience—the purpose of the following *Trojanerinnen* is more pronounced:

> By seeing and observing the complete downfall of great people and entire cities and countries, we indeed feel compassion for them and, out of wistfulness, we can often barely hold back our tears; however, from this constant sight of so much hardship and evil that has befallen others, we also learn how to bear the suffering that we may encounter, with less fear and more strength.[34]

Based on a detailed look at the reception history of Seneca's writings and its traces in the prologue to Opitz's translation of *Troades*, Hans-Jürgen Schings has carved out an image of baroque tragedy as an exercise in interpretation and affect (*Interpretations- und Affektübung*) that is able to turn life's adversities into constancy. His remarks are aimed at a definition of tragedy that— instead of drawing on Aristotle's poetics—is anchored in the literary genre of the consolatory speech, the *consolatio*.[35] Rather than exciting pity and fear, baroque tragedy, as Schings understands it, teaches humans about the *vanitas* of their condition and, more important, about how to overcome it by practicing constancy. Watching other people's misery—this is the lesson one can learn from Opitz's prologue—allows us to face our own with Stoic calm. In what would turn out to be an influential argument for the next decades of scholarship on baroque German tragic drama, Schings called Opitz's analogy between his own situation and the situation of the Trojan women in Seneca's play an exceptional case (*Sonderfall*) of life equaling tragedy in which the close connection with life emphasized the usefulness of the tragedy. Schings expressed his idea mathematically as "*Leben = Trauerspiel*" (life = tragedy).[36]

The axiomatic nature of this thought was most probably part of its appeal. To do justice to the "exceptional case" of Opitz's *Trojanerinnen*, however, the specific form of the equation requires a careful examination. It is necessary to ask how the way in which Opitz deals with time relates to the concepts that are significant in *Troades*. In Seneca's text, the loss of "world," in the sense of a network of semiotic relations, and the loss of world-time, in the sense

---

34. OGW, 430: "In dem wir grosser Leute / gantzer Städte und Länder eussersten Vntergang zum offtern schawen vnd betrachten / tragen wir zwar / wie es sich gebühret / erbarmen mit jhnen / können auch nochmals aus wehmuth die Thränen kaum zu rück halten; wir lernen aber daneben auch aus der stetigen besichtigung so vielen Creutzes vnd Vbels das andern begegnet ist / das vnserige / welches vns begegnen möchte / weniger fürchten vnd besser erdulden." With the exception of quotations from *Majuma*, *á*, *ó*, *ú* have been rendered *ä*, *ö*, *ü* in chapters 6 and 7.

35. Schings, "Consolatio Tragoediae" (1971), 1–44. See also Schings, "Seneca-Rezeption und Theorie der Tragödie," 534–35.

36. See Schings, "Consolatio Tragoediae," 20.

of a temporal space in which these relations can establish themselves, were understood as the main reason for the loss of meaning in the lives of the Trojan women and for their wish for an end of life-time. In his comparison between the situation of the Trojan women and the prisoners of the Thirty Years' War, Opitz transposes the literary problem into his (extraliterary) present. Yet the representation of the world of war depends almost entirely on the Trojan model and does not go into specifics as far as the concrete historical context of the Thirty Years' War is concerned. Seen in this light, the relevance of the literary model cannot be overstated: concrete historical reality of the present only enters into the text in the reference to a previous literary representation. Put otherwise, the tragedy virtually takes the place of the historical reality with which Opitz intends to compare it. Opitz's reliance on this aesthetic model to make sense of the present pushes back on the claim that his main interest was the philosophical content of Seneca's work. From this perspective, one can see that Opitz puts just as much emphasis on systematic and structural comparability as on aesthetic considerations. For example, in the prologue, he reiterates his statement to Buchner that he translated *Troades* for its moral exemplarity but also—and this point actually ranks first in his argument—for its incomparable beauty: "I took it upon myself to translate these Trojan Women into our language: because it is not only the most beautiful among the Roman tragedies, ... but it also seems to perfectly match ... present times."[37]

Moreover, if we refrain from accepting as a matter of course that, in framing his work, Opitz—who is otherwise reluctant to go into specifics about the present war—concentrates on the ruin and the destruction of cities and provinces, then this focus appears to foreground the semiotic collapse that the original depicts. Opitz's translation turns out not to be a simple statement about the vanity of the human condition that can be handled with a reflection on Stoic philosophy or a reinterpretation of the tragic genre. It rather provides insight into an extreme case of *vanitas* that Seneca's text details. The analogy suggests that there is no reason not to assume a loss of "world" and world-time that threatens life-time in Opitz's historical present as well. The difference is that Opitz succeeds in mediating the problem aesthetically. In his translation, Seneca's tragedy takes the structural place of the network of signs in relation to which life-time makes sense.

For the literary model to fulfill this purpose, however, the semiotic relations that were lost in the ruin of Troy first had to be reestablished. The

---

37. OGW, 431: "Habe ich mich vnterwunden hiesige Trojanerinnen in vnsere Sprache zu versetzen: weil sie nicht allein die schönste vnter den Römischen Tragedien ist, ... sondern sich auch auf jetzige Zeiten ... am allerbesten zu fügen scheinet."

translation had to expose its difference from the original, while at the same time bringing aspects of the model's inherent significance to the fore. Instead of taking up Schings's content-based equation of "life = tragedy," we are in a position to recognize the relation between original and translation as a life-nexus in the Benjaminian sense. As I have shown in chapter 2, the term implies that the translation is a form that the original has to take to become itself.

As much as he insisted that he was an admirer and follower of Seneca's aesthetic and philosophical standards, Opitz made several decisions that clearly and consciously set the translation apart from Seneca's text. After all, Opitz's project of establishing German as a literary language that followed idiom-specific rhetorical and poetic rules required that he point out the distinctiveness of German "tragic diction" and make its aesthetic value plausible.[38] Seen in this light, the complex situation that Opitz creates in the dedication to Buchner by referring to the Trojan women as "our prisoners of war" is not only a means to merge his translation and Seneca's tragedy and the temporal dimensions of Troy, Seneca's Rome, and the seventeenth century, but also a way to confidently claim *Troades* for the German context. In the prologue to the reader, Opitz explicitly remarks on his occasional deviation from *Troades* due to linguistic and poetic features, and he explains that he added notes to the translation because "we now write in German and this will require a little explanation until we are more comfortable with it [meaning: the German language]."[39]

The most striking accentuation of a difference, however, is Opitz's translation of the second choral ode.[40] At first glance, nothing alarming occurs at the level of the main text. Opitz takes many—rather innocuous—liberties that are often due to metric considerations:[41]

---

38. Harst, "Germany and the Netherlands," 159.

39. OGW, 431: "Wir schreiben nunmehr Deutsch / da es erstlich einer kleinen Erklerung wil von nöthen seyn / biß wir uns etwas besser werden eingerichtet haben."

40. The poet presumably used the 1621 edition by the Dutch philologist Petrus Scriverius, which in this case—apart from the punctuation—deviates only minimally from the 2018 Harvard edition. See Scriverius, *L. Aenneus Seneca Tragicus*, 193–94: "Non prodest animam tradere funeri, / Sed restat miseris vivere longius? / . . . Quidquid Sol Oriens, quidquid et Occidens / Novit: caeruleis Oceanus fretis / Quidquid vel veniens vel fugiens lavat, / Aetas Pegaseo corripiet gradu.[. . . nec amplius, / Iuratos Superis qui tetigit lacus, / Usquam est . . . / Post mortem nihil est, ipsaque mors nihil, / Velocis spatij meta novissima. / Spem ponant avidi; solliciti metum. / Tempus nos avidum devorat, et chaos." For Opitz's use of this edition, see OGW, 427; Stachel, *Seneca und das deutsche Renaissancedrama*.

41. Harst points out that the use of the Alexandrine in place of the iambic trimeter encouraged Opitz to extend Seneca's short, antithetical structures by reformulating or explaining them; see Harst, "Germany and the Netherlands," 160.

Does the spirit live here anyway and is it not allowed to prepare him a grave? Is it like that? Or do we die with body and soul and everything? ... Where sun and night come into being, that which the ocean, flowing forth and back, floods will dissolve like a stream of water ... Charon's lake does not send any part of us back again ... After this death there is nothing, death itself has to be called nothing; a goal that interrupts our years that flee with us from us. You miserly people abandon all hope, you fearful people drop all supplication ... Time devours us together with the world [*tempus nos avidum devorat, et chaos*].[42]

Opitz translates the sentence about greedy time (*tempus avidum*), which in Seneca opens up a variety of possible interpretations, as "Time devours us together with the world" (*Die Zeit frisst vns mit sampt der Welt*). A less literal translation brings out the meaning that Opitz had in mind: "Time devours us and our individual lives together with the world in which we live." The translation of *chaos* with "world" implies that Opitz was interested in already shaped matter or, in our terms, in a network of signs that gives life a frame. By implication, he knew that in the second choral ode this semiotic point of reference was at stake. Yet unlike the Stoic author of his source, Opitz was not ready to accept the semiotic bankruptcy of the model of the Trojan women, who have neither life nor world, and perhaps not even an immortality of the soul that would function as a guarantor of sense or order.

In an elaborate note, the German poet explains why the choral ode pushed the boundaries of his ideological generosity and why it almost prevented him from carrying out the translation. The note is mysteriously titled "About the chorus: if it is true." Opitz takes for granted that the speakers of the choral ode are the Trojan women:

> The rhymes are iambic, and the first and third verse have eight syllables, the second and fourth verse nine, and so on. It is the chorus and the chorus alone that almost scared me away from the translation. Because in it, the mortality of the soul is expressed in utterly pagan words. But given that no Christian who is grounded solely in their faith could turn to such words or writings, I was a little less concerned about the translation. However, the chorus is made up of Trojan women whose bodies and souls are captured: for they agree that

---

42. OGW, 439–50: "Lebt dan der Geist doch gleichwol hier / Vnd darff man jhm kein Grab nicht machen? / Ist's also? Oder sterben wir / Mit Leib' und Seel' vnd allen Sachen / ... Daß wo die Sonn' und Nacht entsteht / Das was die See pflegt zu begiessen / Die für sich oder rückwerts geht / Wird als ein Wasserstrom verfliessen. / ... des Charons See / Schickt nachmals nichts mehr von vns wieder. / ... Nach diesem Tod' ist nichts mehr nicht / Der Tod ist selber nichts zu nennen; / Ein Ziel das vns die Jahr' abbricht / Die mit vns flüchtig von uns rennen. / Ihr Geitzigen stellt Hoffnung ein / Ihr Furchtsamen laßt ewer Flehen. / ... Die Zeit frißt vns mit sampt der Welt."

body and soul must perish together and that after this life there is nothing to fear or hope for.[43]

It is difficult to grasp the exact meaning of this passage because Opitz remains somewhat ambiguous in his attempt to criticize Seneca and exonerate him at the same time. The sentence that poses the greatest problem is the one in which Opitz seems to claim that the immortality of the soul is an undeniable fact that everyone, including Seneca, has to acknowledge, but that this fact can take the wrong form. In the case of *Troades* it assumes the form of "pagan words." Opitz then proceeds to explicitly criticize Seneca for his contradictory stance with respect to what seems to Opitz to be a clear and self-evident truth. He brings up the first chorus that imagines Priam in Elysium as a contrast to the second choral ode and therefore makes the case for an afterlife of the soul. Confused about Seneca's inconsistencies, Opitz ponders whether the Stoic is just an opportunist who follows common opinion in each given situation or if, by nature, he completely lacks the consistency of the Christian worldview. Opitz finally settles on calling Seneca a "half-Christian," adding the peculiar interjection "God preserve us!" in parentheses: "Now let us hear the half-Christian philosopher (God preserve us!), whose letters to Paul still exist."[44] The comment expresses the extent to which Opitz is torn between his willingness to align himself with his predecessor and his bewilderment over Seneca's fundamental deviation from Opitz's own Christian beliefs, which made the addition of the note necessary in the first place. Above all, however, the note itself is what most clearly distinguishes the translation from the original and reveals its particularity—in other words, its form-being and the way in which it exceeds mere imitation.[45] The comment is a hermeneutic addition and a paratextual supplement, aimed at overcoming Seneca's *vanitas* or the loss of what Opitz translates as "world" via the Christian idea of an afterlife of the soul.

43. OGW, 496: "Vber das Chor: Ob es dann war ist. Die Reime sind Jambisch; vnd hat der Erste vnd Dritte Verß jedweder Acht / der Andere vnd Vierdte neun Sylben: vnd so ferner. Das Chor ist welches mich fast allein von der Verdolmetschung abgeschreckt hätte; weil darinnen die Sterblichkeit der Seelen so gar mit Heydnischen Worten außgedruckt wirdt. Angesehen aber sich kein Christ / der nur in seinem Glauben gegründet ist / an dergleichen Worte oder Schrifften kehren kan: so habe ich destoweniger wegen der Vbersetzung Bedencken getragen. Es bestehet aber dieser Chor von Trojanischen Weibern; die beydes an Leibe und Vernunfft gefangen sind: dann sie einhellig vorgeben / daß nur zugleiche Leib und Seel vntergehen müsten / vnd daß nach diesem Leben weiter nichts zu hoffen oder zu fürchten sey."
44. OGW, 498–99: "Jetzundt wollen wir den halb-Christlichen Philosophen (Gott behüte vns!) hören; dessen Episteln an den Paulus noch vorhanden seyn; wo sie jemandt darvor halten wil."
45. See chapter 2 on form and translation in Benjamin.

It is by way of these subtle differences that Opitz reinstates the semiotic points of reference in the form of the translation. In that sense, Seneca allows Opitz not only to represent the present by putting the drama in the place of an explicit engagement with the contemporary world of the Thirty Years' War but also to open up a "beyond" within this representation that contravenes the implicit nothingness of the world death at the center of Seneca's play. In turn—and once again put in Benjaminian terms—Opitz establishes a life-nexus between Seneca's Rome and the German lands of the Thirty Years' War, between *Troades* and *Trojanerinnen*. According to Benjamin, this nexus is an essentially historical relation in which the translation enables the original to live on in another form. The afterlife of Seneca's *Troades* is realized as a semiotic network that establishes a point of reference for meaningful life-time: a network of reference that will persist even in the face of the most extreme form of world annihilation. Opitz's *Trojanerinnen* itself constitutes this site of emergence from the ruins of war.

Walter Benjamin wrote that "the religious man of the Baroque era clings so tightly to the world because of the feeling that he is being driven along to a cataract with it" (*OGD*, 66). The obsession with death, the brooding over the bits and pieces of lost meaning, the accumulation of objects and the inclination to exaggerate and embellish forms (e.g., poetic forms)—and at this point Benjamin clearly has in mind the materiality of form as opposed to content—result from a baroque sense that eschatological hope for redemption of the world and humankind would be in vain and that immanence is all there is. The hereafter, thus Benjamin inverses the argument, "is emptied of everything which contains the slightest breath of this world" (*OGD*, 66).

Instead, what appears in Opitz's text is not so much an insistent holding on to the world or a static immersion into its material and visible forms in the face of threatening decline caused by the war. It is not an exercise in Stoicism or a genre theory in disguise. Guided by a hermeneutics that takes its cues from the semiotic ruin of Seneca's tragedy, Opitz's approach reshapes the world as a network of signs in the form of his translation. His insight into the manipulability of time and its conditions finally reinstates the aesthetic form, which becomes the condition for life's continuance. It even transgresses the limits of the here and now. For at the end Opitz offers an outlook on a new world, on an afterworld in which the soul lives on and the world that went before still breathes. In defiance of all the characterizations of the baroque that have consigned the artificially construed period to its constant remembrance of death, the poetic form of the translation asserts the idea of an afterlife. It reveals a sudden "invasion" of eschatology, not its disappearance.

IV

The Battleground of Time

7

Johann Jacob Breitinger, Andreas Gryphius, and the Reconsideration of Allegory

Was dauert, ist das seltsame Detail der allegorischen Verweisung: ein Gegenstand des Wissens, der in den durchdachten Trümmerbauten nistet.

What has survived is the extraordinary detail of the allegorical references: an object of knowledge which has settled in the consciously constructed ruins.

WALTER BENJAMIN

About halfway through his critical discourse on the nature, purpose, and use of similes (*Critische Abhandlung von der Natur, den Absichten und dem Gebrauche der Gleichnisse*; 1740) and after having depicted a decline in rhetorical and stylistic ability from Homer to Seneca, the Swiss philologist Johann Jacob Breitinger turns to the baroque German tragic dramas with a gesture of reluctant conscientiousness. "I take up this task unwillingly," he informs his readers, "because I anticipate that—if I do not restrict my honesty that likes to express itself as best it can—I will, with my judgment, outrage my nation [*meine Nation*], who prides itself on articulateness and poetry just as much as other peoples [*Völker*]."[1] What follows, however, is an admonishment of the boastful poets Andreas Gryphius and Daniel Casper von Lohenstein that does not have the slightest scruples about being cruelly direct.

Breitinger embarks on his criticism by condemning the failure of German dramatists to create plays with a proper tragic effect. "If only I think of Lohenstein's mourning plays [*Trauerspiele*]," he laments, "I shudder with disgust [*überfällt mich Frost und Ekel*] . . . The most patient human being, if they are not stupid, must be taken ill with consumption while reading these tragedies [*Tragödien*]" (*CAG*, 212).[2] The verdict over Gryphius is equally damning.

---

1. For the German original, see Breitinger, *Critische Abhandlung von der Natur, den Absichten und dem Gebrauche der Gleichnisse* ([1740] 1967; hereafter cited as *CAG*), 219: "Ich gehe sehr ungerne an dieses Stück, weil ich voraus sehe, dass ich meine Nation, die sich in dem Punct der Wohlredenheit und Poesie eben so viel einbildet, als andre Völker, mit meinem Urtheil erzörnen werde, wofern ich meiner Aufrichtigkeit, die gerne redet, wie sie es verstehet, keine Gewalt anthun soll." All translations are mine.

2. In the *Origin of German Tragic Drama*, Walter Benjamin has differentiated clearly between form and content of the *Tragödie* (tragedy) and the *Trauerspiel* (mourning play). In my

Breitinger finds that it is not the author's literary characters but his "vulgar ineptitude" that evokes the reader's pity (*CAG*, 223).

Breitinger's discontent had its precursor in an influential model. When he wrote his treatise, Johann Christoph Gottsched had already spilled much ink over the purpose of reforming German literature. The elimination of baroque mannerisms was one of his most strenuously pursued goals. In *Critical Poetics* (*Critische Dichtkunst*) from 1729, Gottsched had identified the misuse of stylistic devices and especially of allegory as the reason for the weak tragic effect of baroque dramas. He emphatically rejected the excessive application of tropes in general and particularly with respect to the representation of affects. The combination of affect and allegory, he thought, could only result in implausible pomposity.[3] Gottsched's judgment, which had a fatal impact on the reception of German baroque literature, clearly resounds in Breitinger's rebuke of baroque dramatic mediocrity:

> How could you even suspect that these scholarly figurative speeches and slogans befit an intelligent human being, when he [Lohenstein] sometimes quarrels with himself in nothing but similes [*Gleichnisse*] and metaphors, sometimes foolishly and pompously . . . courts a beauty . . . [or] when he suddenly throws around parables [*Gleichnisse*] and the like beyond measure. In all this, Andr.[eas] Gryphius is little better than him. (*CAG*, 212–22)

The tirade has achieved some renown in literary scholarship. It was discussed extensively in the 1970s, and efforts have been made over the years to square its scathing bluntness with Breitinger's otherwise more or less favorable opinion of allegory. Some interpretations saw the contradictions as part of a general reorientation in literary criticism that took place between late baroque and early Enlightenment. The implicit understanding was that the rejection of allegory—or at least of a specific use—revealed Breitinger's ability to adapt to the new requirements of reason, while the affirmation of the trope positioned him alongside conservative philologists.[4] The negative stigma attached to baroque allegory that Walter Benjamin had worked to reduce by rethinking the relation between allegory and symbol proved its resilience, and the idea of its abolition was linked ever more tightly to intellectual clarity, stylistic refinement, and poetic sophistication.

---

own translations, I will follow the German original. I will otherwise use the terms *mourning play* and *tragic drama* as synonyms.

3. The references to Gottsched can be found in Alt, *Begriffsbilder*, 358, 368–70, 391.

4. See, e.g., Hermann, *Nachahmung und Einbildungskraft*; Schöne, *Emblematik und Drama im Zeitalter des Barock*; Bender, *Johann Jakob Bodmer und Johann Jakob Breitinger*; Martino, *Daniel Casper von Lohenstein*.

Starting with a reconsideration of the sheer vehemence of Breitinger's criticism of similes, this chapter will focus on allegory as the figurative aspect of ruins in the Benjaminian sense but with an emphasis on epistemological issues. Benjamin's distinction between allegories and ruins that attributes the former to the realm of thoughts and the latter to the realm of things has often been misunderstood as a rigorous distinction between an abstract and a concrete side of fragmentation and decay.[5] The term *figurative* is therefore intended to highlight that the point of allegories is precisely that they are both abstract (figurative) and concrete (figure). Allegories are forms that illustrate and interpret, represent and signify. Or as Benjamin put it, ruins are the material of allegories.[6] My main claim draws on the established observation that allegories played a specific role with respect to the status of cultural knowledge in the ambiguous historical situation of the so-called baroque era. The long war of the seventeenth century took place in a time that collected, organized, archived, and represented all the components of an expansive body of knowledge in a seemingly countless number of emblem books, catalogs of hieroglyphs, allegorical encyclopedias, and biblical commentaries.[7] The coherence of knowledge that the baroque claimed in a sometimes totalizing manner was threatened by the destruction, fragmentation, and dispersion of its elements on the battlefield of Europe.[8] Breitinger's intervention was targeted against the perceived attempt of baroque authors to gain control of a simultaneously fragmented and abundant amount of knowledge with the help of allegory.

Had Breitinger's view of Andreas Gryphius been less prejudiced and had he allowed his attention to be distracted away from the tragic dramas and onto other works by the Silesian poet, then he might have seen that Gryphius was not a staunch proponent of allegorical representation but that he carefully weighed its potential and disadvantages. In fact, he seems to have implicitly shared some of Breitinger's skepticism, even if he drew different conclusions. In his play *Majuma*, which he wrote in 1653, virtually on the

---

5. "Allegories are in the realm of thoughts what ruins are in the realm of things" (*OGD*, 178). See my remarks on this relation in chapter 2.

6. This thought is for example expressed in his *Origin of German Tragic Drama* (*OGD*, 177–78).

7. The relation between allegory and the collection and organization of knowledge is not a phenomenon that is specific to the early modern period. For its medieval roots, see Meyer, "Zum Verhältnis von Enzyklopädik und Allegorese im Mittelalter," 290–313.

8. See, e.g., V. Meid, *Die deutsche Literatur im Zeitalter des Barock*, 70–73; Enenkel, *Invention of the Emblem Book*. For the background of this understanding in the medieval notion of a world in which not only words but also things carried meaning and were connected in expansive networks of signs and significations, see Ohly, "Vom geistigen Sinn des Wortes im Mittelalter," 1–31.

threshold between war and peace, Gryphius explores whether and how historical knowledge can be structured through allegory in a time of transition. Comparable to Martin Opitz's unorthodox promotion of the idea of afterlife in an environment obsessed with transience, Gryphius suggests that allegory, despite being a broken aesthetic form, can shape the precarious passage from one historical state to the next. As I will show, *Majuma* is an allegorizing endeavor to establish historical continuity between past and present knowledge and, most important, to open a gateway toward the future. As in Opitz's translation, there is in *Majuma* an element of salvation-historical temporality at work. But while in *Trojanerinnen* it carries the play across the obstacles of pure immanence and past the threats of an uncompromising immersion in material objects, it appears in *Majuma* more like a concession to the challenges of an allegorical approach to historicity. However, we will see that Gryphius ultimately goes further and explores areas beyond both salvation-historical temporality and allegory. His play gives room to an open aesthetic form that uncloses new possibilities for knowledge to manifest itself.

In many ways, Gryphius's play is an instance of overcoming the stereotypes of the so-called baroque. It defies what Hartmut Böhme called Benjamin's "bitterness" in the face of allegories. What Böhme had in mind was Benjamin's melancholy admission of an insurmountable allegorical gap between signifier and signified and his assumption that the allegorical semiotic process mirrored the decay of the world of things or rather used it as its material.[9] In that sense, *Majuma* is a corrective to the new conventions that Benjamin's rehabilitation of allegory—and of baroque literature and art—introduced into the discussion of the trope. Benjamin's appreciation of the "amorphous fragment" that he set against the "organic totality" of the symbol (*OGD*, 176) has left its mark on scholarship, which since the late 1920s has adhered to a notion of early modern allegorical thinking that was supposedly unable to overcome its own commitment to immanence and mortality and to the ruin and fragmentation of forms. Needless to say, Benjamin, who had expressly pointed out that the inclination to rescue things for eternity was "one of the strongest impulses in allegory" (*OGD*, 223), is only partly responsible for this line of interpretation. In *Majuma*, the shattered forms of allegory make space for both the marks of continuity and the signs of decay. The play sets forth that the significance of the things we can know about the history of the world and of human life grows in the interstice.

Based on the conceptual history of allegory as well as evidence from the texts that are of interest here, I will henceforth take the terminological liberty

---

9. Böhme, "Ruinen–Landschaften" (1988), 334–79.

of speaking about allegory with respect to emblematic figures and vice versa, and I will also—with Breitinger—use the term *simile* to denote related phenomena. The purpose of this practice is not to level out differences but to emphasize a common characteristic or pattern that underlies all the examined figures and tropes. The pattern as I understand it is an aporia between "representation" and "signification," between "figuration" and "abstraction" that cannot be resolved but is part of the medial, semiotic, and semantic complexity of the discussed figurative and linguistic forms.[10] The following considerations will show that it can be grasped in miscellaneous aspects of ostentatious imagery and in particular operations of comparison, exchange, variation, and invention, and that it is present in the distinct ways in which the relation between poetic figures and history is negotiated.[11]

The Limits of Allegory

Breitinger's rejection of the "confused writers [*verwirrte Scribenten*]" Lohenstein and Gryphius, together with their allegorical profusion and their contrived wordy learnedness (*CAG*, 223–24), was rooted in a poetological concept that tied the use of poetic means to the imitation of nature.[12] In other words, imagination was required to abide by the laws of probability.[13] Within these limits, a successful invention of figurative speech was deemed possible. It depended on the coincidence and the harmonious interplay between fantasy and reason. Breitinger reverts to a thought by the philosopher Christian Wolff, who considered ingenuity (*Witz*) to be the intellectual and creative capacity that enabled poets to recognize similarities.[14] In Breitinger's adaptation of this idea, imagination reproduces as images the sensory impressions that it receives from reality. *Witz*, which is a faculty of reason, then looks around the gallery (*Bilder-Saal*) of fantasy, recognizes similarities between the images, and combines them accordingly (*CAG*, 10). If the correlation succeeds, pictorial (*mahlerisch*)

---

10. See Strätling, *Allegorien der Imagination*, 275.

11. For the rhetorical tradition, see Freytag, "Allegorie, Allegorese," 330–92. For the aesthetic tradition, see Haverkamp and Menke, "Allegorie," 49–104. Albrecht Schöne has discussed the difference between allegories and emblems in some detail in Schöne, *Emblematik und Drama im Zeitalter des Barock*, 32–35.

12. It is possible that *Scribent* already had a derogatory connotation and meant something like "scribbler." As the *Brothers Grimm Dictionary* indicates, the term had achieved this pejorative meaning by the nineteenth century. See Grimm and Grimm, *Deutsches Wörterbuch*.

13. Alt, *Begriffsbilder*, 372–86.

14. Alt, *Begriffsbilder*, 361; Möller, *Rhetorische Überlieferung und Dichtungstheorie im frühen 18. Jahrhundert*, 51.

figures of speech ensue that Breitinger alternatively calls "similes," "metaphors," "symbolic figures," and "emblematic images."[15] These figures adorn speech, lend clarity and emphasis to concepts, and move the soul.[16]

With his description, Breitinger has the poetically beautiful in mind, upon which poets touch if they demonstrate good taste and choose their figures from the realm between the "common" (*das Gemeine*) and the "unbelievable" (*das Unglaubliche*). As he argues in *Critische Dichtkunst* (*Critical Poetics*), a work that was published in the same year as Breitinger's treatise on similes, poets approach beauty if they invent their images by combining the unbelievable and the miraculous with what is thematically and logically probable:

> This judgment, which is called good taste, [is] a force that furthermore serves us with respect to the affiliation of select things and circumstances instead of a compass, with the help of which we can happily avoid the two hurdles, the common and the unbelievable. Adjacent and in between lies the poetically beautiful . . . This selective judgment therefore teaches us to combine the miraculous and the common artificially. It is thanks to it [the judgment] that one never loses sight of nature and adequacy [*Wohlstand*]; it guards imagination from excesses, it ensures that neither brevity becomes obscure, nor grace puerile, nor richness exaggerated, nor the magnificent bombastic.[17]

Breitinger perceives the miraculous as the periphery of novelty (*äusserste Staffel des Neuen*), a point so unfamiliar and so remote from truth and verisimilitude that it is in constant danger of turning into their opposite. The miraculous, Breitinger writes, seems to contradict the known order of things by masking the truth. Even though it distorts reality, however, the mask is transparent (*eine ganz fremde aber durchsichtige Maske*; CD, 130).

---

15. Breitinger, *Fortsetzung der Critischen Dichtkunst* (1740), 332, 334; quoted in Schöne, *Emblematik und Drama im Zeitalter des Barock*, 120.

16. Volker Meid spoke of Breitinger's understanding of similes as an "art of moving the soul" (*Gemütserregungskunst*); V. Meid, *Die deutsche Literatur im Zeitalter des Barock*, 906.

17. Breitinger, *Critische Dichtkunst* ([1740] 1966; hereafter CD), 430–31: "Dieses Urtheil, welches . . . der gute Geschmack genannt wird [ist] eine Kraft, die uns anderntheils auch in der Verbindung der ausgelesenen Dinge und Umstände statt eines Compasses dienet, vermittelst dessen wir denen zwo Klippen, dem Gemeinen und dem Unglaublichen, zwischen denen das poetische Schöne lieget, und an welche es ziemlich nahe gräntzet, glücklich entgehen können . . . Dieses wehlende Urtheil lehret uns demnach das Wunderbare und Wahrscheinliche künstlich mit einander verbinden, ihm hat man es zu dancken, dass man die Natur und den Wohlstand niehmals aus den Augen setzet, es hinterhält die Einbildung vor Ausschweiffungen, es macht, dass die Kürtze nicht dunckel, das Zierliche nicht schülerhaft, das Reiche nicht übermässig, das Prächtige nicht schwülstig, wird." Translations of this source are mine. See also Möller, *Rhetorische Überlieferung und Dichtungstheorie*, 67.

Breitinger's examples ultimately convey that the miraculous is the probable, hidden behind the mask of allegorical images. The images of poetic fantasy have to remain permeable so that probability can shine through. Probability, in turn, needs the zest of astonishing wonders to capture the attention of the recipients and have a lasting impact on their affects. Balanced in this way, the poetically beautiful—in a free adaptation of Horace's doctrine that poets are supposed to instruct or delight—is capable of pleasing, moving, and teaching those who perceive it: "The enhancement of our knowledge therefore never happens without delight" (*CD*, 61).[18]

In view of the fact that Breitinger almost loses his composure over Lohenstein's and Gryphius's works, this last point is particularly important, for Breitinger ultimately has anthropological reasons to justify his underlying hidden confidence in similes. Humans, thus his argument, are naturally curious, and their curiosity can be addressed and satisfied with the help of allegories and their affinity to truth—that is, with their proximity to reality and probability. In *Critische Dichtkunst*, in the chapter that deals with the mimesis of nature, Breitinger writes:

> Humans by nature have an innate, insatiable curiosity that extends to that which is probable as well as to that which is real . . . ; that which is wrong, improbable or in a certain sense impossible must naturally cause repugnancy and disgust for human reason as soon as it is perceived because it mocks the aspiration of man's natural curiosity and impairs the progress of cognition.[19]

A few chapters later, Breitinger discusses novelty and its relation to poetic beauty: "In this way we can see what poetic beauty consists of; it is a brightly shining beam of truth that affects senses and souls with such force that we cannot resist . . . ; our innate, bold desire for knowledge [*Wissenschaft*] is associated [*vergesellschaftet*] with a hatred of all ignorance."[20] Poetry, that much is obvious from these passages, has a relation with truth. Truth, in turn, possesses an ideal

---

18. See verse 333 of Horace's *Ars Poetica: Aut prodesse volunt, aut delectare poetae* (Poets want to either instruct or delight).

19. *CD*, 61–62: "Der Mensch hat von Natur eine angebohrene unersättliche Wissens-Begierde, diese erstrecket sich so wohl auf das Mögliche als auf das Würckliche . . . ; das Falsche, Unwahrscheinliche oder in gewisser Absicht Unmögliche muss dem menschlichen Verstand, so bald es wahrgenommen wird, natürlicher Weise Widerwillen und Eckel verursachen, weil es die angebohrne Wissens-Begierde des Menschen in ihrem Verlangen aufziehet, und den Fortgang in der Erkenntnis unterbricht."

20. *CD*, 112: "So sehen wir zugleich, worinnen das poetische Schöne bestehet, nemlich, es ist ein hell leuchtender Strahl des Wahren, welcher mit solcher Kraft auf die Sinnen und das Gemüthe eindringet, dass wir uns nicht erwehren können . . . ; es ist unsere angebohrene vorwitzige Begierde nach Wissenschaft, mit einem Abscheu gegen alle Unwissenheit vergesellschaftet."

sensual form that has been brought about by way of rational recognition of similarities, and it affects humans in their natural desire for knowledge.[21]

From these considerations, two conclusions can be drawn that are of particular importance for my argument. First of all, the invention of poetic images begins and ends with an act of cognition. Second, truth is something that can potentially be known, and what can be known potentially is always represented in appropriate images. Seen in this light, Breitinger's intervention against Lohenstein's and Gryphius's immoderately amassed, badly placed, and implausible similes looks like a critique of knowledge. Given its insistence and anthropological core, it can be detached from its relation to tragic dramas and understood as a statement of no confidence in allegory's capacity to absorb existing knowledge. Especially the harsh criticism of allegorical abundance appears to refer to a historical context in which knowledge has become voluminous beyond organization and control. In addition to the aforementioned attempt to arrange the body of knowledge in particular kinds of archives and documents, the rhetorical theories of the seventeenth century increasingly treated emblems and allegories in the context of the *ars inveniendi*, the art of invention, as both the premise and the material outcome of the "invention of knowledge."[22] Breitinger finds himself on the outskirts of a development, so to speak, in the course of which the dynamic of accumulation, indication, and reference has acquired a momentum of its own to the extent that the discovery of appropriate images to store and contain knowledge has become a problem and the overall system threatens to implode.

Yet contrary to expectations, Breitinger shares his concerns with Gryphius, the object of his contempt. In the next passage I turn to the way in which the latter examines the limits and uses of allegory poetically and, anachronistically speaking, effectually anticipates a solution for Breitinger's problem.

Allegory and Historical Knowledge: Gryphius's *Majuma*

On May 31, 1653, Archduke Ferdinand IV was elected Roman-German king in Augsburg.[23] The coronation, which secured the imperial crown for the Austrian

---

21. Hans Peter Hermann supports the notion that sensual and rational aspects are intimately intertwined in Breitinger's poetics with the ultimate goal of achieving knowledge; Hermann, *Nachahmung und Einbildungskraft*, 224.

22. Rieger, *Speichern/Merken*, 45.

23. Gryphius, *Majuma* (1991; hereafter cited as *MA*, with act and verse/line number). See especially the commentary by this edition's editor, Eberhard Mannack, on pages 1217–27. All translations are mine. See also Gryphius, *Lustspiele* (1991), especially the preface by this edition's editor, Herman Palm, on pages 173–76; Jöns, "Majuma, Piastus" (1968), 85–301.

Habsburg dynasty and gave the new king a third domain besides Bohemia and Hungary, took place in mid-June in Regensburg. A chronicle from Gryphius's birthplace Glogau suggests that *Majuma* was performed on June 24 in the author's hometown during the coronation festivities. Gryphius seems to have written the piece, which he called a "play of joy" (*Freuden-Spiel*), for this very occasion. In terms of both content and structure, this three-act play draws on the so-called peace plays (*Friedensspiele*) that were produced in large number around 1648 to celebrate the end of the Thirty Years' War. Like the peace plays, *Majuma* features characters from Greek mythology, and in both cases the events revolve around Mars, the god of war, who is held accountable for his decades-long raging. In the preface to the actual play, Gryphius introduces a forest god who describes 1653 as a year affected by the lingering horrors of war and the hesitant harbingers of peace:

> Vnsere Zeiten haben bißhero nichts als die bluttigen Traurspile des Kriges bejammert / und bey den Flammen der verloderten Städte ihre Wunden und der ihrigen Leichen beseufftzet ... Nunmehr aber / nun des Gottes der Götter Schickung den vil tausendmal gewůndscheten Friden eingeruffen; besuchen wir disen Ort unter dessen Schutz ... der nicht nur sich mit dem Bau der Gårte ergetzet / sondern mehr das wůste Land wieder in Blůtte zu bringen sich euserst bemůhet. (*MA*, Prologue)

> Hitherto, our times have nothing but lamented the bloody tragedies of war and bemoaned over the flames of the burned cities their wounds and their dead ... But now that the act of the God of gods has summoned a thousand times wished for peace, we visit this place [Glogau?] under the protection of the one who ... not only delights in the cultivation of gardens but also strives to make this devastated land bloom again.

The one who gives the forest god hope can easily be identified as Ferdinand IV. His appearance coincides with the Roman flower festival Majuma, traditionally a celebration of new beginnings yet simultaneously a reminder of the transience of life that blossoms and withers and requires that humans remember lasting treasures (*immerwehrende Schätze*) while they still can.

At the outset of the play, Gryphius portrays the love affair between the god of the west wind, Zephyr, and the nymph Chloris. He follows Ovid's *Fastorum libri sex*, a description of Roman religious festivals that the author never finished. This beginning is only loosely related to the main plotline about Mars's trial and punishment. The first act opens with Chloris complaining bitterly about Zephyr's alleged infidelity. In dialogue with the nymph Maia and her son, the god Mercury, she contemplates the vicissitude of earthly things and values and especially of Cupid's (i.e., love's) inconsistent nature, which is easily distracted and seduced by youth and beauty (*MA*, 1.1–80). However, Zephyr has not betrayed or left the nymph; he is only delayed. Upon his return, he and Chloris indulge in a fulsome reconciliation, which at the beginning of act 2 is crowned by Zephyr's request to see Chloris's garden, where he wants her to prove to the world that she is lovelier than any of her flowers (*MA*, 2.19–24). This is the point of intersection between the love story and the punishment of Mars. Chloris has nothing to show her beloved, for her garden is a ruin and a wasteland, destroyed by the god of war. Ironically, Chloris is indirectly responsible for Mars's existence. His mother, Juno, conceived with the help of a flower that Chloris provided. Her plea for redemption is therefore primarily directed at the queen of the gods. To Chloris's surprise, her wish is granted and Mars has to account for his deeds. In the passage in which he appears on the scene, Gryphius used dactyls instead of the otherwise prevalent iambs. The meter imparts Mars's speech with a swift, impelling military rhythm:

> Sanfftsinn'ge Göttin / ich muß es bekennen,
> Daß ich gebohren zu brechen und brennen /
> Daß ich erkohren zum Fechten und Rasen
> Daß mir der Himmel den Mut eingeblasen.
> Hôr ich den Klang der behertzten Trompeten
> So wacht mein Anmut zu fechten und tôdten . . .
> Knôrsch ich in Eisen – ergreiff ich die Klingen;
> So will diß Hertze für Kühnheit zuspringen.
> Seh ich die Ordnung der ährenen Ritter;
> Gôttin ich spring' / ich erhitz' / ich erschitter. (*MA*, 2.95–110)

> Gentle-minded goddess, I must admit that I was born to break and burn. I was chosen to battle and rage and heaven has instilled courage in me. When I hear the sound of spirited trumpets, my desire to fence and kill awakes . . . When my iron suit crunches, when I grasp the blade, this heart wants to burst of audacity. When I see the order of brazen knights, goddess, I leap, I sweat, I shake.

It is of no avail to Mars that he tries to blame all the terror he caused on inescapable fate by which he claims to be driven. Chloris condemns him to restore what he ruined in a quid pro quo and cultivate her garden. The last act sees the disarmed god of war marveling at his own transformation—notably in the same meter in which he used to express his enthusiasm for war:

> Welche Veränderung! sehet, ich baue?
> Pflantze / begüsse / versetze / behaue!
> Wer hâtte vermeinet / daß ich im Garten
> Solte der wachsenden Blumen abwarten? (*MA*, 3.91–95)

What a transformation! Look, do I build? I plant, I water, I relocate and I carve! Who would have thought that I would wait in a garden for the flowers to grow?

The overall metamorphosis, however, has only just begun. While Mars is still musing about his new creative forces, Maia, Zephyr, and Chloris turn into flowers—more precisely, into *Fritillaria imperialis*, or kaiser's crowns (emperor's crowns).[24] Mars himself takes on the shape of an eagle, the heraldic animal of the Habsburg dominion, at which point Mercury enters the stage and explains that the transformations are a reference to Ferdinand IV's coronation. A final hymn effusively praises the new emperor (*MA*, 3.101–8).

In the context of his poetological considerations regarding the relation between the miraculous and the probable, Breitinger dedicates some attention to the allegorical use of mythological figures. He acknowledges that mythology is a source of poetic beauty, a provider of images for the poet that give his thoughts a marvelous shape (*CD*, 345–46). Furthermore, in Breitinger's reading, the essential probability of mythological figures is rooted in tradition. "These allegorical characters," he writes, "have gained a general reputation . . . of probability by appearing so often in the works of the poets" (*CD*, 143–44). However, Breitinger also thinks that an allegorical plot cannot be appropriate material for a dramatic work (*keine anständige Materie für ein . . . dramatisches Gedichte*; *CD*, 144). The reason is that allegorical plots bear a secret that requires an explanation from the poet. In other words, allegories, because they are arbitrary, require interpretation. In Breitinger's view, this explanatory task can only be accomplished if the poet speaks for himself, and not through allegorical figures (*CD*, 145). Even though Breitinger here looks at the problem from a different angle, the passage once again ties allegories to the question of how knowledge can be gained and transferred, and Breitinger's skepticism with respect to similes is on display in all its essentiality. Gryphius shares this skepticism and absorbs it into the overall allegorical structure of *Majuma*.

Toward the end of the play, immediately after the metamorphosis of the gods, Mercury initiates his much-discussed praise of Ferdinand. The reason for the attention the sequence received is primarily the first ten verses:

Was uverhoffte Lust! itzt jauchtze Land und Feld /
Jtzt jauchtze Klipp' und See! die hôchst-erfreute Welt /
Spûrt einen neuen May in dem Augustus Stadt /

---

24. The Latin *fritillus* literally means "dice cup" and is an allusion to the shape of the flower.

> Heut außgeführet siht der grossen Götter Rath . . .
> der grosse FERDINAND . . .
> Wird heut mit Carols Schmuck und Kronen Gold gezirt
> Vnd von acht Fürsten selbst auffs Vatern Thron geführt. (*MA*, 3.109–21)

> What an unexpected joy! Land and field, cliff and lake may cheer now! The delighted world senses a new May because today the city of Augustus [Augsburg] sees the realization of the counsel of the great gods . . . Today the great FERDINAND is adorned with Carl's jewels and his crown of gold and eight princes lead him to his father's throne.

The passage raises questions because Gryphius is obviously suggesting that the coronation happened in Augsburg in the month of May, whereas it actually took place in Regensburg in June. One could shrug off this conspicuous detail as a simple mistake by Gryphius, who confused Ferdinand's election with the coronation. However, as Walter Jöns noted, it seems more likely that Gryphius confounded the dates consciously and manipulated historical reality with the goal of rendering it significant. Fashioning the election month of May as the month that marked the beginning of Ferdinand's reign allowed Gryphius, in turn, to interpret the reign allegorically as a sign for a fresh start after the war.[25]

There are several arguments that support this claim. Jöns quotes a sonnet by Gryphius in which the poet antedates his own birthday to make it coincide with the day of the archangel Michael.[26] Furthermore, *Majuma* in its entirety—from the structure to the flower motifs to the content of the plot—seems to be designed to uphold the transition between destruction and reconstruction. As accurate as these points may be, their impact for an understanding of the function of allegories is limited because they suggest that allegories simply bring an additional level of meaning into view. In the specific historical situation in which *Majuma* was composed, however, the liminal space of uncertainty between war and peace and the insecurity about what knowledge contains in a moment of discontinuity are at stake. Allegories are an expression of this indeterminacy and, at the same time, an attempt to come to terms with it. The act of allegorizing is therefore a sort of experimental operation. In the case of *Majuma*, genuinely rhetorical and poetic means are examined with respect to their suitability to derive peace from war.

A telling example for this vicissitude and aesthetic openness of allegories is the transformation of the gods into flowers (kaiser's crowns) that I

---

25. Jöns, "Majuma, Piastus," 288.
26. Jöns, "Majuma, Piastus," 288.

mentioned earlier. There are two aspects to these metamorphoses that lend them a double meaning. The kaiser's crowns, into which the three gods transform, can be understood either as actual flowers or as the three crowns that Ferdinand IV now possesses. On a poetic and rhetorical plane, this means that allegories have either turned into allegories or materialized as historical objects. It is obvious from this passage that allegories, as the broken and receptive forms that they are, teeter on the brink between abstraction and concretization.

At this point, Nicola Kaminski's study of Opitz's *Buch von der deutschen Poeterey* (*Book of German Poetics*) wherein she conceptualizes the Thirty Years' War as a poetological element at the bottom of Opitz's poetics comes to mind once again. Her argument that the German poet transformed the pressing reality of the war poetically and metaphorically and worked it into the *Poeterey* could be reversed with respect to Gryphius.[27] One could posit that roughly thirty years after Opitz and several years after the war, Gryphius reflects on possibilities and limits of aesthetic means to sustain the situation of peace epistemologically. A look at another text passage from *Majuma* will expand on this idea.

The disarming and taming of Mars in the third act of *Majuma* is accompanied by a sort of antiwar statement, once again delivered by Mercury:

> Die Bine ziht hinfort in seinen Sturmhut ein /
> Der Feder-Pusch mag nun der Vögel Schrecken seyn.
> Der Dolch ist gut / im Fall man etwa Bäume ritzt
> Der Zäune gleiche macht / und junge Reben schnitzt.
> Das Schwerdt taug nicht für uns. Stellt es dem Helden zu /
> Dem das gekrönte Haupt der Erden / seine Ruh
> Vnd Sorgen anvertraut / der Lantz und Feder führt
> Vnd den behertzten Schild mit weissen Rosen zirt. (*MA*, 3.13–20)

From now on, the bee will live in his aconite. The hackle [plume] may now scare the birds. The dagger is useful for carving trees, leveling fences and cutting young vines. The sword is useless to us. Give it to the hero, to whom is entrusted the coronated head of the earth, its peace and its sorrows, [give it] to the one who wields the lance and the quill and who adorns the spirited shield with white roses.

As unremarkable as they may seem, the first two verses of the speech invoke a rich cultural context. They are a reference to emblematics, more precisely

---

27. Kaminski, *Ex bello ars oder Ursprung der "Deutschen Poeterey,"* 16–52, 69–80. Recall also Kaminski's observations concerning Opitz's *Buch von der deutschen Poeterey* as discussed in chapter 6.

to emblem 178 in the 1621 edition of Andrea Alciato's collection of emblems (*Emblematum liber*), which Gryphius, in all probability, used as a source.[28] Emblem 178 features the characteristic tripartite composition of *inscriptio* (motto), *pictura* (image), and *subscriptio* (epigram) that constitutes the emblematic interplay of textual and visual forms of signification (figure 4). The Latin motto *Ex bello pax* (Out of war, peace) establishes the frame for the emblem's content. The image shows more or less exactly what Mercury is referring to in Gryphius's poetic version of the emblem. Bees are buzzing around the now abandoned, plumed helmet of a soldier. Finally, the text of the epigram details what Gryphius merely indicates (figure 5):

> Look, a helmet that a brave soldier wore. It used to be often splattered with the blood of enemies. Now, with the beginning of peace, it has surrendered the use of its narrow space to the bees. May the weapons rest in the distance. May it only be right to start a war if you cannot otherwise enjoy the art of peace.

The dynamic of amplification and abbreviation of thoughts and arguments through both text and image is not unidirectional, however. The first edition of Alciato's emblem book from 1531 contains the emblem with the same *inscriptio* and *subscriptio* but a variation of the *pictura* (figure 6).[29] Aside from the fact that we are presented with two different helmet designs, the later edition adds a hackle (i.e., a decorative plume, so named because of its resemblance to the neck plumage of a bird), to which Gryphius explicitly refers. Moreover, Gryphius's mention of a dagger specifies the weapons referred to in the epigram and simultaneously reframes its use by suggesting it as a tool for gardening. At first glance, something similar seems to be at stake with respect to the sword, which has a general point of reference in the weapons of the *subscriptio* and serves Gryphius by bridging the gap between the war and the contemporary historical context in which Ferdinand IV takes center stage.

Scholarship has occasionally understood Gryphius's appropriation of emblems for his poetry as having an exclusively ornamental function.[30] Yet the *subscriptio* of the emblem Gryphius applies in *Majuma* suggests otherwise. It speaks of the *ars pacis*, the art of peace, or, in other words, of the skill of giving a form to the new situation of peace and the things that can be known about it. Gryphius experiments with these forms. For one—thus indicates the closeness of the first two verses of Mercury's speech to the epigram—he tries out a quasi-mimetic alignment with his model and thereby with the attempts

---

28. Alciato, *Emblemata cum commentariis* (1621).
29. Alciato, *Emblematum liber* (1531).
30. See, e.g., Jöns, *Das "Sinnen-Bild"* (1966), 72–74; Jöns, "Majuma, Piastus," 289–90.

FIGURE 4. Ex bello pax detail, *pictura* (image). Andrea Alciato, *Emblemata* (1621). Photograph courtesy of Special Collections Research Center, William and Mary Libraries.

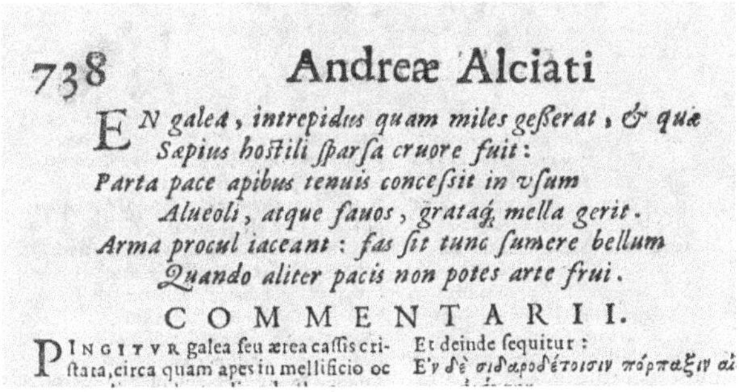

Andreæ Alciati

EN *galea, intrepidus quam miles gesserat , & quæ*
  Sæpius hostili sparsa cruore fuit:
Parta pace apibus tenuis concessit in vsum
  Alueoli, atque fauos, gratáq mella gerit.
Arma procul iaceant: fas sit tunc sumere bellum
  Quando aliter pacis non potes arte frui.

COMMENTARII

PINGITVR galea seu ærea cassis cristata, circa quam apes in mellificio oc— Et deinde sequitur:
Ἐν δὲ σιδαροδέτοισιν πόρπαξιν αἱ

FIGURE 5. Ex bello pax detail, *subscriptio* (epigram). Andrea Alciato, *Emblemata* (1621). Photograph courtesy of Special Collections Research Center, William and Mary Libraries.

FIGURE 6. Ex bello pax, *pictura* and *subscriptio*. Andrea Alciato, *Emblemata* (1531). Photograph courtesy of Augsburg, Staats- und Stadtbibliothek, Phil 34, fol. C3v (urn:nbn:de:bvb:12-bsb11272622-0).

of tradition to represent and process the passage from war to peace. A second option, as the example of the dagger shows, emphasizes the transformation of the source and its allegorical interpretation. Gryphius's third proposal brings the dynamics of metamorphosis to a halt and limits the use of images where the play addresses the historical context directly. There are two elements that constitute this third point. First, and in contrast to the dagger episode, the poet introduces this alternative by abstaining from a transformation or a misappropriation of the sword. Gryphius simply passes the weapon on to the hero of the play and the actual bearer of hope.[31] Second, the final hymn, directed at Ferdinand, is characterized by an insistence on his name that largely renounces poetic images and focuses on verbal designation instead of depiction. The last strophe mentions Ferdinand's name four times in six verses. Gryphius thereby sketches out a state of peace that is increasingly tied to the pure and, as it were, bare and unadorned existence of the new king:

> *FERDINAND! der Erden Sonn!*
> *FERDINAND des Himmels Hoffen!*
> *FERDINAND der Deutschen Wonn!*
> *Vunser Wundsch hat eingetroffen.*
> *Leb! O lebe für und für*
> *FERDINAND der Erden Zir.* (MA, 3.152–57)

> Ferdinand, sun of the earth! Ferdinand, heaven's hope! Ferdinand, bliss of the Germans! Our wish has become true. Live! Oh, live on and on, Ferdinand, the earth's adornment.

Following my hypothesis about Gryphius's attitude toward allegories, the conclusion drawn from this could be that, in *Majuma*, Gryphius passes historical knowledge through different forms and stages of allegorization until, in the last stage, he seems to reduce the imagery to a bare minimum. Knowledge would have reached a state in which it coincides with the existence of the new emperor, who would serve as a point of transition between war and peace and guarantee historical continuity. Yet at the last minute, Gryphius introduces a salvation-historical element into the play. Mercury asks the Austrians to prosper until the coming of the reign of the eternal, unalterable God, and he asks Ferdinand to reconquer Constantinople, the second Rome, from the Turks (*MA*, 3.140–51). At the end of the play and the war, in a moment in which the conditions for peace are at stake, the divine messenger invokes a new reason for a war that would pursue Christian interests into eternity. The question of historical possibility and its allegorical form passes from view.

31. Kaminski, *Ex bello ars oder Ursprung der "Deutschen Poeterey,"* 108.

Yet this is not Gryphius's last word, either. An additional possibility that points beyond the reaches of allegories and salvation history presents itself with respect to the performance of the play. The stage direction at the very beginning of *Majuma* indicates that it was sung (*Auff dem Schauplatz Gesangsweise vorgestellet*). This unmistakable reference to music is the only one of its kind, and even though musical plays (*Singspiele*) of the time were not always explicit about the style of their performance, the scarcity of information in *Majuma* is nonetheless unusual. No notes have been transmitted, there is no mention of the composer or the orchestration, and it remains unclear which parts were actually sung.[32] This lack of detail contrasts starkly with Gryphius's use of a broad variety of meters that seem to increase and support the play's musicality and consequently the likeliness of a musical performance.

The indeterminacy that the single stage direction evokes goes hand in glove with Gryphius's indecisive handling of the allegorical possibilities and his openness for poetic experiments. It also dovetails with the fact that Gryphius's play belongs to a genre of texts that were written for specific occasions. In the *Poeterey*, Martin Opitz had declared the so-called occasional poetry (*Gelegenheitsdichtungen*) volatile and inconsistent.[33] Seen in this light, the vagueness of the musical reference allows for a specific conclusion: To the coronation of the new king—who functions as a symbol of hope but also as a sign for a situation of transition and insecurity—corresponds a medial latency. The realm of musicality is referred to as an option, but it does not materialize. Latency seems to be the adequate frame for knowledge that is not yet stable. Neither abstract nor concrete, it prepares the ground at the margins of aesthetic representation for new aesthetic forms. These open forms, which surpass the visual and poetic traits of allegory but do not drift away into pure abstraction and eternity, are the realm in which Gryphius settles—on the threshold between war and peace and in a moment of crisis for both life-time and world-time. The medial diversification emerges from a poetics and hermeneutics of ruin, but it ultimately leads the way out of the dilemma that Breitinger detected in the fragmentations and simultaneous material excesses of the time between late baroque and early Enlightenment. Latency is what Breitinger's critical gaze overlooked in Gryphius's work but what, in fact, he had in mind when he spoke of the poetically beautiful that, between the probable and the miraculous, generates knowledge in which the future can take hold.

---

32. Jöns, "Majuma, Piastus," 295–96.
33. Kaminski, *Ex bello ars oder Ursprung der "Deutschen Poeterey,"* 105.

8

Thomas Burnet, Georg Wilhelm Friedrich Hegel, and the Realignment of Discourses

> A hideous Ruin ... our little dirty Planet.
> THOMAS BURNET

The Reverend Thomas Burnet crossed the Alps for the first time in 1671 on a grand tour of continental Europe, in tow his young student, the Earl of Wiltshire. The two men were on their way to Italy, where the youth's education was to be enhanced by the actual sight of Europe's cultural legacy, and Burnet's learnedness—acquired mostly from readings—would finally intersect with reality.[1] Yet before the travelers could even lay eyes on the remains of empire and civilization, Burnet's attention was already captured by the view of a different kind of debris. The rough, mountainous landscape that they traversed on their hike over the Simplon Pass would leave a lasting impression on the theologian and challenge his aesthetic perception and scientific inquisitiveness. The world that revealed itself to his awestruck gaze was a ruin.

It would take Burnet many years to come to terms with this experience of decay, irregularity, and disproportion and the feelings of admiration and horror it caused. Burnet had studied at Christ's College in Cambridge, which at the time was the center of the growing Neoplatonist movement. From teachers like Henry More he had adapted the concept of ideal, intelligible forms that inform matter and shape the visible world. He had learned about the "first beauty" through which all things are made beautiful.[2] Burnet's main work, the *Sacred Theory of the Earth* (*Telluris theoria sacra*), appears to be a direct result of the disturbance of his educational background and, at once, a sort of revelation. All of a sudden, Burnet was aware of the broken and torn state of the planet he inhabited. From then onward, the intellectual challenge he faced was to reconcile the world's current condition with God's infallible plan and Neoplatonic as well

---

1. Nicolson, *Mountain Gloom and Mountain Glory*, 207–8.
2. Nicolson, *Mountain Gloom and Mountain Glory*, 219.

as Christian ideas of the beautiful. The inner conflict this caused for Burnet was heightened by the ambivalent sense of grandness and meaninglessness the ruins evoked. The tension is on full display when he writes:

> The greatest Objects of Nature are, methinks, the most pleasing to behold; and next to the great Concave of the Heavens, and those boundless Regions where the Stars inhabit, there is nothing that I look upon with more Pleasure, than the wide Sea and the Mountains of the Earth . . . we do naturally, upon such Occasions, think of God and his Greatness . . . And yet these Mountains we are speaking of, to confess the Truth, are nothing but great Ruins; but such as shew a certain Magnificence in Nature; as from old Temples and broken Amphitheatres of the Romans we collect the Greatness of that People . . . There is nothing doth more awaken our Thoughts, or excite our Minds to enquire into the Causes of such Things, than the actual View of them; as I have had Experience myself, when it was my Fortune to cross, the Alps and Apennine Mountains; for the Sight of those wild, vast and indigested Heaps of Stone and Earth did so deeply strike my Fancy, that I was not easy 'till I could give my self some tolerable Account, how that Confusion came in Nature. (*ST*, 1:188–90)[3]

The "account" that Burnet intended to give came in the form of a literary composition that merged a scientific geological approach with a reading of Genesis. Burnet declared the *Sacred Theory*'s origin in his own "fancy" just as matter-of-factly as he claimed a methodological commitment to reason and thereby framed the work as both a product of imagination and of philosophical and scientific argumentation.[4]

At the outset of his treatise, Burnet explains that the sight of the Alpine wasteland had kindled a desire to understand whether this current form had been intended from the beginning of creation or if the world had changed shape:[5]

> I had always, methought, a particular Curiosity to look back into the Sources and Original of Things; and to view in my Mind, so far as I was able, the

---

3. I am using the sixth edition of the English version of the work: Burnet, *Sacred Theory of the Earth* (1726; hereafter cited as *ST*, with book and page numbers). The first edition appeared in Latin in 1681, followed by an English translation in 1684. The Latin edition was titled *Telluris theoria sacra orbis nostri originem et mutationes generalis, quas aut jam subiit, aut olim subiturus est, complectens; Libri duo priores de deluvio et paradiso*. The two-volume 1726 edition is the English version of Burnet's revised 1689 edition of the Latin text. It contains four books, two more books than the first Latin edition.

4. "'Tis a dangerous thing to engage the Authority of Scripture in Disputes about the Natural World, in Opposition to Reason" (*ST*, 1:xix).

5. Vittoria Di Palma suggests that Burnet "redefined the notion of wasteland for a new generation"; see Di Palma, *Wasteland*, 149.

> Beginning and Progress of a Rising World . . . I carried on my Enquiries further, to try whether this Rising World, when form'd and finish'd, would continue always the same; in the same Form, Structure, and Consistency; or what Changes it would successively undergo . . . and, lastly, what would be its final Period and Consummation . . . But when we speak of a Rising World . . . we speak of the Sublunary World, this Earth, and its Dependencies, which rose out of a Chaos about Six Thousand Years ago. And seeing it hath fallen to our Lot to act upon this Stage, to have our present Home and Residence here, it seems most reasonable, and the Place design'd by Providence, where we should first employ our Thoughts, to understand the Works of God and Nature. (ST, 1:1–3)

Burnet came to the conclusion that the present condition of the earth could not have been God's intention and that the ruin was the result of a major transformation from a previously uncorrupted state. This concern with the versatility of forms would turn out to be at the heart of the *Sacred Theory* and the topic that Burnet would attempt to substantiate both scientifically and theologically. He observed the correlation between the world's changing geological shape and the altering conditions for human life on earth and derived from it a firm belief in historicity as the driving force of all worldly and vital movements.[6] The same adherence to history also guided Burnet's interpretation of the Bible, and it led him to perceive the deluge—theologically a punishment for human sinfulness that resulted in the loss of paradise—as the natural cause for the universal decay. Yet in the *Sacred Theory* and especially in his later work *Archaeologiae Philosophicae*, Burnet also stayed true to his Neoplatonic background and especially to More's emphasis of the simultaneously literal and symbolic sense of Genesis.

Burnet's effort to sustain scientific findings with the help of the biblical account has caused confusion, misunderstandings, and open, sometimes hostile disapproval. Stephen Jay Gould noticed that throughout its reception history, Burnet's work was regularly mischaracterized as an example of the "improper intrusion of religion into scientific matters" or vice versa, and that the juxtaposition—intended to merge theological and scientific views—has often been mistaken for a trigger that kindled the conflict between science and theology. Gould counters that at the time of the *Theory*'s composition, no such divide existed. The disagreement, he states, was rather one between traditionalists and modernists on both sides of the intellectual aisle.[7] Reinhard Zimmermann detailed the nature of the severe temporal conflict that

---

6. Gould, *Time's Arrow, Time's Cycle* (1987), 44.
7. Gould, *Time's Arrow, Time's Cycle*, 24–26.

Burnet's simultaneously geological and biblical rationale for the loss of the first world (and paradise) incited. The tension, Zimmermann argues, was mainly one between science's increasing focus on the slowness of geological processes and the emphasis that the biblical account put on the suddenness of the divine act. In Zimmermann's view, it was particularly the Reverend Burnet's self-imposed task to merge science and theology on the basis of facts that was doomed to fail from the outset. Such an approach was potentially suited to address recent reconsiderations of isolated scientific findings, but it was ineffectual with respect to the comprehensive structural changes that new scientific discoveries induced.[8]

In my own reading of Burnet's theologico-scientific treatise, I will put forward a new understanding of the *Sacred Theory* as a piece of writing that is shaped by the tension between abstraction and concretization. Granted that the two concepts provoked objection or met with approval from different groups of readers, the reception-historical implications are only one aspect of a much more fundamental and far-reaching textual dynamic. Getting to the bottom of this dynamic is the goal of the following considerations. I presuppose that, much as in Andreas Gryphius's *Majuma*, the organization of historical knowledge is at stake in Burnet's *Sacred Theory*. Both authors struggle with yet unsecured concepts and inventories of knowledge in their respective discursive and historical moment. In Gryphius's case, the transition between war and peace created a situation of uncertainty, while for Burnet the issue is the precariousness of epistemological categories in the course of a realignment of scientific and theological discourses. Unlike the concept of reconciliation, which presupposes that there are two opposing sides waiting to be harmonized, the idea of realignment implies that the features of a discourse are in flux and keep taking new shape against the backdrop of the historical context.[9] Realignment is therefore a continuous, interminable process that can be either complicated or else simple or altogether neutral. The relation between discourses is as mutable and multifarious as the discourses themselves. On the following pages, I will speak of both reconciliation and realignment, and while in the first case I intend to express a harmonizing tendency, I emphasize the force of alternation in the second.

In his attempt to control the material excesses of allegory, Gryphius resorted to the realm of medial latency. As we will see, Burnet maneuvers between the concrete and abstract traits of his objects of investigation as well as

---

8. Zimmermann, *Künstliche Ruinen*, 2–3.
9. Also see Tuveson, *Millennium and Utopia*, 113, and his argument against the idea that Burnet tried to reconcile religion and science.

of the methods to examine them. Whether his endeavor was a conscious act or not is of secondary importance for my argument. Instead, I will focus on the indicators that Burnet—intentionally or inadvertently—envisioned the realignment of scientific and theological discourses as a decidedly literary process.[10] For those of Burnet's critics who recognized the literary streak in his *Theory*, it was usually an incentive to denounce his approach as either nonscientific or theologically unorthodox. The transdiscursive *possibilities* of literature and the ways in which they play out with respect to a realignment of discourses of knowledge in Burnet's work is yet to be uncovered by this analysis. They lurk in the ruins and in Burnet's use of theatrical metaphors, both of which unmask the movement between abstraction and concretization as a genuinely literary one.

The struggle for new knowledge always expresses itself, in one way or another, as an altercation between time concepts. As I have already mentioned, Zimmermann indicates as much when he juxtaposes the temporalities of divine disruption and geological duration in the *Sacred Theory*. To what degree Burnet was aware that their simultaneous occurrence caused logical inconsistencies is not entirely clear. He seems to have sought to work around the contradictions by holding, on the one hand, that the deluge had been "one Stroke" and a "single Action" and, on the other, that the material conditions for the great flood had evolved slowly over thousands of years (*ST*, 1:90). Yet the coincidence of continuity and discontinuity is only one element in a complex temporal setting that exposes Burnet's work as a battleground of time. The fiercely contested subject is the matter of historicity, the natural and divine laws of time-conditioned change and transformation and their relation to timelessness and eternity. To make his point that the world and humanity have an origin, Burnet engages in a detailed rebuttal of Aristotle's notion of an eternal cycle of time.[11] It is the purpose of the following deliberations to shine a light on the connection between time and the dynamic of abstraction and concretization.

In the short final section of this chapter, I will make a suggestion as to how we could read Georg Wilhelm Friedrich Hegel's encounter with the "dead masses" of the Swiss Alps more than a century after Burnet as a realignment

---

10. Burnet's literary style has not gone unnoticed. For instance, Stephen Jay Gould repeatedly refers to the narrative or dramatic qualities of the *Sacred Theory*. See Gould, *Time's Arrow, Time's Cycle*, 44–45. Marjorie Nicolson states that Burnet's "real gifts were those of a novelist or dramatist"; see Nicolson, *Mountain Gloom and Mountain Glory*, 192. Neither Gould nor Nicolson, however, asks about the reasons for Burnet's literary style.

11. Gould, *Time's Arrow, Time's Cycle*, 42.

of his own philosophical discourse. I will tentatively explore the idea that at the core of Hegel's philosophy lies the interplay between abstraction and concretization that first makes itself seen in the heaps of broken rocks but ultimately pervades all of the spirit's manifestations.

Theatrum ruinosum

"New found Lands and Countries accrue to the Prince whose Subject makes the first Discovery." In this manner, Thomas Burnet opens his dedicatory letter to King William III, who had requested an English translation of the popular Latin edition of the *Sacred Theory of the Earth*. "And having retriev'd a World that had been lost for some thousands of Years out of the Memory of Man, and the Records of Time," Burnet continues, "I thought it my Duty to lay it at your Majesty's feet." Burnet served in an advisory role by royal appointment as clerk of the closet. The discovery, Burnet admits, will not expand the king's "Dominions" nor enrich his thoughts. It can, at best, provide fodder for the monarch's curiosity about the original state of the first world, of which only fragments remain: "We have still the broken Materials of the first World, and walk upon its Ruins" (*ST*, book 1, Epistle Dedicatory).

Building on this partly religious, partly scientific conviction that the current ruined state of the earth was a consequence of the deluge, Burnet refers, in the preface to the reader, to the flood as one of those "great Turns of Fate" that belong among the major transformations of the natural world. At the same time, they are part of the narrative of the scripture (*ST*, 1:xvii). According to Burnet, these two conditions—the revelations of science and the insights of religion—were "the Hinges upon which the Providence of this Earth" moved, and they qualified an event as simultaneously sacred and historical.

Before the deluge, Burnet tells his readers, the earth was featureless. From a fluid mass, confused, formless, and dark, arose a smooth and regular shape without mountains, "plain as the Elysian fields" (*ST*, 1:72). This was the form of the earth when it first became a "habitable World" and the "Seat of Paradise" (*ST*, 2:238). Burnet claims, in other words, that the world began with a process of formation and that beginning and form coincided, so as to account for the world's historicity:[12]

> And whosoever understands the Progress and Revolutions of Nature, will see that neither the present Form of the Earth, nor its first Form, were permanent or immutable Forms, but transient and temporary by their own Frame and

---

12. Burnet argues against Aristotle's doctrine of the eternity of the world.

Constitution; which the Author of Nature, after certain Periods of Time, had design'd for Change and Destruction. (*ST*, 1:54–55)

Being historical and not eternal is the property of forms and the trait that the world, being a formed entity, shares with works of art: "The Earth, under that Form and Constitution it now hath, could not more be eternal than a Statue or Temple, or any Work of Art" (*ST*, 1:51). Finally, the same condition of mutability, transience, and mortality that applies to the world as form is the historical state of mankind, made up of individual lives:

> There are many particular Marks and Arguments, that the Generations of Men have not been from Everlasting. All History, and all Monuments from Antiquity, of what kind soever, are but of a few Thousand of Years date; we have still the Memory of the Golden Age, of the first State of Nature, and how Mortals liv'd then in Innocency and Simplicity. (*ST*, 1:55)

From an epistemological point of view, history and time are—as Burnet suggests early on in his treatise—the categories that humans are equipped to understand. They are the issues on which intellectual endeavors should be focused, rather than on futile attempts to comprehend nontemporal eternity:

> Whatsoever concerns this Sublunary World in the whole Extent of its Duration, from the Chaos to the last Period, this I believe Providence hath made us capable to understand, and will in its due Time make it known. All I say, betwixt the first Chaos and the last Completion of Time and all Things temporary, this was given to the Disquisitions of Men: On either Hand is Eternity, before the World and after, which is without our reach: But that little spot of Ground that lies betwixt these two great Oceans, this we are to cultivate, this we are Masters of, herein we are to exercise our Thoughts. (*ST*, 1:7)

Naturally, form, world, and life, as they first emerged in perfect, paradisiac symmetry and proportion from the disorder and confusion of matter, did not last. The passage in which Burnet describes how the deluge—God's punishment for the "Wickedness and Degeneracy of Men" (*ST*, 1:130)—put an end to this fragile harmony of Eden's seamless beauty is fashioned as a stage entrance. Addressing his potential readers, Burnet writes, "Draw but the Curtain, and these Scenes will appear, or something very like 'em." (*ST*, 1:90). A sophisticated dramatic representation of the great flood follows a few pages later:

> Thus the Flood came to its height; and 'tis not easy to represent to our selves this strange Scene of Things, when the Deluge was in its Fury and Extremity; when the Earth was broken and swallowed up in the Abyss, whose raging Waters rise higher than the Mountains and fill'd the Air with broken Waves,

with a universal Mist, and with thick Darkness, so as Nature seem'd to be in a second Chaos; and upon this Chaos rid the distress'd Ark, that bore the small Remains of Mankind . . . all the Poetry and all the Hyperboles that are used in the Description of Storms and raging Sea, were literally true in this. (*ST*, 1:134–35)

Burnet's scientific explanation for the drama was based on the report in Genesis that he ascribed to Moses, "the best of Historians" (*ST*, 1:12).[13] Genesis 7:11 mentions that in the "six hundredth year of Noah's life, in the second month, on the seventeenth day . . . all the fountains of the great deep burst forth" and drowned "everything on dry land."[14] Burnet deduced from this description that the surface of the earth had cracked in the drought of an eternal antediluvian summer and allowed the heated water underneath to erupt as in a steam turbine (*ST*, 1:95). From the pressure, the earth, which Burnet imagined as hanging above the deep, broke and fell into the water-filled "Abyss" (*ST*, 1:87–90). The violent displacement of the water caused the void to overflow and the entire earth, from the plains to the highest mountain, was inundated. When the water finally receded after more than a year, one could see "the true Image of the present Earth in the Ruins of the first. The Surface of the Globe would be divided into Land and Sea; the Land would consist of Plains and Valleys and Mountains, according as the Pieces of this Ruin were plac'd and dispos'd: Upon the Banks of the Sea would stand the Rocks, and near the Shore would be Islands, or lesser Fragments of Earth compass'd round by Water . . . the Parts would fall hollow in many Places in this, as in all other Ruins" (*ST*, 1:91) The deluge, Burnet writes, brought "another Face of things, other Scenes, and a new World upon the Stage" (*ST*, 1:122). However, the world did not change in terms of matter and substance, but with respect to "Frame, Form and Composition" (*ST*, 1:54), such that old greatness was still visible in the overall decay. The first world lived on in the second.

At the beginning of book 2, abiding by his literal interpretation of the Bible, Burnet relates the historicity of the world to that of individual life. In comparing the ante- and postdiluvian conditions, one of the differences that is uppermost in his mind is the discrepancy in life-time. "I know no Difference betwixt the Antediluvian World and the present," he writes, "so apt to affect us, if we reflect upon it, as this wonderful Disproportion in the Ages of Men; our Forefathers and their Posterity: They liv'd seven, eight, nine hundred Years and upwards." The miracle of the longevity of our ancestors is

---

13. The assumption that Moses wrote Genesis is of course not a fact established by historical-critical interpretation of the Bible.

14. Gen. 7:11, in Coogan, Brettler, and Newsome, *New Oxford Annotated Bible*.

only matched by the astonishing brevity of our own lives, Burnet marvels: "It is altogether as strange a Thing that Men should have such short Lives as they have now, as they had such long Lives in the first Ages of the World" (*ST*, 2:245–47). Burnet then unites life and world, first by pointing out that the Bible measured the ages of the world in terms of the years lived by the patriarchs, and second by once again using a theatrical metaphor:

> Our Life now is so short and vain, as if we came only into the World to see it and leave it; by the Time we begin to understand ourselves a little, and to know where we are, and how to act our Part, we must leave the Stage, and give place to others as meer Novices as we were ourselves at our first Entrance. (*ST*, 2:252)

There is, as Burnet's somewhat long-winded examination reveals, no easily discernible physical or moral reason for the shift in life expectancy after the flood. And to many of those contemporaries "of Wits and Parts" who had known nothing but the shortness of life-time, the excessively long lives that the patriarchs allegedly enjoyed only made sense, as Burnet observes, if the numbers of years that the Bible mentioned were not taken literally:

> Yet I know some have thought this so improbable and incongruous a Thing, that to save the Credit of Moses and the Sacred History, they interpret these Years of Lunar Years or Months; and so the Ages of these Patriarchs are reduc'd to much what the same measure with the common Life of Men at this Time. (*ST*, 2:246)

In this particular sequence, Burnet ascribes the impulse to interpret the Bible allegorically—in his words, to "depres[s] the Sense of Scripture"—to the necessity of a rational account of what the Bible describes, which is the same as the need for "a Theory" (*ST*, 2:246). Burnet seems to criticize scholars with an inclination toward allegory by insisting that an incorporation of science into an understanding of the sacred text on the basis of history is possible. In this line of argument, the significance of ruins becomes obvious. Ruins, as Burnet does not tire to point out, are the material signs of the mutability and temporality of forms and the historicity of the world. Their objectness links geological to cultural and political history, as the many comparisons between the world as ruin and the ruins of human-made architecture and the remains of empires indicate:

> I confess when this Idea of the Earth is present to my Thoughts, I can no more believe that this was the Form wherein it was first produc'd, than if I had seen the Temple of Jerusalem in its Ruins, when defac'd and sack'd by the Babylonians; I could have persuaded my self, that it had never been in any other Posture, and that Solomon had given Orders for Building it so. (*ST*, 1:212)

In Burnet's attempt to organize knowledge, ruins are the material vehicles of that knowledge, caused by an act of God. They carry physical traces of the constructions (in a broad sense) that they used to be, and they are a sort of tangible comment on the losses and the deprivations of the present. Furthermore, materiality and objecthood are crucial in Burnet's anticipation of the future as well. As he details in books 3 and 4 of the *Sacred Theory*, the dawn of a "new Heaven and a new Earth," first mentioned in book 1, depends on the dissolution of the present ruin in a universal conflagration (*ST*, 1:136).

Burnet's accentuation of reification and historicity was ambivalent, however. There are inconsistencies and sudden turns in his reasoning that reveal an intellectual indecision as to whether the organization of knowledge is rather a matter of the conceptual or the factual characteristics of systems and categories. One of the passages in which he tries to come to terms with the tension occurs in chapter 11 of the first book. In the course of his remarks about the origin of mountains, Burnet explains what a hypothesis is and how we can determine its usefulness. A good hypothesis, he states, is capable of grasping nature in its entirety. But contradicting his own definition, he contends that one could object to the relevancy of hypotheses on principle by arguing that they are "a kind of Fiction or Supposition" that has to be verified in comparison with an observable reality. Burnet admits that under the condition of the limited reach of our sensual perception, we rely on intelligible suppositions to achieve knowledge. He then proceeds to declare his own method with regard to the examination of the ruined state of the world as based on a hypothesis, only to immediately take the proposition back and replace it with a declaration of confidence in the authority of the literal sense of Scripture:

> But to speak the Truth, this Theory is something more than a bare Hypothesis; because we are assured that the general Ground that we go upon is true . . . for besides Reason and Antiquity, Scripture it self doth assure us of that . . . And whereas an Hypothesis that is clear and proportion'd to Nature in every Respect, is accounted morally certain, we must in Equity give more than a moral Certitude to this Theory. (*ST*, 1:203)

Yet the confession of trust in the reifying force of the Bible, which was supposed to lift the *Sacred Theory* above the realm of mere hypothesis and give it a solid foundation in truth, reality, and history, was not Burnet's last word. He clarified that, on the basis of the scripture, the hypothetical status of his claim could be overcome exclusively with respect to the general events. Certainty existed only in terms of the factuality of the flood and the destruction it caused. The evaluation of the details, however, he wanted to keep flexible to be able to accommodate, whenever necessary, new scientific insights: "For as to the Particularities, I look upon them only as problematical, and accordingly I affirm nothing therein but with a Power of Revocation, and a Liberty to change my Opinion when I shall be better inform'd" (*ST*, 1:203). What Burnet called *Theory*—and pronounced to be "chiefly Philosophical" and adhering to reason—was therefore a model of reflection, which, instead of being based on a process of abstraction, was built on an openly displayed ambiguity between concrete and abstract categories. In the following, I will show that the oft-noted theatrical elements of Burnet's work are relevant precisely with respect to this equivocation of *theoria*.

In his essay "Theatrum Theoreticum" (2007), Rodolphe Gasché sets forth how the use of theatrical strategies in philosophical theory exposes the blind spots of theoretical thinking.[15] His point of departure is Hans Blumenberg's reception-historical take on an anecdote famously told by Socrates in Plato's dialogue *Theaetetus*. A Thracian maid laughs at the astronomer Thales of Miletus, who, watching the stars above, falls into a well at his feet.[16] The scene exposes the ludicrousness of the unworldly theoretician, who, striving for knowledge, loses contact with reality. In Blumenberg's terms, Thales and the Thracian woman are protagonists in the "confrontation between theory and lifeworld."[17] Against this backdrop, Gasché concerns himself with the theatricality of theory. Drawing on Blumenberg's claim that the anecdote about the maid and the astronomer is the first instance in the history of philosophy in which theory (Thales's gaze) shows itself to a spectator (the maid's gaze), he asks whether theory necessarily has to be staged. In other words, he wonders if the search for knowledge and truth—that is, *theoria* in the Platonic sense of *episteme*—has to make itself visible to achieve its goals and if it therefore has an intrinsic affiliation with the theater.[18]

Gasché's answer harks back to what he identifies as a prephilosophical relation between the act of seeing and the divine in Greek religious festivals. Supporting his argument by cautiously linking the etymologies of *thea* (seeing) and *theos* (god), he holds that in the context of the sacred feast that served the purpose of human-divine interaction, the theater was the place in which gods, appearing in visible shape, could be viewed by worshipping

---

15. Gasché, "Theatrum Theoreticum," 188–208.

16. Blumenberg, *Laughter of the Thracian Woman* (2015). For the German original, see Blumenberg, *Das Lachen der Thrakerin* (1987).

17. Blumenberg, *Laughter of the Thracian Woman*, 11. For an understanding of life-world as a prephilosophical and pretheoretical state, see Blumenberg's discussion of Husserl in chapter 2.

18. Gasché, "Theatrum Theoreticum," 195–96, 200.

spectators. At the same time, the gods themselves were observers of the performances that people staged in their honor. Therefore, Gasché writes, in the theater "those who [came] to see the gods [were] the objects themselves of a divine gaze."[19] The lingering concern with the relation between *theoria* and the divine in Platonic and Aristotelian thought finally evidenced that the prephilosophical conditions remained relevant for philosophical theory. The knowledge-seeking theoretician, thus Gasché's conclusion, is a performer in front of the gods. In trying to resemble them, he imitates their way of seeing, which is a self-reflexive vision that sees "itself by itself."[20]

Yet emulating the divine vision with the human gaze is an impossibility. Theoretical observation is ultimately unable to observe itself. As Thomas Forrer argues—and as the interaction between Thales and the Thracian woman corroborates—the philosopher relies on being seen if he is to account for his own theoretical reflection. Forrer claims that the impossible immediacy of human theoretical vision as well as the irreducible necessity to distinguish between the viewer and the viewed is the reason why theory can never completely free itself of theatricality. The theater provides the sensual or physical space—in Forrer's terms the "scene" (*Schauplatz*)—that allows for *theoria* to become visible, but without enabling it to see itself. Put otherwise, the only way of theorizing theory—and the closest the human viewpoint can approximate a divine perspective—is via the act of visualization, for which the privileged place is the theater.[21] In Forrer's reading of Gasché, much emphasis lies on the concreteness of the theatrical space in which theory's theory materializes by way of becoming physically visible. There is a strong focus on the act of reification, which emerges as the determining counterpart of theoretical abstraction.

If we adapt this perspective for our analysis of the *Sacred Theory*, then the abundance of theatrical metaphors must be understood as evidence for Burnet's profound insight into the workings and limits of *theoria*. In the so-called early modern period, the theatrical metaphor was, in addition to its possible use with respect to the vanity of human existence, a popular trope to denote the organization—that is, the representation and contemplation—of knowledge.[22] In the royal advisor's historical moment, on the one hand, the organization of knowledge that he is after requires an evaluation of contents and methods of knowing and an affirmation of those elements that are con-

19. Gasché, "Theatrum Theoreticum," 201.
20. Gasché, "Theatrum Theoreticum," 206.
21. See Forrer, *Schauplatz / Landschaft*, 44–45.
22. See, e.g., Friedrich, "Frühneuzeitliches Wissenstheater," 301.

sidered valid and effective; on the other hand, it involves dealing with the unknown. Burnet calls the entirety of this process *theoria*, and he points out its hypothetical nature. Yet he also recognizes that theory cannot do without the factuality, the historicity, and the visibility that ground what is fictional and speculative about it in tangible, material, and observable reality.

Structurally and systematically, this is the point at which theater and ruin intersect and establish a relation to historical time, and it is here that the significance of Burnet's work as a literary discourse emerges. Walter Benjamin wrote in *The Origin of German Tragic Drama* that "in the ruins history has physically merged into the setting"—"as script [*Schrift*]" (*OGD*, 177–78). The setting is the theatrical scene, the *Schauplatz* of the tragic drama (*Trauerspiel*). In it, history appears as "nature-history" (*Naturgeschichte*), for which it is characteristic that it "does not assume the form of a process of an eternal life" but, quite on the contrary, that of "irresistible decay" (*OGD*, 166). In that sense, the references to theater in Burnet's *Theory* put the history of the world in front of the readers' eyes. What they see is script, or, more precisely, what Benjamin called "characters of transience" (*Zeichenschrift der Vergängnis*), ruins and allegories, the means of the literary discourse and of art that "declares itself to be beyond beauty" (*OGD*, 178). Unlike Benjamin, however, and in accordance with the Greek spectacle for the gods, Burnet establishes a connection between theater and the all-seeing deity. The stage of the world, he writes, is a place "design'd by Providence" (*ST*, 1:3).

There is one conspicuous instance in Burnet's *Sacred Theory* in which many of the elements that participate in the dynamic of abstraction and concretization—the significance of ruins, a scene of spectatorship and implicit theatricality, the hypothetical situation of an experiment, and the tension between attaining new knowledge and preserving the old—are intertwined. Burnet imagines a situation in which a sleeping man from the flatlands is abandoned on the top of a mountain. Upon awakening, he has a visual experience that is not relatable to anything familiar and for which he has no epistemological categories: "At his Feet, it may be, an Heap of frozen Snow in the midst of Summer. He would hear the Thunder come from below, and see the black Clouds hanging beneath him." From the displaced man's perspective, the world presents itself in ruinous disorder. Burnet almost scornfully remarks that it would "not be easy" for the spectator to convince himself of the reality of what he saw. Yet interestingly, the same objects that are, at first, responsible for the disconnect between the viewer and the viewed and evoke in the man from the flatlands the impression that he has been subject to enchantment ("he wou'd think himself in an enchanted Country") eventually enable the transformation of the perceived illusion into the acceptance of a visibly broken but concrete world. The man, Burnet writes, "would be convinc'd, at least, that there are some Regions . . . strangely rude, and ruin-like, and very different from what he had ever thought of before" (*ST*, 1:192). Persuaded by the ruins of the world, the protagonist of the thought experiment turns from a victim of abstract fiction into a witness of empirical truth.

Looking back at Burnet's use of the Bible in the context of his explanation of hypotheses, one might be inclined to suggest that the scripture reliably stepped in when scientific speculation threatened to spin out of control and therefore needed to be entrenched in verifiable—that is, biblically supported—facts. However, the situation is more complicated than that. The indetermination between abstraction and concretization concerned the interpretation of the Bible itself. In fact, it played a vital role in the conspicuously mixed reactions to the *Sacred Theory* from its initial publication to the last editions after the author's death. The widely read and popular work was a frequent target of criticism and attacks from clerics and scientists alike, while, at the same time, it did not lack apologists and admirers. Marjorie Nicolson speaks of the "Burnet controversy" in which, for several years after the *Sacred Theory* had been published, the author participated only indirectly by way of extending his work from two to four books. He joined the debate in 1690 after Erasmus Warren in his work *Geologia* had contradicted Burnet's view of the world as a ruin and thereby indirectly criticized his aesthetics.[23]

The broadsides against Burnet came from a variety of fields, and they were aimed at various aspects of his *Theory*. However, in addition to a very critical reception of his scientific claims that, for example, earned him the title of an ardent Cartesian,[24] one of the main stumbling blocks for contemporary readers was indeed Burnet's inconclusive handling of the question as to whether the Bible and especially Genesis should be interpreted according to the historical or the allegorical sense of scripture. The problem was evident to Burnet's first reader, who happened to be Isaac Newton. Burnet had probably made Newton's acquaintance at the University of Cambridge, where he was a senior proctor when the younger scholar completed his master of arts degree in 1668. Before publishing the Latin version of the *Sacred Theory*, Burnet sent Newton parts of the first two books and asked for his opinion.[25]

---

23. Nicolson, *Mountain Gloom and Mountain Glory*, 187, 233–37.

24. On Burnet as an ardent Cartesian, see Mandelbrote, "Isaac Newton and Thomas Burnet,"156.

25. Mandelbrote, "Isaac Newton and Thomas Burnet," 157; Newton, *Correspondence of Isaac Newton* (1960; hereafter cited as *CIN*, with volume and page numbers), 2:319–34.

Many scholars have deemed Newton's overall friendly and reassuring response an explicit alignment of his thoughts on creation with Burnet's. "I think the main part of your Hypothesis as probable as what I have here written, if not in some respects more probable," Newton writes in a lengthy letter from January 1680/81, referring to Burnet's scientific claims (*CIN*, 2:329). He also agreed with Burnet on the supposition that Moses had accommodated the biblical language to the understanding of his original audience (*CIN*, 2: 331)—an argument Burnet and other thinkers in his surroundings had adopted from Saint Augustine's commentary on the literal meaning of Genesis. Underneath this conciliatory surface, however, Newton's skepticism seems to have been more distinct. Scott Mandelbrote observed that for Newton one subject of contention was the true nature of Moses's authority. From his point of view, Burnet's method ultimately amounted to a rejection of the prophet's account. Even though Newton was not opposed to an allegorical interpretation of Genesis that could potentially reveal truths about creation that a literal understanding was unable to grasp, Mandelbrote opined that he remained unconvinced that Burnet had succeeded in offering such a reading. In his letter, Newton suggests to Burnet that he should "consider . . . whether any one who understood the process of ye creation & designed to accommodate to ye vulgar not an Ideal or poetical but a true description of it as succinctly & theologically as Moses has done, without omitting any thing material wch ye vulgar have a notion of . . . could mend that description wch Moses has given us" (*CIN*, 2:333). For Mandelbrote, the passage indicates that Newton perceived Burnet's *Sacred Theory* as an ideal and therefore inaccurate description of the biblical events.[26]

Drawing on this notion, I would like to highlight a different possible thrust of the letter. Newton points to a challenge that every account and interpretation of the Bible faces. Somewhat tautologically speaking, it is accurate only if it is true, mindful of the concrete context of its audience ("any thing material") and guarded against the temptations of abstraction. One could conclude that for Newton a narrative about creation that claims to be remotely comparable to Moses's account must stick closely to the historical facts and be neither ideal (abstract) nor poetic (abstract as well). Yet the way in which Newton articulates his invitation to Burnet to "consider" whether someone who adhered to all these rules "could mend" Moses's narrative says nothing about Newton's own attitude toward the issue, nor does it indicate what the right answer might be. It is therefore plausible that Newton's rhetorical question implies that mending Moses's report by avoiding abstraction is

---

26. Mandelbrote, "Isaac Newton and Thomas Burnet," 157–58.

impossible. The continuation of the passage supports this view, for Newton proceeds to declare Moses's language poetic. "If it be said," he writes, "that ye expression of making and setting two great lights in ye firmament is more poetical then natural: so also are some other expressions of Moses." The signifiers can be poetic as long as "the things signified by such figurative expressions are not Ideall [sic] or moral but true" (*CIN*, 2:333).

With respect to Genesis and the practice of biblical interpretation, Newton makes explicit by pointing out the relevancy of both history and allegory, of facts and their poetic description, what Burnet implicitly realizes about the workings of science and its relation to the Bible. In his analysis of the ruined state of the earth, Burnet practices a juxtaposition of concrete and abstract arguments but tries to bring them into line with a pronouncedly historical point of view. Newton finds that the act of securing what we know about the formation of life and the world, as well as what we can add to this knowledge, depends on the recognition of the textual interplay between abstraction and concretization, their synergy and their antagonistic dynamic. His criticism of Burnet is ultimately aimed at a hermeneutic imbalance that he detects in the *Sacred Theory* rather than at the royal advisor's failure to deliver an accurate allegorical reading of Genesis. Put chiastically, Burnet's methodical problem, as far as Newton is concerned, is that he does not acknowledge clearly enough that there is poetry in science and science in poetry, that history requires allegory and allegory history, and that only through an alliance of these perceived counterparts can the realignment of theology and science materialize.

If this is indeed what Newton intended to convey, then the fate of the *Sacred Theory* as well as the damage that Burnet's reputation would suffer in the wake of the publication would prove the younger scholar right, but not in the way he might have expected. The reactions to the treatise put Burnet on the defensive to an extent that most of his later writings appeared like a response to the critics of his earlier work. The clerk of the closet seemed to realize that the rejections had much to do with his handling of *historia* and *allegoria*. But the insight did not translate into a compromise between abstraction and concretization or the explicit recognition of his own discourse as a literary one. To "save" the *Theory*, Burnet ultimately abandoned his focus on a literal understanding of creation for a decidedly allegorical approach.[27] In 1692, his advocacy for an allegorical interpretation of Genesis in *The Ancient Doctrine Concerning the Originals of Things* (*Archeologiae Philosophicae*) finally earned him the pitiless scorn of orthodox theologians, some of whom

---

27. Nicolson, *Mountain Gloom and Mountain Glory*, 238.

accused him of deism. The "scandal" ended his career at King William III's court, and it excluded him from any further consideration for church office.[28]

Why Burnet ultimately defected to the abstract realm of allegorical liberty is understandable as an act of self-defense or, as Zimmermann suggested, as an insight into the epistemological limits of literality. That the new method failed so utterly, however, is not only owing to the conservatism of Burnet's contemporaries but must, at least partly, be ascribed to his misjudgment of the discursive possibilities of his time. As Newton saw clearly, the organization of new knowledge about life and the world required a form of discourse that was able to absorb both "the realm of thoughts" and the "realm of things" described by Benjamin (*OGD*, 178). It had to be a discourse, suited to render the tension between the imaginary and the factual, the concreteness of ruins and the paradoxical abstract concreteness of allegories, productive. That literature was that space in which new knowledge could be imagined and reified but also interpreted, categorized, realigned, and dismissed shines through much of Burnet's writing, but it never enters the sphere of conscious strategies. This is all the more surprising because some of Burnet's harshest critics recognized the potential, even if they used it as an argument against him. In 1698, the mathematician John Keill launched a devastating and comprehensive rebuke of Burnet's scientific findings in *An Examination of Dr. Burnet's Theory of the Earth*. On the last page, however, the diatribe suddenly metamorphoses into the most appreciative acknowledgment of Burnet's aesthetics. Burnet, Keill admits, is a poet:

> For as I believe, never any Book was fuller of Errors and Mistakes in Philosophy, so none ever abounded with more beautiful Scenes and more surprising Images of Nature; but I write only to those who might perhaps expect to find a true Philosophy in it. They who read it as an Ingenious Romance, will still be pleased with their Entertainment.[29]

Burnet himself ultimately settled for a declaration of goodwill: "I formerly designed to handle these Matters particularly, and clearly, to the utmost of my Ability: but old Age invades me and Death approaches." Burnet spoke of having erected, in a "short Warfare," only "a slender Monument of a Life not spent in Idleness." And almost as a consolation he predicted a "happy Age" in which everything that he had dealt with would appear "in the most beautiful Light."[30]

---

28. Gould, "Reverend Thomas' Dirty Little Planet" (1977), 145.
29. Keill, *Examination of Dr. Burnet's Theory of the Earth*, 176–77.
30. Burnet, *Archeologiae Philosophicae* (1736), viii.

Beyond what was likely an expression of hope for afterlife and redemption, one could be tempted to attribute to Burnet the uncanny feat of having anticipated the aesthetic admiration for ruins in following generations. For even if the notion of beauty was diametrically opposed to Burnet's perception of what he called a "broken world," his ruins had left their mark on a literary discourse that guided the realignment of science and theology, from which future thinkers would proceed.

Toward a Philosophical System: Hegel's Encounter with the Alps

This final section of the chapter is conceived as an afterthought to my examination of Thomas Burnet's *Sacred Theory*. From Hegel's short but detailed travel journal that he kept while on a hike to the Swiss Bernese Alps in 1796, I derive a decidedly heuristic model, intended to shed light on the function of Hegel's excursion to the mountains for the history of his own philosophy.[31] Burnet and Hegel have in common that their view of the Swiss mountainscape was largely unfavorable and, at first glance, this seems to be about as far as the similarities go.[32] In fact, the differences appear to outweigh the overlaps by far; for instance, Hegel never uses the term *ruin*, and the sentiment evoked by the sight of rocks and stones is neither shock nor awe but boredom and occasional indifference. Hegel is not interested in the details of the natural causes for the disorder, nor does he reflect on the biblically sustainable reasons. Instead, he offers a meticulous description of every single sight, but mostly without lingering on individual prospects. Quick to judge what he sees, he cannot hide a certain irritation over the fact that the experience of the sublime, in which the nature watchers of his time indulge, appears to pass him by. The mountains Eiger, Mönch, and Jungfrau, each about 13,000 feet high, simply did not leave the expected impression of grandness, majesty, and grandeur, Hegel writes (*Reisetagebuch*, 474). Besides, he is just as invested in a survey of the Alpine dwellers' customs, food, language, and political rights—in short, their cultural accomplishments—as he is in a portrayal of their natural environment.[33]

---

31. The text has been edited by one of Hegel's first biographers; see Rosenkranz, *Georg Wilhelm Friedrich Hegels Leben*, 470–90. Excerpts from the journal can be found in: Hegel, *Frühe Schriften* (1986), 614–18. In what follows, I will quote from Rosenkranz's 1844 edition and indicate the document as *Reisetagebuch*.

32. On the basis of this negative view, Burnet and Hegel have been grouped together before. See, e.g., Flubacher, "Gefühlswelten und Gebirgslandschaften," E1–E15.

33. Jaeschke, *Hegel-Handbuch*, 74–75.

Otto A. Böhmer argued that following his experience in the Alps, Hegel turned away from nature and toward the spirit. In Böhmer's narrative, the philosopher, who at the time had not yet made a name for himself, realized that nature in general, and especially in the shape of constricting cliffs, hindered the spirit's free movement.[34] Drawing on this position, I propose that the pivotal significance of the travel journal for the formation of Hegel's philosophy and its goal of attaining knowledge can be pinpointed in a subtle dynamic engendered by a shifting focus on abstraction and concretization, which would finally unfold its comprehensive significance in Hegel's theory of absolute idealism. Here is precisely where the scarce resemblances between Burnet and Hegel become meaningful. My suggestion is that the movement between abstraction and concretization as it plays out in Hegel's text can be gathered from similar motifs that are at stake in Burnet's *Sacred Theory*. This comparison reveals a certain continuity between the two thinkers, which coexists with the numerous discontinuities and is by no means historical but systematic. In what follows, I explicitly argue within the confines of a hypothesis and a thought experiment. Nevertheless, speaking of *abstraction* and *concretization* with respect to Hegel's work warrants a little elaboration, even if the terms are applied to a period before the emergence of Hegel's philosophical system.

To begin with, abstraction, as is well known, has its specific place in Hegel's philosophy, where it occupies the first stage in his dialectic. As such, it occurs only in correspondence with two other moments, the dialectical and the speculative. Abstraction is the step in which "the understanding postulates something unconditioned or something absolute."[35] In that sense, it fulfills a methodical necessity on the way to cognition. However, Hegel has criticized and even mocked notions of its exclusiveness. In 1807, shortly after the publication of the *Phenomenology of Spirit*, Hegel discussed the meaning of abstract thinking in his essay "Wer denkt abstrakt?" ("Who Thinks Abstractly?"). His verdict is that the subject of pure abstraction is not the philosopher but the uneducated person, who forgets that universals exist only in particular things.[36] Consequently and conversely, the concrete is not the sensuous opposite of the spiritual abstract. In his *Lectures on Aesthetics* (*Vorlesungen über Ästhetik*) of 1835, Hegel writes that everything truthful or significant is concrete in itself, no matter whether it pertains to the realm of the

---

34. Böhmer, "Der Geist in den Alpen," 129–38.

35. Beiser, *Hegel*, 167.

36. Hegel, "Wer denkt abstrakt?" (1979), 575–81; Hegel, *Enzyklopädie der philosophischen Wissenschaften im Grundriss I* (1979), §24.

spirit or to that of nature (*alles Wahrhaftige des Geistes sowohl als der Natur ist in sich konkret*).[37] Friedemann Barniske has therefore spoken of "speculative depth" (*spekulative Tiefe*) as a characteristic feature of the concrete in Hegel's aesthetics.[38]

If, in the course of my considerations, I retain the terms *abstraction* and *concretization* from my analysis of Burnet's *Theory*, then it is also with an eye toward the complexities of Hegel's elaboration of the concepts, especially in the *Phenomenology of Spirit* but also in the *Lectures on Aesthetics*. The terms are intended to capture what Hegel shares with Burnet and to absorb some of the antinomies that Hegel dealt with systematically and methodically in his later work. In the travel journal, we can observe a sort of dialectical process in which the universal and the particular negotiate their relation. As I will show, the adventurer guides his readers through stages of simple perception, of revelation and momentary experiences of beauty that seem to imply steps in the process of what Hegel would define theoretically as reality's self-revelation to consciousness.[39] In a sense, the travel journal seems to illustrate just what Beiser claimed with respect to Hegel's methodology: that it emerges from the "'self-organization' of the subject matter" and of its "'inherent movement,'" rather than being an a priori means to approach the inner form of an object.[40] To touch upon the inherent movement of the inner form of the subject matter is the goal of the ensuing snapshots from Hegel's journey.

In the year of the mountain trek, Hegel held a position as a private tutor for the two young sons of the Bernese patrician family Steiger von Tschugg. Hegel had moved to Switzerland in 1793, after finishing his studies of philosophy and theology in Tübingen. His nineteenth-century biographer Rudolf Haym noted that Hegel's teachers dismissed him with the verdict that he appeared to be a man of pleasant disposition but limited insight or ambition, a bad orator and "an idiot in philosophy" (*ein Idiot in der Philosophie*).[41] Hegel had indeed not yet achieved the height of his philosophical sophistication. The fame that he attained in later years seems to have altogether surprised old acquaintances.[42]

---

37. Hegel, *Vorlesungen über Ästhetik I* (1970), 100.
38. Barniske, *Hegels Theorie des Erhabenen*, 20–22.
39. See Hegel, *Phänomenologie des Geistes* (1986), especially the preface; Marx, *Hegels Phänomenologie des Geistes*.
40. Beiser, *Hegel*, 160.
41. Haym, *Hegel und seine Zeit*.
42. Rosenkranz, *Georg Wilhelm Friedrich Hegels Leben*, 30.

Little is known about Hegel's personal circumstances during the years he spent abroad, yet based on his writings from that period, Haym declared the Swiss sojourn as a time of unprecedented intellectual formation that advanced the methodological development of Hegel's thinking toward a philosophical system.[43] Haym, who is mostly interested in Hegel's early theological writings, does not mention the travel journal to support his claim. But Hegel's account contains glimpses of a systematizing, conceptualizing intention that is in line with Haym's observations and implicitly also refers back to Burnet's late seventeenth-century theoretical endeavor.[44]

The first indicator of such a complex constellation occurs in a passage at the beginning of the journal, when Hegel, using the third person, describes the experience of estrangement that visitors from the flatlands would be bound to have among the mountains. The narrow valleys frighten and confine them. And while they long for expansion and an opening of the landscape, their gaze hits rocky walls wherever it wanders (*Reisetagebuch*, 471–72). Vaguely reminiscent of Burnet's sleeper on the top of a mountain, this spectator has replaced a sense of enchantment when facing the ruins with a feeling of fear. He has substituted the acceptance of a concrete, broken world with the desire to escape or to free himself from it, as the literal meaning of the Latin *abstrahere* conveys. At the outset of his travelogue, Hegel sets up a conflict-laden, tense dynamic between the promise of abstraction in the sense of liberation and the threat of concretization as a confining sensual perception.

Further into the text and into the mountainscape, Hegel's focus shifts to the dullness of the wasteland that he and his three companions traverse. The four men have reached Guttannen, and, as Hegel points out—evoking a sense of them having reached the edge of the world—it is the last Bernese village before the border with the canton of Valais. The trail outside the village is wild and monotonous (*öde*), with the same sad (*traurig*), rough (*rauh*) cliffs towering on both sides along the way. The ground is covered in granite boulders, and Hegel cannot recognize the slightest hint of usefulness or purpose in this hostile environment. Toward the evening, they reach a stony hut in a bleak (*öde*), sad (*traurig*) stone desert (*Steinwüstenei*), and Hegel takes stock of his impressions—or rather lack thereof. For neither his eyes nor his imagination (*Einbildungskraft*), Hegel writes, are able to find purchase on the formless masses (*formlose Massen*). The viewer is deprived of pleasure (*Wohlgefallen*), astonishment (*Staunen*), or admiration (*Bewunderung*). The landscape seems

---

43. Haym, *Hegel und seine Zeit*, 40–41.
44. With this I do not mean to claim that there is a direct influence between Hegel and Burnet.

potentially appealing only to a mineralogist, who could find abundant material for study. Hegel curiously states that the scientist's findings would likely just result in deficient geological hypotheses. Finally, Hegel relinquishes his attempt to recognize the sublime in what he calls the "eternally dead masses" (*die ewig toten Massen*). He concludes that the only feeling they generate in him is the unchanging and in the long run boring notion that "this is the way it is" (*es ist so*; *Reisetagebuch*, 482–83).

The description Hegel gives of the landscape strangely hovers between the emphasis of random fragments and shapeless pieces and an evocation of an equally formless whole. In contrast to Burnet, who ties ruins to transformation, Hegel sees parts and masses that are radically static and atemporal. As I echo Barniske's words, the concreteness Hegel depicts seems to lack speculative depth. The universal and the particular have no meeting point. And while Burnet's efforts are aimed at a theory in which the abstract and the concrete are juxtaposed in a dynamic relation, they appear to be irreconcilable in Hegel's text. They do not even merge in the hypothesis of a mineralogist, whose assumptions between empirical evidence and theory Hegel dismisses as flawed before they can materialize.

There is only one instance over the course of the entire excursion that seems to halfway compensate Hegel for his disappointed expectations. The moment comes as a sort of aesthetic revelation at the sight of a waterfall.[45] From the rim of the abyss into which the water cascades, the audience (*Zuschauer*) has an overview of the majestic spectacle (*majestätisches Schauspiel*) of falling waves that draw the spectators' gaze downward, yet without ever allowing the eye to pursue or fix them. The waves' shapes (*Gestalt*) dissolve at every moment and are constantly replaced by new ones. The beholder therefore perpetually sees the same image and knows, at once, that it is never the same. Hegel is finally satisfied. Eternal death and static passivity that the rocks and stones represented have been replaced by tremendous activity (*gewaltige Regsamkeit*) and eternal life (*ewiges Leben*) and transformation. Imagination is in flux, driven by the movement toward spaces that are invisible from the observer's vantage point.

The concreteness of this visual experience, which Hegel sustains with theatrical metaphors and the self-liberation of the imaginative force that expands into the realm of the unknown, could be understood as having attained a sort of productive equilibrium if it were not for Hegel's last thought in this

---

45. For an interpretation of the passage with respect to the problem of representation in Hegel's aesthetics, see Gammon, "Modernity and the Crisis of Aesthetic Representation in Hegel's Early Writings," 145–70.

passage. It is dedicated to the impossibility of capturing the simultaneously concrete and abstract drama of eternal change on canvas. Hegel suggests that—much like the cliffs of the Alpine wasteland—the sensual presence of a painting (*sinnliche Gegenwart des Gemäldes*) would prevent imagination from transcending its immediate object. The "sensible appearing of the idea" was not yet conceptually mastered.[46] It held itself ready in the wasteland, however, as if waiting for Hegel's discourse to be properly realigned.

---

46. Hegel, *Vorlesungen über Ästhetik I*, 25.

V

Futures and Ruins

9

Johann Wolfgang von Goethe, Georg Simmel, and the Provisionality of Forms

> *Hier lernt man heiter schreiben:*
> *über den Schutt der Zeiten*
> *geht immergrün die Zeit dahin.*
>
> Here one learns how to stride lightheartedly:
> time passes evergreen
> across the debris of times.
>
> RICHARD DEHMEL

"Now, at last, I have arrived in the First City of the world!"[1] These were the words of excitement Johann Wolfgang von Goethe noted in his travel report when, after a month of journeying through Italy, he finally arrived in Rome on November 1, 1786. Goethe's enthusiasm was evoked by two seemingly opposing experiences. One was that he sensed that in the Eternal City his aesthetic education was about to be animated. "Now I have arrived, I have calmed down," Goethe writes. "All the dreams of my youth have come to life . . . and everything I have known for so long through paintings, drawings, etchings, woodcuts, plaster casts and cork models is now assembled before me." The other experience was that of an entirely new existence initiated by the encounter with Rome: "It could well be said that as soon as one sees with one's own eyes the whole which one had hitherto known inside and out but in fragments, a new life begins."[2] Goethe can therefore say that wherever he goes, he finds "a familiar object in an unfamiliar world" (*wohin ich gehe, finde ich eine Bekanntschaft in einer neuen Welt*; IJ, 129; IR, 168). Whatever he sees is exactly how he imagined it and, at the same time, new. The novelty that

---

1. Goethe, *Italian Journey* (2004; hereafter cited as *IJ*), 128. For the German original, see Goethe, *Italienische Reise* (1976; hereafter cited as *IR*), 167: "Ja, ich bin endlich in dieser Hauptstadt der Welt angelangt!"

2. Goethe, *Italienische Reise*, 168: "Denn es geht, man darf wohl sagen, ein neues Leben an, wenn man das Ganze mit Augen sieht, das man teilweise in- und auswendig kennt." Translation modified.

Goethe detects in old ideas stems from the sudden precision and coherence they acquire when placed within Roman reality (*IJ*, 129; *IR*, 168).

One week after his arrival, Goethe reports that he has gained a general idea of the city (*nach und nach tritt in meiner Seele der allgemeine Begriff dieser Stadt hervor*) by comparing its past and present state (*ich mache mir die Plane des alten und neuen Roms bekannt*). It is a slow process that leads to the affirmation of the newfound consistency and liveliness of Goethe's observations. His attention is first captured by intact and ruined architecture, and he repeatedly returns to the places where he found the most noteworthy monuments (*die grössten Merkwürdigkeiten*). Mapping the city in this way—by separating the old Rome from the new (*das alte Rom aus dem neuen herausklauben*)—is a "difficult and melancholy business," but it affords the beholder an experience of magnificence (*Herrlichkeit*) and devastation (*Zerstörung*) that evades conceptualization. Goethe grapples to reconcile the two sides of Rome; on the one hand, its multiple transformations over more than two thousand years and, on the other, its unchanging identity. The course of time has altered everything, Goethe muses, but then again, we walk upon the same ground and often even see the same columns and the same walls that have been here for centuries. The effect on the visitor is that one feels like a witness to the "great decrees of destiny" that have afflicted the city. But one cannot shake off one's bewilderment over Rome's unfathomably complex historicity and temporality (*IJ*, 133; *IR*, 173–74).

Goethe was likely alluding to these impenetrable layers of time when he stated that in Rome one is confronted with a monstrosity (*dieses Ungeheure wirkt ganz ruhig auf uns ein*). But there is another aspect that he had in mind. In Rome, he writes, we do not have to look for the meaningful (*das Bedeutende*) (*IJ*, 133; *IR*, 174).[3] Instead, it besieges and overwhelms us, creating the most multifarious landscape in the smallest possible space—a scenery that, while it cannot be conceptualized, seems to lend itself to aesthetic representation:

> Anderer Orten muss man das Bedeutende aufsuchen, hier werden wir davon überdrängt und überfüllt. Wie man geht und steht zeigt sich ein landschaftliches Bild aller Art und Weise, Paläste und Ruinen, Gärten und Wildnis, Fernen und Engen, Häuschen, Ställe, Triumphbögen und Säulen, oft alles zusammen so nah, dass es auf ein Blatt gebracht werden könnte. (*IR*, 174)

---

3. *Italian Journey* editors W. H. Auden and Elizabeth Meyer translate *das Ungeheure* as "immensity." With my translation as "monstrosity," I try to keep the potentially unsettling aspect of the experience. Auden and Meyer translate *das Bedeutende* as "important points of interest."

In other places one has to search for the meaningful; here it crowds in on one in profusion. Wherever one stands and walks, a manifold scenic image presents itself; palaces, ruins, gardens, wilderness, small houses, stables, triumphal arches, columns—all of them often so close together that they could be sketched on a single sheet of paper. (*IJ*, 133, translation modified)

However Rome's significance, as lavish as it may be, is also fragmented. Studying the city in its entirety requires that the student piece together (*zusammenstoppeln*) the whole from superabundant yet endless ruins (*unendliche, obgleich überreiche Trümmer*; *IJ*, 164; *IR*, 214). Meaning is so plentiful that one pen alone, as Goethe says, cannot do it justice. To grasp what Rome in fact represents, "one would need a thousand styluses to write with" (*Man müsste mit tausend Griffeln schreiben*; *IJ*, 133; *IR*, 174). Goethe suggests, in other words, that the dispersion of significance be met with a multiplication of aesthetic means.

The connection between decay and aesthetic production that so distinctly suggested itself to Goethe once he stepped on Roman soil had in fact set the tone of the *Italian Journey* early on, even if in an indirect and anecdotal manner. At the beginning of the trip, Goethe is involuntarily stranded in the town of Malcesine on Lake Garda. Forced by the weather to stay ashore, he decides to make creative use of the unplanned layover. Goethe stays in the medieval Scaligero Castle and starts drawing the old tower. While sketching his subject, he is soon surrounded by a group of curious onlookers, one of whom makes the artist aware that his activity is unlawful. The local magistrate is summoned and a peculiar conversation unfolds in which Goethe, attempting to justify his actions, indicates that the castle is a ruin and has therefore sparked his aesthetic interest, whereas the magistrate, oblivious of the aesthetic value of ruins, suspects that Goethe's artistic effort has a political goal. The only reason for ruin gazing that the magistrate can imagine is espionage for the Austrian Empire. The incident ends well for Goethe, yet he seems to breathe a sigh of relief when the winds finally allow him to depart from Malcesine. The place, he writes—confidently self-identifying with Odysseus— could have easily become "the coast of the Laestrygones" (*lästrygonisches Ufer*) for him (*IJ*, 44–48; *IR*, 42–48).[4]

Even before the Italian journey, ruins were a recurring motif in Goethe's artistic as well as his fictional and nonfictional literary work. Katharina Grätz stated with respect to the early poem "Der Wanderer" ("The Wanderer")

---

4. The mythological Laestrygonians were a tribe of cannibalistic giants who attacked Odysseus, destroyed most of his ships, and ate many of his men when he made a stopover in their land on his way to Ithaca.

FIGURE 7. Johann Heinrich Wilhelm Tischbein, *Goethe in der römischen Campagna* (1787). Oil on canvas. Photograph courtesy of Collection Database / Digital Collection, Städel Museum, Frankfurt am Main.

from 1772 that Goethean ruins mainly have a cultural-poetical function. Situated in the interface between history, art, and nature, they are indicators and "catalysts" of changing cultural settings and relations. Ruins have been associated with Goethe's image as an artist and writer ever since 1786, when Johann Heinrich Wilhelm Tischbein portrayed him in the Roman Campagna, reclining on the remains of an Egyptian obelisk, surrounded by debris from several periods of ancient art (figure 7).[5] The portrait is without a doubt the most famous and influential painting ever made of the poet. It gained iconic status soon after it was composed. Tischbein, whom Goethe had befriended on his trip through Italy, had told the Swiss poet and physiognomist Johann Caspar Lavater that his intention was to paint Goethe "life-sized" among the ruins and "reflecting upon the fate of human works."[6] The composition suggests

---

5. Grätz, " 'Erhabne Trümmer,' " 157. "Der Wanderer" features a dialogue between a walking traveler and a young peasant woman who with her family lives among the ruins of an antique temple. Grätz described the poem as a poetic composition of the Italian journey *before* the Italian journey (153).

6. Lenz, *Tischbein: Goethe in der Campagna di Roma*, 9: "Ich habe sein Porträt angefangen

Goethe's crucial role in this fate. The figure of the poet is placed in the foreground, facing away from the antique objects and the landscape at his back. The ruins seem to remind the beholder of the cultural heritage on which Goethe builds—a tradition that he revives and surpasses at the same time. Rudolf Bisanz spoke of the "birth of a myth" that was only marginally due to the painting's art-historical significance. More important, the portrait was broadly received in German cultural history. Since the beginning of its reception, Bisanz notes, it was "entangled" in a host of "extra-pictorial associations" such as "literature, the classics, history, archaeology, physiognomy, art theory and politics."[7] One could say that the veneration of Goethe as an icon of the classical German humanistic ideal and the father figure of German literature in general is literally built on remains of the past.

Despite the obvious importance of ruins for Goethe's work and in spite of their role in the context of his reputation as the epitome of German literature and culture, there have (so far) been no attempts in scholarship to conceptualize the ruin as a model for Goethe's reflections on literature and art. The reluctance to assign to ruins a poetological or art-theoretical function is certainly not without reason. For one, it often seems as if Goethe kept the ruin strictly within the confines of a secondary motif. In other words, whether ruins set the stage for a broader discussion about nature and culture or if they serve to trigger reflections on history and time, their purpose appears to be limited and inconstant.[8] To be sure, ruins are dispersed across Goethe's work with a certain regularity, and he does not fail to recognize their semiotic complexity. Yet it is difficult to see a consistency of usage that goes beyond motivic aspirations and that could rightly be interpreted as pursuing a systematic and structural intention. In Goethe's "thousand styluses" that do not suffice to capture the dispersed pieces of the city, one can nevertheless glimpse a possible new function of ruins in which fragmentation and aesthetic production are intertwined. However, Goethe does not linger on the idea but instead concludes the report by referring to his exhaustion and traveler's fatigue: "And then, in the evening, one feels exhausted after so much looking and admiring [*und dann ist man abends müde und erschöpft vom Schauen und Staunen*]" (*IJ*, 133; *IR*, 174).

---

und werde es in Lebensgrösse machen, wie er auf den Ruinen sizet und über das Schicksaal der Menschligen Wercke nachdencket."

7. Bisanz, "Birth of a Myth," 187–99.

8. E.g., as in the Joseph episode of *Wilhelm Meisters Wanderjahre* (*Wilhelm Meister's Journeyman Years*) from 1821.

238　　　　　　　　　　　　　　　　　　　　　　　　　　　　CHAPTER NINE

The somewhat precarious status of ruins within Goethe's work comes into view more pronouncedly when compared to one of the poet's preferred models of artistic reflection—namely, architecture.⁹ An example that stands in close vicinity to the ruin passages in the *Italian Journey* is Goethe's visit to Vicenza only five days after his departure from Malcesine. The anecdotal tone in which he retells the incident of the ruin of the old northern Italian castle gives way to a stern, almost solemn analysis of Palladio's buildings and suggests an intrinsic affinity between the skill of the architect and that of the poet:

> Once one actually sees those works, one recognizes their great value. For they are supposed to fill the eye [*das Auge füllen*] with their actual size and physicality and they are meant to satisfy the spirit with the beautiful harmony of their dimensions and with the perspectival back and forth [*Vordringen und Zurückweichen*], not just with an abstract outline. Therefore I say about Palladio that he was a man who was truly from within an intrinsically great man [*ein recht innerlich und von innen heraus grosser Mensch*]. The major problem with which this man, like all newer architects, grappled, is how to make proper use of the order of columns . . . But how he joined this together [*wie er das unterainander gearbeitet hat*], how he impresses [us] with the tangible presence of his creations and makes [us] forget that all he does is to persuade [*überreden*]! There is something truly divine about his talents, utterly like the power [*völlig wie die Force*] of a great poet who, out of truth and falsehood, creates a third whose borrowed existence enchants us. (*IJ*, 63–64; *IR*, 70–71; translation modified)¹⁰

Dorothea von Mücke has associated this appreciation of architecture as a form of art and the acknowledgment of its role in the context of aesthetic theory with Goethe's pamphlet *Von deutscher Baukunst* (*On German Architecture*) from 1772. As is well known, the text uses the example of the Strasbourg Cathedral and its architect Erwin von Steinbach to address the idea of real (i.e., characteristic) art that emerges from the artist's individuality. The essay has been subject to a host of interpretations, and many have placed it in the context of an eighteenth-century Gothic revival and a discussion of the concept of original genius. In contrast to these positions, von Mücke emphasizes the pamphlet's significance as the index of a paradigm shift in the

---

9. Another one is the tableau.

10. Scholarship has pointed to Goethe's obvious identification with Palladio that is more apparent in later passages of the *Italian Journey*—for instance, when Goethe praises the architect for having educated himself by studying antiquity or when he pities him for having had to deal with the "petty narrow-mindedness of his time" (*IJ*, 81). See, e.g., Mehne, *Bildung versus Self-Reliance?*, 45.

arts. Her argument is that Goethe "turns to architecture as the model object of art" in a moment in which art is about to move beyond models of mimetic representation.[11]

Against this backdrop, the following reading of Goethe's 1828 short story "Novelle" ("Novella") and Georg Simmel's 1907 essay "Die Ruine" ("The Ruin") introduces yet another paradigm shift, one that applies to both literature and philosophy in the early nineteenth century as well as in the first decades of the twentieth century. With respect to Goethe, I will deduce, with reference to both the writing process of "Novelle" and a close reading of the text, the emergence of an aesthetic reflection that, late in Goethe's life, led to a focus on decay and ultimately suggested that provisionality is a fundamental trait of forms. Unlike the related concept of ephemerality, provisionality does not focus on the transience of forms in the first place. It rather emphasizes the meaning of transformability or translatability in the Benjaminian sense. In other words, provisionality is about the reconciliation of identity and becoming but, as we will see, without drawing on the idea of synthesis. The same point was made by Simmel a century later, albeit in reference to a cultural-philosophical problem and, as it seems, almost inadvertently. The short but dense essay on the ruin distinguishes Simmel as a thinker whose considerations reach beyond dialectic oppositions and into neglected or underestimated realms of philosophy. Goethe's and Simmel's texts have both received scholarly interpretations that emphasize the significance of the ruin as a means of aesthetic and conceptual synthesis. I will show that quite the opposite is true: the ruin can be understood as a liminal figure between form and life, between ideal and disruption, and it is precisely through this undermining of synthesis that ruins keep philosophical thinking as well as creative processes in motion and enable an afterlife—or a future—of forms and ideas.

Moreover, my approach attempts to shed light on each work's respective status in the broader context of literary history and the history of philosophy, and I will provide some impulse toward rethinking Goethe's perspective on aesthetic theory, as well as the perception of Simmel as a promoter of what Theodor Adorno contemptuously called "Wald- und Wiesenmetaphysik" (armchair metaphysics).[12] What I have called *world* in previous chapters now refers to both the history of literature and the history of philosophy.

---

11. Von Mücke, "Beyond the Paradigm of Representation," 6. The tableau, of which Goethe made ample use in his work, can also be read primarily as a mode of complicating the notion of representation. See, e.g., Solanki, "Book of Living Paintings," 245–70.

12. Adorno, "Henkel, Krug und frühe Erfahrung" (2003), 564. It is a well-known fact that throughout his entire life Simmel struggled to be taken seriously as a philosopher.

In what follows, I will first situate Goethe's "Novelle" in the context of a decades-long formation process—of both the author and his work. I will then turn to the text itself and—within an abundance of motifs, themes, forms, images, and unheard-of events, which Goethe famously foregrounded as the primary characteristic of the genre and incorporated into the novella—focus on the ruin and on how it introduces a contradiction between the prospect of synthesis, at the level of content, and antagonistic division, at the level of structure. In a second step, I will argue that Georg Simmel was torn between two options of employing the ruin for his own cultural-theoretical, philosophical, and aesthetic purposes: as a synthesis between the opposing, dialectical elements of *form* and *life*, on the one hand, and as a symptom of the impossibility of that very synthesis, on the other. I will show that the course of Simmel's argument runs against his declared goal to synthesize the antagonistic forces in what he calls the "tragedy of culture" and supports an understanding of the ruin as a flexible, ever-shifting figure of thought (*Denkfigur*) instead.

The Coming Poesie: Goethe's "Novelle"

In January 1829, several months after the printing of "Novelle," his last extensive prose narrative, Goethe wrote to his friend, the Prussian councillor of state Christoph Ludwig Friedrich Schultz:

> Meanwhile, it gives me the most pleasant sensation that the novella is being received favorably; one feels that it detached itself from the bottommost depths of my being [*dass sie sich vom tiefsten Grunde meines Wesens losgelöst hat*]. The conception is more than thirty years old; there must be traces of it in the correspondence [with Schiller]. And your appreciation of precisely that correspondence is completely appropriate.[13]

Schultz had read "Novelle" and, along with the exchange of letters between Goethe and Friedrich Schiller that had recently been published, had praised it as a heavenly piece of writing, too subtle and pure to resonate with an earthly audience (*BGS*, 356–57). Goethe's response—even as it expresses joy over Schultz's enthusiastic reaction and explicitly acknowledges his admiration for the letters—conveys an ambivalent attitude toward German literature and its protagonists of the late eighteenth century, including his own work and persona. "One could say that I am very naive to have something like this printed," Goethe writes about his correspondence with Schiller. "But I specifically

---

13. Düntzer, *Briefwechsel zwischen Goethe und Staatsrath Schultz* (1853; hereafter cited as *BGS*), 361. Translations from the correspondence with Schultz are mine.

considered the present moment appropriate to once again showcase that epoch where you, venerated friend, and many other excellent people were young, and strove, and tried to educate yourselves [*strebten und sich zu bilden suchten*]; where we, the older ones, aspired [*aufstrebten*] and tried to educate ourselves as well [*uns auch zu bilden suchten*] and occasionally acted clumsily [*ungeschickt*] enough" (*BGS*, 361). In particular, Goethe casts an ironic look back at Schiller's monthly literary journal *Die Horen* (*The Hours*), which was issued between 1795 and 1797. It serves him as an example of how authors tried to outperform one another's literary productivity and erudition, and how their sophomoric fervor led to unintentionally comic results. From a safe distance, the years of immaturity are seen in a favorable light. But this generous gesture is nonetheless accompanied by the wish that those days never return: "May God prevent that anyone should once again envision [*sich wieder vergegenwärtige*] the state of German literature of that time—even though I do not want to underestimate its merits; but if an agile spirit [*ein gewandter Geist*] does it [envision the past], he will not hold it against me that I did not seek salvation there [*dass ich hier kein Heil suchte*]" (*BGS*, 361–62). At the same time, Goethe recognizes that if thirty years ago younger and older writers had not felt the urge and compulsion to put the significance of their contemporary moment on paper, German literature would have taken a different direction.[14] In his letter, the poet fails to give a clear reason why the late 1820s are the right time to do some soul searching and grappling with the past, and the reader is—at least for the time being—left to ascribe the impulse to Goethe's old age and his wish to take stock of a lifelong, extensive literary output.

In this ambiguous constellation in which Goethe both values and distances himself from the past, the role of "Novelle" is remarkable. It features the revival of an old concept in a new form and thereby accounts for both past days of immature eagerness and the proper realization of an existing idea at the right time.[15] What Goethe only touches upon in his letter to Schultz had been the topic of extensive conversations with Johann Peter Eckermann two years earlier. Goethe is quoted by his interlocutor on January 15, 1827:

> I was going to treat the subject [of "Novelle"] thirty years ago and have carried it in my head ever since. The work went on oddly enough ... I meant to treat it in an epic form and in hexameters, and had drawn up a complete outline with

---

14. On the long period of composition, see Wagenknecht, *Erläuterungen und Dokumente*, 63–87.

15. In this context of an old concept in a new form, Goethe draws a distinction between form and content, which is different from my understanding of form. Goethe's focus on transformation is, however, in line with my point of view.

> this view. But when I now took up the subject again, not being able to find my old outline, I was obliged to make a new one ... Now my work is ended, the old outline is again found, and I am glad I did not have it earlier.[16]

The new form, through which the old content seems to have finally asserted itself to Goethe's satisfaction, is prose. But even this claim of a late success has to be taken with a grain of salt. After all, Goethe speaks of "Novelle" as having "detached itself from the bottommost depth of [his] being." The German verb is *loslösen*, and its use has two opposing implications: Goethe might have intended to emphasize that he strongly identified with his creation, which he saw as an independent but essential part of his innermost person. Or he might have wanted to point out that the detachment had to be understood as a sort of alienation. This alternative bears consequences for the question of how aesthetic form and detachment are related. One option is that Goethe was suggesting that finding the right aesthetic form for a specific content is always a process that evolves from the core of the creator's being. The other possibility is that Goethe's comments to Schultz and Eckermann insinuate that the appropriate aesthetic form comes at the cost of authenticity, and conversely that authenticity goes hand in glove with a deficient form. Regardless of whether this ambiguity can be resolved, Goethe's invocation of it suggests that, with respect to "Novelle," there is no real closure in sight. Over time, the story both varied and remained unchanged—a tension that led to somewhat contradictory judgments of the earlier and later stages of development by Goethe and exposed "Novelle" to potential future transformation.

But what exactly is it about "Novelle" that Goethe kept reshaping and rethinking? My hypothesis is that, as a work that emerged over time and is explicitly and closely linked to Goethe's evolution as an author, "Novelle" documents the challenges that merging the demands of art with a theoretical impulse posed for Goethe. By *theoretical impulse*, I mean a writing process that evolves from the formulation of an idea and leads to the materialization of the work of art modeled on this idea. "Novelle"—in terms of its genesis as well as its textual characteristics—supports the idea that aesthetic theory is neither a hindrance for nor an irrelevance to aesthetic production, but that, on the contrary, it inspires and advances it. Admittedly, there is a whole range of reasons why one might discard this claim from the outset. Goethe's own aesthetic mutability, his heterodox approach to concepts and normative aesthetic criteria, but most of all his open disdain for any kind of aesthetic theory are just the most obvious ones. On January 6, 1798, Goethe writes to Schiller,

---

16. Goethe, *Conversations of Goethe with Eckermann and Soret*, 320. For the German original, see Eckermann, *Gespräche mit Goethe*.

"As long as a work of art does not exist, no one has an idea of its possibilities."[17] A few years earlier, he had declared that the poet always precedes the critic.[18] And in a direct comment on the difficult origins of "Novelle" in the *Tag- und Jahreshefte* from 1797, Goethe had stated:

> The plan was thought through in all its details, which unfortunately I did not conceal from my friends. They advised me against it and I am still saddened that I followed their advice, because the poet alone can know what lies in a subject matter [*der Dichter allein kann wissen, was in einem Gegenstande liegt*] and what kind of charm and grace he can draw from it.[19]

All three statements—the third one in contradistinction to Goethe's later assessment of German literature of the 1790s—reject the idea of a priori concepts that shape literary production. The Goethe biographer Karlheinz Schulz has emphasized the self-reflexive significance that aesthetic thought had for Goethe. He points out that for the author, aesthetics is the equivalent of reflection on an already existing work of art. It ultimately defines Goethe's understanding of education (*Bildung*) in the broad sense of cultivation of one's intellect and self. Goethe's theoretical interest is, in other words, retrospective and educational in hindsight.[20] Theory has a reflexive function with no significant influence on the creative process.[21] It seems as if, with regard to "Novelle," Goethe tried to make this point particularly clear. As quoted earlier from his letter, Goethe reports to Eckermann that the story was written from scratch even though he had an old outline that he could not find at the time. He then points out that the eventual discovery of the first outline revealed that it had little in common with the second one.[22] What Goethe seems to emphasize is the originality of "Novelle" and its freedom from whatever preconception or process of reflection could potentially have influenced its creation.

Yet this adherence to originality is put into perspective by the "double nature" of "Novelle." Goethe states that a process of education took place

---

17. See *BGS*, 536: "So lange ein Kunstwerk nicht da ist hat niemand einen Begriff von seiner Möglichkeit."
18. Goethe, *Werke* (1911), 110.
19. Goethe, "Poetische Werke," 53. Translation mine.
20. Schulz, *Wandlungen und Konstanten in Goethes Ästhetik und literarischer Laufbahn*, 3. Schulz claims that for Goethe, aesthetics mostly fulfilled the function of self-reflection and, in a broad sense, of education.
21. Schulz, *Wandlungen und Konstanten in Goethes Ästhetik und literarischer Laufbahn*, 1–2.
22. The first outline has not been preserved. There are, in Goethe's other correspondences, statements that contradict this claim. In 1826 he wrote to Wilhelm Humboldt that he found the old plan and carried it out in prosaic form; see Witte and Schmidt, *Goethe-Handbuch: Prosaschriften*, 253.

between the emergence of the idea and the finding of the right form for it. While Goethe's first attempt at penning the story coincided with an attempt at self-education by two generations of German authors, he makes the second effort—which finally succeeds—after a time lapse during which education seems to have advanced and the earlier stage in the creation of "Novelle" can be dismissed. Instead of education being the result of a process of reflection, initiated by the analysis of an existing aesthetic object, the theoretical impetus seems to subtend aesthetic production. In fact, education in the sense of theoretical reflection was geared toward the future, in which the idea of "Novelle" finally materialized. In other words, theory preceded art. The unusual and puzzling title of the story seems to support this assumption: before the events are told, we face an abstract label and a genre-theoretical question.[23] And yet, even if it is the case that with "Novelle" Goethe abandoned his premise to always give art priority over the reflection about art, this does not mean that the work is an aesthetic fulfillment of a methodological, critical, or theoretical claim. The theoretical expectation—understood as an educational aspiration—remains as unfulfilled as the artistic ideal. "Novelle" provides the insight that theory and art are both endeavors yet to be realized, and the ruin is the token that indicates the contradictions of this process.

"Novelle" opens with the departure of a young prince and his hunting party from the castle of a prosperous town. The prince has only reluctantly bid farewell to his wife, whom he recently married and has now committed to the care of his uncle and a nobleman named Honorio. Left behind, the princess withdraws to her chambers and gazes after the hunting party through a telescope:

> Sie fand das treffliche Teleskop noch in der Stellung wo man es gestern Abend gelassen hatte als man, über Busch, Berg und Waldgipfel, die uralten Ruinen der alten Stammburg betrachtend, sich unterhielt, die in der Abendbeleuch-

---

23. As is well known, Goethe's own account of the title emphasizes the novelty of the events. See Goethe, *Conversations of Goethe with Eckermann and Soret*, 346:

> "I'll tell you what," said Goethe, "we will call it 'The Novel (Die Novelle);' for what is a novel but a peculiar and as yet unheard-of event? This is the proper meaning of this name; and much which in Germany passes as a novel is no novel at all, but a mere narrative, or whatever else you like to call it. In that original sense of an unheard-of event, even the 'Wahlverwandtschaften' may be called a 'novel.'"

Answering his question about the final title of the piece, Goethe wrote to his publisher that the title was "Novelle" and that he had reasons not to put *a* (*eine*) in front of it. See Witte and Schmidt, *Goethe-Handbuch: Prosaschriften*, 252.

tung merkwürdig hervortraten, indem alsdann die grössten Licht- und Schattenmassen den deutlichsten Begriff von einem so ansehnlichen Denkmal alter Zeit verleihen konnten. (GN, 516)

She found the excellent telescope still in the position where it had been left the preceding evening when, looking over bush, hill and forest, they entertained themselves by examining the lofty ruins of the ancient ancestral castle. It stood out remarkably in the evening light because then the greater masses of light and shadow could give the most distinctive concept of such an imposing monument of olden times. (FT, 104)[24]

In a single, almost excessively long sentence, Goethe establishes the relation between the new and the old castle as one that is characterized by spectatorship. The ruins of the past are an object of aesthetic admiration by the beholders of the present. The sentence is constructed in a way that mentions the observers in the middle of a description of the ruins and thereby disrupts the flow of the account. It almost seems as if the unusual syntax reveals a certain precariousness of the aesthetic perception of ruins. However, the next scene not only presents ruins and their entanglement with nature as an object of aesthetic apprehension but also as material for aestheticization. Friedrich, the prince's uncle, enters the room with a draftsman who carries a portfolio with drawings of the old castle. Presenting these drawings sheet by sheet to the princess, Friedrich, following ekphrastic tradition, describes and interprets the images on display:[25]

"We shall show you here the views of the ancestral castle [*Ansichten der Stammburg*], drawn so as to make clear [*anschaulich*] from different sides how the mighty offensive and defensive construction [*Trutz- und Schutzbau*] has resisted [*entgegengestemmte*] for ages the weathering [*Witterung*] of the years and how, here and there, its walls had to give way and collapse in jumbled ruin [*in wüsten Ruinen zusammenstürzen musste*]."

In explaining the individual sheets, the prince continued: "Here, where we come up the narrow road through the outer wall to reach the castle itself, there rises one of the most formidable rocks in all these mountains. On it stands a tower, but no one could tell where nature's stone ends and that of skillful handicraft begins . . . Just see how our master draftsman has expressed this

---

24. For the German original, see Goethe, "Novelle" (hereafter cited as GN, with page number); the English version is in Goethe, *Fairy Tales, Short Stories, and Poems* (hereafter cited as FT, with page number).

25. Bernhard Zimmermann has shown that the pastoral romance *Daphnis and Chloe* by second-century Greek author Longos was the main source for Goethe's ekphrastic passages. See B. Zimmermann, "Goethes Novelle und der Hirtenroman des Longos," 101–12.

characteristic feature on paper. How distinctly [*kenntlich*] the different trunks and roots are entwined in the stonework and the mighty boughs are woven through the breaches in the walls!" (*FT*, 105; GN, 517)

In front of the reader's and the princess's eyes, an antagonistic encounter between ever-active, living nature and a collapsing monument of human culture unfolds in a transmedial—literary and pictorial—spectacle:

> "It is a wilderness like no other, a unique area [*ein zufällig einziges Lokal*] where one can see the ancient vestiges of the long-vanished power of man [*die alten Spuren längst verschwundener Menschenkraft*] in conflict [*in dem ernstesten Streit*] with an ever-living and constantly active nature [*mit der ewig lebenden und fortwirkenden Natur*]."
>
> Displaying another sheet, he went on: "What do you say about the courtyard, that because of the collapse [*das Zusammenstürzen*] of the gate tower is inaccessible and has not been trod by anyone since time immemorial? . . . Here and there mighty trees have been able to take root. They grew slowly but resolutely and now they extend their branches into the galleries, where the knights once walked to and fro. They have indeed become the masters here, and they may remain so." (*FT*, 105–6; GN, 517–18)

The images are meant to make the wilderness accessible to the mind of the beholder and inspire in her the wish to see the site of the colliding forces—in other words, to make the step from representation to actual presence.[26] Friedrich concludes:

> "We should therefore thank the skillful artist who in various pictures portrays everything for us in such a laudable fashion that we feel as if we were there [*als wenn wir gegenwärtig wären*]. He used the finest hours of the day . . . and moved about these subjects for weeks . . . But now that everything is sketched so neatly and accurately, he will finish his work down here in comfort. With these pictures we shall adorn our garden hall, and no one will look at our carefully arranged flower beds, arbors and shady paths without wishing to be really up there, observing the old and the new [*in dem wirklichen Anschauen des Alten und Neuen*]: what is rigid, unyielding, indestructible and that which is fresh, pliant, irresistible." (*FT*, 106; GN, 518)

This calculated impact is not lost on the princess, who has never seen the ruins up close and proposes a ride to the forest. Yet Friedrich denies her request, denouncing it as untimely: "Not yet, my dear . . . What you saw here is what it can and will become . . . Art must first complete its task if it is

---

26. Dorothea von Mücke sees architecture as a "medium of emphatic presence" for Goethe; Von Mücke, "Beyond the Paradigm of Representation," 6.

not to become ashamed of nature" (*FT*, 106). At first sight, Friedrich's answer seems reasonable enough. It has been read as evidence that Goethe valued the forces of nature over the persuasive skills of art and meant to set himself apart from the ekphrastic tradition that tends to emphasize the opposite, or the refinement of nature through art.[27] Nevertheless, there are glaring ambiguities in the uncle's response that can be reconciled only with difficulty. First, he claims that the artist's drawings already evoke the sense that the viewer is on-site and one might ask why, under these circumstances, the immediate experience of the place is even necessary. Second, it is puzzling that the uncle praises the drawings so highly, making them commensurate with reality ("as if we were there") if simultaneously he argues that they have yet to be completed. If this remark is a statement that intends to highlight the importance of potentiality and possibility, of change and transformation, then, third, it is unclear why art should have to be completed to serve as a mediator for the princess's encounter with the real world. Finally, in a very basic sense, it is not quite evident why nature should require art's mediation in the first place. The only plausible explanation is that the uncle, having raised the princess's expectations, does not want her to be disappointed. Yet how could one be disappointed by nature if it is superior to art and if the artist's drawings are so accurate that they make us feel "as if we were there"? I will come back to these contradictions in Friedrich's ekphrasis. For the moment, let us state that they point to a complex relationship between art and nature and that, once again, the ruin lies at the center of the tension.

Despite Friedrich's objection, the princess insists that they ride at least to the foot of the castle hill to catch a glimpse of the beautiful landscape. Accompanied by Honorio, they take the route through town, where a fair is being held with countless booths and attractions. The travelers have already reached a vantage point with a view of the surrounding area when they see that a fire has broken out in the town. In the ensuing chaos, a tiger and a lion have managed to escape from their cages. Defending the princess, Honorio kills the tiger. Meanwhile the lion hides among the ruins of the ancestral castle. A young boy calms and tames him with music and singing and leads him back to his cage. The last words we read are the lyrics of his alluring song:

> Und so geht mit guten Kindern
> Sel'ger Engel gern zu Rat,
> Böses Wollen zu verhindern,

---

27. This is certainly the case for Longos, Goethe's main point of reference. See B. Zimmermann, "Goethes Novelle und der Hirtenroman des Longos," 109. See also Kaiser, "Zur Aktualität Goethes," 13–36.

> Zu befördern schöne Tat.
> So beschwören, fest zu bannen
> Liebem Sohn ans zarte Knie
> Ihn, des Waldes Hochtyrannen,
> Frommer Sinn und Melodie. (GN, 534)
>
> Thus do blessed angels guide
> children when in time of need;
> they attempt to turn aside
> harm and further some fine deed.
> Good intent and melody
> captivate and gently bring
> him, the forest's mighty king
> to the small boy's little knee. (FT, 122)

The German poet Gottfried Benn had a famously scornful reaction to "Novelle" and especially the ending, which, from the point of view of sarcastic criticism, confirmed the perception of Goethe as a champion of synthesis but also laid bare some of the reasons why the unity that Goethe supposedly established was not necessarily credible:

> Eine Menagerie fängt Feuer, die Buden brennen ab, die Tiger brechen aus, die Löwen sind los—und alles verläuft harmonisch . . . Das Säuseln eines Knaben besänftigt die Natur . . . Es muss nur ein Knabe mit der Flöte kommen! Sehr richtig! Aber er kommt eben nicht. Wir sehen ihn nicht kommen. Geschwätz! Narrheit! Geheimratsbehaglichkeit . . . Gigantisch das Ganze, aber faul![28]
>
> A menagerie catches fire, the booths burn down, the tigers escape, the lions are on the loose—and everything ends harmoniously . . . The susurration of a boy soothes nature . . . Nothing but a boy with a flute has to come! Exactly! Only he does not come. We do not see him coming. Nonsense! Folly! Comfort of a privy council! Gigantic, the whole thing, but lazy!

Even Eckermann found himself somewhat abashed when Goethe asked him his opinion about the ending of the novella. "I did not know what to say," he writes in *Conversations*. "It seemed to me that the conclusion was too simple, too ideal, too lyrical, and that at least some of the other figures should have reappeared."[29] Goethe of course had an explanation ready:

> To find a simile [*Gleichnis*] to this novel . . . imagine a green plant shooting up from its root, thrusting forth strong green leaves, from the sides of its sturdy stem,

---

28. Gottfried Benn quoted in Witte and Schmidt, *Goethe-Handbuch: Prosaschriften*, 263–64. English translation mine.

29. Goethe, *Conversations of Goethe with Eckermann and Soret*, 331–32.

and at last terminating in a flower. The flower is unexpected and startling, but come it must— nay, the whole foliage has existed only for the sake of that flower, and would be worthless without it ... The purpose of this novel was to show how the unmanageable and the invincible [*das Unbändige, Unüberwindliche*] is often better restrained by love and pious feeling than by force ... This is the ideal [*das Ideelle*]—this is the flower. The green foliage of the extremely real introduction is only there for the sake of this ideal, and only worth anything on account of it. For what is the real in itself [*was soll das Reale an sich*]? We take delight in it when it is represented with truth [*mit Wahrheit dargestellt*]—nay, it may give us a clearer knowledge of certain things, but the proper gain to our higher nature [*der eigentliche Gewinn für unsere höhere Natur*] lies alone in the ideal [*Ideal*], which proceeds from the heart of the poet [*das aus dem Herzen des Dichters hervorging*].[30]

The ideal that Goethe mentions with regard to the ending of the story—and whose source he again locates deeply within the poet—has been understood as the utopian reconciliation of the content-based opposites that the beginning of "Novelle" establishes: the juxtaposition of the old and new castles that introduces a dialectical tension between past and present, old and new, human activity and the force of nature.[31]

However, the resolution of the dialectic tension has not always been attributed to the ending of the story. Katharina Grätz has argued that in the ekphrasis passage the underlying claim is a possible synthesis between art and nature, based on the assumption that the ruin is a form of mediation between the two.[32] Friedrich's description of the opposition and concurrent indiscernibility of nature and the human-made castle, according to Grätz, is based on the dominant cultural-historical paradigm that the ruin is a figure or form in which an antagonism between upward-striving forces of the spirit and downward-sinking forces of nature is at work. Christian Cay Lorenz Hirschfeld writes in his *Theory of Garden Art* from 1780 that nature tends to triumphantly reclaim the places that architecture took from it as soon as their inhabitants abandon them.[33] Georg Simmel states in "Die Ruine" that ruins are the setting in which nature forms and transforms cultural artifacts and the power relation between spirit and nature is turned upside down.[34] In

---

30. Goethe, *Conversations of Goethe with Eckermann and Soret*, 332–33.

31. Witte and Schmidt, *Goethe-Handbuch: Prosaschriften*, 260–61. Dieter Borchmeyer interpreted "Novelle" in the context of Goethe's examination of the French Revolution; see Borchmeyer, *Höfische Gesellschaft und Französische Revolution bei Goethe*, 333–50.

32. Grätz, "'Erhabne Trümmer,'" 165.

33. Hirschfeld, *Theorie der Gartenkunst*, 113, quoted in Grätz, "'Erhabne Trümmer,'" 151.

34. Simmel, "Die Ruine," 287–295. For an English translation of the essay, see Simmel, *Georg Simmel, 1858–1918: A Collection of Essays*, 259–66 (1959; hereafter cited as *GS*, with page number).

"Novelle," by offering the prospect that the artistic effort of the draftsman will finally match the demands of nature, Friedrich implies, according to Grätz, that the conflict can become aesthetically productive, or, in other words, that it can be settled with the help of art. Friedrich's aspiration to acquire the perfect work of art, one that is suitable for competing with the reality of the ancestral castle, she interprets as an indicator that in "Novelle" there is fulfillment in art because art can create the perfect ruin: a timeless sign of unity between the old and the new, nature and the artifice.[35]

The accuracy of these observations aside, the assumption that the first passage on ruins implies a synthesis of antagonistic forces not only disregards the considerable problems that Friedrich's ekphrasis poses in terms of the somewhat inconsistent line of arguments, but it also neglects a decisive structural feature. As far as its place in the narrative is concerned, the passage stands out as cumbersome and unwieldy—as if its function within the story had been reconsidered several times. Initially it aligns itself thematically with the prince's farewell—insofar as the telescope through which the princess watches her departing husband is introduced as the same tool that allowed a view of the ancestral castle. But just as if the princess had subverted the purpose of the telescope by looking at the wrong object, the scene is abruptly interrupted by the entry of Friedrich, who, without any further reference to the parting hunters or the events of the previous night, begins his ruin monologue and ekphrastic speech. The passage is detached from its context like a painting in a frame, without any real continuity with the previous sequence but also strangely isolated with respect to the subsequent story. It seems as though Friedrich's dismissive response to the princess's request for a visit to the castle ultimately prevented the ruin from evolving into a plot motif.

The following occurrences further support the notion that the ruin is neither a structural connecting piece nor the site of a final unity between art and nature. "Novelle" ends with some of its main characters gathered in the ruin of the ancestral castle. Observers turn into participants, artistic representation that was intended to kindle the wish to visit the ruin into actual presence *in* the ruin. Yet the unheard-of events that brought everyone here did not allow for the well-prepared, artistically mediated encounter with reality that Friedrich envisioned. Consequently, the object that was tied to the prospect of synthesis and that appeared as the focus of every gaze is mentioned only in passing, and Goethe turns away from the visual arts and toward music to conclude his tale:

---

35. Grätz, "'Erhabne Trümmer,'" 168.

Finally the flute was heard again. The child stepped forth from the hole, his eyes shining with satisfaction; the lion followed, but slowly and apparently with some difficulty. Now and then he seemed to want to lie down, but the boy led him in a semicircle through the trees, that still held some of their colorful leaves, until at last the boy sat down as if transfigured in the last rays that the sun sent through a gap in the ruins. (*FT*, 121)

Whether one considers "Novelle" as too simple, too ideal, carefully calculated, highly symbolic or lazy, the irritation that this late work by Goethe caused among recipients derives from the perceived promise of synthesis or an ideal that seemed bound up with the ruin but that the ruin's structural and thematic development failed to fulfill.[36] And yet, even though Goethe's self-justification with respect to the novella's ending says otherwise, one has to ask whether the expectation of an ideal or a synthesis was misdirected all along. The question is whether Goethe set up the ruin as a semantically, temporally, and aesthetically open form to introduce an inconclusive ending that he had prepared in the ekphrasis passage and whether he thereby postponed the realization of the ideal that he claimed to have wrested from the foliage of the story. Against the backdrop of the long genesis of "Novelle" and its status as an object of methodological and artistic interest, the thought seems plausible that, in more than one way, the final form was yet to arrive. The implications of this supposition are far-reaching: in "Novelle," Goethe established a hermeneutics of the ruin that emphasizes the discontinuous character of formation. Unusual about this suggestion is not that Goethe had an interminable process of becoming in mind. After all, Goethe's form concept is linked to notions of "cultivation and transformation," form is "minted," it "lives" and "grows."[37] The innovation in "Novelle" is that it does not promise an ideal but thinks of transformation in terms of breaks and inconsistencies. Arising from the ruin, "Novelle" heralds the incessant future coming of forms of poetic production without end point or goal.

Building Up and Breaking Down: Georg Simmel's "Die Ruine"

In Georg Simmel's essay "Die Ruine," there are numerous indicators that suggest his acquaintance with "Novelle." However, he does not mention the work explicitly, and even though we seem to be confronted with a genuine reception of Goethe, one has to resist the temptation to read Simmel's treatise as

---

36. For the charge that "Novelle" is too simple, too ideal, carefully calculated, see Conrady, *Goethe: Leben und Werk*, 979–81.

37. For Goethe's understanding of form, see Wellbery, "Romanticism and Modernity," 276.

the theory that explains Goethe's literary text. Instead, the juxtaposition of the two works and thinkers is intended to examine the comparability of their understanding of the function of ruins and render each position productive with respect to their own historical and discursive context. It is, however, likely that Simmel recognized the important role Goethe had ascribed to the ruin and that he based the thrust of his own argument on this observation. What is more, Goethe is at the center of Simmel's reflections in two longer works that he composed before and after he wrote "Die Ruine" and that examine related ideas: "Kant und Goethe" ("Kant and Goethe") and "Goethe."

Simmel begins his essay by describing architecture as the "only art[form] in which the great struggle between the will of the spirit and the necessity of nature issues into real peace." It is—as Simmel understands it—a balance between upward-striving and downward-drawing forces, between matter and "artistic thought," nature and spirit (*GS*, 259). Unlike in music, literature, or painting, where matter serves an idea that is "conceivable only in the human soul" (*GS*, 259), in architecture the act of formation through the spirit causes matter to release the visibility of the idea. This early passage indicates that the treatise has to be read with an eye toward Simmel's philosophy of life and the concept of a tragedy of culture in which the antagonism between form and life is emphasized, a perspective I outlined in chapter 2. In the context of detailing the opposing forces, Simmel engaged extensively with Immanuel Kant and Goethe and the idea that they represent two sides of the "cosmic enmity" between spirit and nature. In his 1906 essay "Kant und Goethe," Simmel maps out the ideal of a potential unity between philosophy and art, concept and thing—in short, between Kant and Goethe—that he predicts for his own and future generations. Simmel undoubtedly intended a clear distinction between the two thinkers and their function as representatives of philosophical and literary or artistic points of view. However, it would be an oversimplification to assume that he was unambiguous in ascribing conceptual thinking to Kant and what he called "a feeling for nature, the world and life" to Goethe. That the relation is more complex becomes obvious early in the essay when, in referring to Goethe, Simmel uses the terms *philosophy* and *art* synonymously. Moreover, in the course of his argument, he increasingly focuses on the poet alone.[38] This focus indicates that the synthesis between Kant and Goethe—which Simmel saw as a means to overcome the conflict between subjective life and its objective expression at the core of his own theory—was not one that would have been easily achievable or self-evident.

---

38. Simmel, "Kant und Goethe" (1995), 126–27. For the complex relationship that Simmel establishes between Kant and Goethe, see Prica, "Ruine" (2014), 273–97.

In 1913, Simmel wrote a monograph on Goethe. The tension and possible synthesis between Kant and Goethe that he had examined in the earlier essay was now applied to Goethe of the classical period and to his understanding of the beautiful as a form of correspondence between the self and the world, art and nature, subject and object.[39] The paradigm at work here matches the one present in Friedrich's description of the ruins of the ancestral castle in "Novelle," and it is opposed to what, in "Kant und Goethe," Simmel described as a violent act of reason against nature, a stance associated with the philosopher.[40] In the monograph, Simmel seeks to determine "the intellectual [*geistig*] meaning of Goethe's existence" by which he means "the relationship between Goethe's form of being [*Daseinsart*] and what he said about the big categories of art and intellect, praxis and metaphysics, nature and soul—and the advancement of these categories through him."[41] In other words, Simmel is interested in the synthesis between Goethe's life and his work that realizes itself in the poet's genius. Subjective life, thus Simmel's assessment of Goethe, naturally merges into objectively valuable products and overcomes the tragedy of culture, the necessity that life expresses itself in cultural forms that can never fully contain it.[42]

"Die Ruine" was published between these two in-depth examinations of Kant, Goethe, and their possible synthesis, and the obvious question is what the 1907 essay adds to the argument. Before I turn to the short piece, it is important to my point to mention the criticism that Simmel received ex cathedra, so to speak, for his preoccupation with unity. In 1966, Theodor Adorno in his engagement with Hegel's dialectic in "Negative Dialektik" ("Negative Dialectics") took a stand against philosophy's inherent preference for comprehensive systems of thought and demanded attention toward that which had hitherto been neglected: the nonconceptual, the singular, and the particular.[43] That said, it would be a misunderstanding of Adorno's intention to see it as an attempt to abolish concepts. His declared goal was to exceed concepts with concepts—in other words, to accept their limited range but at the same time use them to approach reality as closely as possible. This would leave room for nonconceptual—above all, *aesthetic*—perception.[44] In this context, Adorno acknowledged Georg Simmel's dedication to concrete objects, which

---

39. Simmel, "Goethe" (2003).
40. Simmel, "Kant und Goethe," 136.
41. Simmel, "Goethe," 9. Translation mine.
42. Simmel, "Goethe," 14.
43. Adorno, "Negative Dialektik" (1970).
44. Adorno, "Negative Dialektik," 24.

he understood as a corrective to "the chattering of epistemology and intellectual history [*das Klappern von Erkenntniskritik und Geistesgeschichte*]."[45] But he soon saw his hopes for an orientation toward the "incommensurability of the object" disappointed. In Adorno's view, Simmel's commitment to "things" was halfhearted at best and betrayed an interest in instrumentalizing the particular for insights into the general. Adorno rejected Simmel's characterization of works of art as ideational entities as being completely detached from reality. In sum, Adorno denounced Simmel as an undialectical, unworldly thinker. This judgment was important for Simmel's reputation and status as a philosopher—a situation that cannot be blamed on the accuser alone. Simmel's work promotes a "severe metaphysics of art" that excludes historical dimensions, follows idealism with respect to its terminology, and claims a radical autonomy of the artwork.[46] And yet, despite Adorno's dismissal and even in contrast to his self-perception, Simmel can be conceived as a dialectician at the very least. His analysis of the ruin will prove to be exactly what Adorno required but overlooked in Simmel's work: a restoration of the conceptual that converged with an acknowledgment of the nonconceptual.

As I have already mentioned, the first paragraph of "Die Ruine" seems to reaffirm the reconciliation of dichotomies that Simmel had proposed with respect to Kant and Goethe, but this time he relates them to architecture as a particular form of art. From here, Simmel quickly proceeds to the instant when an architectural construction collapses and the equilibrium of natural forces and spiritual forces is disturbed. Only the "unity of the form," he declares, can uphold the peace between matter and spirit, thing and concept. If the form breaks, the old enmity comes to the fore. In what follows, Simmel sets out to show how it is possible that, in the ruin, an aesthetic allure asserts itself, which—despite the decay—remains tied to the notion of integrity. First, Simmel mentions a ruin-related inversion of the relationship between nature and spirit. The human spirit that usually forms and builds up surrenders its product to the downward-tearing forces of the natural world until the human artifice starts to look like a work of nature. Again, the possible source of this thought in Goethe's "Novelle" is obvious. Second, Simmel points out that the conflict between nature and spirit involves an ethical dimension. A new whole emerges when nature, rebelling against violation by the spirit, reclaims its inherent right. This retributive justice eventually engenders an aesthetic of ruins. It imbues the decaying building with meaning and prevents it from

---

45. Adorno, "Henkel, Krug und Frühe Erfahrung."
46. Quotation from editor Ingo Meyer's afterword in Simmel, *Jenseits der Schönheit*, 420.

being seen as a mere consequence of futile contingency. In Simmel's terms, the spirit returns home to nature, and peace surrounds the building's sinking back into the landscape. This kind of peace paradoxically finds its final explanation in a third form of antagonism that takes place within the human soul, which in Simmel's understanding is nature and spirit at once. Within the soul, an interminable moral process is at work that causes the soul to permanently change its shape. Simmel juxtaposes this inexhaustible dynamic and restless rhythm with the desire of the aesthetic perception for an equilibrium and combines the affinity between ethics and aesthetics with the definition of peace that surrounds the ruin:

> The profound peace, which, like a holy charmed circle [*heiliger Bannkreis*], surrounds the ruin, conveys a sense of this constellation, of the obscure antagonism which determines the form of all existence [*die Form alles Daseins*], now acting among merely natural forces, now occurring only within psychic life, and now, as in the present case, taking place between nature and matter. This antagonism—although here too it is in disequilibrium [*nicht zum Gleichgewicht versöhnt*] in that it lets one side preponderate as the other sinks into annihilation [*Vernichtung*]—nevertheless offers us a quietly abiding image [*ruhig verharrendes Bild*], secure in its form. The aesthetic value of the ruin combines the disharmony, the eternal becoming of the soul struggling against itself, with the satisfaction of form [*formale Befriedigtheit*], the firm limitedness [*Umgrenztheit*], of the work of art. (GS, 265)

This passage suggests that the ruin does not simply resolve the conflict between subjective and objective forces that the disintegration of the form unleashes. New unity does not equal a new equilibrium like the one typical of a complete architectural structure. Instead, the antagonism between upward-striving and downward-sinking forces manifests itself openly but still under the aspect of form. What Simmel claims is that only fragmentary forms can coalesce with the restless pulsation of life.

However, Simmel reaches this conclusion late in the text. What precedes it is a somewhat disjointed, nebulous argument, which is complicated by the author's tendency to bring up the tension between subject and object in rapidly changing contexts without explaining the transitions. The function of the ruin shifts with the setting in which it appears. It manifests itself as a physical work of art, as a symbol of nature and as a token of the human soul:

> On the one side of that typical conflict stood the purely external form or symbolism [of the ruin]: the contour of the mountain as defined by the building-up [*Aufbau*] and the breaking-down [*Einstürzen*]. But in respect to the other pole of existence, [the conflict] lives entirely within the human soul—that

> battlefield between nature, which the soul is itself, and spirit, which the soul is itself. The forces which one can designate only by the spatial simile of upward striving [*Aufwärtsstreben*] are at work continuously in our soul, continuously interrupted, deflected, overcome by other forces which work in us. (*GS*, 264)

This strategy is, on the one hand, complemented by a mode of potentiality that suggests that the text as a whole has to be understood as figurative speech. On the other hand, the essay repeatedly proceeds assertively. In the end, the question remains whether this text is about the eponymous ruin after all, given that the ruin constantly eludes the observer. Such a question raises the suspicion that, rather than being the subject matter, the ruin is a symptom that points to what concerns philosophy in general and Simmel's philosophical thinking in particular: the basic antagonism that determines the form of all existence. This solution would seem plausible if it were not so evident that in Simmel's text, the ruin is not just a symptom but a concrete object as well. It is a third entity between thing and concept, between art and philosophy, and as such it is situated beyond the dictates of form, totality, identity, and even dialectics. Its purpose is not to synthesize or mediate but to keep the basic tension alive, which becomes obvious at the end of the essay. In conclusion, Simmel supports his own claim of the peacefulness of ruins with one last argument, suggesting that in ruins the past becomes aesthetically accessible and therefore present. At the sight of ruins, Simmel writes:

> Such profound and comprehensive energies of our soul are brought into play that there is no longer any sharp division between perception and thought. Here psychic wholeness [*Ganzheit*] is at work, seizing, in the same way that its object fuses the contrast of present and past into one united form [*Einheitsform*], on the whole span of physical and spiritual vision in the unity of aesthetic enjoyment, which, after all, is always rooted in a deeper than merely aesthetic unity. (*GS*, 266)

Two things are remarkable about this difficult passage. On the one hand, it sounds like a celebration of unity on a variety of levels: within our souls, between thought and perception, present and past, and of course nature and spirit. On the other hand, by distinguishing between the psychic wholeness of the soul and the united form of its object, Simmel seems to attempt a clear distinction between the ruin and the soul as the object and the subject of perception. It is an effort that comes too late, because at this point Simmel has already multiplied the dichotomies and rendered a simple division into subject and object unthinkable. For instance, the contrast between nature and spirit is not only relevant and effective within ruins or within the soul, merely rendering them commensurate, but it also binds them and relates them directly.

The movement of thought that seeks to comprehend a basic antagonism of existence is thereby kept in permanent suspense.

Adorno did not recognize the potential that lay in Simmel's figure of the ruin. He did not see that the ruin, being neither concept nor image and both at the same time, was a counterstatement against the idea of synthesis and not its affirmation. Asserting its critical and creative potential, the liminal figure of the ruin reached beyond the dualism of philosophy and art, decay and unity, metaphysics and materiality, form and life. Had he seen it, Adorno might have been forced to admit that Simmel's thinking deserved its rightful place in the history of philosophy not only for doing justice to Adorno's own call for a philosophical dialectic that took into account conceptual and nonconceptual approaches but also because it reached beyond the dialectical, keeping philosophical thinking in motion and in close proximity to aesthetic considerations.

Georg Simmel's "Die Ruine" and Johann Wolfgang von Goethe's "Novelle" both speak of the denial of an ideal and a continuously postponed realization of the final form. In his old age, Goethe turns toward an aesthetics and hermeneutics of ruin and secures the continuation of German literature by representing it as incomplete on the basis of a broken form. Simmel's ultimate rejection of unity in his consideration of the ruin bespeaks his flexibility as a thinker. It also underscores the significance of his short essay within the history of philosophy—an essay that asks questions about life beyond the safety of systems and the routine of dialectics. Only by suspending complete synthesis can a future for philosophy and poetry remain imaginable.

Epilogue

> The man could hear him playing. A formless music for the age to come. Or perhaps the last music on earth called up from out of the ashes of its ruin.
>
> CORMAC MCCARTHY, *The Road*

In Don DeLillo's 1982 novel *The Names*, the narrator James Axton is an American risk analyst based in Greece who works for a company that sells insurances to multinational corporations, protecting their investments against political turmoil. Axton leads the typical life of an expatriate, culturally and emotionally detached from both his roots and his new living environment, yet at the same time equipped with considerable confidence that the role he plays in history is meaningful: "This is where I want to be. History. It's in the air . . . We're right in the middle. We're handlers of huge sums of delicate money . . . Analysts of risks . . . The world is here."[1] The degree of involvement that this statement suggests almost hides the fact that the world in which Axton claims to be living is in no way exposed to the same kind of political change or instability experienced by those countries farther east in which his company's clients invest. The world he is talking about is Athens, geographically close enough to the region where hazard is real but far enough away to provide a protected space in which fictions of Western political superiority can prosper: "Here was our own model of democratic calm" (*TN*, 96). In Axton's terms, to be in the middle of history and the world mostly means to be at the center of a financial transaction.

Yet from the protagonist's perspective, even the safe haven of Athens has a blind spot, an object that, in his world but out of place, paradoxically appears in plain sight. Like a trauma with which he fails to cope, the view of the Acropolis haunts his movements in the modern city. Wherever he goes, the presence of the Parthenon seems inescapable. But he blocks out its existence

---

1. DeLillo, *The Names* (1989; hereafter cited as *TN*), 97–98.

EPILOGUE

in a masterly act of sublimation, successfully pretending that the traces of the historical past on the hill have nothing to do with him:

> For a long time I stayed away from the Acropolis. It daunted me, the somber rock. I preferred to wander in the modern city, imperfect, blaring. The weight and moment of those worked stones promised to make the business of seeing them a complicated one. So much converges there . . . The ruins stood above the hissing traffic like some monument to doomed expectations. (*TN*, 3)

It takes the entire length of the novel and an assault on the narrator's life to prepare him for an encounter with the decayed landmark. What he finds, when he finally faces the ruins and his own anxiety, is unexpected:

> I walk to the east face of the temple, so much space and openness, lost walls, pediment, roof, a grief for what has escaped containment. And this is what I mainly learned up there, that the Parthenon was not a thing to study but to feel. It wasn't aloof, rational, timeless, pure. I couldn't locate the serenity of the place, the logic and steady sense. It wasn't a relic species of dead Greece but part of the living city below it. This was a surprise. I'd thought it was a separate thing, the sacred height, intact in its Doric order. I hadn't expected a human feeling to emerge from the stones but this is what I found, deeper than the art and mathematics embodied in the structure, the optical exactitudes. I found a cry for pity. This is what remains to the mauled stones in their blue surround, this open cry, this voice that we know as our own. (*TN*, 330)

The experience is one of surprising continuity. Among the ruins, Axton discovers that the past is part of the contemporary world and that the two are connected by way of a single emotion. All that ruin gazers ever felt (admiration, nostalgia, fear, regret, melancholy, disbelief, aesthetic pleasure, creative inspiration, or despair) and every insight they ever had (into life, death, history, form, the divine and the human, and the workings of time) has been replaced, in the late twentieth century, by pity. Pity seems to be all we can hope for, in a ruined state.

And in a state of ruin we appear to be. The political, ecological, and economic events of the past few decades have contributed to a renewed obsessive fascination with ruins.[2] Decay, whether in the concrete or figurative sense, is the cultural signature feature of a crisis-ridden globalized present. For some observers, ruins are symptoms and signs of a nearing apocalyptic scenario. These circumstances have contributed to an unprecedented variety of ruins that characterize the present moment. War-related devastation occurs side by side with destruction through natural disaster and the slow disintegration of

---

2. See Boym, "Ruinophilia" (2017), 43–47.

relatively recently abandoned centers of the industrial age;[3] shifting politics, demographics, and economics leave empty buildings behind, some of which will never be reused; utopian artistic or social architectural projects run out of money; natural resources dwindle, bad investments fail, and people move on, as all the while their deserted infrastructure disintegrates;[4] nuclear reactors explode; empires still fall. These so-called modern ruins are both "belated and contemporary," confounding what we think we know about time and duration.[5] They are anachronistic in the proper sense.[6]

In scholarly and public debates, two dominant lines of argument have emerged that conceptualize the present experience of decay, and they both expose the discourse of ruins as closely linked to economic considerations. The first argument combines ruination and regeneration according to the model of "creative destruction." Decay appears as the prerequisite for the recapture of space by nature or artists and similarly imaginative minds. The basis for this point of view is Joseph Schumpeter's economic theory in which he describes creative destruction as a "process of industrial mutation that incessantly revolutionizes the economic structure from within, incessantly destroying the old one, incessantly creating a new one."[7] Schumpeter's position is based on his reading of Karl Marx's thoughts on the forces of capitalism, and, while in accordance with his object of study he acknowledges that capitalism ultimately undermines its own "institutional framework" and is therefore bound to implode, he clearly emphasizes the aspect of creativity, and reception has followed him in this.[8] Those who adhere to the second approach to contemporary ruins have raised objections against this trait of endless productivity in Schumpeter's theory. Here, the focus lies on ruin as a teleological process that leads to an irreversible break in the system of capitalism and has profound social consequences. In the wake of the most recent financial crisis, proponents of this thesis heralded the end of the middle class.[9]

The prototypical example in which both positions coincide and illustrate the tension that is inherent to the present perception of ruins in the Western

3. The most famous example is of course Detroit. I will come back to it later in this epilogue.
4. E.g., Kolmanskop in Nigeria or Fordlandia in the Amazon.
5. Boym, "Ruinophilia," 44.
6. On the anachronistic ghostliness of the American postindustrial rural landscape, see Largier, "Land of the Walking Dead," 201–4.
7. Schumpeter, *Capitalism, Socialism and Democracy* (1994), 82–83. For the German original, first published in 1942, see Schumpeter, *Kapitalismus, Sozialismus und Demokratie* (2005).
8. Schumpeter, *Capitalism, Socialism and Democracy*, 139.
9. With a pop-cultural and journalistic streak and with respect to Detroit, see Kullmann, *Rasende Ruinen*.

world is the city of Detroit. Stricken by the decline of the automotive industry since the 1950s and providing fertile ground for administrative and governmental failures, not least to resolve enduring issues such as racist housing policies or the so-called white flight to the suburbs, the metropolis endured an exodus of 25 percent of its overall population between the 2000 and 2010 census counts.[10] The drastic decline was dubbed a "demographic catastrophe . . . without parallel in the modern world."[11] When in 2013 Detroit had to file for bankruptcy, the city was in a state of severe urban decay, with an estimated number of eighty-five thousand abandoned houses.[12] Those forced to stay were left to dwell in a ruinscape on the brink of being reclaimed by nature.[13]

Concurrently with nature, its competitor and accomplice, the world of art also invaded the wasteland. Detroit's ruins have been photographed from all angles.[14] Every remote corner has featured in a documentary film.[15] Performance artists together with tourists from around the globe have posed in front of the gigantic carcass of Michigan Central Station, turning the city into a spectacle and an icon of beautiful decay (figure 8).[16]

John Patrick Leary categorized these emerging "conquerors" of the Detroit wilderness into two groups who share a fascination for the anti-imperialistic implications of ruins, their potential—in other words—to represent the history of the disadvantaged. One group consists of those who indulge in elegiac lament over the destroyed city and display a peculiar interest in loss and the seemingly marginal vestiges "that we have of our twentieth-century history."[17] Suggestions to keep the ruins to serve as monuments to a perished society like the remains of European antiquity might be included here.[18] So might the melancholy of the brooders preoccupied with the symbolic value of bankrupt

10. Seelye, "Detroit Census Confirms a Desertion Like No Other."
11. "So Cheap, There's Hope."
12. Davey and Williams, "Billions in Debt, Detroit Tumbles Into Insolvency."
13. See the discussion of Detroit's recent history in Sugrue, *Origins of the Urban Crisis*; Davey, "A Picture of Detroit Ruin, Street by Forlorn Street." For the number of abandoned homes, see Orr, "Financial and Operating Plan"; Larson et al., "Exploring the Impact of 9,398 Demolitions on Neighborhood-Level Crime in Detroit, Michigan," 57–63.
14. One of the famous examples is the photo volume by Marchand and Meffre, *Ruins of Detroit*. For a critical view of Detroit in photography and film, see Arnold, "Urban Decay Photography and Film," 326–39.
15. An example is Julien Temple's *Requiem for Detroit?* (United Kingdom, 2010).
16. See Apel, *Beautiful, Terrible Ruins*.
17. Leary, "Detroitism."
18. Sugrue, "City of Ruins."

FIGURE 8. Michigan Central Station in Detroit (2015). Photograph by the author.

Detroit.[19] An excess of this mournful attitude has been called "ruin porn," described by Leary in 2011 as a gaze that aestheticizes decay "without inquiring of its origins, [that] dramatizes spaces but never seeks out the people that inhabit and transform them, and romanticizes isolated acts of resistance without acknowledging the massive political and social forces aligned against the real transformation."[20] In some cases, the impulse to aestheticize enters a somewhat odd symbiosis with a sober survey of the harsh economic and social reality of Detroit. Rebecca Solnit's 2007 article in *Harper's Magazine*—

19. Steinmetz, "Colonial Melancholy and Fordist Nostalgia," 294–320.

20. Leary, "Detroitism." See also Malone, "Case against Economic Disaster Porn." The first person to use the expression *ruin porn* was allegedly journalist and photographer James D. Griffioen. See his interview with *Vice Magazine* journalist Thomas Morton: Morton, "Something, Something, Something, Detroit."

titled, with a self-reflexive gesture, "Detroit Arcadia"—juxtaposes a chronicle of the misery with a rhetoric worthy of a pastoral romance. "Detroit is still beautiful," she writes, "both in its stately decay and in its growing natural abundance."[21]

The other group that Leary identified are the utopians, who document and defend "the city's possibilities," focusing on art projects that are intertwined with the reuse of abandoned land. From this point of view, Detroit's "renaissance" is on the horizon, and there is unfaltering confidence in the city's relentless creative drive. Utopians are eager to cultivate, but it is often their own lifestyle that they seek to foster and improve. Their utopia is a concept that is primarily imported from elsewhere, unconsciously mimicking the possibilities that other places offer.[22]

The views of these two groups are compatible with those of the Schumpeterians and their opponents. The dynamic of rise and fall in the case of creative decline can, first, be compared to a utopian perception of ruins. Second, the anticapitalist perspective on the force of an incessant fall is comparable to the attitude of lamenters over the ruins of their time.[23] These views coexist in the perception of Detroit, and they can overlap. More often than not, they contribute to an understanding of the city as a commodity whose value is determined by aestheticized collapse.

For Leary, the offending aspect regarding the contemporary perceptions of ruins from the industrial age is that they radically decontextualize their object, or, in our terms, detach them from discourses. Representations of the ruins of Detroit, he argues, are resistant to "narrative content or explication." They are detached from the social and political reality and offer no path to an understanding of how we relate to the decay in front of our eyes. The result is a kind of art for art's sake that is always exploitative and does not contribute in any way to the political debate. The interest in history is nothing but a "vague sense of historical pathos."[24]

Whether or not this assessment can do justice to the diversity of ruin-related artistic outputs in twenty-first-century Detroit is of course questionable. In a politically and socially highly charged environment, Leary rightly criticizes art that is oblivious of its ethical responsibility. Yet his objections, although expressed with the purpose of advocating for historical accuracy,

21. Solnit, "Detroit Arcadia."
22. Leary, "Detroitism."
23. My intention is not to imply that the lamenters are anticapitalists whereas the utopians are capitalists.
24. Leary, "Detroitism."

seem to reiterate the long-standing stereotype that ruins, throughout their history, have been hotbeds of semantic abundance and that only now, in so-called modernity, has this prolific efficiency found its decadent end. As I laid out in the introduction, such a notion neglects that ruins, for all their semantic possibilities, have always been open to semantic emptiness and that it is by way of this confluence of meaning and meaninglessness that historical distinctiveness can be grasped.

The developments of recent years even suggest that Leary might have focused on the wrong issues altogether. Between 2014, when the first large scale demolition of abandoned houses took place, and November 2019, when the city council voted down a bond sale proposed by the mayor to finance complete blight removal within five years, nineteen thousand structures were demolished—compared with nine thousand that were refurbished.[25] The city's new plan was criticized for being focused on "tearing down" instead of "building up" and was seen as an appalling document of a lack of imagination in dealing with the problem of affordable housing.[26] It was also a way to obliterate the memory of decay.

The zeal with which the city government invested in erasing the traces of ruin was blatantly concrete and symbolic at once, and it had an unlikely precedent in earlier examples of fervent construction work. Unsurprisingly, Detroit's architectural history suggests a coincidence between industrial and constructional productivity. Yet architecture has also been used as a sort of antidote against the threat of economic and social instability or else a décor to mask dissolution that has already occurred. One example was the construction of John Portman's Renaissance Center in downtown Detroit that Henry Ford II initiated with the intention of curbing the "white flight" during the 1970s.[27] Other examples are more recent. Since the beginning of the twenty-first century, a number of new investments have left the impression that Detroit consists of little more than the downtown area with its business edifices and skyline, captivating enough to make the spectator forget the dilapidation that dominates throughout the rest of the city.[28]

25. City of Detroit, "Mayor Outlines $250M Bond Program to Eliminate Residential Blight"; Larson et al., "Exploring the Impact of 9,398 Demolitions," 57–63.

26. Givens, "Opinion: Detroit Demo Bond Doesn't Address Blight Root Causes." Givens's numbers regarding the renovated homes differ from those disclosed by the chief financial officer of the city of Detroit.

27. Desiderio, "Catalyst for Downtown," 83–112.

28. Most famously, the mortgage lending company Quicken Loans moved its headquarters to Detroit in 2011. Some of the projects had to be canceled or put on hold—for instance, the Cadillac Center that failed to meet the standards of the Detroit Economic Growth Corp.

Against the background of this tendency to suppress and sublimate the reality of destruction, Leary's criticism of decontextualized art seems to underestimate that some of the artworks clearly played a role in a process of concretization and historicization that went beyond a superficial sentiment and stemmed from an endeavor to keep the evidence of decay instead of eliminating it. These works of art are part of a transformation that does not erase the ruin or reconstruct its former state but collaborates with it instead. Thus art, even in its politically unconscious forms, creates historical significance merely by acknowledging the collapse.[29]

The fact that Leary did not accept historical relevancy without political sustainability and had little patience for what he considered to be a sort of capricious emptiness in contemporary "ruinophilia" does not diminish—and maybe it even emphasizes—his crucial insight.[30] He saw clearly that the perception and interpretation of ruins needs to be based on discourses and constellations. Ultimately, his intervention is one against a simplistic, monodiscursive view of decay and affirms that, in the most fundamental sense, ruins are sites of conglomerations, intersections, and multiple dimensions of time. In the course of this book, I explored some of these discourses and the constellations that informed them on a long journey through time and space and from ruin to ruin: from the remains of Troy to those of Greece, Rome, and the Holy Roman Empire; from the Alps to Poliphilo's dreamland of antiquity, Goethe's nameless, dilapidated ancestral castle, and Detroit's urban decay. Along the way, I laid bare the vulnerability and precariousness of existence, the perpetual endangerment of human desire for duration, closure, and totality. In doing so, the impositions of history came to the foreground. The difficult concept of *world* and its complicated relation with *life* was uncovered. Yet through the lens of a textuality of ruins, possibilities started to emerge; surprising and unexpected discursive options, historiographical, philosophical, and poetic forms that reflected on continuity despite disruption, and afterlife despite the limits of temporality. This point of view allowed for an analysis that was driven by the inclusion of texts and historical contexts that are not necessarily part of the literary, historiographical, and philosophical canon, and it enabled a new view on those works and authors that have become firmly established as representatives of specific periods.

At the center of my reading of Petrarch and the *Hypnerotomachia Poliphili* was the propitious moment, a time concept that brought the poetic and

---

29. Boym, "Ruinophilia," 45.
30. For the use of the term in the sense of an appreciation of ruins, see Boym, "Ruinophilia."

historical force to light that hides in postponement and the practice of lingering delay and reveals how ruins of the past survive. Hildebert of Lavardin and Ferdinand Gregorovius dealt with the challenge of how to live on after the experience of disruption, and whereas Hildebert offered a semiotic solution, Gregorovius claimed continuity by aesthetically linking world-time and his own life-time. Living on was Martin Opitz's concern as well. By reshaping Seneca's poetic world in his translation, he established the aesthetic form as the condition for life's continuance. On the battleground of time, between the concreteness and abstraction of ruin, Johann Jacob Breitinger and Andreas Gryphius tried to grasp the core of historical knowledge and its implications for the future to come, while Thomas Burnet and G. F. W. Hegel struggled to conceptually realign the competing, overlapping, and emerging discourses of their historical (and biographical) present. Johann Wolfgang von Goethe and Georg Simmel, in an antithetical move against synthesis, secured the continuity of literature and philosophy.

In each case examined here, historical milestones were relocated, authoritative figures dethroned. There was no movement toward closure, no striving toward a goal. Yet at each stage, the ruin was the site of ongoing living history, replete with discourses of the past and the future, always receptive, always changing. In that sense, this journey does not end at the threshold to modernity or in the realm of its aftermath. The dilapidated twenty-first-century city of Detroit gives evidence of yet another constellation that arranges discourses around ruins. Some of these discourses are old, like the lament over a broken world or the melancholy of life after loss. Other discourses arise from the contemporary moment, like the discourse of financial economy. They offer semiotic frameworks to deal with crises, change, and transformation that are different from the interpretive patterns familiar from tradition. Yet while the constellations are in themselves complex, related to the most intricate notions of time, transforming our view of history and existence and reshaping our notion of form, some of what converges in the ruins stays the same. Their textuality manifests a recurring triad of world-time, life-time, and form that remains stable over the centuries. It accounts for the fact that the present has always been the past's ruined future. The triad ultimately seems to justify the comparison between the historically and thematically disparate objects and contexts examined here. In that sense, the constellation of world-time, life-time, and form evinces that ideas about ruins and perceptions of decay have always been ancient and modern at once.

This might ultimately be the reason why Don DeLillo's James Axton recognizes the voice of the stones on the Acropolis as his own. Amid a world of profit and transactions, the constellation aligns to spawn, out of the ruin, a unifying emotion of great simplicity and the highest ethical sophistication. What emerges is familiar, even though it has lived on by being reshaped, reconstructed, rewritten, reimagined, rethought. Sometimes what emerges is pity, sometimes it is music. It always is a new and ancient form, built from the rubble of the ages "for the age to come."

Acknowledgments

This book has undergone many transformations over the past few years. It traveled with me from one continent to another while changing shape, content, and language, ultimately to be completed in North Carolina during a global pandemic. The one constant in uncertain times, however, was the network of countless professional relations and personal friendships on both sides of the Atlantic that made this book possible. I am grateful and humbled by the immense generosity and ceaseless help that I have received along the way.

I was fortunate enough to have the opportunity to work on this book while teaching in the Department of Germanic and Slavic Languages and Literatures at the University of North Carolina at Chapel Hill. It has been an incomparably enjoyable working place and the ideal environment for me to thrive as a scholar. I owe most special thanks to Richard Langston, whose wise mentorship, tireless support, and positive encouragement not only exceedingly improved the book but also taught me a great deal about academic life in the United States and helped me handle every challenge with confidence. One could not wish for a better, more reliable teacher, colleague, and friend. I also owe special thanks to Nicholas Jones, who is the only person who read every single word of every draft of the manuscript. His impressive bilingualism and his subtle sense for the right measure of editorial intervention greatly advanced the book linguistically, while letting me keep my own voice. I owe thanks to all my smart and supportive colleagues in the Department of Germanic and Slavic Languages and Literatures, especially Gabriel Trop, Ruth von Bernuth, Eric Downing, Tin Wegel, and Jonathan Hess, whom I remember most fondly, and outside the department to Maggie Fritz-Morkin and Brett Whalen. I thank my students both at UNC and in the

Carolina-Duke Graduate Program in German Studies who have discussed some of the chapters with me and given me insightful feedback.

I owe thanks to the two anonymous readers who reviewed this manuscript for the University of Chicago Press. Their thorough, analytically and historically perspicacious feedback challenged and motivated me to reset some of my parameters, and it was an invaluable asset in my effort to improve the book. I thank my editor, Randy Petilos, whose exceptionally patient, reliable, and efficient guidance made the publishing process an uncomplicated and pleasant one. Lori Meek Schuldt copyedited the manuscript with the greatest possible competence and care.

To the Institute for the Arts and Humanities at UNC, I am grateful for granting me a semester of leave to complete this book and to discuss results and prospects with a group of dedicated fellows. Lutz Koepnick I thank for his invitation to Vanderbilt University and the opportunity to discuss chapter 1. His interest in my work and his friendship are two wonderful pieces of good luck. I thank Dorothea von Mücke for her invitation to Columbia University as well as her useful comments on chapter 9, and Jocelyn Holland for inviting me to Caltech and introducing me to the medievalists at the Division of the Humanities and Social Sciences who gave me feedback on chapter 5. Niklaus Largier, Markus Stock, and Kathryn Starkey gave me the opportunity to participate in the Colloquium on Medieval German Studies in Stanford and Berkeley, and they were most generous with practical support and advice.

My fascination with ruins predates my move to North Carolina. As a visiting postdoc at the Department of Germanic Studies at the University of Chicago, I had the opportunity to share initial ideas and first papers with faculty and graduate students. I am most grateful to Christopher Wild, who was my host and my most important interlocutor. His ideas on the concept of "living on" deeply influenced my perspective on baroque German literature and found entrance into part 2 of this book. His and David Wellbery's support and advice were crucial for the next phase of my professional trajectory. In Chicago, I met Helmut Puff, whose work on ruins has been a model and a guiding principle for my own thinking and clarified my goals. Among the many graduate students and postdocs in Chicago who helped me with talks and papers and who enriched my social life, I would like to single out Tamara Kamatović and David Egan.

I am grateful to Julia Weitbrecht, Maximilian Benz, and my dissertation advisor Christian Kiening, who facilitated a dialogue about several chapters of this book with an audience in Germany and Switzerland. Benno Wirz gave me the first opportunity to write about ruins in an edited volume, and his input and unmatched open-mindedness have moved this project forward more than once. Wendelin Brühwiler has been a careful reader and critic.

ACKNOWLEDGMENTS

I thank my friends and family in the United States and Europe who contributed to this book through their interest, encouragement, and sometimes surprising thoughts. I am particularly grateful to Eliane Spahni, Michaela Schönenberger, Barbara Jenni, Michael Bühler, Safia Swimelar, Adi Džumhur, Sheila and Bob Breitweiser, Katharina Flieger, Mario Lüscher, Teresa Gruber, Elisabetta Antonelli, Dragana Drmić, Patrick Kühnis, Nicole Meier, Karl Wagner, Thomas Möckli, Douglas Whitcher, Florian Keller, Fabio Soldati, and Sibylle Marti. I thank my brother, Dimitrije Prica, for his spirited, good-humored presence in my life, and my parents, Ursula and Pantaleon Prica, to whom I owe more than I can say. Finally, I thank Robbie Breitweiser for his companionship and support over the past five years. It has been a privilege to have him by my side.

*

Chapter 4 originally appeared in print, in different form, as "Lingering: Visions of Past and Future in the *Hypnerotomachia Poliphili*" in *Temporality and Mediality in Late Medieval and Early Modern Culture* (Cursor Mundi 32), edited by Christian Kiening and Martina Stercken (Turnhout, Belg.: Brepols, 2018), 229–54, and a German version of portions of chapter 7 appeared as "Limes-Gestalten: Über Zeit und Form in der Troja-Literatur," in *Letzte Dinge: Deutungsmuster und Erzählformen des Umgangs mit Vergänglichkeit im Horizont heterochroner Zeitsemantiken in Mittelalter und Früher Neuzeit*, edited by Julia Weitbrecht, Andreas Bihrer, and Timo Felber, 143–61 (Göttingen: V&R unipress, 2020). A longer version of the section on Georg Simmel in chapter 9 appeared in German as "Ruine: Versuch über die philosophische Kehrseite bei Georg Simmel," in *Philosophische Kehrseiten: Eine andere Einleitung in die Philosophie*, edited by Natalie Pieper and Benno Wirz, 273–97 (Freiburg im Breisgau: Verlag Karl Alber, 2014).

Bibliography

Adorno, Theodor W. 1970. *Negative Dialektik: Jargon der Eigentlichkeit*. Vol. 6 of *Gesammelte Schriften*. Frankfurt am Main: Suhrkamp Verlag.
———. 2003. "Henkel, Krug und Frühe Erfahrung." In *Gesammelte Schriften*, vol. 11, *Noten zur Literatur*, 556–66. Frankfurt am Main: Suhrkamp Verlag.
Agamben, Giorgio. 1999. "The Dream of Language." In *The End of the Poem: Studies in Poetics*, 43–61. Stanford, CA: Stanford University Press.
Albrecht, Michael von, ed. 1997. *A History of Roman Literature: From Livius Andronicus to Boethius*. Vol. 2. Leiden: Brill.
Alciato, Andrea. 1531. *Emblematum liber*. Augsburg: Heinrich Steyner.
———. 1621. *Emblemata cum commentariis*. Patauij [Padua]: Apud Petrum Paulum Tozzium.
Alt, Peter André. 1995. *Begriffsbilder: Studien zur literarischen Allegorie zwischen Opitz und Schiller*. Tübingen: Niemeyer Verlag.
Apel, Dora. 2015. *Beautiful, Terrible Ruins: Detroit and the Anxiety of Decline*. Newark, NJ: Rutgers University Press.
Aristotle. 1984. "Problemata Physica." In *The Complete Works: The Revised Oxford Translation*, vol. 2, edited by Jonathan Barnes. Princeton, NJ: Princeton University Press.
Arnold, Sarah. 2015. "Urban Decay Photography and Film: Fetishism and Apocalyptic Imagination." *Journal of Urban History* 41 (2): 326–39.
Assmann, Aleida. 1999. *Erinnerungsräume: Formen und Wandlungen des kulturellen Gedächtnisses*. Munich: C. H. Beck.
Assmann, Aleida, Monika Gomille, and Gabriele Rippl, eds. 2002. *Ruinenbilder*. Munich: Wilhelm Fink Verlag.
Baker, David Weil. 2003. "Ruin and Utopia." *Moreana* 40 (155): 49–66.
Barański, Zygmunt G. 2009. "Petrarch, Dante, Cavalcanti." In Barański and Cachey, *Petrarch and Dante*, 50–113.
Barański, Zygmunt G., and Theodore J. Cachey, eds. 2009. *Petrarch and Dante: Anti-Dantism, Metaphysics, Tradition*. Notre Dame, IN: University of Notre Dame Press.
Barniske, Friedemann. 2019. *Hegels Theorie des Erhabenen: Grenzgänge zwischen Theologie und philosophischer Ästhetik*. Tübingen: Mohr Siebeck.

Barolini, Teodolinda. 1989. "The Making of a Lyric Sequence: Time and Narrative in Petrarch's *Rerum vulgarium fragmenta*." *Modern Language Notes* 104:1–38.
———. 2009. "The Self in the Labyrinth of Time." In *Petrarch: Critical Guide*, 33–62.
Barthes, Roland. 1988. "Textual Analysis of Poe's *Valdemar*." In *Modern Criticism and Theory*, edited by David Lodge, translated by Geoff Bennington, 172–95. Harlow: Longman.
———. 1990. *S/Z*. Translated by Richard Miller. Oxford: Blackwell.
Bartsch, Shadi, and Alessandro Schiesaro, eds. 2011. *The Cambridge Companion to Seneca*. Cambridge: Cambridge University Press.
Baum, Constanze. 2013. *Ruinenlandschaften: Spielräume der Einbildungskraft in Reiseliteratur und bildkünstlerischen Werken über Italien im 18. und frühen 19. Jahrhundert*. Heidelberg: Winter Verlag.
Becker-Contarino, Barbara. 2002. "Opitz und der Dreissigjährige Krieg." In *Martin Opitz (1597–1439): Nachahmungspoetik und Lebenswelt*, edited by Thomas Brogstedt and Walter Schmitz, 38–52. Tübingen: Max Niemeyer Verlag.
Beiser, Frederick. 2005. *Hegel*. New York: Routledge.
Bender, Wolfgang. 1973. *Johann Jakob Bodmer und Johann Jakob Breitinger*. Stuttgart: J. B. Metzler.
Benjamin, Walter. 1972. "Die Aufgabe des Übersetzers." In *Gesammelte Schriften*, vol. 4, pt. 1, edited by Tillmann Rexroth, 9–21. Frankfurt am Main: Suhrkamp Verlag.
———. 1973. "Some Motifs in Baudelaire." In *Charles Baudelaire: A Lyric Poet in the Era of High Capitalism*. London: New Left Books.
———. 1975. "Eduard Fuchs: Collector and Historian." *New German Critique* 5:27–58.
———. 1980. "Über den Begriff der Geschichte." In *Gesammelte Schriften*, vol. 1, pt. 2, *Abhandlungen*, edited by Rolf Tiedemann and Hermann Schweppenhäuser, 691–704. Frankfurt am Main: Suhrkamp Verlag.
———. 1991. "Das Passagen-Werk." In *Gesammelte Schriften*, vol. 5, edited by Rolf Tiedemann. Frankfurt am Main: Suhrkamp Verlag.
———. 1991. "Eduard Fuchs, der Sammler und der Historiker." In *Gesammelte Schriften*, vol. 2, pt. 2, *Aufsätze, Essays, Vorträge*, edited by Rolf Tiedemann and Hermann Schweppenhäuser, 465–505. Frankfurt am Main: Suhrkamp Verlag.
———. 1991. "Über einige Motive bei Baudelaire." In *Gesammelte Schriften*, vol. 1, pt. 2, *Abhandlungen*, edited by Rolf Tiedemann and Hermann Schweppenhäuser. Frankfurt am Main: Suhrkamp Verlag.
———. 1991. *Ursprung des deutschen Trauerspiels*. In *Gesammelte Schriften*, vol. 1, pt. 1, *Abhandlungen*, edited by Rolf Tiedemann and Hermann Schweppenhäuser, 203–430. Frankfurt am Main: Suhrkamp Verlag.
———. 1998. *The Origin of German Tragic Drama*. Translated by John Osborne. London: Verso.
———. 2002. *Arcades Project*. Translated by Howard Eiland and Kevin McLaughlin. Cambridge, MA: Harvard University Press.
———. 2002. "The Task of the Translator." In *Selected Writings*, vol. 1, *1913–1926*, edited by Marcus Bullock and Michael W. Jennings, 253–63. Cambridge, MA: Harvard University Press.
———. 2006. "On the Concept of History." In *Selected Writings*, vol. 4, *1938–1940*, translated by Edmund Jephcott, Howard Eiland, and Michael W. Jennings, 389–400. Cambridge, MA: Harvard University Press.
Bisanz, Rudolf M. 1988. "The Birth of a Myth: Tischbein's Goethe in the Roman Campagna." *Monatshefte* 80 (2): 187–99.

Blaise, Albert. 1975. *Lexicon Latinitatis medii aevi: Praesertim ad res ecclesiasticas investigandas pertinens*. Turnhout, Belg.: Brepols.

Blumenberg, Hans. 1971. "Wirklichkeitsbegriff und Wirkungspotential des Mythos." In *Terror und Spiel: Probleme der Mythenrezeption*, Poetik und Hermeneutik 4, edited by Manfred Fuhrmann, 11–66. Munich: Wilhelm Fink Verlag.

———. 1979. *Arbeit am Mythos*. Frankfurt am Main: Suhrkamp Verlag.

———. 1983. *The Legitimacy of the Modern Age*. Cambridge, MA: MIT Press.

———. 1985. *Work on Myth*. Translated by Robert Wallace. Cambridge, MA: MIT Press.

———. 1987. *Das Lachen der Thrakerin: Eine Urgeschichte der Theorie*. Frankfurt am Main: Suhrkamp Verlag.

———. 1988. *Matthäuspassion*. Frankfurt am Main: Suhrkamp Verlag.

———. 1997. *Paradigmen zu einer Metaphorologie*. Frankfurt am Main: Suhrkamp Verlag.

———. 2001. *Lebenszeit und Weltzeit*. Frankfurt am Main: Suhrkamp Verlag.

———. 2006. *Beschreibung des Menschen*. Frankfurt am Main: Suhrkamp Verlag.

———. 2010. *Paradigms for a Metaphorology*. Translated by Robert Savage. Ithaca, NY: Cornell University Press and Cornell University Library.

———. 2015. *The Laughter of the Thracian Woman: A Protohistory of Theory*. Translated by Spencer Hawkins. New York: Bloomsbury Academic.

Böhme, Hartmut. 1988. "Kritik der Melancholie und Melancholie der Kritik." In *Natur und Subjekt*, 256–73. Frankfurt am Main: Suhrkamp Verlag.

———. 1988. "Ruinen-Landschaften: Zum Verhältnis von Naturgeschichte und Allegorie in den späten Filmen von Andrej Tarkowskij." In *Natur und Subjekt*, 334–79. Frankfurt am Main: Suhrkamp Verlag.

———. 1989. "Die Ästhetik der Ruinen." In *Der Schein des Schönen*, edited by Dietmar Kamper and Christoph Wulf, 287–304. Göttingen: Steidl Verlag.

Böhmer, Otto A. 2018. "Der Geist in den Alpen: Hegel und der Aufstieg zur Philosophie." In *Lichte Momente*. Munich: Deutsche Verlags-Anstalt.

Bolz, Norbert, and Willem Van Reijen, eds. 1996. *Ruinen des Denkens—Denken in Ruinen*. Frankfurt am Main: Suhrkamp Verlag.

Borchmeyer, Dieter. 1977. *Höfische Gesellschaft und Französische Revolution bei Goethe: Adliges und bürgerliches Wertsystem im Urteil der Weimarer Klassik*. Kronberg im Taunus, Ger.: Athenäum.

Borsi, Stefano. 1995. *Polifilio Architetto: Cultura architettonica e teoria artistica nell' Hypnerotomachia Poliphili di Francesco Colonna, 1499*. Rome: Officina.

Bosco, Umberto. 1971. *Francesco Petrarca*. Bari: Laterza.

Boym, Svetlana. 2001. *The Future of Nostalgia*. New York: Basic Books.

———. 2017. "Ruinophilia." In *The Off-Modern*, 43–47. New York: Bloomsbury.

Braun, Manuel. 2007. "Kristallworte, Würfelworte: Probleme und Perspektiven eines Projekts 'Ästhetik mittelalterlicher Literatur.'" In *Das Fremde Schöne: Dimensionen des Ästhetischen in der Literatur des Mittelalters*, edited by Manuel Braun and Christopher Young, 1–40. Berlin: De Gruyter.

Breitinger, Johann Jacob. 1740. *Fortsetzung der Critischen Dichtkunst: Worinnen die Poetische Mahlerey In Absicht auf den Ausdruck und die Farben abgehandelt wird*. With an introduction by Johann Jacob Bodmer. Zurich: Conrad Orell & Co. and Joh. Fried. Gleditsch.

———. (1740) 1966. *Critische Dichtkunst*. Vol. 1. Facsimile of the 1740 edition. Stuttgart: J. B. Metzler.

———. (1740) 1967. *Critische Abhandlung von der Natur, den Absichten und dem Gebrauche der Gleichnisse*. Facsimile of the 1740 edition. Stuttgart: J. B. Metzler.

Buchheim, Iris. 2011. "Heidegger." In *Hölderlin-Handbuch: Leben—Werk—Wirkung*, edited by Johann Kreuzer, 432–38. Stuttgart: J. B. Metzler.
Bühlbäcker, Hermann. 1999. *Konstruktive Zerstörungen: Ruinendarstellungen in der Literatur zwischen 1774 und 1832*. Bielefeld, Ger.: Aisthesis.
Burckhardt, Jacob. 1958. *The Civilization of the Renaissance in Italy*. 2 vols. Translated by S. G. C. Middlemore. New York: Harper & Row.
Burke, Peter. 1969. *The Renaissance Sense of the Past*. London: Edward Arnold.
Burnet, Thomas. 1726. *The Sacred Theory of the Earth: Containing an Account of the Original of the Earth and of All the General Changes Which It Hath Already Undergone or Is to Undergo, till the Consummation of All Things*. 2 vols. London: John Hooke.
———. 1736. *Archeologiae Philosophicae: Or, the Ancient Doctrine Concerning the Originals of Things*. London: Printed and sold by J. Fischer.
Burton, Robert. 2001. *The Anatomy of Melancholy*. Reprinted with an introduction by William H. Gass. New York: New York Review of Books. First published 1621.
Cachey, Theodore J. "Between Petrarch and Dante: Prolegomenon to a Critical Discourse." In Barański and Cachey, *Petrarch and Dante*, 3–49.
Caferro, William. 2018. *Petrarch's War: Florence and the Black Death in Context*. Cambridge: Cambridge University Press.
Calder, William M. III. 1970. "Originality in Seneca's *Troades*." *Classical Philology* 65 (2): 75–82.
Calvesi, Maurizio. 1996. *La Pugna d'amore in sogno di Francesco Colonna romano*. Rome: Lithos.
Caprio, Vincenzo. 1987. *Poesia e poetica delle rovine di Roma: Momenti e problemi*. Rome: Istituto Nazionale di Studi Romani.
Casella, Maria Teresa, and Giovanni Pozzi, eds. 1959. *Francesco Colonna: Biografia e opere*. 2 vols. Padua: Antenore.
Cassirer, Ernst. 1963. *The Individual and the Cosmos in Renaissance Philosophy*. Translated by Mario Damandi. Oxford: B. Blackwell.
Celenza, Christopher S. 2017. *Petrarch: Everywhere a Wanderer*. London: Reaction Books.
City of Detroit. 2019. "Mayor Outlines $250M Bond Program to Eliminate Residential Blight from All Neighborhoods by Mid-2025." Published September 16. https://detroitmi.gov/news/mayor-outlines-250m-bond-program-eliminate-residential-blight-all-neighborhoods-mid-2025.
Colonna, Francesco. 1998. *Hypnerotomachia Poliphili*. 2 vols. Edited by Marco Ariani and Mino Gabriele. Milan: Adelphi.
———. 1999. *Hypnerotomachia Poliphili: The Strife of Love in a Dream*. Translated by Jocelyn Godwin. London: Thames & Hudson.
Conrady, Karl Otto. 1999. *Goethe: Leben und Werk*. Düsseldorf: Artemis & Winkler.
Coogan, Michael D., Marc Z. Brettler, and Carol Newsom, eds. 2010. *The New Oxford Annotated Bible: New Revised Standard Version with the Apocrypha; An Ecumenical Study Bible*. 4th ed. Oxford: Oxford University Press.
Cooper, John M. 2012. *Pursuits of Wisdom: Six Ways of Life in Ancient Philosophy from Socrates to Plotinus*. Princeton, NJ: Princeton University Press.
Cotts, John D. 2009. *The Clerical Dilemma: Peter of Blois & Literate Culture in the Twelfth Century*. Washington, DC: Catholic University of America Press.
Cowdrey, Herbert E. J. 2004. *Pope Gregory VII, 1073–1085*. Oxford: Clarendon Press.
Cupperi, Walter. 2002. *Senso delle rovine e riuso dell'antico*. Pisa: Classe di Lettere e Filosofia.
Curran, Brian A. 2016. "Teaching and Thinking (About) the High Renaissance: With Some Observations on its Relationship to Classical Antiquity." In *Rethinking the High Renaissance:*

The Culture of the Visual Arts in Early Sixteenth-Century Rome, edited by Jill Burke, 27–55. London: Routledge.

Czapla, Ralf Georg. 1998. "Zur Topik und Faktur postantiker Romgedichte (Hildebert de Lavardin, Joachim du Bellay, Andreas Gryphius): Mit einem Exkurs über die Rezeption von Hildeberts *carmen 36 Scott* in der Frühen Neuzeit." *Daphnis* 27 (1): 141–83.

Dällenbach, Lucien, and Christiaan L. Hart Nibbrig, eds. 1984. *Fragment und Totalität*. Frankfurt am Main: Suhrkamp Verlag.

Dante Alighieri. 2000. *Inferno*. Translated by Robert Hollander and Jean Hollander. New York: Doubleday.

Davey, Monica. 2014. "A Picture of Detroit Ruin, Street by Forlorn Street." *New York Times*, February 17. https://www.nytimes.com/2014/02/18/us/detroit-tries-to-get-a-clear-picture-of-its-blight.html.

Davey, Monica, and Mary Williams Walsh. 2013. "Billions in Debt, Detroit Tumbles into Insolvency." *New York Times*, July 18. https://www.nytimes.com/2013/07/19/us/detroit-files-for-bankruptcy.html.

Deger, Ernst. 1976. *Joachim Du Bellay: Die Römischen Sonette*. Munich: Wilhelm Fink Verlag.

Dekkers, Midas. 2000. *The Way of All Flesh: A Celebration of Decay*. London: Harvill Press.

DeLillo, Don. 1989. *The Names*. New York: Vintage Books.

De Man, Paul. 1983. *Blindness and Insight: Essays in the Rhetoric of Contemporary Criticism*. 2nd ed. Theory and History of Literature 7. Minneapolis: University of Minnesota Press.

De Nolhac, Pierre. 1907. *Pétrarque et l'humanisme*. Vol 2. Paris: Honoré Champion.

Derrida, Jacques. (1967) 1997. *On Grammatology*. Translated by Gayatri Chakravorty Spivak. Baltimore: Johns Hopkins University Press.

Desiderio, Francis. 2009. "A Catalyst for Downtown: Detroit's Renaissance Center." *Michigan Historical Review* 35 (1): 83–112.

Diderot, Denis. 1876. "Observations sur la sculpture et sur Bouchardon (1763)." In *Œuvres complètes de Diderot*, edited by Jules Assézat, vol. 13, 40–47. Paris: J. Claye.

———. 1995. *On Art II: The Salon of 1767*. Edited and translated by John Goodman. New Haven, CT: Yale University Press.

Didi-Huberman, Georges. 2003. "Artistic Survival: Panofsky vs. Warburg and the Exorcism of Impure Time." Translated by Vivian Rehberg and Boris Belay. *Common Knowledge* 9 (2): 273–85.

———. 2017. *The Surviving Image: Phantoms of Time and Times of Phantoms; Aby Warburg's History of Art*. Translated by Harvey L. Mendelsohn. University Park: Pennsylvania State University Press. Original French edition, *L'image survivante: Histoire de l'art et temps des fantômes selon Aby Warburg*, published 2002.

Dillon, Brian, ed. 2011. *Ruins: Documents of Contemporary Art*. Cambridge, MA: MIT Press.

Dillon, Matthew, and Lynda Garland, eds. 2010. *Ancient Greece: Social and Historical Documents from Archaic Times to the Death of Alexander the Great*. London: Routledge.

Dilthey, Wilhelm. 1927. "Der Aufbau der geschichtlichen Welt in den Geisteswissenschaften." In *Gesammelte Schriften*, vol 7. Leipzig: Verlag von B. G. Teubner.

———. 2002. *The Formation of the Historical World in the Human Sciences*. Edited by Rudolf A. Maakkreel and Frithjof Rodi. Princeton, NJ: Princeton University Press.

Di Palma, Vittoria. 2014. *Wasteland: A History*. New Haven, CT: Yale University Press.

Dotti, Ugo. 1978. *Petrarca e la scoperta della coscienza moderna*. Milan: Feltrinelli.

Du Cange, Charles du Fresne, Sieur. 1883–1887. *Glossarium mediae et infimae Latinitatis*. Edited by G. A. Louis Henschel, Pierre Carpentier, Christoph Adelung, and Léopold Favre. 3 vols. Niort: L. Favre.

Düntzer, Heinrich, ed. 1853. *Briefwechsel zwischen Goethe und Staatsrath Schultz*. Leipzig: Dyk.

Du Pérac, Etienne, and Rudolf Wittkower, eds. 1963. *Disegni de le ruine di Roma e come anticamente erono*. Milan: A. Pizzi.

Dutschke, Dennis. 1981. "The Anniversary Poems in Petrarca's *Canzoniere*." *Italica* 58 (2): 83–101.

Eckermann, Johann Peter. 1999. *Gespräche mit Goethe in den letzten Jahren seines Lebens 1823–1832*. Edited by Christoph Michel. Frankfurt am Main: Deutscher Klassiker Verlag.

Eco, Umberto. 1988. *The Aesthetics of Thomas Aquinas*. Translated by Hugh Bredin. Cambridge, MA: Harvard University Press.

Edwards, Catharine. 2011. "Imagining Ruins in Ancient Rome." *European Review of History—Revue européenne d'histoire* 18 (5–6): 645–66.

Eisner, Martin. 2007. "Petrarch Reading Boccaccio: Revisiting the Genesis of the *Triumphi*." In *Petrarch and the Textual Origins of Interpretation*, edited by Teodolinda Barolini and H. Wayne Storey, 131–46. Leiden: Brill.

Emden, Christian J. 2002. "Walter Benjamins Ruinen der Geschichte." In Assmann, Gomille, and Rippl, *Ruinenbilder*, 61–87.

Emmerson, Richard K., ed. 2006. *Key Figures in Medieval Europe: An Encyclopedia*. London: Routledge.

Enenkel, Karl A. E. 2019. *The Invention of the Emblem Book and the Transmission of Knowledge, ca. 1510–1610*. Leiden: Brill.

Fantham, Elaine. 1982. *Seneca's "Troades": A Literary Introduction with Text, Translation and Commentary*. Princeton, NJ: Princeton University Press.

Fenzi, Enrico. 2013. "Petrarca e l'esilio: Uno stile di vita." *Arzanà: Cahier de littérature médievale italiennne* 16–17:365–402.

Ferri, Rolando. 2014. "Transmission." In *Brill's Companion to Seneca: Philosopher and Dramatist*, edited by Gregor Damschen and Andreas Heil, 45–49. Leiden: Brill.

Figal, Günter. 2016. *Martin Heidegger: Zur Einführung*. Hamburg: Junius Verlag.

Finotti, Fabio. 2009. "The Poem of Memory: *Triumphi*." In Kirkham and Maggi, *Petrarch: Critical Guide*, 63–84.

Flubacher, Silvia. 2019. "Gefühlswelten und Gebirgslandschaften." In *Montan-Welten: Alpengeschichte abseits des Pfades*, edited by Tina Asmussen, E1–E15. Zurich: Intercom Verlag.

Földenyi, László. 2016. *Melancholy: Melankólia*. Translated by Tim Wilkinson. New Haven, CT: Yale University Press. Original Hungarian edition, *Melankólia*, published 1984.

Forero-Mendoza, Sabine. 2002. *Le temps des ruines: Le goût des ruines et les formes de la conscience historique à la Renaissance*. Sayssel, Fr.: Champ Vallon.

Forrer, Thomas. 2013. *Schauplatz / Landschaft: Orte der Genese von Wissenschaften und Künsten um 1750*. Göttingen: Wallstein Verlag.

Freccero, John. 1975. "The Fig Tree and the Laurel: Petrarch's Poetics." *Diacritics* 5 (1): 34–40.

Freud, Sigmund. 1940. "Jenseits des Lustprinzips." In *Gesammelte Werke*, vol. 13, 3–69. Frankfurt am Main: S. Fischer Verlag.

———. 1964. "New Introductory Lectures on Psycho-Analysis and Other Works." In *The Standard Edition of the Complete Psychological Works of Sigmund Freud*, edited and translated by James Strachey, vol. 12. London: Hogarth Press.

———. 1978. "Brief an Romain Rolland (Eine Erinnerungsstörung auf der Akropolis). " In *Gesammelte Werke*, vol. 16, 250–57. Frankfurt am Main: S. Fischer Verlag.

———. 1995. "An Autobiographical Study." In *The Standard Edition of the Complete Psychological Works of Sigmund Freud*, edited and translated by James Strachey, vol. 20, 7–74. London: Hogarth Press.

———. 1995. "Beyond the Pleasure Principle." In *The Standard Edition of the Complete Psychological Works of Sigmund Freud*, edited and translated by James Strachey, vol. 18, 7–74. London: Hogarth Press.

———. 1999. *Civilization and its Discontents*. In *The Standard Edition of the Complete Psychological Works of Sigmund Freud*, edited and translated by James Strachey, vol. 21, 59–146. London: Hogarth Press.

———. 1999. "Delusion and Dream in Wilhelm Jensen's 'Gradiva.'" In *The Standard Edition of the Complete Psychological Works of Sigmund Freud*, edited and translated by James Strachey, vol. 9, 7–95. London: Hogarth Press.

———. 1999. "Fragment of an Analysis of a Case of Hysteria." In *The Standard Edition of the Complete Psychological Works of Sigmund Freud*, edited and translated by James Strachey, vol. 7, 3–122. London: Hogarth Press.

———. 1999. *The Interpretation of Dreams (First Part)*. In *The Standard Edition of the Complete Psychological Works of Sigmund Freud*, edited and translated by James Strachey, vol. 4. London: Hogarth Press.

———. 2007. *Unser Herz zeigt nach Süden: Reisebriefe 1893–1926*. Edited by Christfried Tögel. Berlin: Aufbau Verlag.

Freytag, Wiebke. 1992. "Allegorie, Allegorese." In *Historisches Wörterbuch der Rhetorik*, vol. 1, edited by Gert Ueding, 330–92. Tübingen: Niemeyer Verlag.

Friedlander, Eli. 2012. *Walter Benjamin: A Philosophical Portrait*. Cambridge, MA: Harvard University Press.

Friedrich, Markus. 2015. "Frühneuzeitliches Wissenstheater." In *Wissensspeicher der Frühen Neuzeit: Formen und Funktionen*, edited by Frank Grunert and Anette Syndikus, 297–328. Berlin, Boston: Walter De Gruyter.

Fritzsche, Peter. 2004. *Stranded in the Present: Modern Times and the Melancholy of History*. Cambridge, MA: Harvard University Press.

Furno, Martine. 2003. *Une "Fantasie" sur l'antique: Le goût pour l'épigraphie funéraire dans l'Hypnerotomachia Poliphili de Francesco Colonna*. Geneva: Droz.

Gagnebin, Jeanne Marie. 2011. "'Über den Begriff der Geschichte.'" In Lindner, *Benjamin-Handbuch*, 284–300.

Gammon, Martin. 2000. "Modernity and the Crisis of Aesthetic Representation in Hegel's Early Writings." In *Hegel and Aesthetics*, edited by William Maker, 145–70. Albany: State University of New York Press.

Gamper, Michael, and Helmut Hühn. 2014. "Einleitung." In *Zeit der Darstellung: Ästhetische Eigenzeiten in Kunst, Literatur und Wissenschaft*, edited by Michael Gamper and Helmut Hühn, 7–23. Hannover: Wehrhahn Verlag.

Gampp, Axel. 2011. "Rom zwischen Tivoli und Washington: Die Visualisierung des antiken Rom in der Frühen Neuzeit." In *Das antike Rom und sein Bild*, edited by Hans-Ulrich Cain, Annette Haug, and Yadegar Asisi, 225–43. Berlin: De Gruyter.

Gasché, Rodolphe. 2007. "Theatrum Theoreticum." In *The Honor of Thinking: Critique, Theory, Philosophy*, 188–208. Stanford, CA: Stanford University Press.

Geimer, Peter. 2003. "Frühjahr 1962: Ein Touristenschicksal." In *Verwindungen: Arbeit an Heidegger*, edited by Wolfgang Ullrich, 45–61. Frankfurt am Main: S. Fischer.

Georges, Karl Ernst. 1998. *Ausführliches lateinisch-deutsches Handwörterbuch.* Vol. 2. Darmstadt: Wissenschaftliche Buchgesellschaft.

Gibbon, Edward. 1802. *The History of the Decline and Fall of the Roman Empire.* Vol. 12. London: Printed for T. Cadell and W. Davis.

———. 1986. *The Autobiographies.* Edited by John Murray. London: William Clowes and Sons.

Gibson, Bruce. 2017. "Hildebert of Lavardin on the Monuments of Rome." In "Word and Context in Latin Poetry: Studies in Memory of David West," edited by A. J. Woodman and J. Wisse. Special issue, *Cambridge Classical Journal: Proceedings of the Cambridge Philological Society* 40:131–78.

Ginsberg, Robert. 1970. "The Aesthetics of Ruins." *Bucknell Review* 18 (3): 89–103.

———. 2004. *The Aesthetics of Ruins.* Amsterdam: Rodopi.

Givens, Donna. 2019. "Opinion: Detroit Demo Bond Doesn't Address Blight Root Causes." *Deadline Detroit,* November 14. https://www.deadlinedetroit.com/articles/23711/opinion_detroit_demo_bond_doesn_t_address_blight_s_root_causes_reject_it.

Goethe, Johann Wolfgang von. 1850. *Conversations of Goethe with Eckermann and Soret.* Translated by John Oxenford. London: Smith, Elder.

———. 1911. *Werke.* Edited at the behest of Grand Duchess Sophie of Saxony. Vol. 51. Weimar: H. Böhlau.

———. 1973. "Poetische Werke: Autobiographische Schriften 4." In *Berliner-Ausgabe,* vol. 16. Berlin: Aufbau Verlag.

———. 1976. *Italienische Reise.* Frankfurt am Main: Insel Verlag.

———. 1980. "Urworte. Orphisch." In *Goethes Werke,* vol. 1, pt. 3. Weimar: Böhlau Verlag.

———. 1998. *Fairy Tales, Short Stories, and Poems.* Edited and translated by J. W. Thomas. New York: Peter Lang.

———. 2004. *Italian Journey.* Translated by W. H. Auden and Elizabeth Meyer. London: Penguin Classics.

———. 2007. "Novelle." In *Werke,* vol. 2, edited by Dieter Borchmeyer et al. Leipzig: Insel Verlag.

Gosetti-Ferencei, Jennifer Anna. 2009. *Heidegger, Hölderlin, and the Subject of Poetic Language: Toward a New Poetics of Dasein.* New York: Fordham University Press.

Gould, Stephen Jay. 1977. "The Reverend Thomas' Dirty Little Planet." In *Ever Since Darwin: Reflections in Natural History,* 141–46. New York: W. W. Norton.

———. 1987. *Time's Arrow, Time's Cycle: Myth and Metaphor in the Discovery of Geological Time.* Cambridge, MA: Harvard University Press.

Grätz, Katharina. 2004. "'Erhabne Trümmer': Zur kulturpoetischen Funktion der Ruine bei Goethe." In *Auf klassischem Boden begeistert: Antike-Rezeptionen in der deutschen Literatur,* edited by Olaf Hildebrand and Thomas Pittrof, 145–69. Freiburg im Breisgau: Rombach Druck- & Verlagshaus.

Gregorovius, Ferdinand. 1894–1902. *History of the City of Rome in the Middle Ages.* Vols. 1–8. Translated by Annie Hamilton. London: G. Bell & Sons.

———. 1907. *The Roman Journals 1852–1874.* Translated by Annie Hamilton. London: G. Bell & Sons.

———. 1988. *Geschichte der Stadt Rom im Mittelalter: Vom V. bis XVI. Jahrhundert.* 4 vols. Edited by Waldemar Kampf. Munich: C. H. Beck.

———. 1991. *Römische Tagebücher 1852–1889.* Edited by Hanno-Walter Kruft and Markus Völkel. Munich: C. H. Beck.

Grimm, Jakob and Wilhelm. 2021. *Deutsches Wörterbuch*. Wörterbuchnetz, Trier Center for Digital Humanities. Accessed February 27. https://www.woerterbuchnetz.de/DWB. Digitized version of *Deutsches Wörterbuch* (Leipzig: Salomon Hirzel, 1854-1960).

Grossmann, Andreas. 2004. "The Myth of Poetry: Heidegger's 'Hölderlin.'" *Comparatist* 28:29–38.

Gryphius, Andreas. 1878. *Lustspiele*. Edited by Hermann Palm. Tübingen: Bibliothek des literarischen Vereins in Stuttgart.

———. 1991. *Majuma*. In *Dramen*, edited by Eberhard Mannack. Frankfurt am Main: Deutscher Klassiker Verlag.

Guest Lapraik, Clare. 2016. *The Understanding of Ornament in the Italian Renaissance*. Leiden: Brill.

Guignon, Charles. 2005. "The History of Being." In *A Companion to Heidegger*, edited by Hubert L. Dreyfus and Mark A. Wrathall, 392–406. Malden, MA: Blackwell.

Habel, Sabrina. 2019. "Die Eskalation der Zeit: Hans Blumenberg als konservativer Diagnostiker der Moderne." *Geschichte der Gegenwart*, January 9, https://geschichtedergegenwart.ch/die-eskalation-der-zeit-hans-blumenberg-als-konservativer-diagnostiker-der-moderne/.

Habermas, Jürgen. 1985. *Der philosophische Diskurs der Moderne: Zwölf Vorlesungen*. Frankfurt am Main: Suhrkamp Verlag.

———. 1987. *The Philosophical Discourse of Modernity: Twelve Lectures*. Translated by Frederick Lawrence. Cambridge, MA: MIT Press.

Hainsworth, Peter. 1988. *Petrarch the Poet: An Introduction to the "Rerum Vulgarium Fragmenta."* London: Routledge.

Harst, Joachim. 2016. "Germany and the Netherlands: Tragic Seneca in Scholarship and on Stage." In *Brill's Companion to the Reception of Senecan Tragedy*, edited by Eric Dodson Robinson, 149–73. Leiden: Brill.

Haverkamp, Anselm, and Bettine Menke. 2000. "Allegorie." In *Ästhetische Grundbegriffe: Historisches Wörterbuch*, vol 1, edited by Karlheinz Barck, 49–104. Stuttgart: J. B. Metzler.

Haym, Rudolf. 1857. *Hegel und seine Zeit: Vorlesungen über Entstehung und Entwicklung, Wesen und Werth der Hegel'schen Philosophie*. Berlin: Verlag von Rudolf Gärtner.

Heckscher, Wilhelm Sebastian. 1936. *Die Romruinen: Die geistigen Voraussetzungen ihrer Wertung im Mittelalter und in der Renaissance*. Würzburg: Richard Mayr.

———. 1938. "Relics of Pagan Antiquity in Medieval Settings." *Journal of the Warburg Institute* 1 (3): 204–20.

Hegel, Georg Wilhelm Friedrich. 1970. *Vorlesungen über Ästhetik I*. Vol. 13 of *Werke*. Frankfurt am Main: Suhrkamp Verlag.

———. 1979. *Enzyklopädie der philosophischen Wissenschaften im Grundriss I*. Vol. 8 of *Werke*. Frankfurt am Main: Suhrkamp Verlag.

———. 1979. "Wer denkt abstrakt?" In *Jenaer Schriften 1801-1807*, vol. 2 of *Werke*, 575–81. Frankfurt am Main: Suhrkamp Verlag.

———. 1986. *Frühe Schriften*. Vol. 1 of *Werke*. Frankfurt am Main: Suhrkamp Verlag.

———. 1986. *Phänomenologie des Geistes*. Vol. 3 of *Werke*. Frankfurt am Main: Suhrkamp Verlag.

Heidegger, Martin. 1954. *Was heisst Denken?* Tübingen: Max Niemeyer Verlag.

———. 1968. *What Is Called Thinking?* Translated by Fred D. Wieck and J. Glenn Gray. New York: Harper & Row.

———. 1981. *Erläuterungen zu Hölderlins Dichtung*. Vol. 4 of *Gesamtausgabe*. Edited by Friedrich-Wilhelm von Herrmann. Frankfurt am Main: Vittorio Klostermann.

———. 1985. *Phänomenologische Interpretationen zu Aristoteles: Einführung in die phänomenologische Forschung.* Vol. 61 of *Gesamtausgabe.* Edited by Walter Bröcker and Käte Bröcker-Oltmanns. Frankfurt am Main: Vittorio Kolstermann.

———. 1986. "Brief an Erhart Kästner, 1.1.1954." In *Martin Heidegger/Erhart Kästner: Briefwechsel 1953–1974,* edited by Heinrich W. Petzer. Frankfurt am Main: Insel Verlag.

———. 1989. *Beiträge zur Philosophie (Vom Ereignis).* Vol. 65 of *Gesamtausgabe.* Edited by Friedrich-Wilhelm von Hermann. Frankfurt am Main: Vittorio Klostermann.

———. 2000. *Elucidations of Hölderlin's Poetry.* Translated by Keith Hoeller. Amherst, NY: Humanity Books.

———. 2000. *Zu Hölderlin, Griechenlandreisen.* Vol. 75 of *Gesamtausgabe.* Edited by Curt Ochwadt. Frankfurt am Main: Vittorio Klostermann.

———. 2001. *Being and Time.* Translated by John Macquarrie and Edward Robinson. Oxford: Blackwell.

———. 2002. *Off the Beaten Track.* Edited and translated by Julian Young and Kenneth Haynes. Cambridge: Cambridge University Press.

———. 2005. *Sojourns: The Journey to Greece.* Translated by John Panteleimon Manoussakis. With a foreword by John Sallis. Albany: State University of New York Press.

———. 2009. *Phenomenological Interpretations of Aristotle: Initiation into Phenomenological Research.* Translated by Richard Rojcewicz. Bloomington: Indiana University Press.

———. 2012. *Contributions to Philosophy (Of the Event).* Translated by Richard Rojcewicz and Daniela Vallega-Neu. Bloomington: Indiana University Press.

Heidenreich, Felix. 2005. *Mensch und Moderne bei Hans Blumenberg.* Munich: Wilhelm Fink Verlag.

Heil, Andreas. 2013. *Die dramatische Zeit in Senecas Tragödien.* Leiden: Brill.

Hell, Julia. 2010. "Imperial Ruin Gazers, or Why Did Scipio Weep?" In Hell and Schönle, *Ruins of Modernity,* 169–92.

———. 2019. *The Conquest of Ruins: The Third Reich and the Fall of Rome.* Chicago: University of Chicago Press.

Hell, Julia, and Andreas Schönle. 2010. Introduction to Hell and Schönle, *Ruins of Modernity,* 1–14.

Hell, Julia, and Andreas Schönle. 2010. *Ruins of Modernity.* Durham, NC: Duke University Press.

Hennigfeld, Ursula. 2008. *Der ruinierte Körper: Petrarkistische Sonette in transkultureller Perspektive.* Würzburg: Königshausen & Neumann.

Hermann, Hans Peter. 1970. *Nachahmung und Einbildungskraft: Zur Entwicklung der deutschen Poetik von 1670 bis 1740.* Berlin: Gehlen.

Hildebertus. 2001. *Hildebertus Cenomanensis Episcopus, Carmina minora.* 2nd ed. Edited by A. Brian Scott. Leipzig: K. G. Saur.

Hirsch, Alfred. 2011. "Die Aufgabe des Übersetzers." In Lindner, *Benjamin-Handbuch,* 609–25.

Hirschfeld, Christian Cay Lorenz. 1780. *Theorie der Gartenkunst.* Vol. 2. Leipzig: Weidmann Verlag.

Hölderlin, Friedrich. 1999. *Sämtliche Gedichte und Hyperion.* Edited by Jochen Schmidt. Frankfurt am Main: Insel Verlag.

Horn, Eva. 1998. *Trauer schreiben: Die Toten im Text der Goethezeit.* Munich: Wilhelm Fink Verlag.

Hui, Andrew. 2016. *The Poetics of Ruins in Renaissance Literature.* New York: Fordham University Press.

Husserl, Edmund. 1970. *The Crisis of European Sciences and Transcendental Phenomenology.* Translated by David Carr. Evanston, IL: Northwestern University Press.

———. 2012. *Die Krise der europäischen Wissenschaft und die transzendentale Phänomenologie.* Annotated edition. Hamburg: Felix Meiner Verlag.

Hüttig, Albrecht. 1990. *Macrobius im Mittelalter: Ein Beitrag zur Rezeptionsgeschichte der "Commentarii in somnium Scipionis."* Frankfurt am Main: Peter Lang.

Irvine, William B. 2009. *A Guide to the Good Life: The Ancient Art of Stoic Joy.* Oxford: Oxford University Press.

Jaeschke, Walter, ed. 2010. *Hegel-Handbuch: Leben–Werk–Schule.* Stuttgart: J. B. Metzler.

Jöns, Dietrich Walter. 1966. *Das Sinnen-Bild: Studien zur allegorischen Bildlichkeit bei Andreas Gryphius.* Stuttgart: J. B. Metzler.

———. 1968. "Majuma, Piastus." In *Die Dramen des Andreas Gryphius: Eine Sammlung von Einzelinterpretationen*, edited by Gerhard Kaiser, 285–301. Stuttgart: J. B. Metzler.

Jung, Werner. 1990. *Georg Simmel: Zur Einführung.* Hamburg: Junius Verlag.

Kaiser, Gerhard. 1991. "Zur Aktualität Goethes: Kunst und Gesellschaft in seiner Novelle." In *Mutter Natur und die Dampfmaschine: Ein literarischer Mythos im Rückbezug auf Antike und Christentum*, 13–36. Freiburg im Breisgau: Rombach.

Kaminski, Nicola. 2004. *Ex bello ars oder Ursprung der "Deutschen Poeterey."* Heidelberg: Winter Verlag.

Kantorowicz, Ernst H. 1957. "Man-Centered Kingship: Dante." In *The King's Two Bodies: A Study in Medieval Political Theology*, 451–95. Princeton, NJ: Princeton University Press.

Karmon, David. 2011. *The Ruin of the Eternal City: Antiquity and Preservation in Ancient Rome.* New York: Oxford University Press.

Keill, John. 1698. *An Examination of Dr. Burnet's Theory of the Earth.* Oxford: Printed at the Theater.

Kern, Manfred, and Alfred Ebenbauer. 2003. Introduction to *Lexikon der antiken Gestalten in den deutschen Texten des Mittelalters*, edited by Manfred Kern and Alfred Ebenbauer, ix–lvii. Berlin: De Gruyter.

Kirkham, Victoria, and Armando Maggi, eds. 2009. *Petrarch: A Critical Guide to the Complete Works.* Chicago: University of Chicago Press.

Klibansky, Raymond, Erwin Panofsky, and Fritz Saxl. 1964. *Saturn and Melancholy: Studies in the History of Natural Philosophy, Religion and Art.* London: Thomas Nelson & Sons.

Kocziszky, Eva, ed. 2011. *Ruinen in der Moderne: Archäologie und die Künste.* Berlin: Reimer Verlag.

Koerner, Joseph Leo. 1985. "The Mortification of the Image: Death as Hermeneutic in Hans Baldung Grien." *Representations* 10:52–101.

Kohl, Karl-Heinz. 2003. *Die Macht der Dinge: Geschichte und Theorie sakraler Objekte.* Munich: C. H. Beck.

Köhn, Eckhardt. 2003. "Hans Blumenberg liest Walter Benjamin: Philologische Splitter." In *Medien und Ästhetik: Festschrift für Burkhardt Lindner*, edited by Harald Hillgärtner and Thomas Küpper, 83–102. Bielefeld, Ger.: Transcript Verlag.

Kornbluh, Anna. 2019. *The Order of Forms: Realism, Formalism and Social Space.* Chicago: University of Chicago Press.

Koschorke, Albrecht. 2008. "Nicht-Sinn und die Konstitution des Sozialen." In *Erleben, Erleiden, Erfahren: Die Konstitution sozialen Sinns jenseits instrumenteller Vernunft*, edited by Kay Junge et al., 319–32. Bielefeld, Ger.: Transcript Verlag.

Koselleck, Reinhart. 1982. "Begriffsgeschichte and Social History." *Economy and Society* 11 (4): 409–27.

———. 2004. *Futures Past: On the Semantics of Historical Time*. Translated by Keith Tribe. New York: Columbia University Press.
Kretzulesco-Quaranta, Emanuela. 1976. *Les jardins du songe: "Poliphile" et la mystique de la Renaissance*. Paris: Les belles lettres.
Kruft, Hanno-Walter. 2004. *Geschichte der Architektur-Theorie*. Munich: C. H. Beck.
Kullmann, Katja. 2012. *Rasende Ruinen: Wie Detroit sich neu erfindet*. Berlin: Suhrkamp.
Kurdzialek, Marian. 1971. "Chaos." In *Historisches Wörterbuch der Philosophie*, vol. 1, edited by Joachim Ritter, 980–81. Basel: Schwabe Verlag.
Lacroix, Sophie. 2007. *Ce que nous disent les ruines: La fonction critique des ruines*. Paris: L'Harmattan.
Lactantius. 2005. *Divinarum institutionum libri septem*. Book 2. Edited by Eberhard Heck. Berlin: De Gruyter.
Largier, Niklaus. 2017. "The Land of the Walking Dead: Fragments of a Conversation." In *Gespenster des Wissens*, edited by Ute Holl, Claus Pias, and Burkhardt Wolf, 201–4. Zurich: Diaphanes.
Larson, Matthew, Yanqing Xu, Leah Ouelett, and Charles F. Klahm. 2019. "Exploring the Impact of 9,398 Demolitions on Neighborhood-Level Crime in Detroit, Michigan." *Journal of Criminal Justice* 60 (January–February): 57–63.
Leary, John Patrick. 2011. "Detroitism." *Guernica: A Magazine of Art and Politics*, January 15. https://www.guernicamag.com/leary_1_15_11/.
Lenz, Christian. 1979. *Tischbein: Goethe in der Campagna di Roma*. Frankfurt am Main: Städelsches Kunstinstitut.
Levine, Caroline. 2015. *Forms: Whole, Rhythm, Hierarchy, Network*. Princeton, NJ: Princeton University Press.
Lindner, Burkhardt, ed. 2011. *Benjamin-Handbuch: Leben—Werk—Wirkung*. Stuttgart: J. B. Metzler.
Littlewood, Cedric A. 2015. "Theater and Theatricality in Seneca's World." In Bartsch and Schiesaro, *Cambridge Companion to Seneca*, 161–73.
Loud, Graham A. 2000. *The Age of Robert Guiscard: Southern Italy and the Norman Conquest*. London: Pearson Education.
Luhmann, Niklas. 1996. *Social Systems*. Translated by John Bednarz Jr. with Dirk Baecker. Stanford, CA: Stanford University Press.
Macaulay, Rose. 1953. *Pleasure of Ruins*. London: Weidenfeld & Nichols.
Macrobius, Ambrosius Theodosius. 1981. *Macrobii Ambrosii Theodosii Commentariorum in Somnium Scipionis libri duo*. Edited and translated by Luigi Scarpa. Padua: Livinia.
Makarius, Michel. 2004. *Ruins*. Paris: Édition Flammarion.
Malone, Noreen. 2011. "The Case Against Economic Disaster Porn." *New Republic*, January 22. https://newrepublic.com/article/81954/detroit-economic-disaster-porn.
Mandelbrote, Scott. 1994. "Isaac Newton and Thomas Burnet: Biblical Criticism and the Crisis of Late Seventeenth Century England." In *The Books of Nature and Scripture: Recent Essays on Natural Philosophy, Theology, and Biblical Criticism in the Netherlands of Spinoza's Time and the British Isles of Newton's Time*, edited by James E. Force and Richard H. Popkin, 149–78. International Archives of the History of Ideas 139. Dordrecht, Neth.: Springer.
Marchand, Yves, and Romain Meffre. 2010. *The Ruins of Detroit*. Göttingen, Ger.: Steidl Verlag.
Marino, Rosanna. 1996. "Il secondo coro delle *Troades* e il destino dell'anima dopo la morte." In *Nove studi sui cori tragici di Seneca*, edited by Luigi Castagna, 57–73. Milan: Publicazioni dell' Università Cattolica.

Martinelli, Bortolo. 1972. "Feria sexta aprilis: La data sacra del Canzoniere del Petrarca." *Rivista di Storia e Letteratura Religiosa* 8:449–89.

Martino, Alberto. 1978. *Daniel Casper von Lohenstein: Geschichte seiner Rezeption.* Vol. 1, *1661–1800.* Tübingen: Max Niemeyer Verlag.

Marx, Werner. 1971. *Hegels Phänomenologie des Geistes: Die Bestimmung ihrer Idee in "Vorrede" und "Einleitung."* Frankfurt am Main: Vittorio Klostermann.

Maskarinec, Malika. 2018. *The Forces of Form in German Modernism.* Evanston, IL: Northwestern University Press.

Mayer, Roland. 2007. "Impressions of Rome." *Greece and Rome* 54 (2): 156–77.

Mazzotta, Giuseppe. 1978. "The *Canzoniere* and the Language of the Self." *Studies in Philology* 75 (3): 271–96.

———. 1993. *The Worlds of Petrarch.* Durham, NC: Duke University Press.

Mehne, Philipp. 2008. *Bildung versus Self-Reliance? Selbstkultur bei Goethe und Emerson.* Würzburg: Königshausen & Neumann.

Meid, Christopher. 2012. *Griechenland-Imaginationen: Reiseberichte im 20. Jahrhundert von Gerhart Hauptmann bis Wolfgang Koeppen.* Berlin: De Gruyter.

Meid, Volker. 2009. *Die deutsche Literatur im Zeitalter des Barock: Vom Späthumanismus zur Frühaufklärung, 1570–1740.* Munich: C. H. Beck.

Melehy, Hassan. 2001. "Du Bellay's Time in Rome: The *Antiquitez*." *French Forum* 26 (2): 1–22.

———. 2003. "Spenser and Du Bellay: Translation, Imitation, Ruin." *Comparative Literature Studies* 40 (4): 415–38.

———. 2005. "Antiquities of Britain: Spenser's 'Ruines of Time.'" *Studies in Philology* 102 (2): 159–83.

Meltzer, Françoise. 2019. *Dark Lens: Imaging Germany, 1945.* Chicago: University of Chicago Press.

Meyer, Heinz. 1990. "Zum Verhältnis von Enzyklopädik und Allegorese im Mittelalter." *Frühmittelalterliche Studien* 24:290–313.

Michel, Alain. 1986. "Rome chez Hildebert de Lavardin." In *Jerusalem, Rome, Constantinople: L'image et le mythe de la ville*, edited by Daniel Poirion, 197–203. Paris: Presses de l'Université de Paris-Sorbonne.

Möller, Uwe. 1983. *Rhetorische Überlieferung und Dichtungstheorie im frühen 18. Jahrhundert: Studien zu Gottsched, Breitinger und G. Fr. Meier.* Munich: Wilhelm Fink Verlag.

Mommsen, Theodor E. 1959. "Petrarch's Conception of the 'Dark Ages.'" In *Medieval and Renaissance Studies*, edited by Eugene F. Rice Jr., 106–29. Ithaca, NY: Cornell University Press.

Mortier, Roland. 1974. *La poétique des ruines en France: Ses origines, ses variations de la Renaissance à Victor Hugo.* Geneva: Librairie Droz.

Morton, Thomas. 2009. "Something, Something, Something, Detroit." *Vice Magazine*, July 31. https://www.vice.com/en_us/article/ppzb9z/something-something-something-detroit-994-v16n8.

Moxter, Michael. 2014. "Trost." In *Blumenberg lesen: Ein Glossar*, edited by Daniel Weidner and Robert Buch, 337–49. Frankfurt am Main: Suhrkamp Verlag.

Müller, Hans-Peter. 1949. "Die Ruine in der deutschen und niederländischen Malerei des 15. und 16. Jahrhunderts." PhD diss., Heidelberg University.

Müller-Funk, Wolfgang. 2013. *Die Dichter der Philosophen: Essays über den Zwischenraum von Denken und Dichten.* Munich: Wilhelm Fink Verlag.

Münkler, Herfried. 2017. *Der Dreissigjährige Krieg: Europäische Katastrophe, deutsches Trauma (1618–1648).* Berlin: Rowohlt Verlag.

Newton, Isaac. 1960. *The Correspondence of Isaac Newton*. Vol. 2, *1676–1687*. Edited by H. W. Turnbull. Cambridge: Cambridge University Press.

Nicholls, Angus. 2015. *Myth and the Human Sciences: Hans Blumenberg's Theory of Myth*. New York: Routledge.

Nicolson, Marjorie Hope. (1959) 1997. *Mountain Gloom and Mountain Glory: The Development of the Aesthetics of the Infinite*. Reprint, Seattle: University of Washington Press.

Niethammer, Lutz. 1989. *Posthistoire: Ist die Geschichte zu Ende?* Reinbek, Ger.: Rowohlt Taschenbuch Verlag.

Norden, Eduard. 1918. *Die antike Kunstprosa: Vom VI. Jahrhundert v. Chr. bis in die Zeit der Renaissance*. Vol. 2. Leipzig: B. G. Teubner.

Oechslin, Werner. 2000. "Traum, Liebe, Kampf: Die *Hypnerotomachia Poliphili*; Von der Zerlegung des Textes und vom Sinn des Ganzen." *NZZ: Neue Zürcher Zeitung*, March 11.

Ohly, Friedrich. 1983. "Vom geistigen Sinn des Wortes im Mittelalter." In *Schriften zur mittelalterlichen Bedeutungsforschung*, 1–31. Darmstadt: Wissenschaftliche Buchgesellschaft.

Opitz, Martin. 1979. *Gesammelte Werke: Kritische Ausgabe; Die Werke von 1621–1626*, vol. 2, pt. 2, edited by George Schulz-Behrend. Stuttgart: Anton Hiersemann.

———. 2011. *Lateinische Werke 2 (1624–1631)*. Edited by Gert Roloff. Berlin: De Gruyter.

Orr, Kevyn. 2013. *Financial and Operating Plan, May 12, 2013*. Detroit: City of Detroit Office of Emergency Manager. https://www.michigan.gov/documents/treasury/City_of_Detroit_-_Final_Financial__Operational_Plan__45_Day_Plan_051313_420882_7.pdf.

Ortiz Delgado, Francisco Miguel. 2017. "La moderacion de las pasiones o indicios de estoicismo en las *Troyanas* de Seneca." *Revista de Filosofia* 73:193–209.

Owen, William H. 1970. "Time and Event in Seneca's Troades." *Wiener Studien*, n.s., 40:118–37.

Oxford Latin Dictionary. 1968. Oxford: Clarendon Press.

Panofsky, Erwin. 1972. *Renaissance and Renascences in Western Art*. New York: Harper & Row.

Pelosi, Olimpia. 1988. *Il sogno di Polifilo: Una quête dell' umanesimo*. Salerno: Edisud.

Petrarca, Francesco. 1581. "Epistolae de rebus senilibus." *Opera quae extant omnia*. 4 vols. Basileae [now Basel]: per Sebastianum Henricpetri.

———. 1962. *The Triumphs of Petrarch*. Translated by Ernest Hatch Wilkins. Chicago: University of Chicago Press.

———. 1974. *Le Familiari I-XI*. 2 vols. Translated and with an introduction by Ugo Dotti. Urbino: Argalia.

———. 1975. *Opere latine*. Vol. 1. *A cura di Antonietta Bufano*. Turin: Unione tipografico-editrice torinese.

———. 1992. *Letters of Old Age: Rerum senilium libri I-XVIII*, vol. 1, books 1–9. Translated by Aldo S. Bernardo, Saul Levin, and Renata A. Bernardo. Baltimore: Johns Hopkins University Press.

———. 1996. *The "Canzoniere," or "Rerum Vulgarium Fragmenta."* Translated by Mark Musa, with an introduction by Barbara Manfredi. Bloomington: Indiana University Press.

———. 1996. *Trionfi, Rime estravaganti, Codice degli abbozzi*. Edited by Vinicio Pacca and Laura Paolino. Milan: Mondadori.

———. 2014. *Letters on Familiar Matters: Rerum Familiarum Libri I-XVI*. 2 vols. Translated by Aldo S. Bernardo. New York: Italica Press.

Pfau, Thomas. 2013. *Minding the Modern: Human Agency, Intellectual Traditions, and Responsible Knowledge*. Notre Dame, IN: University of Notre Dame Press.

Plato. 1981. *Timaeus, Critias, Cleitophon, Menexenus and Epistles*. Translated by A. G. Bury. Cambridge, MA: Harvard University Press.

Polybios. 1995. *The Histories*. Vol. 6. Translated by W. R. Paton. Cambridge, MA: Harvard University Press.

Prica, Aleksandra. 2014. "Ruine." In *Philosophische Kehrseiten: Eine andere Einleitung in die Philosophie*, edited by Natalie Pieper and Benno Wirz, 273–97. Freiburg im Breisgau: Karl Alber Verlag.

———. 2018. "Lingering: Visions of Past and Future in the *Hypnerotomachia Poliphili*." Translated by Jake Fraser. In *Temporality and Mediality in Late Medieval and Early Modern Culture*, Cursor Mundi 32, edited by Christian Kiening and Martina Stercken, 229–52. Turnhout, Belg.: Brepols.

Probst, Peter, and Franz Josef Wetz. 1998. "Traum." In *Historisches Wörterbuch der Philosophie*, vol. 10, edited by Joachim Ritter and Karlfried Gründer, 1461–73. Basel: Schwabe Verlag.

Puff, Helmut. 2014. *Miniature Monuments: Modeling German History*. Berlin: De Gruyter.

Ranson, Susan. 2021. "Brod und Wein; Bread and Wine." German Literature. Accessed February 25. https://sites.google.com/site/germanliterature/19th-century/hoelderlin/brot-und-wein-bread-and-wine.

Reck, Hans Ulrich. 2005. "Traum." In *Ästhetische Grundbegriffe*, vol. 6, edited by Karlheinz Barck et al., 171–201. Stuttgart: J. B. Metzler.

Rehm, Walter. (1939) 1960. *Europäische Romdichtung*. Reprint, Munich: M. Hueber.

Rieger, Stefan. 1997. *Speichern/Merken: Die künstlichen Intelligenzen des Barock*. Munich: Wilhelm Fink Verlag.

Rosenkranz, Karl. 1844. *Georg Wilhelm Friedrich Hegels Leben*. Berlin: Verlag von Duncker & Humblot.

Rouse, Richard H. 1971. "The A Text of Seneca's Tragedies in the Thirteenth Century." *Revue d'Histoire des Textes* 1:93–121.

Ruin, Hans. 2012. "Thinking in Ruins: Life, Death and Destruction in Heidegger's Early Writings." *Comparative and Continental Philosophy* 4 (1): 15–33.

Rushworth, Jennifer. 2017. *Petrarch and the Literary Culture of Nineteenth-Century France: Translation, Appropriation, Transformation*. Woodbridge, UK: Boydell Press.

Schedler, Matthaeus. 1916. *Die Philosophie des Macrobius und ihr Einfluss auf die Wissenschaft des christlichen Mittelalters*. Münster: Aschendorffsche Verlagsbuchhandlung.

Scherer, Burkhard. 1999. "Zur Funktion des zweiten Chorlieds der *Troades* des Seneca." *Mnemosyne*, 4th ser., 52:572–78.

Schings, Hans-Jürgen. 1971. "Consolatio Tragoediae: Zur Theorie des barocken Trauerspiels." In *Deutsche Dramentheorien*, vol. 1, edited by Reinhold Grimm, 1–44. Frankfurt am Main: Athenäum Verlag.

———. 1974. "Seneca-Rezeption und Theorie der Tragödie: Martin Opitz' Vorrede zu den *Trojanerinnen*." In *Historizität in Sprach- und Literaturwissenschaft: Vorträge und Berichte der Stuttgarter Germanistentagung 1972*, edited by Walter Müller-Seidel, 521–37. Munich: Wilhelm Fink Verlag.

———. 1977. *Melancholie und Aufklärung: Melancholiker und ihre Kritiker in Erfahrungsseelenkunde und Literatur des 18. Jahrhunderts*. Stuttgart: J. B. Metzler.

Schmidt, Dorothea. 1978. *Untersuchungen zu den Architekturekphrasen in der "Hypnerotomachia Poliphili": Die Beschreibung des Venus-Tempels*. Frankfurt am Main: R. G. Fischer.

Schmücker, Reinhold. 1992. "Monologisches Gespräch: Heideggers Vorlesung über Hölderlins Hymne *Andenken*." *Zeitschrift für Germanistik*, n.s., 2 (3): 550–68.

Schöne, Albrecht. 1964. *Emblematik und Drama im Zeitalter des Barock*. Munich: C. H. Beck.

Schöning, Matthias. 2009. "Zeit der Ruinen: Tropologische Stichproben zu Modernität und Einheit der Romantik." *Internationales Archiv für Sozialgeschichte der deutschen Literatur* 34 (1): 75–93.

Schramm, Percy Ernst. 1929. *Kaiser, Rom und Renovatio: Studien und Texte zur Geschichte des römischen Erneuerungsgedankens vom Ende des Karolingischen Reiches bis zum Investiturstreit*. 2 vols. Leipzig: Teubner.

Schulz, Karlheinz. 2010. *Wandlungen und Konstanten in Goethes Ästhetik und literarischer Laufbahn*. Munich: Universitätsbibliothek Johann Christian Senckenberg. http://www.goethe zeitportal.de/fileadmin/PDF/db/wiss/goethe/schulz_wandlungen_konstanten.pdf.

Schumpeter, Joseph A. 1994. *Capitalism, Socialism and Democracy*. London: Routledge.

———. 2005. *Kapitalismus, Sozialismus und Demokratie*. Tübingen: A. Francke.

Scott, A. Brian 1968. "Peter von Moos, 'Hildebert von Lavardin 1056–1133: Humanitas an der Schwelle des Höfischen Zeitalters.'" *Medium Aevum* 37:185–88.

———. 1968. "The Poems of Hildebert of Le Mans: A New Examination of the Canon." *Medieval and Renaissance Studies* 6:42–83.

Scriverius, Petrus. 1621. *L. Aenneus Seneca Tragicus*. Leiden: Ex recensione et museo Petri Scriverii. Ex officina Ioannis Maire.

Seelye, Katherine Q. 2011. "Detroit Census Confirms a Desertion Like No Other." *New York Times*, March 23. https://www.nytimes.com/2011/03/23/us/23detroit.html.

Seneca. 2001. *Troades*. Introduction, text, and commentary by Atze J. Keulen. Leiden: Brill.

———. 2005. *On the Shortness of Life*. Translated by C. D. N. Costa. New York: Penguin Books.

———. 2018. *Tragedies: Hercules, Trojan Women, Phoenician Women, Medea, Phaedra*. Vol. 1. Edited and translated by John G. Fitch. Cambridge, MA: Harvard University Press.

Siegmund, Andrea. 2002. *Die romantische Ruine im Landschaftsgarten: Ein Beitrag zum Verhältnis der Romantik zu Barock und Klassik*. Würzburg: Königshausen & Neumann.

Simmel, Georg. 1959. *Georg Simmel, 1858–1918: A Collection of Essays*. Translated by Kurt H. Wolff. Columbus: Ohio State University Press.

———. 1995. "Kant und Goethe: Zur Geschichte der modernen Weltanschauung." In *Gesamtausgabe*, vol. 10, *Philosophie der Mode, Die Religion, Kant und Goethe, Schopenhauer und Nietzsche*, edited by Michael Behr, Volkhard Krech, and Gert Schmidt, 119–66. Frankfurt am Main: Suhrkamp Verlag.

———. 1996. "Der Begriff und die Tragödie der Kultur." In *Gesamtausgabe*, vol. 14, *Hauptprobleme der Philosophie, Philosophische Kultur*, edited by Rüdiger Kramme and Otthein Rammstedt, 385–416. Frankfurt am Main: Suhrkamp Verlag.

———. 1996. "Die Ruine." In *Gesamtausgabe*, vol. 14, *Hauptprobleme der Philosophie, Philosophische Kultur*, edited by Rüdiger Kramme and Otthein Rammstedt, 287–95. Frankfurt am Main: Suhrkamp Verlag.

———. 1997. "The Concept and Tragedy of Culture." In *Simmel on Culture: Selected Writings*, edited by David Frisby and Mike Featherstone, 55–75. London: Sage.

———. 1999. "Lebensanschauung." In *Gesamtausgabe*, vol. 16, *Der Krieg und die geistigen Entscheidungen, Grundfragen der Soziologie, Vom Wesen des historischen Verstehens, Der Konflikt der modernen Kultur, Lebensanschauung*, edited by Gregor Fitzi and Otthein Rammstedt, 209–425. Frankfurt am Main: Suhrkamp Verlag.

———. 2003. "Goethe." In *Gesamtausgabe*, vol. 15, *Goethe, Deutschlands innere Wandlung, Das Problem der historischen Zeit, Rembrandt*, edited by Uta Kösser, Hans-Martin Kruckis, and Otthein Rammstedt, 7–270. Frankfurt am Main: Suhrkamp Verlag.

———. 2008. "Briefe 1912–1918." In *Gesamtausgabe*, vol. 23, *Briefe 1912–1918, Jugendbriefe*, edited by Otthein Rammstedt and Angela Rammstedt. Frankfurt am Main: Suhrkamp Verlag.

———. 2008. *Jenseits der Schönheit: Schriften zur Ästhetik und Kunstphilosophie*. Edited by Ingo Meyer. Frankfurt am Main: Suhrkamp Verlag.
———. 2010. *The View of Life: Four Metaphysical Essays with Journal Aphorisms*. Edited and translated by John A. Y. Andrews and Donald N. Levine. Chicago: University of Chicago Press.
Simmen, Jeannot. 1980. *Ruinen-Faszination in der Graphik vom 16. Jahrhundert bis in die Gegenwart*. Dortmund: Harenberg.
Smolak, Kurt. 2002. "Beobachtungen zu den Rom-Elegien Hildeberts von Lavardin." In *Latin Culture in the Eleventh Century: Proceedings of the Third International Conference on Medieval Latin Studies, Cambridge, 9–12 September 1998*, vol. 2, edited by Michael W. Herren, Christopher James McDonough, and Ross Gilbert Arthur, 371–84. Turnhout, Belg.: Brepols.
"So Cheap, There's Hope: The Parable of Detroit." 2011. *Economist* 401 (8756). https://www.econ omist.com/united-states/2011/10/22/so-cheap-theres-hope?fsrc=scn%2Ftw%2Fte%2Far% 2Fsocheaptheres hope.
Solanki, Tanvi. 2016. "A Book of Living Paintings: Tableaux Vivants in Goethe's *Die Wahlverwandtschaften*." *Goethe Yearbook* 23:245–70.
Solnit, Rebecca. 2007. "Detroit Arcadia: Exploring the Post-American Landscape." *Harper's Magazine*, July. https://harpers.org/archive/2007/07/detroit-arcadia/.
Sommer, Manfred. 2014. "Lebenswelt." In *Blumenberg lesen: Ein Glossar*, edited by Daniel Weidner and Robert Buch, 160–70. Frankfurt am Main: Suhrkamp Verlag.
Speer, Albert. 2005. *Erinnerungen*. Berlin: Ullstein.
Spencer-Brown, George. 1969. *Laws of Form*. London: Allen & Unwin.
Stachel, Paul. 1907. *Seneca und das deutsche Renaissancedrama*. Berlin: Meyer & Müller.
Stadler, Ulrich. 2002. "Bedeutend in jedem Fall: Ein Panorama-Blick auf die Ruinen." In Assmann, Gomille, and Rippl, *Ruinenbilder*, 271–87.
Stäheli, Urs. 2012. "The Hegemony of Meaning: Is There an Exit to Meaning in Niklas Luhmann's Systems Theory?" *Revue internationale de philosophie* 1 (259): 105–22.
Staley, Gregory Alan. 2010. *Seneca and the Idea of Tragedy*. Oxford: Oxford University Press.
Steinberg, Justin. 2009. "Dante *Estravagante*, Petrarch *Disperso*, and the Other Woman." In Barański and Cachey, *Petrarch and Dante*, 263–89.
Steinmetz, George. 2010. "Colonial Melancholy and Fordist Nostalgia: The Ruinscapes of Namibia and Detroit." In Hell and Schönle, *Ruins of Modernity*, 294–320.
Stewart, Susan. 2020. *The Ruins Lesson: Meaning and Material in Western Culture*. Chicago: University of Chicago Press.
Stewering, Roswitha. 2000. "Architectural Representations in the *Hypnerotomachia Poliphili* (Aldus Manutius 1499)." *Journal of the Society of Architectural Historians* 59 (1): 6–25.
Stierle, Karlheinz. 2003. *Francesco Petrarca: Ein Intellektueller des 14. Jahrhunderts*. Munich: Carl Hanser Verlag.
Stoler, Ann Laura, ed. 2013. *Imperial Debris: On Ruins and Ruination*. Durham, NC: Duke University Press.
Strätling, Susanne. 2005. *Allegorien der Imagination: Lesbarkeit und Sichtbarkeit im russischen Barock*. Munich: Wilhelm Fink Verlag.
Stroh, Wilfried. 2014. "Troas." In *Brill's Companion to Seneca: Philosopher and Dramatist*, edited by Gregor Damschen and Andreas Heil, 435–47. Leiden: Brill.
Sugrue, Thomas. 2010. "City of Ruins." In Marchand and Meffre, *Ruins of Detroit*, 9–15.

———. 2014. *The Origins of the Urban Crisis: Race and Inequality in Postwar Detroit.* Princeton, NJ: Princeton University Press.

Summit, Jennifer. 2000. "Topography as Historiography: Petrarch, Chaucer, and the Making of Medieval Rome." *Journal of Medieval and Early Modern Studies* 30 (2): 211–46.

———. 2003. "Monuments and Ruins: Spenser and the Problem of the English." *English Literary History* 70 (1): 1–34.

Sweet, Rosemary. 2012. *Cities and the Grand Tour: The British in Italy, c. 1690–1820.* Cambridge: Cambridge University Press.

Syndram, Dirk, ed. 1988. *Römische Skizzen: Zwischen Phantasie und Wirklichkeit.* Mainz: Verlag Philip von Zabern.

Tertullianus. 1947. *De anima.* Edited by J. H. Waszink. Amsterdam: J. M. Meulenhoff.

Tilliette, Jean-Yves. 1995. "Tamquam lapides vivi . . . : Sur les 'Élégies Romains' d' Hildebert de Lavardin (ca. 1100)." *Collection de l'école française de Rome* 204:359–80.

Torelli, Mario. 2017. "From Ruins to Reconstruction: Past and Present." *Archeologia e Calcolatori* 28 (2): 27–45.

Trillitzsch, Winfried. 1978. "Seneca tragicus: Nachleben und Beurteilung im lateinischen Mittelalter von der Spätantike bis zum Renaissancehumanismus." *Philologus* 112 (1–2): 120–36.

Trinacty, Christopher. 2015. "Senecan Tragedy." In Bartsch and Schiesaro, *Cambridge Companion to Seneca,* 29–40.

Tschumi, Bernard. 1994. *Architecture and Disjunction.* Cambridge, MA: MIT Press.

Turner, Bryan S. 1992. "Ruine und Fragment: Anmerkungen zum Barockstil." In Reijen, *Allegorie und Melancholie,* 202–23.

Tuveson, Ernest Lee. 1949. *Millennium and Utopia: A Study in the Background of the Idea of Progress.* Berkeley: University of California Press.

Ullman, Walter. 2003. *A Short History of the Papacy in the Middle Ages.* London: Routledge.

Ussani, Vicenzo. 1955. *Insomnia: Saggio di critica semantica.* Rome: Signorelli.

Valk, Thorsten. 2002. *Melancholie im Werk Goethes: Genese–Symptomatik–Therapie.* Tübingen: Max Niemeyer Verlag.

Van Reijen, Willem, ed. 1992. *Allegorie und Melancholie.* Frankfurt am Main: Suhrkamp Verlag.

———. 2004. "Heideggers ontologische Differenz: Der fremde Unterschied in uns und die Inständigkeit im Nichts." *Deutsche Zeitschrift für Philosophie* 52 (4): 519–39.

Vinken, Barbara, ed. 2001. *Du Bellay und Petrarca: Das Rom der Renaissance.* Tübingen: Niemeyer Verlag.

Vöckler, Kai. 2009. *Die Architektur der Abwesenheit: Über die Kunst, eine Ruine zu bauen.* Berlin: Parthas.

Vogel, Hans. 1948. *Die Ruine in der Darstellung der abendländischen Kunst.* Kassel, Ger.: Winter.

Vogl, Joseph. 2011. *On Tarrying.* London: Seagull Books.

Von Grimm, Friedrich Melchior Freiherr, ed. 1815. *Historical and Literary Memoirs and Anecdotes, selected from the correspondence of Baron de Grimm and Diderot with the Duke of Saxe-Gotha, and many other distinguished persons, between the years of 1753 and 1790.* Vol. 1. Translated by Robert Bland and Anne Plumptre. London: Printed for H. Colburn.

Von Moos, Peter. 1965. *Hildebert von Lavardin (1056–1133): Humanitas an der Schwelle des höfischen Zeitalters.* Stuttgart: Anton Hiersemann.

———. 1979. "Par tibi, Roma, nihil: Eine Antwort." *Mittellateinisches Jahrbuch* 14:119–26.

———. 2019. "Homo creans in den Romgedichten Hildeberts von Lavardin." In *Fleur de Clérgie: Mélanges en l'honneur de Jean-Yves Tilliette,* edited by Olivier Collet, Yasmina

Foehr-Janssen, and Jean Claude Mühletaler, 170–93. Geneva: Rayon Histoire de la Librairie Droz.

Von Mücke, Dorothea E. 2009. "Beyond the Paradigm of Representation: Goethe on Architecture." *Grey Room* 35 (Spring): 6–27.

Wagenknecht, Christian. 1982. *Erläuterungen und Dokumente: Johann Wolfgang Goethe; Novelle.* Stuttgart: Reclam.

Wagner-Egelhaaf, Martina. 1997. *Die Melancholie der Literatur: Diskursgeschichte und Textfiguration.* Stuttgart: J. B. Metzler.

Weber, Samuel. 2008. *Benjamin's -abilities.* Cambridge, MA: Harvard University Press.

Weidmann, Heiner. 1992. *Flanerie, Sammlung, Spiel: Die Erinnerung des 19. Jahrhunderts bei Walter Benjamin.* Munich: Wilhelm Fink Verlag.

Weidner, Daniel. 2011. "Fort-, Über-, Nachleben: Zu einer Denkfigur bei Walter Benjamin." In *Benjamin-Studien 2*, edited by Daniel Weidner and Sigrid Weigel, 161–78. Munich: Wilhelm Fink Verlag.

———. 2012. "Life After Life: A Figure of Thought in Walter Benjamin." Paper presented at the conference Afterlife: Writing and Image in Walter Benjamin and Aby Warburg, Universidad Federal de Minais Gerais, Belo Horizonte, Brazil, October. www.zfl-berlin.org/tl_files/zfl/downloads/personen/weidner/life_after_life.pdf.

Weigel, Sigrid. 2012. "Jenseits des Todestriebs: Freuds Lebenswissenschaft an der Schwelle von Natur- und Kulturwissenschaft." *KulturPoetik* 12 (1): 41–57.

Weinrich, Harald. 2008. *On Borrowed Time: The Art and Economy of Living with Deadlines.* Translated by Steven Rendall. Chicago: University of Chicago Press.

Wellbery, David. 2010. "Romanticism and Modernity: Conceptual Continuities and Discontinuities." *European Romantic Review* 21 (3): 275–89.

———. 2014. "Form und Idee: Skizze eines Begriffsfeldes um 1800." In *Morphologie und Moderne: Goethes "Anschauliches Denken" in Geistes- und Kulturwissenschaften*, edited by Jonas Maatsch, 17–42. Berlin: De Gruyter.

Wetz, Franz Josef. 2004. *Hans Blumenberg: Zur Einführung.* Hamburg: Junius Verlag.

Whately, Thomas. 2016. *Observations on Modern Gardening: An Eighteenth-Century Study of the English Landscape Garden.* Edited by Michael Symes. Suffolk: Boydell & Brewer.

Wild, Christopher. 2013. "'They haver their exits and their entrances': Überlegungen zu zwei Grunoperationen im *theatrum mundi*." In *Theatrum Mundi: Die Metapher des Welttheaters von Shakespeare bis Beckett*, edited by Björn Quiring, 89–131. Berlin: August Verlag.

Wilkins, Ernest Hatch. 1960. *Petrarch's Correspondence.* Padua: Antenore.

———. 1961. *The Life of Petrarch.* Chicago: University of Chicago Press.

Wilson. Peter H. 2011. *The Thirty Years War: Europe's Tragedy.* Cambridge, MA: Harvard University Press.

Witte, Bernd, and Peter Schmidt, eds. 1997. *Goethe-Handbuch: Prosaschriften.* Vol 3. Stuttgart: J. B. Metzler.

Woodward, Christopher. 2001. *In Ruins.* London: Random House.

Zadek, Elise. 2005. "Der Palatin in den Publikationen Hieronymus Cocks: Ruinen und ihre frühneuzeitlichen Darstellungen im Bild." Humboldt Universität zu Berlin. Published May 13. https://edoc.hu-berlin.de/handle/18452/14720.

Zak, Gur. 2010. *Petrarch's Humanism and the Care of the Self.* Cambridge: Cambridge University Press.

Zanker, Paul. 1999. "Die Ruine: Vom Baumaterial zur Erzeugung starker Gefühle." *NZZ: Die Neue Zürcher Zeitung*, December 4, 85.

Zimmermann, Bernhard. 1999. "Goethes Novelle und der Hirtenroman des Longos." In *Goethes Rückblick auf die Antike: Beiträge des deutsch-italienischen Kolloquiums. Rom 1998*, edited by Bernd Witte and Mauro Ponzi, 101–12. Berlin: Erich Schmidt Verlag.

Zimmermann, Reinhard. 1989. *Künstliche Ruinen: Studien zu ihrer Bedeutung und Form*. Wiesbaden: Verlag L. Reichert.

Ziolkowski, Jan M. 2004. "*Hildebertus Cenomannensis episcopus, Carmina minora* by Hildebertus, A. Brian Scott." *Speculum* 79 (1): 203–5.

Zucker, Paul. 1968. *Fascination of Decay: Ruins; Relic–Symbol–Ornament*. Ridgewood, NJ: Gregg Press.

Zwierlein, Otto. 1966. *Die Rezitationsdramen Senecas*. Meisenheim am Glan, Ger.: Hain Verlag.

Index

Note: Page numbers in italics refer to illustrations.

absolutism of reality, 53–54
abstraction and concretization: of allegory, 191, 201; Hegel on, 225–26; as irreconcilable, 227–29; of ruins, 254, 256; of *theoria*, 217–20
Adorno, Theodor, 239; "Negative Dialektik," 253–54
aesthetics: of architecture, 238–39, 252; Goethe's theory of, 242–44; of ruins, 12–13, 35, 207–8, 235, 245, 254–57, 261–63; as term, 13n32
afterlife: in allegory, 70–71; in fame, 63–64, 101, 110; of history, 57–58, 63, 66, 72; of originals in translation, 62–64, 71, 185; in supplementation, 38–39, 46; as term, 8–9, 58–59. *See also* death
Alciato, Andrea, *Emblematum liber*, 202, *203*, 204
allegory: Benjamin on, 18, 19, 70–71, 158, 191, 192; as both abstract and concrete, 191, 201; criticism of, 189–90; and emblems, 201–2; historical continuity and historical knowledge through, 191–92, 199–200, 205–6; vs. literal sense of Scripture, 215–17, 220–22; and mythology, 199; reason and truth in, 193–96
Ambrose of Milan, 150
antediluvian world, 212–15
antithesis, 145–46, 149
anxiety and fear, 53, 162
Appian, *Punic Wars*, 1
archaeology, and psychoanalysis, 41–42
architecture, and art, 238–39, 252
Ariani, Marco, 117
Aristotle, *Problemata Physica*, 156
art: afterlife of, 63; and architecture, 238–39, 252; and nature, 247, 249–50; and philosophy, 252, 256
art history, ruin scholarship, 2, 4–5
artificial ruins, 20–21
Assmann, Aleida, 91

atemporality and eternity, 63, 70–71, 109–10, 111, 123, 149, 150

Barański, Zygmunt, 103, 104
Barniske, Friedemann, 226, 228
Barolini, Teodolinda, 82, 83, 88
baroque style: allegory, 70–71, 158, 190 (*see also* Gryphius, Andreas, *Majuma*); criticism of, 189–90; stereotypes of, 177, 192; tragedy, 180, 189 (*see also* Opitz, Martin, *Trojanerinnen*)
Barthes, Roland, 145, 149
Baudelaire, Charles, *Les Fleurs du Mal*, 61
beauty. *See* aesthetics
Being: and two beginnings of philosophy, 31, 32, 37; as unconcealed concealment, 33, 37, 38; and *Verfallenheit*, 67
Below, Nicolaus von, 48
Benjamin, Walter, 56–64; on allegory, 18, 19, 70–71, 158, 191, 192; *Arcades Project*, 64; and Blumenberg, 64–65; on *Erfahrung*, 61–62; on eschatology, 157; on fame, 63–64, 101; on forms, 62, 71–72; on history, 57–58, 63, 66, 69–70, 72, 219; mentioned, 3, 182, 185, 223; "On the Concept of History," 57–58; *The Origin of German Tragic Drama*, 70, 189n2, 219; reception of, 56–57; "Some Motifs in Baudelaire," 61; "The Task of the Translator," 62–64, 66, 71; on translation, 62–64, 71
Benn, Gottfried, 248
Bisanz, Rudolf, 237
Blumenberg, Hans, 48–55; on absolutism of reality, 53–54, 162; on awareness of divide between life-time and world-time, 49–50, 52; *Beschreibung des Menschen*, 66; on consolation, 66,

Blumenberg, Hans (*cont.*)
  151; on fame, 64–65, 101; on form, 65; *Lebenszeit und Weltzeit*, 48, 49–50, 54; *Legitimacy of the Modern Age*, 92n27; on life-world-experience, 50–52; mentioned, 167, 168, 179; on narcissists, 48–49, 162; on Petrarch, 92n27; reception of, 54–55; on theory, 217; *Work on Myth*, 53
Boccaccio, Giovanni, 101, 102; *Amorosa visione*, 102n46
Boethius, *Consolatio Philosophiae*, 175
Böhme, Hartmut, 2–3, 22, 158, 192
Böhmer, Otto A., 225
Borchmeyer, Dieter, 249n31
Boym, Svetlana, 4
Breitinger, Johann Jacob, 189–96; on allegory and mythology, 199; on allegory and reason, 193–94; *Critische Dichtkunst*, 194–96; on Lohenstein and Gryphius, 189–90
Buchner, August, 177
Burckhardt, Jacob, 91n25, 139–40, 153
Burke, Peter, 12
Burnet, Thomas, 207–24; *Archaeologiae Philosophicae*, 209, 222–23; and Hegel, 224, 225, 227, 228; *Sacred Theory of the Earth* (*see* Burnet, Thomas, *Sacred Theory of the Earth*)
Burnet, Thomas, *Sacred Theory of the Earth*: abstraction and concretization of *theoria*, 217, 218–20; on allegorical vs. literal sense of Scripture, 215–17, 220–22; on antediluvian world, 212–15; overview, 207–9; realignment of scientific and theological discourses, 210–11; reception of, 209–10, 220–23
Burton, Robert, 157

Celtis, Conrad, 175
chaos, 172–73, 183
Charles IV (Holy Roman emperor), 85
Christianity: conflicted view of ruins, 17; paradox of the cross, 146–51, 159; and Seneca, 174; view of afterlife, 60–61, 184. *See also* theological-scientific discourse
Clement III (pope), 135–36
Cola di Rienzo, 78–79, 85–86, 94
Colonna, Francesco, 113
Colonna, Giovanni, Cardinal, 78, 89–90, 91
Colonna, Giovanni, Fra, 91, 92–94
consolation, 66, 146, 151, 172, 180
continuity: in allegory, 191–92, 200, 205–6; in discontinuity, 108–9, 153–54; as impossible, 173–74; medieval conception of, 13, 150; in paradox of the cross, 148, 150–51; and replacement, 17
Cooper, John M., 163n2
Cristiani, Luca, 81
cross, paradox of, 146–51, 159
culture, paradox of, 59–60

Dante Alighieri, 102–4, 111n61; *Divina Commedia*, 102, 103, 105, 118n17
Dasein. *See* Being
death: and brevity of life, 87, 88, 100–101, 106–8, 162; drives of, 68–69; as integral to life, 60–61, 66–67, 72; nothingness and finality of, 170, 172, 173, 183, 185; postponement of, 118–19; and ruinance, 67–68. *See also* afterlife
decay, as term, 7, 8
Dekkers, Midas, 8
DeLillo, Don, *The Names*, 258–59
Delrío, Martín, 176n23
Derrida, Jacques, 46, 90
Detroit, MI, 261–65, 262
Diderot, Denis, 19–20, 21, 22
Didi-Huberman, Georges, 8–9
Dilthey, Wilhelm, 58–59; *Das Erlebnis und die Dichtung*, 61–62
Dionigi di Borgo San Sepolcro, 90
Di Palma, Vittoria, 208n5
dreams: interpretation of, 119–20; and labyrinths, 117–19
Du Bellay, Joachim, 3
Dürer, Albrecht, 114

Eckermann, Johann Peter, 241–42, 248
economic ruin, 260–61
education, and reflection, 243–44
Edwards, Catharine, 2n4
Eisner, Martin, 102n46
elegy genre, 138. *See also* Hildebert of Lavardin
emblems, 201–2, 203, 204
empiricist realism, 2
Erfahrung (experience), 61–62
eroticism, 115
eternity and atemporality, 63, 70–71, 109–10, 111, 123, 149, 150
Etruscus Laurentianus, 175
Euripides: *Hecuba*, 174; *Troades*, 174

fame, 63–64, 101, 103, 104, 106–7, 110
Farnabius, Thomas, 176n23
fear and anxiety, 53, 162
Fenzi, Enrico, 83–84
Ferdinand IV (king of the Romans), 196–97, 199–200, 205
Ficino, Marsilio, 157
Finotti, Fabio, 108
Fitch, John G., 165
Földenyi, László, 157, 159n66
follies (fake ruins), 20–21
Forero-Mendoza, Sabine, 122n26
forms: broad conceptualization of, 71–72; semiotic status of, 93, 181–83, 185; of significance, 53, 55; texts as, 6–7; translations as, 62, 71

INDEX 295

Forrer, Thomas, 218
Fortunatus, Venantius, *Vexilla regis*, 147, 148
fragments and fragmentation: of discourses, 22; greatness of Rome despite, 15n42, 140–45; necessity of, 34–35; and paradox of the cross, 146–51, 159; of Petrarch's works, 87–88, 92; and restless life, 255; as semiotically and semantically unstable, 93, 96, 142; and supplementation, 35, 38–39
Freccero, John, 80n6
Freud, Sigmund, 40–47; on archaeology and psychoanalysis, 41–42; and Blumenberg, 48; *Civilization and Its Discontents*, 42; on convergence of past and present, 42, 45–46; "Delusion and Dream in Wilhelm Jensen's 'Gradiva,'" 41; on derealization, 44; on drives, 68–69; "Fragment of an Analysis of a Case of Hysteria," 41; *The Interpretation of Dreams*, 46; *Jenseits des Lustprinzips*, 68–69
Friedlander, Eli, 56–57

Gabriele, Mino, 117
Gagnebin, Jeanne Marie, 57n29
Gallio, Lucius Junius Annaeanus, 174
Garibaldi, Giuseppe, 133, 134
Gasché, Rodolphe, 217–18
Gehlen, Arnold, 52n14
Geimer, Peter, 30n4
Gibbon, Edward, *The History of the Decline and Fall of the Roman Empire*, 78, 155
Gibson, Bruce, 142
Ginsberg, Robert, 3, 4n12
Goethe, Johann Wolfgang von, 233–51; ambivalent view of aesthetic theory, 242–44; on architecture, 238; *Italian Journey*, 233–35, 238; "Novella" (*see* Goethe, Johann Wolfgang von, "Novella"); portrait of, 236–37, 236; and Simmel, 252–54; visit to Rome, 233–35; *Von deutscher Baukunst*, 238–39; "Der Wanderer," 235–36
Goethe, Johann Wolfgang von, "Novella": ekphrastic passage, 245–47, 249, 250; ending, 248–49; origins, 240–44; reception of, 240, 248; ruin as synthesizing force, 249–50; ruin as unfulfilled future, 250–51
Gombrich, Ernst, 8
Gottsched, Johann Christoph, *Critical Poetics*, 190
Gould, Stephen Jay, 209, 211n10
grand gestures, 21, 91n23
Grassi, Leonardo, 112–15
Grätz, Katharina, 235–36, 249, 250
greatness: as function of time, 21–22; of Rome despite ruins, 15n42, 140–45; of Rome in paradox of the cross, 146–51, 159
Greece: Freud's visit to, 43–47; Heidegger's visits to, 29–35

Gregorovius, Ferdinand, 132–38, 151–61; on continuity of history, 153–54; depression and melancholy, 154–55, 156–59; *Geschichte der Stadt Rom im Mittelalter*, 89, 133, 134–35, 152–56, 159–60; on Hildebert, 137, 146, 151; on Investiture Controversy, 135–37; "Krieg der Freischaren um Rom," 134n3; on Petrarch, 89, 92n27; on Risorgimento, 133–35; *Roman Journals*, 133, 134–35, 152
Gregory VII (pope), 135–37
grief and lament, 13–14, 115, 163–65. *See also* melancholy
Griffioen, James D., 262n20
Gronovius, Johann Friedrich, 176n23
Grossmann, Andreas, 31n7
Grotius, Hugo, 176
Gryphius, Andreas, 196–206; criticism of, 189–90; *Majuma* (*see* Gryphius, Andreas, *Majuma*); and Seneca, 176
Gryphius, Andreas, *Majuma*: context, 196–97, 200; emblems in, 201–2; historical continuity and historical knowledge through allegory, 191–92, 199–200, 205–6; overview, 197–99
Guidobaldo di Montefeltre, 112–13
Guiscard, Robert, 17, 133, 135–37

Habermas, Jürgen, 36
Haffner, Sebastian, 49
Hainsworth, Peter, 82–83
Harst, Joachim, 182n41
Haym, Rudolf, 226, 227
Heckscher, Wilhelm Sebastian, 2, 3, 12, 14, 17n44, 35, 138
Hegel, Georg Wilhelm Friedrich, 224–29; *Lectures on Aesthetics*, 225–26; *Phenomenology of Spirit*, 225, 226; "Wer denkt abstrakt?," 225
Heidegger, Elfride, 29
Heidegger, Martin, 29–40; *Aufenthalte*, 30–31; *Being and Time*, 67; and Blumenberg, 53; *Contributions to Philosophy*, 31–32, 37; criticism of, 35–36; dialogue with Hölderlin's poetry, 30–31, 36, 37–39; first impressions of Greece, 32–33; on necessity of fragments, 34–35; *Phänomenologische Interpretationen zu Aristoteles*, 67–68; on ruinance, 67–68, 72n76; on second beginning of philosophy, 31–32, 33–34, 36, 37, 40
Heidenreich, Felix, 52n12
Heil, Andreas, 171
Heinsius, Daniel, 176
Hell, Julia, 1–2, 4, 5, 23, 35n17, 36n22, 41–42
Henry IV (Holy Roman emperor), 135–36
Hermann, Hans Peter, 196n21
Hildebert of Lavardin, 138–51; and antithesis, 145–46, 149; *Carmina minora*, 139; on greatness of Rome despite ruins, 15n42, 140–45; on greatness of Rome in paradox of the cross, 146–51,

Hildebert of Lavardin (*cont.*)
159; Gregorovius on, 137, 146, 151; reception of, 138–40, 150; visit to Rome, 137
Hirschfeld, Christian Cay Lorenz, 249
history. *See* time and history
Hitler, Adolf, 48, 54, 64
Hölderlin, Friedrich, 30–31, 36, 37–39
Homer, *Iliad*, 1
Hui, Andrew, 10, 79n4, 80n5, 93n28, 115
humanism, 139–40
Humboldt, Wilhelm, 243n22
Husserl, Edmund, 50–51, 54n19; *The Crisis of European Sciences and Transcendental Phenomenology*, 51
Hypnerotomachia Poliphili, 112–29, *124*, *125*, *128*; act of interpretation in, overview, 119–20, 129; architectural ekphrasis of pyramid and obelisk, 121–26; architectural ekphrasis of temple of unhappy lovers, 126–29; authorship, 113; as labyrinth, 116–19; lingering in, 116, 119, 126, 127–28, 129; overview, 115; patronage, 112–13; title, 113–14

imagination: and memory, 21; and reason, 193–94
Immisch, Otto, *Das Nachleben der Antike*, 58n34
Investiture Controversy, 135–37

Jöns, Walter, 200
Jung, Carl Gustav, 61

kairos, 80, 88–89, 94–96, 99–100, 107–9, 111
Kaminski, Nicola, 176–77, 201
Kampf, Waldemar, 152–53
Kant, Immanuel, 252
Kästner, Erhart, 30n3
Keill, John, *An Examination of Dr. Burnet's Theory of the Earth*, 223
Keyserling, Hermann Graf, 59
Klages, Ludwig, 61
Koepnick, Lutz, 36
Koselleck, Reinhart, 6, 50n3
Kruft, Hanno-Walter, 122, 134, 136n8
Kurdzialek, Marian, 173n13

Lacroix, Sophie, 4n12
Lactantius (Christian author), 174
lament and grief, 13–14, 115, 163–65. *See also* melancholy
language: hybrids, 113–14; vernacular, 101, 103–4
Lavater, Johann Caspar, 236
Leary, John Patrick, 261, 262, 263–64, 265
life: bound in cultural forms, 59–60; brevity of, 87, 88, 100–101, 106–8, 162; death as integral to, 60–61, 66–67, 72; drives of, 68–69; as labyrinth, 117–19; and living on, 137, 151–54, 160–61; philosophy of, 58–61; ruinance of factical, 67–68. *See also* afterlife; time and history

life-time and world-time: and absolutism of reality, 54; in anti- vs. postdiluvian world, 214–15; awareness of divide between, 49–50, 52; and chaos of worldlessness, 172–73; and disappearance of world-reference, 165–70; and life-world-experience, 50–52; melancholic conception of, 160; of narcissists, 48–49
lingering, 116, 119, 126, 127–28, 129, 159
Lipsius, Justus, 176
Lohenstein, Daniel Casper von, 189, 190
Longos, *Daphnis and Chloe*, 245n25, 247n27
Ludwig van Kempen, 87
Luhmann, Niklas, 24, 143

Macaulay, Rose, 3
Macrobius, 119
Mandelbrote, Scott, 221
Manutius, Aldus, 112
Marx, Karl, 260
meaning: abundance in Rome, 234–35; and antithesis, 145; loss of, in modernity, 22; and marked vs. unmarked sides of a distinction, 143; and meaninglessness, 24; survival of, in modernity, 23–24
medieval thought: on allegory, 70–71; indifferent perception of ruins, 12–13; on time, 50, 91
Meid, Volker, 194n16
melancholy: and consolation, 66, 146, 151, 172, 180; definitions of, 156–58; and Detroit's ruins, 261–63; and empiricist realism, 1–2; Gregorovius's experience of, 154–55, 156, 158–59; lament and grief, 13–14, 115, 163–65; and semiotic status, 158–60; and world-time, 160
Melanchthon, Philipp, 175
Meltzer, Françoise, 5, 46n43
Migne, Jacques Paul, *Patrologia Latina*, 139
Mommsen, Theodor, 91
More, Henry, 207, 209
Moritz of Orange, 176
mortality. *See* death
Müller-Funk, Wolfgang, 39n30
mythology, and allegory, 199

narcissists, 48–49, 162
nature: and art, 247, 249–50; unity with spirit, 254–57
Nelli, Francesco, 77, 79, 84–86
Neoplatonism, 207
Newton, Isaac, 220–21
Nicolson, Marjorie, 211n10, 220
Niethammer, Lutz, 57n27
Norden, Eduard, 139

Oedipal conflict, 42, 45–47
Opitz, Martin, 176–85; *Buch von der deutschen Poeterey*, 176, 201, 206; *Trojanerinnen* (*see* Opitz,

Martin, *Trojanerinnen*); war's influence on, 176–77
Opitz, Martin, *Trojanerinnen*: note on second choral ode, 183–84; restoration of semiotic points of reference, 181–83, 184–85; Scriverius edition, 173n14, 182n40; temporal merging of past and present, 179–81, 182, 185; time motif in dedication, 177–79
Osborne, John, 70n72
Ovid: *Fastorum libri sex*, 197; *Metamorphoses*, 174

Palladio, Andrea, 238
Panofsky, Erwin, 8, 13, 115
paradox: of the cross, 146–51, 159; of culture, 59–60
Paul, Saint, 174
Pelosi, Olimpia, 120n20
perfection, 144
periodization, 79n4
Peter of Blois, 138–39
Petrarch, 77–111; on brevity of life, 87, 88, 100–101, 106–8; *Canzoniere*, 81, 87; characterized as modern, 13–14, 91–92; on Dante, 102–4; *De vita solitaria*, 100; *Epistolae Familiares*, 87–88; first trip to Rome, 89–90; fragmented works of, 87–88, 92; and fragmented gesture, 21; hope for restored Rome, 78–79, 84–86, 87, 94–96, 97–99; in literary studies, 3; love lyrics to Laura, 81–83, 104–6, 110; on poetic standards, 85, 86–87, 103–4; as poet laureate, 90–91; on potentiality and postponement of kairos, 80, 88–89, 94–96, 99–100, 107–9, 111; relocation to Italy, 96–97; *Rerum senilium libri*, 98; *Rerum vulgarium fragmenta*, 81–83, 94–96, 97, 110n59; on Roman history, 92–93; and Seneca, 175–76; *Trionfi*, 100, 101–2, 104–11; on Vaucluse, 80–81, 83–84
Philippe de Cabassole, 80–81
philosophy: and art, 252, 256; mutual supplementation of poetry and, 38–39; two beginnings of, 31–32
Pietro di Parenzo, 77–78, 103
pity, 259
Plato, *Theaetetus*, 217
Polybios (Greek historian), 1
Prudentius, Aurelius Clemens, 174
psychoanalysis, and archaeology, 41–42
Puff, Helmut, 25

Ranke, Leopold, 136n8
reality: absolutism of, 53–54; consolation as survival strategy, 66
reason, and allegory, 193–96
relics, 14, 147
religion. *See* Christianity; theological-scientific discourse
Risorgimento, 133–35
Robert, Hubert, 12, 21, 22

Robert Guiscard, 17, 133, 135–37
Robert of Anjou, 90
Rolland, Romain, 40, 43
Roma quanta fuit ipsa ruina docet, 15
Rome: Goethe's visit to, 233–35; greatness of, despite ruins, 15n42, 140–45; greatness of, in paradox of the cross, 146–51, 159; Hildebert's visit to, 137; and Investiture Controversy, 135–37; Petrarch's first trip to, 89–90; Petrarch's hope for restored, 78–79, 84–86, 87, 94–96, 97–99; and Risorgimento, 133–35; semiotic status of, 93–96, 143–44
Ruin, Hans, 68n66
ruinance, 67–68, 72n76
Ruinen des Denkens—Denken in Ruinen (Bolz and Van Reijen), 3–4
ruin porn, 262
ruins: etymology, 7–8; as forms, 71–72
ruin scholarship, 2–5, 260
Ruins of Modernity (Hell and Schönle), 4

Scaliger, Joseph Justus, 176
Schiller, Friedrich, 240–41, 242–43; *Die Horen*, 241
Schings, Hans-Jürgen, 180
Schmidt, Dorothea, 121, 126
Schönle, Andreas, 4
Schramm, Percy Ernst, 146n37
Schultz, Christoph Ludwig Friedrich, 240
Schulz, Karlheinz, 243
Schumpeter, Joseph, 260
scientific discourse. *See* theological-scientific discourse
Scipio Africanus the Younger, 1
Scott, A. Brian, 139, 140
Scriverius, Petrus, 173n14, 176n23, 182n40
semiotic status: and continuity, 150, 154, 160–61; of the cross, 147–49; of forms, 93, 181–83, 185; fragility of, 93–94, 111, 142–43; and melancholy, 158–60; of Rome, 93–96, 143–44; of Troy, 165–69; of the world, 149–50, 165–67, 169–70, 180, 185
Seneca, Lucius Annaeus, 163–74; *De brevitate vitae*, 163; reception of, 174–76; *Troades* (*see* Seneca, Lucius Annaeus, *Troades*)
Seneca, Lucius Annaeus, *Troades*: chaos of worldlessness, 172–73; disappearance of world-reference, 165–70; Hecuba's grief, 163–65; nothingness of death, 170, 172, 173; scholarly debate on second choral ode, 170–71. *See also* Opitz, Martin, *Trojanerinnen*
Seneca the Elder, 175
Sidonius Apollinaris, 174
Simmel, Georg, 251–57; "Der Begriff und die Tragödie der Kultur," 59–60; criticism of, 239, 253–54; "Goethe," 253; "Kant und Goethe," 252; "Lebensanschauung," 59, 60–61; on life, 59–61, 72,

Simmel, Georg (*cont.*)
  252, 253; mentioned, 3, 144n31; "Die Ruine," 249, 251–52, 254–57; on unity of nature and spirit, 254–57
Smolak, Kurt, 147–48
sojourns, 31–32, 33–34, 40
Solnit, Rebecca, 262–63
Speer, Albert, 24
Spencer-Brown, George, *Laws of Form*, 143
Spengler, Oswald, *The Decline of the West*, 23
Spenser, Edmund, 3
Steinbach, Erwin von, 238
Steinberg, Justin, 104n50
Stewart, Susan, 5, 10
Stierle, Karlheinz, 21, 79n4, 80, 82–83, 91n23, 93, 97, 100, 102, 106
Stoicism, 163, 167, 169, 170, 173
supplementation, 35, 38–39, 46

Tarkovsky, Andrei, 3
Tertullian, *De anima*, 174
theater, 217–18
theological-scientific discourse: abstraction and concretization of *theoria*, 217, 218–20; allegorical vs. literal sense of Scripture, 215–17, 220–22; antediluvian world, 212–15; Burnet's, overview, 208–9; criticism of, 209–10; realignment of, 210–11
theoria, 217–20
Thirty Years' War, 176, 177, 179–81, 182, 185
Thomas Aquinas, Saint, 12–13
Thucydides (Greek historian), 21n52
Tilliette, Jean-Yves, 151
time and history: abolition of, 67–68; afterlife of, 57–58, 63, 66, 72; antediluvian world, 212–15; and artistic production, 177–79; and chaos, 172–73, 183; continuity and knowledge through allegory, 191–92, 199–200, 205–6; continuity as impossible, 173–74; continuity through discontinuity, 108–9, 153–54; continuity through paradox of the cross, 148, 150–51; convergence of past and present, 42, 45–46, 179–81, 182, 185; and drive theory, 69; eternity and atemporality, 63, 70–71, 109–10, 111, 123, 149, 150; and fame, 64–65; and lingering, 116, 119, 126, 127–28, 129, 159; and literal sense of Scripture, 215–17, 220–22; and modernity, 91; potentiality and postponement of kairos, 80, 88–89, 94–96, 99–100, 107–9, 111; ruins as medium for continuity of past and present, 123, 126, 129; sojourns as transitional space, 31–32, 33–34, 40; and two beginnings of philosophy, 31–32, 33–34, 36, 37, 40; and unity of form, 88. *See also* afterlife; death; life; life-time and world-time
Tischbein, Johann Heinrich Wilhelm, *Goethe in der römischen Campagna*, 236–37, 236
Todverfallenheit (falling toward death), 66–67, 70
tragedy genre. *See* Opitz, Martin, *Trojanerinnen*; Seneca, Lucius Annaeus, *Troades*
transformation: from first to second beginnings of philosophy, 31–32, 33–34, 36, 37, 40; unfulfilled, 251
translation: originals in, 62–64, 71, 182–86; and time, 177–79
Trillitzsch, Winfried, 175
Trinacty, Christopher, 169n6
Troy, 163–69

Ullman, Walter, 136n7
Urban V (pope), 97–100
utopia, 122, 263

vanitas, 173, 177, 180, 181
Vellutello, Alessandro, 82
Verfallenheit (fallenness, subjugation), 67
vernacular language, 101, 103–4
Virgil, *Aeneid*, 163n3, 174
Visconti, Giovanni, 97
Völkel, Markus, 134
von Moos, Peter, 138n15, 139–40, 144, 150
von Mücke, Dorothea, 238–39, 246n26

Wagner-Egelhaaf, Martina, 158
Warburg, Aby, 8, 9
war motif. *See* Gryphius, Andreas, *Majuma*; Opitz, Martin, *Trojanerinnen*; Seneca, Lucius Annaeus, *Troades*
Warren, Erasmus, *Geologia*, 220
Weber, Samuel, 62, 63n52, 66, 70n72, 71
Weidner, Daniel, 56–57, 59, 64, 101n42
Wetz, Frantz Josef, 54n19
Whately, Thomas, *Observations on Modern Gardening*, 21
William III (king of England), 212
Wolff, Christian, 193
Woodward, Christopher, 155
world-time. *See* life-time and world-time

Zak, Gur, 92n27
Zimmermann, Reinhard, 2, 3, 12n30, 20n47, 209–10, 223, 245n25
Zucker, Paul, 2

www.ingramcontent.com/pod-product-compliance
Lightning Source LLC
Chambersburg PA
CBHW051350290426